The Bloomsbury Companion to Phonetics

Edited by
Mark J. Jones and
Rachael-Anne Knight

Bloomsbury Companions

Bloomsbury Academic
An imprint of Bloomsbury Publishing Plc

B L O O M S B U R Y
LONDON · OXFORD · NEW YORK · NEW DELHI · SYDNEY

Bloomsbury Academic
An imprint of Bloomsbury Publishing Plc

50 Bedford Square
London
WC1B 3DP
UK

1385 Broadway
New York
NY 10018
USA

www.bloomsbury.com

BLOOMSBURY and the Diana logo are trademarks of Bloomsbury Publishing Plc

First published in paperback 2015

First published 2013

© Mark J. Jones, Rachael-Anne Knight and Contributors, 2013, 2015

Mark J. Jones and Rachael-Anne Knight have asserted their right under the
Copyright, Designs and Patents Act, 1988, to be identified as the Editors of this work.

British Library Cataloguing-in-Publication Data
A catalogue record for this book is available from the British Library.

ISBN: PB: 978-1-4742-3727-7
HB: 978-1-4411-4606-9
ePub: 978-1-4411-5454-5
ePDF: 978-1-4411-1611-6

Library of Congress Cataloging-in-Publication Data
A catalog record for this book is available from the Library of Congress.

Typeset by Newgen Imaging Systems Pvt Ltd, Chennai, India
Printed and bound in Great Britain

The Bloomsbury Companion to Phonetics

Bloomsbury Companions

The Bloomsbury Companion to Cognitive Linguistics, edited by Jeannette Littlemore and John R. Taylor

The Bloomsbury Companion to Lexicography, edited by Howard Jackson

The Bloomsbury Companion to M.A.K. Halliday, edited by Jonathan J. Webster

The Bloomsbury Companion to Stylistics, edited by Violeta Sotirova

The Bloomsbury Companion to Syntax, edited by Silvia Luraghi and Claudia Parodi

Continuum Companion to Discourse Analysis, edited by Ken Hyland and Brian Platridge

Available in Paperback as *Bloomsbury Companion to Discourse Studies*

Continuum Companion to Historical Linguistics, edited by Silvia Luraghi and Vit Bubenik

Available in Paperback as *Bloomsbury Companion to Historical Linguistics*

Continuum Companion to Phonology, edited by Nancy C. Kula, Bert Botma and Kuniya Nasukawa

Available in Paperback as *Bloomsbury Companion to Phonology*

Continuum Companion to the Philosophy of Language, edited by Manuel García-Carpintero and Max Köbel

Available in Paperback as *Bloomsbury Companion to the Philosophy of Language*

Continuum Companion to Second Language Acquisition, edited by Ernesto Macaro

Available in Paperback as *Bloomsbury Companion to Second Language Acquisition*

Contents

Contents

List of Figures

Introduction

Rachael-Anne Knight and Mark J. Jones

While editing this volume, we have aimed to produce a book that will be useful to people with a good basic knowledge of phonetics, but who quickly need to appreciate the state-of-the-art in a particular subfield. Phonetics is an increasingly large and disparate science, and, correspondingly, it is increasingly difficult to be an expert in the breadth and depth of every subfield. For the newcomer to the subject, the array of different subfields, research techniques and theoretical considerations must be baffling as well as exciting, and we hope that this book will bridge the gap between the introductory textbooks and the more specialist volumes and primary literature. Phonetics can be viewed as focusing on the meeting point between physical-biological, cognitive and linguistic aspects of speech, but there is room for a lot of leeway around this point. The exact scope of phonetics depends on how it is defined in relation to allied disciplines like phonology, but also in relation to disciplines such as linguistics, of which phonetics may or may not form a part (e.g. Ohala, 2004). Similar questions are also raised in these fields, see, for example, papers in Burton-Roberts et al. (2000) for questions concerning the relationship of phonology to linguistics.

One of the reasons that phonetics (particularly experimental phonetics, in Ohala's (2004) terms) is such a large field is that it encompasses several distinct parts of the speech chain (Denes & Pinson, 1993), which models the processes which occur when speech is used to transfer a message from one person to another. Traditional descriptions of phonetics often describe articulatory phonetics, relating to the movements of the vocal tract, acoustic phonetics, relating to the properties of the sound waves produced and auditory phonetics, relating to the perception of those sound waves. Chapters in this volume cover all these areas of phonetics, often linking two or more, and sometimes referring to the wider questions of the relationship of phonetics to phonology, and linguistics in general. Despite the increased fragmentation and specialization evident within phonetics, the links between chapters reinforce the idea that everything is connected. We cannot consider what speech is without also asking what speech does, and vice versa.

Heselwood, Hassan and Jones begin by providing a history of the discipline of phonetics. The chapter is in two sections. The first, covering our knowledge of phonetics until the formation of the International Phonetics Association (IPA) in 1886, considers the earliest endeavours of phoneticians across the globe. The second covers the formation of the IPA and the development of the phonetic alphabet, the rise of acoustic phonetics, computer technologies and instrumental analysis.

The next four chapters present different methods used in the study of phonetics, with the aim of providing technical and practical advice. Knight and Hawkins present research methods in speech perception. The authors do not individually describe the large number of paradigms used in the field, but instead note the many considerations that must be taken into account so that perception experiments can be designed without confound, independent of the paradigm used.

A similar line is taken in Tabain's chapter, which focuses on research methods for speech production and notes that no single technique can provide data on every aspect of articulation. After a consideration of general methods for gathering data on articulation, a detailed discussion is focused on electropalatography (EPG), electromagnetic articulography (EMA) and ultrasound, and the pros and cons of each. These sections reinforce the limits of each technique, but give a useful checklist that will enable researchers to pick the best method for a particular topic of investigation.

Butcher describes the practical considerations involved in conducting phonetic fieldwork. Topics include the planning and preparation involved, the equipment needed, how to prepare speech material and work with native-language informants and additional ways of eliciting data (such as articulatory and perceptual experiments). Stepping outside the lab is fraught with dangers, and Butcher's chapter provides tips on everything from avoiding cultural misunderstandings to getting a good night's sleep, as well as how to get the best data in the field.

Watt discusses research methods in acoustic analysis, using the typical freeware packages currently available. The focus is on making valid and reliable measurements of the key acoustic properties of speech sounds, particularly duration and frequency, but the chapter also discusses what to do with the data before comparisons are made and conclusions drawn. Normalization techniques for vowel formants are illustrated.

The next nine chapters present the state-of-the-art in various subfields of phonetics. Hazan begins with a survey of speech perception development. Taking a somewhat historical perspective, she examines the early experiments in infant perception from the 1970s, before moving on to consider not only what infants can perceive but also the ways in which they might develop skills in speech perception. The shift away from questions about 'what' infants do to 'how' they do it raises questions which are echoed in later chapters by Simpson and by Smith.

Esling considers the subdiscipline of voice and phonation. The chapter covers air stream mechanisms, states of the larynx, voice qualities and phonation types. The articulatory details of these are considered alongside how they are used in the languages of the world, both to create meaning and paralinguistically. This chapter clearly shows how the application of speech production techniques can provide new insights into aspects of speech already considered well-understood.

Astruc discusses aspects of prosodic phenomena, including stress, rhythm and intonation. She describes the functions of prosody, such as conveying syntactic information and structuring other aspects of phonology. The chapter also considers the phonetic correlates of the various prosodic subsystems, how these subsystems interact and their relationship to segmental systems.

Jones considers universal patterns in phonetics, and phonetic variation related to biological and physical aspects of speech production. He explores when variation reflects speaker choices, and when it is a by-product of universalist mechanisms. The chapter also covers how we make crosslinguistic comparisons and where potential phonetic variation might arise from physical-biological sources.

Simpson describes work relating to the (still) largely undiscovered territory of spontaneous speech, such as how it can be elicited, how it is different to other types of speech (such as read speech), its patterns and explanations for those patterns. He also considers the phonetic organization of conversation, such as talk-in-interaction, and the way phonetics is used to carry out interactional functions.

The next four chapters underline how phonetics is not just an area of theoretical relevance, but how phonetic knowledge can be applied. Starr-Marshall, Martin and Knight explain how phonetics is used in the clinic, with a focus on the assessment and diagnosis of children with speech sound disorders. Topics include how to gather a speech sample, the role of phonetic transcription, types of analysis, categorization of disordered speech and, briefly, how phonetic aspects can influence the type of intervention provided.

French and Stevens present the types of work undertaken by forensic speech scientists, with a focus on the task of speaker comparison. They describe the importance of variation within and between speakers, the different methodologies available for speaker comparison and how findings can be formulated as conclusions to be expressed in court. The chapter also presents a vital snapshot of current issues in forensic phonetics, such as the use of automatic techniques alongside traditional analysis.

Ashby and Ashby note that there is little established work on phonetics pedagogy, and that which exists is often focused on pronunciation and second language learning. They explore distinctions such as whether phonetics is being learnt for its own sake, or for another purpose, such as to improve pronunciation. They also discuss the relationship between phonetic pedagogy and general pedagogical theory. These are issues which often go undiscussed, and raise questions about what the next generation(s) of phoneticians and speech scientists need to know in order to carry out solid work.

Huckvale considers technological applications which rely on phonetics, such as established text-to-speech systems, and emerging technologies, such as translation systems. He describes the types of phonetic representations that are used, and how these representations are processed from the acoustic signal, through various other levels, to the utterance. Finally he describes how these features are instantiated in the architecture of selected modern applications. Here too the potential for phonetics to be applied to real-world problems is highlighted, as well as the way that approaches to speech analysis can inform ideas about what speech is.

The final two chapters of the volume consider the future of the field. While several of the chapters in the central section make reference to future progress, they do so in relation to fairly narrow areas and subfields. The two final chapters take the wider perspectives of speech production and speech perception as a starting point to describe probable future trends in thinking and research.

Smith takes a broad view of speech perception, encompassing linguistic as well as social and interactional meaning. She considers the types of variability that can be found in the speech signal and how listeners can exploit these in order to interpret meaning. She also considers how such variation can be utilized by the psychological and neural mechanisms underlying speech processing.

Harrington, Hoole and Pouplier describe two views of speech production: how the speaker's intended message is related to the acoustic signal, and why certain patterns of production occur in languages. Throughout the chapter they consider the importance of speech dynamics in relation to coarticulation, assimilation and consonant clusters, and the perceptual consequences of these areas of investigation.

Throughout the volume the authors consider some of the fundamental questions in phonetics, such as the relationship between phonetics and other levels of language, the importance of variability and how it can be described, accounted for and used by listeners, the necessity of describing both the patterns that arise in speech and *how* they arise and the relationship between production and perception of speech. We hope that the volume goes some way towards bridging gaps between subdisciplines in the increasingly broad and disparate field of phonetics.

Rachael-Anne Knight and Mark J. Jones

July 2012

1 Historical Overview of Phonetics

Chapter Overview

This historical overview is in two parts. The first part identifies certain important milestones in the development of phonetics from earliest historical times up to the formation of the International Phonetic Association (IPA) in 1886. The second part reports on key advances in the discipline from that time to the present.

Phonetics from Ancient Times up to the IPA

Barry Heselwood

1 The Ancient World

1.1 Egypt

A hieroglyphic alphabet was in use for representing Ancient Egyptian consonants by the end of the fourth millennium BCE (Coulmas, 2003, pp. 173–5). Examples of rebus writing also date from this time (Baines, 2004, p. 163). Signs for vowels started to make sporadic appearances during the third millennium BCE (Gelb, 1963, p. 168). These developments require some analysis of pronunciation, albeit a pre-theoretical one. Rebus writing relies on recognition of the phonetic identity of homonyms but not on phonetic theory.

Acrophony may have played a significant role in the spread of writing in the ancient Near East (Gardiner, 1916). In acrophony a logogram becomes an alphabetic letter when it is used to represent the first sound of the word instead of the whole word, its signifying function shifting from lexis to phonology. For this to happen, there has to be recognition of the same sound in other word-forms.

The hieroglyphic alphabet, rebus writing and acrophony indicate that from the earliest known examples of written language deliberate pairing not only of words and written symbols but also of sounds and written symbols has been undertaken.

1.2 India

Probably the first systematic framework for the analysis of speech was developed in India in the early part of the first millennium BCE (Allen, 1953, p. 5; Varma, 1961, p. 4). Sanskrit consonants and vowels were classified according to articulatory criteria of place, manner and voicing in much the same way as the modern IPA, with the functions of active and passive articulators identified. Sounds were also quantified into mora-like units, consonants being half a unit, short vowels one and long vowels two (Varma, 1961, p. 89). They made discoveries of how voicing is generated in the larynx, theorized about syllabification and consonant-vowel dependencies, studied connected speech phenomena under the heading *sandhi* – a term still used in modern phonology – attended to the use of voice-pitch for tone and tried to account for the relationship of tone to quantity. Concerning tempo, they noted speech could be fast, medium or slow (ibid., p. 170).

When the work of the Indians became known in the West, it had a significant influence on phoneticians such as Alexander J. Ellis and Henry Sweet (Allen, 1953, p. 4).

1.3 Greece

The rudiments of a science of phonetics can be seen in the writings of Plato and Aristotle in the fourth century BCE. Plato, in his *Theaetetus* (202e–203c), mentions the differences between consonants and vowels and their combination into syllables. Allen (1953, p. 36) claims that Aristotle may have appreciated the role of the larynx in providing voicing for speech. However, when he says 'we cannot use voice when breathing in or out, but only when holding the breath' (*De Anima*, II.8.420[b]7), he displays crucial lack of understanding of the process.

The Stoic grammarians in the third to second centuries BCE distinguished between the signified and the signifier. The Aristotelian doctrine concerning writing that 'written marks [are] symbols of spoken sounds' (*De Interpretatione*, 16ᵃ3) meant that speech sounds were seen as the primary signifiers and became objects of study. They arranged consonants and vowels into nonsense sequences, venturing outside the constraints of Greek phonotactics (Robins, 1990, p. 28). Greek letters were thus being used less as a spelling system and more as a phonetic notation system with an embryonic body of phonetic theory behind it. Further development of Greek phonetic theory can be seen in the *Téchnē Grammatiké* attributed to Dionysius Thrax (ca. 170–ca. 90 BC). Sounds are cross-classified on the basis of shared manner features such as stop, continuant and aspiration. Thrax recognized in Greek three triads of aspirated-voiced-unaspirated plosives although he fell short of an accurate account of voicing as did all Greek and Roman commentators (Matthews, 1994, pp. 13–14).[1] Terminology relating to manner of articulation was used with explicit phonetic definitions although, despite descriptions of labial, dental and velar stops (ibid., p. 13), no technical terms were coined by the Greeks for denoting places of articulation (Allen, 1981, pp. 119–21).

2 The Middle Ages

2.1 The Arab Grammarians

Although their descriptions of Arabic sounds tend to be brief and can sometimes be difficult to interpret, it is clear from the works of scholars such as Al-Khalīl (718–86 CE), Sībawayh (ca.750–796 CE), Ibn Jinnī (933–1002 CE) and Ibn Sīnā (Avicenna) (980–1037 CE) that a fruitful phonetic tradition existed in the Middle East at this time.

Like the Greeks, the Arabs did not understand voicing but they went further than the Greeks in developing a framework and terminology for classifying sounds and arrived at insights such as Ibn Jinnī's analogy between the vocal tract and a flute in the way sounds are made by forming closures at various points while forcing air through (Mehiri, 1973, p. 166).

Sībawayh developed a typology of connected speech phenomena, distinguishing different kinds and degrees of assimilation (Al-Nassir, 1993, pp. 56–80) very like modern discussions of gradient and categorical assimilation (e.g. Ellis & Hardcastle, 2002), and setting up a strength hierarchy in which greatest strength was assigned to sounds which most resist assimilation.

In the Arab treatises we encounter phonetic descriptions of dialectal differences, sociolinguistic variation and speech errors (Anwar, 1983). We also find a concern with methods of observation, data elicitation and the control of contextual variables of both a phonetic and a social nature (Alhawary, 2003). This

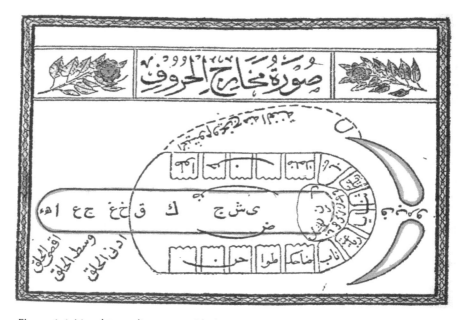

Figure 1.1 Vocal tract diagram entitled *S ?ūrat makhārij al-h?urūf* 'Picture of the exits of the letters' from *Miftāh? al-'Ulūm* 'The Key to the Sciences' by Al-Sakkāki. Dotted line indicates the nasal passage with a nostril above the lip.

empirical emphasis on observation under controlled conditions, together with many accurate descriptions of phonetic phenomena, marks the work of the medieval Arab phoneticians as a valuable contribution in the history of the discipline (see Heselwood & Hassan, forthcoming).

The Arab tradition produced what is probably the earliest diagram of the vocal tract. It appeared in the late twelfth or early thirteenth century CE and is reproduced in Figure 1.1 (from Bakalla, 1982, p. 87). Arabic letters are arranged at the places of articulation of the corresponding sounds, thus giving the letters the function of phonetic symbols.

2.2 Europe

Very little study of phonetics went on in Europe in the Middle Ages (Robins, 1990, p. 87). Observations of how Latin sounds were influenced by local vernaculars were couched mostly in impressionistic terms and were largely confined to remarking on the effects of context on sound quality. For example, lenition processes were noted, as was a tendency for voiceless fricatives to become voiced intervocalically (see the accounts of various treatises of the time in Vineis & Maierú, 1994, pp. 190–7).

The anonymous *First Grammatical Treatise*, from twelfth-century Iceland, has been cited as representing the most advanced phonetic analysis of the medieval period in Europe (Robins, 1990, p. 82; Vineis & Maierú, 1994, p. 187). It offers a comprehensive componential analysis of vowel qualities in Old Norse, distinguishes nasalized and non-nasalized vowels, short and long vowels, degrees of vowel openness, adduces minimal pairs to prove the existence of these distinctions and provides new letters for them by diacritical modifications to the five Latin vowel letters (Haugen, 1972, pp. 15–19, 34–41). However, there is no mention of lip-shape in vowels and, apart from distinguishing singletons and geminates, there is no attempt at a phonetic classification of consonants.

Common to phonetics in all periods before the Renaissance was a focus on the pronunciation of a particular language – Sanskrit, Greek, Latin, Arabic, Norse – with some limited attention to dialectal variants. The concept of a 'general phonetics' had yet to emerge.

3 Renaissance Europe

The issue of whether to write Romance vernaculars so that spellings reflected vernacular pronunciation or Latin etymology became important in Renaissance Europe, the debate often dividing strongly along religious and ideological lines (Tavoni, 1998, pp. 18–29). The Calvinist Louis Meigret (ca.1500–1558) viewed spellings which were not true to pronunciation as 'superstitions' and developed his own phonetically reformed orthography for French. Concern with spelling reform and orthographic invention, in eastern as well as western Europe (Gandolfo, 1998, pp. 111–14), raised practical and theoretical questions about the representation of speech sounds.

The late fifteenth century also saw diachronic and comparative examination of classical and vernacular languages, treating them as linguistic equals subject to the same phonetic laws (Tavoni, 1998, pp. 46–7), but we have to wait another century for Jacob Madsen's *De literis libri duo* (1586) before we have the first known publication taking an explicitly general phonetics perspective (Kemp, 2006, p. 473). The vocal tract and the sounds it can produce, rather than the pronunciations of particular languages, increasingly become objects of study in subsequent works (ibid., pp. 476–7).

Western general phonetic theory made significant strides in England through the work of Sir Thomas Smith (1513–77), John Hart (ca.1500–1574) and other sixteenth- and seventeenth-century scholars. They are the early figures in what has, since Sweet's coining of the phrase, become known as 'the English school of phonetics' (Firth, 1957).

Both Hart and Smith augmented the Latin alphabet with some letters of their own devising. While Smith employed experimental methods of phonetic self-observation (e.g. Smith, 1568, pp. 34–5), he displayed an absence of adequate analytic terms in his ostensive definitions of sounds. His achievement was to set out a system of phoneme-grapheme correspondences for English (Cecioni, 1980, p. 91). Hart makes the greater contribution to phonetic theory by describing speech-sound production in some detail and grouping sounds together on the basis of shared phonetic parameters (e.g. Hart, 1569, pp. 41–2). Danielsson (1955, p. 220) credits him as the first European to note anticipatory assimilation across word boundaries in connected speech. We must remember, however, that insofar as Hart developed a phonetic theory it was to serve as a justification for spelling reform.

4 Seventeenth Century

Robert Robinson's 1617 *The Art of Pronuntiation* contains perhaps the earliest example of a vowel chart (see Figure 1.2). It shows the position of the high point of the tongue in relation to the palate for five vowel qualities with symbols to represent short and long versions. He devised a complete set of new

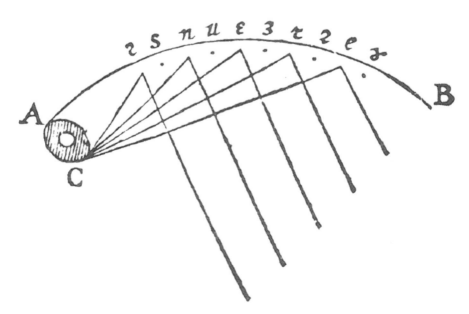

Figure 1.2 Robinson's 1617 vowel chart. A = glottis, B = front of palate, C = tongue root.

symbols instead of adapting or adding to alphabetic letters, treated voicing as a prosody and classified sounds according to an original scheme in which the vocal tract is divided into 'outward', 'middle' and 'inward' regions with four manner distinctions corresponding to plosive, nasal, fricative and approximant (Dobson, 1957, pp. 23–4). Although the assigning of sounds to the regions is sometimes counter to modern phonetics, and his symbols may be 'easier to forget than to learn' (ibid., p. xi), Robinson's work shows an advance towards a phonetics free from the letter-based thinking of the past, with a marriage of taxonomy and notation of the kind that underpins the modern IPA system.

John Wallis (1616–1703) in his *Tractatus de loquela* of 1653 presents tables arranged so that sounds appear as the products of intersecting categories (see Kemp, 1972, pp. 196–7) as they do on IPA charts (IPA, 1999, p. 159). The significance of a chart with intersecting dimensions is that it becomes a model of phonetic space rather than, in the case of Robinson's chart, a model of the vocal tract. It is therefore more abstract and the dimensions can take on the status of autonomous components.

The teenage Isaac Newton (1643–1727) set out a classification of consonants and vowels and devised an original set of symbols to represent them systematically. He also reported an experiment in which 'The filling of a very deepe

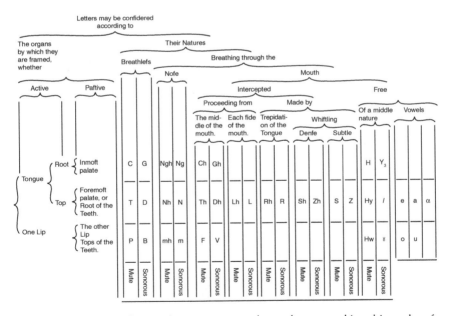

Figure 1.3 Wilkins' chart with consonants and vowels arranged in a hierarchy of binary distinctions. Reproduced with the permission of the Brotherton Collection, Leeds University Library.

flaggon wth a constant streame of beere or water sounds ye vowells in this order w, u, ω, o, a, e, i, y' (Elliott, 1954, p. 12).

John Wilkins (1614–72), Bishop of Chester, was influential in the movement to establish a set of sounds for the pronunciation of a universal language, a preoccupation of the time (Robins, 1990, pp. 126–30). Viewed as a model of phonetic space, Wilkins' cross-classificatory chart (see Figure 1.3) is more sophisticated than Wallis's. It is structured by a hierarchy of binary distinctions, incorporates both vowels and consonants, and shows a more detailed appreciation of articulatory structures and processes. An innovative feature of Wilkins' work is his design of an 'organic alphabet' of symbols as iconic representations of articulatory-aerodynamic properties of sounds (Wilkins, 1668, p. 378; see also Allbright, 1958, pp. 8–10). Organic symbols explicitly identify sounds as objects of study independently of any writing system and therefore imply the possibility of phonetics as a language-independent discipline drawing on the disciplines of anatomy and physiology. Wilkins also designed letters systematically based on the component features of sounds (Wilkins, 1668, p. 376), similar to Newton's and to the universal alphabet designed by Francis Lodwick (see below).

William Holder (1616–97) in his *Elements of Speech* offers the first substantial account of voicing since the time of the Indian grammarians. In a passage worth quoting in full, Holder provides the conceptual rudiments of what we know as the aerodynamic-myoelastic theory of phonation, and the source-filter model of speech production (original spelling and italics):

> The *Larynx* both gives *passage* to the Breath, and also, as often as we please, by the force of Muscles, to bear the sides of the *Larynx* stiffe and near together, as the Breath passeth through the *Rimula* [=glottis], makes a vibration of those Cartilaginous Bodies which forms that Breath, into a vocal sound or Voice, which by the *Palate*, as a *Chelis* or shell of a Lute, is sweetened and augmented. (Holder, 1669, p. 23)

Francis Lodwick (1619–94) in *Essay towards an Universal Alphabet* grouped sounds according to shared articulatory properties, but their tabular arrangement only partly follows the structure of the vocal tract and lacks anatomical labels. Lodwick aimed to provide the means to represent any sound in any language, anticipating the IPA in stating 'that no one Character have more than one Sound, nor any one Sound be expressed by more than one Character' (Lodwick, 1686, p. 127).[2]

By the late seventeenth century, phonetics had become defined as a subject with a significant degree of independence from orthography. It had developed a terminology and a theoretical framework, although the further efforts needed to more firmly establish its methods and principles did not really come until the nineteenth century.

5 Eighteenth Century

Curiously little seems to have been done in phonetics in the eighteenth century, until the last quarter. Joshua Steele's (1700–91) *An Essay towards Establishing the Measure and Melody of Speech* of 1775 addressed issues concerning the prosodic structure of speech and its representation. Terms and notational devices from music are employed in the analysis of rhythmic, intonational and other dynamic features. Steele's approach went largely unappreciated at the time (Sumera, 1981, p. 103), but some of his resources have made a reappearance in the extensions to the IPA, for example *allegro, f(orte), p(iano)* (Duckworth et al., 1990); there are also resemblances to later interlinear intonational transcriptions.

A 'vowel triangle' was a feature of the 1781 *Dissertatio physiologico-medica de formatione loquelae* of Christoph Hellwag (1754–1835). It is one of the first representations of vowels in an abstract vowel space of this kind (Kemp, 2001, pp. 1469–70) which has clear similarities to the cardinal vowel system of Daniel Jones (e.g. Jones, 1972, pp. 31–9) and the modern IPA vowel quadrilateral.

A number of English pronouncing dictionaries appeared with various ways of representing consonants and vowels as well as word-accent (Beal, 2009). Thomas Spence (1750–1814) produced in his *Grand Repository of the English Language* of 1775 what Abercrombie (1965, p. 68) has described as 'a genuine, scientific, phonetic alphabet'. It comprises modifications of the roman alphabet presented in alphabetical order with keyword exemplifications but no phonetic descriptions. Spence really adds nothing to general phonetic science, and his regularization of the grapheme-phoneme correspondences of English into a 'broad phonemic system' (Beal, 1999, p. 89) was no advance on Smith's work of two centuries earlier.

Of greater fame than Spence was John Walker (1732–1807), his *A Critical Pronouncing Dictionary* appearing in 1791. However, Walker's classification scheme shows no advance on that of Wilkins or Holder, and his phonetic descriptions are in some respects less perceptive: he does not appear to have understood Holder's account of voicing; his description of labiodental fricatives being produced 'by pressing the upper teeth upon the under lip' (Walker, 1791, p. 6) is careless in attributing active and passive roles; he seems unsure whether [ʃ, ʒ] are single sounds or not (ibid., p. 4). Unlike Spence, Walker does not venture much beyond the graphic resources of the 26-letter roman alphabet to represent sounds, except for a system of superscript numerals to distinguish vowel qualities. While he had an acute ear for fine shades of sound, especially in vowels, he lacked a corresponding concern for phonetic theory.

The eighteenth century was not as fruitful in its explorations and development of phonetics as the previous century had been, or as the following century would prove to be.

6 Nineteenth Century

6.1 Phonetic Notation

A distinction which has proved of lasting value in phonetic transcription is that between 'narrow' and 'broad' (Laver, 1994, pp. 550–61; IPA, 1999, pp. 28–30). It first appears in the *Palaeotype* and *Glossotype* systems designed by Alexander J. Ellis (1814–80). The purpose of the former was 'to indicate the pronunciation of any language with great minuteness' (Ellis, 1869, p. 1), the latter being for linguists who wish 'to indicate pronunciation with some degree of exactness, but do not care to enter upon general phonetic investigations' (ibid., p. 13). Basing his symbols on the letters of the roman alphabet had not only the advantage of familiarity, but also of arbitrariness, mirroring the arbitrary relation between word-form and meaning which gives human language its power as a semiotic system. Arbitrarinesss means that symbol definitions can be adjusted as phonetic theory changes, new symbols can be added to the stock and the transcriber can choose how much detail to include in a transcription. The broad-narrow distinction, and the use of roman-based symbols, was continued by Henry Sweet (1845–1912) in his *Broad* and *Narrow Romic*, the former embodying the phoneme principle in all but name (Collins & Mees, 1999, pp. 43–44), and by the IPA. Two other important notation systems in the mid-nineteenth century were the *Standard Alphabet* of the Egyptologist Richard Lepsius (1810–84) and the *Visible Speech* system designed by Alexander

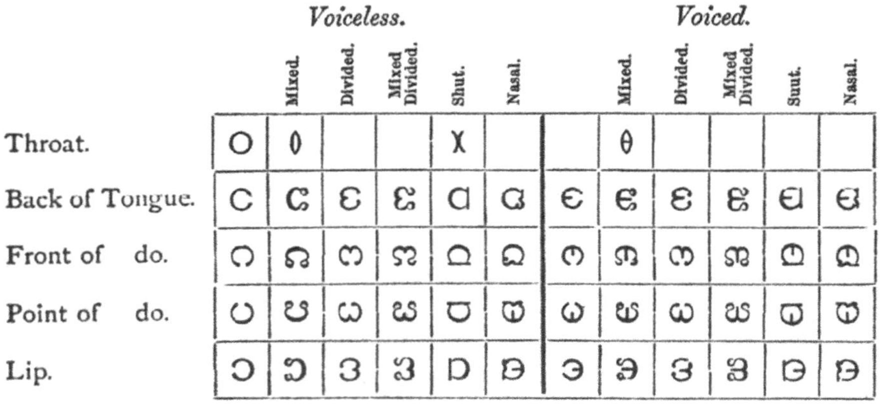

	Voiceless.					*Voiced.*				
	Mixed.	Divided.	Mixed Divided.	Shut.	Nasal.	Mixed.	Divided.	Mixed Divided.	Shut.	Nasal.
Throat.	O	0		X		θ				
Back of Tongue.	C	Ϲ̦	Ɛ	Ɛ̦	ꓷ	ꓷ	Ɛ	Ɛ̦	Ɛ	Ɛ̦	Ꮛ	Ꮛ
Front of do.	ꓛ	ꓛ̦	ꝏ	ꝏ̦	Ꙩ	Ꙩ	ꙩ	ꙩ̦	ꝏ	ꝏ̦	Ꙩ	Ꙩ
Point of do.	�	ꚇ	ꙍ	ꚇ̦	ꙅ	ꙅ̦	ꙍ	ꚇ̦	ꙍ	ꚇ̦	Ꙍ	Ꙍ
Lip.	Ɔ	ꙅ	3	ʒ̦	ꓓ	ꓷ	ꙅ	ꙅ̦	3	ꙅ̦	Ꙅ	Ꙅ

Figure 1.4 Bell's table of organic symbols for voiceless and voiced consonants showing systematic relationship between symbol structure and phonetic features (Bell, 1867, p. 66).

Melville Bell (1814–80). Lepsius' system was conceived principally as a universal orthography which could be applied to hitherto unwritten languages (Lepsius, 1863, pp. 26–30), rather than as an expression of theoretical phonetic categories – we see in it the preoccupations of the philologist more clearly than those of the phonetician. When it is lexical items which are to be represented rather than categories of sound, there is no call for a broad-narrow distinction. Bell's system, however, was highly focused on phonetic processes and was an experiment in organic alphabet creation, reminiscent of Wilkins, such that 'all Relations of Sound are symbolized by Relations of Form' (Bell, 1867, p. 35) in an iconically motivated fashion; Figure 1.4 shows examples. However, it is difficult to apply the broad-narrow distinction using organic notation systems, and, as Sweet recognized, if phonetic theory changes then the symbols have to change. In addition to their unfamiliarity, another practical disadvantage of organic and systematic notation systems is that symbols look very similar, making them more difficult to read.

6.2 Instrumental Phonetics

Explorations in instrumental phonetics were carried out in the nineteenth century by physical scientists rather than linguists. They approached speech more as a mechanical product of the vocal tract, rather than as the manifestation of abstract language. Hermann von Helmholtz (1821–94) identified pharyngeal and buccal resonances and experimented with synthetic speech (Kemp, 2001, p. 1471). A laryngoscope was invented by Benjamin Babington in 1829 (Bailey, 1996) and refined by Max Oertel in 1878 by adapting stroboscopy, enabling observation of vocal fold vibration (Peter, 1996). Instruments for making aerodynamic measurements included the manometer and spirometer, and sound-waves were first represented graphically by Édouard Scott on his Phonautograph in 1859 – they were transmitted via a membrane to a pencil which drew them on a rotating drum (Tillmann, 1995). First experiments in direct palatography were carried out in 1872 by a London dentist, J. Oakley Coles. A few years later another dentist, Norman W. Kingsley of New York, invented the artificial palate, making it easier to inspect patterns of linguo-palatal contact (Abercrombie, 1965, p. 125). The invention of sound recording by Thomas Edison in 1877 enabled repeated listening to the same utterance more than once, and collection and storage of speech for later analysis.

By the time of the IPA's formation, phonetic theory, notation systems and the scientific understanding of speech sounds were sufficiently advanced to be forged into a comprehensive science of phonetics, although this was not to happen fully until the twentieth century.

Historical Chapter IPA to Modern Period

Zeki Majeed Hassan and Mark J. Jones

This section is necessarily brief given the huge expansion in the scope of phonetic science and the range of subdisciplines and specializations, covering fundamental questions like the evolution of the vocal tract and the nature of speech to areas of major psychological interest with practical applications like multimodal speech perception. Detailed overviews of some specific subareas are provided in the specialist chapters in this volume. The story of phonetics from the late nineteenth century to the present day is one of increasing reliance on experimentation and technological innovation, and the development of hypotheses and testable models of speech production and perception.

At the beginning of the twentieth century, the stage was set for phonetics to develop into a comprehensive and coherent science. There were two strands to this development, one more experimental, one more taxonomic, but both continued the work of early 'proto-phoneticians'. Descriptions of speech sounds were being founded upon a growing understanding of their articulatory basis, with a regularized terminology. Physiological alphabets like Bell's *Visible Speech* gave way to alphabets which used articulation to organize sets of more or less holistic symbols (rather than iconic composites), leading to the IPA, which is almost certainly the most widely used and widely understood phonetic alphabet. The IPA performs the dual function of classification, in a kind of phonetic periodic table of the elements, and transcription. Just like the periodic table of the elements, the IPA system has been used to predict what sounds might be possible. It grew from a system of representing speech sounds largely with language teaching in mind – showing again the practical applications and origins of phonetics – to a system which was intended to represent all the sounds possible in human languages. Transcription systems like the IPA provide a symbolic classification system, as well as a means for representing speech sounds in writing. Much of this groundwork was prompted by considerations of historical sound change such as Sievers' *Grundzüge der Phonetik* (1905) and by interest in dialects such as Ellis (1869) and Sweet (1877). This aim was no doubt furthered by contact with more 'exotic' languages in European colonies and as North American linguists described indigenous languages. By the 1930s, the descriptive phonetic techniques which had been applied to languages like English (Jones, 1918 (1972)) were being applied to languages like (Chi) Shona (Doke, 1931), Efik (Ward, 1933), and to Khoisan languages (Beach, 1938).

The IPA has stood the test of time as a useful tool for describing and categorizing speech sounds, and is de facto the universal phonetic script having overshadowed other systems, both alphabetic and physiological, like Bell's 'visible speech'.

Consonant sounds are classified in terms of voice, place and manner, and vowels are classified in terms of height, fronting and rounding. Basic symbols can be modified by the use of multiple diacritics. The IPA continues to be managed by the International Phonetic Association (also abbreviated as IPA). The system of IPA symbols itself has been expanded and revised several times to include, for example, consonants produced using different airstream mechanisms and to make it more internally consistent, though a few inconsistencies remain, such as the basic symbol for a voiced labiodental nasal having no basic counterparts among the plosives (the dental diacritic must be applied to the bilabial symbols). The latest revision took place in 2005 and added the symbol for a voiced labiodental flap (see Olson & Hajek, 1999), and there has been recent discussion concerning low vowels (Barry & Trouvain, 2008; Ball, 2009; Recasens, 2009). Classification is impressionistic, and the IPA is rarely used in mainstream phonetic work for data collection, the symbols instead being used as labels for more detailed instrumental analyses, though it continues to be used in clinical work and outside phonetics. An extended IPA (ExtIPA) specifically for use in clinical work has been devised (Duckworth et al., 1990). Since 1886 the IPA has published a journal specifically for phonetics, now called the *Journal of the International Phonetic Association*.

At the same time that the IPA was being developed, experimental work on phonetics continued, utilizing existing equipment such as the kymograph, a device for recording pressure variations (such as blood pressure, but equally oral air pressure) on a revolving drum. The kymograph utilized a device much like the mouthpiece of a brass instrument to transfer vibrations through a hose to a very delicate stylus. The stylus recorded the movements by wiping a clean line onto soot-blackened paper as the drum holding the paper was rotated. Several styli could be combined on one sheet. In the Menzerath and Lacerda study mentioned below, the drum had a circumference of 250 cm to record longer utterances, and was about 18 cm deep to allow multiple simultaneous tracings for time (from a 100 Hz electrical tuning fork), lip movements (one line each), movements of the lower jaw, as well as nasal and oral airflow. The kymograph was used extensively in early experimental phonetic work by Rousselot (1897–1908), Scripture (1906) and Panconcelli-Calzia (1924), and used by Stetson (1951, originally published 1928) in his study of motor control (Stetson, 1951, p. 25 mentions using the original white-on-black kymograph tracings as negatives for making photographic plates). Many other ingenious devices were adapted or developed for experimental phonetic work, as depicted in Rousselot, Scripture and Panconcelli-Calzia. Many of these devices look cumbersome and, frankly, terrifying to modern eyes, but they represent the high point of phonetic devices from the 'age of engineering', and as indicated above many were still in use at the time of Stetson 1951. Experimental phonetic work was also inspired to some extent by contact with non-European languages, as attested by the contributions Panconcelli-Calzia made to journals like *Zeitschrift für Eingeborenensprachen* (later *Zeitschrift für Kolonialsprachen*), such as the kymographic tracings of voiceless nasals in Kizaramo (Dzalamo, Tanzania) reproduced in Panconcelli-Calzai (1924, p. 47). Several short-lived journals for experimental phonetics were founded, such as *Vox* (Berlin, 1916–22), *Archives néerlandaises de phonétique expérimentale* (Haarlem, 1927–47) and the *Zeitschrift für Experimentalphonetik* (Leipzig, 1930–2). By this time, phonetics was clearly regarded as a science, and the discipline had a wide enough following to permit the holding in 1932 of the first *International Congress of Phonetic Sciences* (ICPhS) in Amsterdam, which was attended by 136 delegates from more than a dozen countries (Pols, 2004).

Married to these technological advances, new ways of analysing and thinking about phonology within the nascent discipline of linguistics were providing a growing appreciation of the links between various levels of analysis such as the phoneme and physical instantiations in varying contexts. As phonological analysis also developed, it became clear(er) that the term 'speech sound' is potentially ambiguous. Different kinds of transcription were recognized based on developing themes of abstraction and realization. A narrow phonetic transcription would involve the greatest attention to detail, whereas a broad phonemic transcription would involve the use of IPA symbols (almost) completely devoid of precise phonetic content. Some tension appears to have arisen between experimentalists and those (perhaps not all phoneticians) who sought to develop an all-embracing phonetic alphabet. It was already well-known that speech sounds were not 'static and immobile like letters standing next to each other' ('starr und unlebendig wie die Buchstaben nebeneinander stehen', [my translation]; Panconcelli-Calzia, 1924, p. 69, quoting Meinhof, 1918), and that the relationship between phonetic script and speech was 'loose' ('locker', Panconcelli-Calzia, 1924, p. 68). Scripture and Daniel Jones both referred to the adjacent influences of speech sounds upon one another, and in 1933 the term 'coarticulation' (Koartikulation) was formally introduced in Menzerath and Lacerda's experimental monograph (Menzerath & Lacerda, 1933; Hardcastle, 1981). Coarticulation and the relationship between dynamic speech and a more abstract (and possibly invariant) target has of course been a major topic in experimental phonetic research ever since, and this is unlikely to change.

There was interest in speech perception too in the early years of the twentieth century; Panconcelli-Calzia (1924, p. 111) refers to an experiment involving the tones of Ewe sentences, which were whistled rather than spoken, with identification of the original sentences tested, but sound recording techniques (rather than kymography) were still relatively underdeveloped. Recording to vinyl discs allowed a recording to be preserved relatively well, but was time-consuming and inflexible. Magnetic tape would eventually allow for physical manipulation in the form of tape-splicing techniques, but more sophisticated speech perception experiments only really became possible in the age of electronics. In the 1930s, the Vocoder, the first speech synthesizer had been developed at Bell Telephone Labs in the United States of America, where later still the spectrograph would be developed, but it was not until the 1950s that speech synthesis really came of age at Haskins Labs (founded in the 1930s, and increasingly specializing in speech from the 1940s onwards).

If phonetics in the period before 1940 was mainly – but not exclusively – concerned with transcription and speech production, research ever since has been dominated by the insights made possible by the invention of the sound spectrograph and the rise of acoustic phonetics. The ability to visualize the speech signal in linear acoustic terms has revolutionized approaches to speech. The acoustic signal is the bridge between speaker and listener. The kymograph had been adapted from its initial and more medical applications and applied to speech. In the 1940s various new technologies were developed, mainly within the growing field of telecommunications, including a machine developed at Bell labs in the United States of America for representing speech in real time (and temporarily) as glowing images on a moving band treated with phosphor (the images faded rapidly and were deliberately erased by 'quenching lamps' before the next image was applied; see Dudley & Gruenz, 1946). The sound spectrograph was also developed at Bell labs in the United States of America (Koenig et al., 1946), and this is the machine that has come to dominate acoustic analysis. In its original form, the spectrograph was limited to recording 2.4 seconds (2,400 ms) of speech on tape, which was then run repeatedly through a filter whose frequency response was changed manually. The signal from the filter was amplified and burned a permanent image onto paper, in a reversal of the kymographic technique of removing a soot-blackened layer. Once the entire frequency range had been analysed by successive replays, the image could be removed from the drum for manual analysis of frequency and duration. The image showed time along the horizontal axis, frequency on the vertical axis and the darkness of the image showed amplitude. The spectrograph is rarely referred to now, and has become a virtual part of the phonetician's arsenal in the form of speech analysis software, but spectrograms and spectra remain a vital part of speech analysis. In their modern form, they can be produced to any desired length, and manipulated post-hoc by zooming in and altering various settings for greater time or frequency resolution and amplitude.

The age of electricity also allowed for more sophisticated speech synthesis, and also acoustic modelling of the vocal tract. In the 1940s Chiba and Kajiyama used modelling of the vocal tract as electrical circuits to investigate the nature of the vowel (Chiba & Kajiyama, 1941), and later, Gunnar Fant developed the first comprehensive theory of speech acoustics, utilizing data from x-rays and vocal tract area functions as well as modelling (Fant, 1960). This work has continued, perhaps most famously (apart from Fant's work) in the work of Ken Stevens at MIT which has produced the modern-day 'speech acoustics' Bible *Acoustic Phonetics* (1998). Work with spectrograms at Haskins in the 1950s led to the development of the pattern playback device, a device which 'read' real and (importantly) artificial stylized spectrograms, using light reflected through grooves to build up a synthetic speech signal (e.g. Delattre et al., 1955). Work with pattern playback laid the foundations for modern speech perception research.

Modern experimental phonetics can draw on a whole range of articulatory tracking and imaging techniques as well as airflow acoustic analysis and more longstanding investigations of airflow. Modern techniques include electropalatography (Hardcastle, 1972), electrolaryngography (Fourcin & Abberton, 1971), electromagnetic midsagittal accelerometry (e.g. Perkell et al., 1992), ultrasound tongue imaging (e.g. Keller & Ostry, 1983) as well as Magnetic Resonance Imaging or MRI (even in real-time, Byrd et al., 2009) and techniques which also permit brain function to be indirectly imaged (e.g. fMRI).

The future of work in phonetics will involve a synthesis of experimental techniques to investigate physical speech movements, their aerodynamic and acoustic consequences and their underlying control mechanisms.

Notes

1. In the second century CE Galen, regarded as the founder of experimental physiology, characterized voicing as 'breath beaten by the cartilages of the larynx' (Kemp, 2006, p. 472), which is perhaps the closest anyone came to an account of voicing in the ancient Western world.
2. The first principle of the IPA as given in 1888 is: 'There should be a separate letter for each distinctive sound'.

2 Research Methods in Speech Perception

Rachael-Anne Knight and Sarah Hawkins

1 Introduction

Speech perception refers to how humans process spoken language. Some definitions restrict the process to identification of sound units (phonology); but this chapter takes a broader view. In most natural listening situations our main job is to turn the acoustic waveform produced by a speaker into a meaningful message. This process takes into account not only individual speech sounds but also the changing pitch of the voice (intonation), the word order (syntax), the meanings of individual words (semantics) and our knowledge of the speaker and the situation (pragmatics). Despite the number of variables involved, for most of us speech perception is an easy task which we can do even in difficult listening conditions, such as when there is background noise from other people talking, or other types of noise. Human listeners are much better than computers at understanding speech in noise and at interpreting whole discourses (Kewley-Port, 1999), indicating how much we have yet to learn about how humans perceive speech. Due to space limitations, this chapter is confined to research involving auditory perception of word-sized units or smaller. We will not consider comprehension related to syntax, semantics or pragmatics, although, as noted by Smith (this volume), the future of speech perception research probably lies in understanding how speech perception functions at these levels and beyond. We assume familiarity with the basic questions and foci of interest in speech perception. These issues are covered in textbooks and chapters such as Hawkins (1999a and 1999b).

Research into speech perception is challenging because the processes of perception cannot be directly observed. Some information about these processes can be gleaned in everyday situations from misunderstandings or slips of the ear (see Boyd, 2008), from neuropsychological data and from the perceptual abilities of people after strokes or head injuries (see Badecker, 2008). However, the vast majority of research in this area is experimental in nature. In a typical speech perception experiment, a researcher presents a person (known as the subject, listener or participant) with stimuli, and the participant makes some kind of judgement or decision about the stimuli, or is subjected to techniques which allow for perception to be monitored without a conscious response. Experiments allow the researcher to have precise control over the stimuli the participant hears, and also to measure their responses accurately.

Like all experiments, those in speech perception involve the researcher manipulating aspects of the world, and measuring how people react to these manipulations. Aspects of the experiment that can vary are called variables. Variables manipulated by the researcher are called independent variables, while those that the researcher measures are called dependent variables. Other variables that are known or suspected to affect what is being measured must be held constant so they do not affect results; these are known as control variables. If such variables are not controlled then they, rather than the independent variables, might be responsible for the results, in which case we say that the uncontrolled variable and one or more independent variables are confounded. Chapters 2 and 3 of Snodgrass et al. (1985) provide useful discussion of these and other aspects of experimental design.

The following sections discuss speech perception experiments using the subsections that are common in journal articles, including participants and stimuli (which largely relate to independent variables), procedures and the various dependent variables that can be measured and analysed.

2 Participants

Some important independent variables relate to the characteristics of the listeners involved in the study. We might be interested in differences between speech perception skills of men and women, or monolinguals and bilinguals, or children and adults. As a researcher cannot assign sex, languages spoken or age to a listener, these variables are manipulated by the way listeners are selected. A researcher might construct two groups of listeners, one group of men, and one group of women, and then compare the groups' results on the same task. It is important to note that, even if participant factors are not independent variables in the experiment, they might still need to be controlled by the experimenter, to avoid introducing variables which would confound the results. There are many participant variables, some more obvious than others, which can affect speech perception.

2.1 Age

Speech perception abilities change across the lifespan, with infants learning to tune into the patterns used in their native language/s (Werker & Tees, 1984). While they do much of this in the first year of life, these abilities do change over time, and so experiments with young children must distinguish fairly narrow age bands. It is generally assumed that speech perception does not vary much during adulthood, and thus many speech perception experiments use convenience samples of university students, which restrict listeners to a range of 18–35 years, for example. However, elderly listeners have different speech perception abilities and strategies from younger adults, partly because hearing typically deteriorates with age, yet vocabulary does not. Most types of distortion to stimuli affect elderly listeners more than young listeners, especially when more than one type of distortion is applied simultaneously (Gordon-Salant & Fitzgibbons, 1995).

2.2 Languages Spoken

Many studies restrict listeners to those who are monolingual in the language of testing. Bilingual speakers may perform differently to monolingual speakers of either language, and add unwanted variation to the results. For example, even early bilinguals and trilinguals are poorer than monolingual speakers of that language at perceiving their second language in noise (Tabri et al., 2011). If the focus of research is bilingual speakers then care needs to be taken to control the age at which they first learnt their languages, the amount of exposure they had to each language during acquisition and how much they use it in daily life (e.g. Flege, 1999), as all these factors affect speech perception abilities (Best & Tyler, 2007).

2.3 Clinical Diagnosis

Many studies of speech perception focus on listeners who have 'no reported difficulties of speech or hearing'. Individuals who have hearing impairments perceive differently to hearing individuals, so are usually excluded from research on hearing populations. Less obviously, other disorders can also affect speech perception. For example, children with dyslexia are more affected by hearing speech in noisy conditions than children without dyslexia (Ziegler et al., 2009). Of course the speech perception abilities of those with clinical diagnoses can be the focus of research; comparing the abilities of those with Williams Syndrome to those of typically developing controls (Majerus et al., 2011), or the abilities of those with bilateral versus unilateral cochlear implants (Dunn et al., 2010), are just two examples.

2.4 Accent

There is much evidence that it is easier to understand speech presented in your own accent than in an unfamiliar accent (e.g. Floccia, et al., 2006). Therefore it is often useful to restrict listeners to those who share the accent of the test stimuli; in some circumstances, such as clinical testing, it can be valuable to create different versions of stimuli suitable for the accent of the listeners to be tested. There is also evidence, however, that speakers of non-standard accents are not as impaired when listening to the media standard (such as Standard Southern British English or General American) as speakers of the media standard are when listening to non-standard accents (e.g. Adank et al., 2009). This is presumed to be due to exposure via the media, and contact with speakers of the standard accent, although this is yet to be demonstrated.

2.5 Sex/Gender

We know that there are differences between the speech produced by men and women, such as phonation, pitch and articulation, and that these differences occur for both biological and social reasons (see Simpson, 2009 for a review). Differences between the sexes might also be found in perception, as women appear to be more sensitive to phonetic variables that carry social information. For example, Hay et al. (2006) asked participants to listen to synthetic vowels and indicate which vowel they had heard. The sheets on which they indicated their responses included the name of one of two accents, although listeners' attention was not explicitly drawn to this information. Women's responses were influenced by the expected accent, while men's were not. In addition, Liederman et al. (2011) indicate that women are more reliant on contextual information than men when listening to distorted speech.

3 Stimuli

Variables related to how stimuli or their presentation vary are called stimulus variables. Unlike some participant variables, these are under the direct control of the researcher. People unfamiliar with speech research are often surprised at how many factors need to be considered to ensure that there are no confounding variables. It makes good sense to spend time, care and attention on designing stimuli, so that all relevant factors are taken into account.

3.1 Initial Decisions about Stimuli

3.1.1 Levels of Language
An experimenter is typically interested in a particular linguistic level that bears a label drawn from linguistic theory: for example, segment (often called phoneme), syllable, word or sentence. However, no segment of sound functions solely as a phoneme: even an isolated vowel such as [ɑ] can be considered as simultaneously a bundle of features, a syllable nucleus, a syllable, an intonational phrase and an entire utterance with a particular function – perhaps an 'ah!' of discovery, or an 'ah' of sympathy. As the experimenter, it is important that you ensure that you design your experiment so that listeners' responses really do tap into the linguistic level you hope to target. An experiment in which the task is to identify a syllable as /bɑ/ or /dɑ/ might be tapping into features or phonemes, but also, in a non-rhotic accent, it contrasts a word with a non-word ('bar' vs. /dɑ/).

3.1.2 Natural or Synthetic Stimuli
The stimuli used in speech perception experiments are often tokens of natural speech recorded in excellent conditions using high quality equipment (see www.phon.ucl.ac.uk/resource/audio/recording.html). Natural stimuli are desirable because, unlike most synthesized stimuli used for perception experiments, they are produced by a human vocal tract, and are therefore closer to the speech heard in everyday listening situations. However, speech produced for experiments (so-called lab speech) rarely mirrors spontaneous speech, since the speaker has been told what to say and has been observed while saying it. Nevertheless, lab speech is crucially important in current speech perception research because of the systematic control it imposes on stimuli (Xu, 2010). Researchers can minimize the unnaturalness of lab speech by acclimatizing speakers to the recording situation, using natural-sounding dialogues rather than isolated words or sentences, and giving time to practice, while checking recordings for any unnaturalness.

As an alternative to natural speech, synthetic stimuli can be created (see Holmes & Holmes, 2001). Tokens can be created by combining already existing speech in new ways (using concatenative synthesis or by splicing parts of speech from different natural signals together), or from scratch using formant or articulatory synthesis. More commonly, natural tokens of speech can be manipulated in various ways. Freeware such as PRAAT (Boersma & Weenink, 2011) allows researchers to manipulate aspects of a natural speech signal such as duration, formant transitions or the pitch contour, and resynthesize the signal so that it still sounds natural. One advantage of synthetic stimuli is that it allows cues to combine in ways that do not occur naturally. For example, Summerfield and Haggard (1977) investigated the role of Voice Onset Time (VOT) and F1 frequency for the voiced/voiceless distinction. Using synthetic syllables allowed them to vary VOT and F1 onset precisely, and to combine them in ways that do not occur in natural speech. While synthetic speech has many advantages, it is usually harder to understand than natural speech even when it sounds natural (see, for example, Ogden et al., 2000).

3.1.3 Segmental Factors

As noted, many experiments focus on individual segments or phonemes. There is a great deal of evidence that different features of sounds contribute differently to perception in different situations. For example, in a classic experiment, Miller and Nicely (1951) asked listeners to name English consonants heard in different degrees of noise. While voicing and nasality information were preserved even in very noisy conditions, place of articulation was severely affected by noise.

Even when segments are not the focus of the experiment, they must still be considered to ensure that confounding variables are not introduced. For example, when an experiment focuses on intonation, a number of aspects of the segmental string need to be controlled (see Wichmann et al., 2000 for details). Voiceless segments will disrupt the intonation contour, and other types of segmental variables are associated with microprosodic variations. Vowel height and F0 interact, with open vowels having a lower F0 than closed vowels. Furthermore the duration of syllabic constituents (such as the onset and rhyme) can influence how the intonation contour is realized.

3.2 Lexical Factors

Many of the factors considered in this section are also issues for research with written words. Note however that results gained from written stimuli may not generalize to spoken stimuli. In particular, they might have very limited relevance to perception of connected or rapid speech.

3.2.1 Words versus Non-words

Many speech perception experiments present single words as stimuli, but tokens need not be real words in the participants' native language: such tokens are called pseudowords, nonwords or nonsense words (or syllables). These terms are used somewhat interchangeably across disciplines, but we will call those words that follow the phonology of the language in question pseudowords. Responses to words are normally faster than responses to pseudowords (e.g. Rubin et al., 1976), and the lexical status of stimuli also affects perception of individual speech sounds. Ganong (1980) demonstrated that the same ambiguous sound is classified differently according to whether it is presented as part of a word or pseudoword. So, an ambiguously voiced alveolar plosive might be classified as /d/ at the start of /ɪʃ/ (as 'dish' is a word but 'tish' is not) but as /t/ at the start of /ɪf/ (as 'tiff' is a word, but 'diff' is not).

3.2.2 Lexical Frequency

Words that are common, or more frequent, are generally processed more quickly and easily (e.g. Howes, 1957; Grosjean, 1980), but there is some debate about how frequency interacts with factors such as word length (see Bradley & Forster, 1987 for discussion).

3.2.3 Age of Acquisition

Humans learn words at different times in their lives, and this variable, correlated with lexical frequency, is known as 'age of acquisition'. Clearly it does not make sense to present children with words that are not yet in their vocabularies, but age of acquisition may need to be taken into account even for adults. Age of acquisition may affect processing speed, particularly when lexical frequency is controlled (e.g. Garlock et al., 2001) suggesting that words acquired early might be more robustly represented.

3.2.4 Imageability

Production studies will often choose imageable (picturable) stimuli, so that these can be presented pictorially for naming. However, there is also evidence that speech perception can be affected by the imageability of words; Tyler et al. (2000) indicate that subjects can respond more quickly to words that are highly imageable.

3.2.5 Neighbourhood Density

Neighbourhood density is the number of words that differ from a word or pseudoword by a single segment. Words from sparse neighbourhoods are processed more quickly and accurately (Luce & Pisoni, 1998). This is the opposite to findings in visual word recognition where low-frequency words from dense neighbourhoods are recognized more quickly (see Goldinger et al., 1992 for discussion). Neighbourhood density effects are an important illustration of how findings can differ substantially between modalities.

3.2.6 Length/Duration
The length of a stimulus can be thought of in terms of its duration, or the number of segments or syllables it contains. Word duration affects several performance factors, including how many words can be remembered from a list (e.g. Baddeley et al., 1975).

3.2.7 Prosodic Factors
In Germanic languages, strong syllables are often taken to mark the start of words (e.g. Van Donsellar et al., 2005), reflecting the statistically greater likelihood of this pattern. This distinction is one of the first cues to word segmentation: it is present in children as young as seven and a half months (e.g. Jusczyk, 1999). Listeners are sensitive to other aspects of the rhythm of language with infants as young as four days old discriminating between languages from different rhythm classes, such as syllable and stress-timed (Mehler et al., 1988). This means that perceptual experiments need to consider the rhythm class of any languages used for comparison.

We noted above that vowels have an intrinsic F0, which affects the pitch contour. Conversely, altering the F0 can affect which vowels are perceived, either directly, in the same way as formant frequencies, or indirectly by affecting listeners' impression of the speaker's size and gender (see Barreda & Nearey, 2012).

3.3 Contextual Factors and Priming

The way we recognize sounds and words takes into account not just the acoustic stimuli, but a whole host of other considerations, one of which is the context in which stimuli are presented (Frauenfelder & Tyler, 1987 discuss different types of context). For example, Warren and Warren (1970) demonstrated that, when a sound is replaced with noise, listeners use the rest of the sentence to interpret the word which includes the noise. Thus, the identical acoustic chunk '*eel', where '*' is some irrelevant noise, is heard as 'wheel' in a sentence like 'the *eel was on the axle', but 'peel' in 'the *eel was on the orange', a finding known as the phoneme restoration effect. The sentence structure and the listening situation can also affect perception (see Smith this volume for a fuller discussion). Thus the context must be taken into consideration when designing experiments.

Priming techniques can be used to investigate how perception of one stimulus is affected by presentation of another, and is thus used to examine, for example, influences of meaning and phonological relationships between words (semantic and phonological priming respectively). Two items are presented, both auditorily, both visually or cross-modally. The first item is called the *prime*, and the second the *target*. In semantic priming, their relationship varies such that researchers can compare responses to those that are semantically related (such as *dog* and *cat*) and unrelated (such as *pan* and *cat*). Typically, processing is facilitated by prior presentation of a related or identical prime, so, for example, 'cat' will be processed more quickly and easily after 'dog' than after 'pan'.

4 Reduction of Stimulus Information

To avoid ceiling effects (where participants score as well as possible in all conditions) we can degrade stimuli in various ways, the most popular method being to present speech in background noise. The signal intensity compared with the degree of background noise (the signal to noise ratio or SNR) is a crucial determinant of how well speech can be understood. The effects of SNR are themselves influenced by factors such as the type of noise (Simpson & Cook, 2005), whether participants listen to foreign- or native-accented speech (Bradlow & Alexander, 2007) and the predictability of the word from its preceding context (Kalikow et al., 1977).

Other methods of reducing the information present in, or available from, the stimuli include presenting stimuli at low volumes (e.g. Cutler & Butterfield, 1992) or in reverberation (e.g. Nabelek, 1988), or filtered to remove particular frequencies that differentially degrade particular types of linguistic information (e.g. Fletcher, 1953 in Assmann & Summerfield, 2004; Mehler et al., 1988). Relatedly, to foreground prosodic patterns, segmental variability can be reduced by using 'reiterant speech' where every syllable is replaced by /ma/ (Larkey, 1983), or, more recently, by 'saltanaj' (Ramus & Mehler, 1999), so-called because, for example, all fricatives are replaced with /s/, all vowels with /a/, all liquids with /l/ and so on.

Gating techniques reduce information in the time domain. Typically, a series of stimuli are made from a single recorded word by removing increasingly large portions from its end. So the first section, or gate, may be only 20–30 ms long (Grosjean, 1996) and the final gate contains the whole word. Gating allows researchers to identify how much of a word needs to be heard before it is recognized, and to compare this in different environments, such as when the word is presented in isolation or in context (e.g. van Petten et al., 1999).

5 Procedures

Procedures, or paradigms, go under a variety of names, which often identify the task of the listener (auditory lexical decision, shadowing, word spotting), sometimes the way stimuli were modified (gating) and sometimes the way the dependent variables are measured (eye tracking). Nevertheless, the paradigms share a number of commonalities and therefore, rather than looking at each one individually, we take a step backwards to think more about these commonalities. For more about particular paradigms, see the 1996 special issue of *Language and Cognitive Processes*.

5.1 Repetitions

The number of times each stimulus is repeated will vary according to the experimental design, but, when possible, it is advisable to include a fairly large number of repetitions, usually 10–20. This is so that spurious effects, such as listeners' momentarily losing attention, do not unduly influence the results, since the more trials listeners hear, the smaller the effect of an atypical answer (see Sawsuch, 1996). Stimuli are typically presented so that repetitions of the same stimulus are separated by other stimuli (or by filler items, used so that the purpose of the experiment is not obvious) in order to avoid fatigue or perseveration in responses. Continuously presenting the same stimulus can result in changes in perception. Warren (1968), for example, indicates that playing the same item continuously for three minutes can lead to as many as 30 changes (known as verbal transformation effects) in the word perceived, dependent on factors such as word complexity. In intelligibility tests, however, each stimulus can normally only be heard once since priming effects influence responses to later repetitions.

5.2 Randomization and Counterbalancing

Many experiments are designed so that every participant serves in every condition. For example, it is usual for a single participant to be exposed to both real and pseudowords, or words presented at several SNRs. It is therefore important to consider carefully the order in which stimuli are presented. Presenting all the real words at the start of the experiment, and all the pseudowords at the end, might lead to better performance for the words, as people tire during the experiment, or, alternatively, better performance for the pseudowords as people improve with practice (a confound). To avoid these problems, stimuli are randomized or counterbalanced. Randomization means that stimuli are mixed up so that listeners cannot predict which type (e.g. word or pseudoword) comes next. Counterbalancing, by contrast, systematically varies the order in which the conditions appear so that different groups of participants do the conditions in different orders and all orders are completed. These types of design decisions can be complicated; they affect whether you have 'between' or 'within' group designs, and the statistics you use. See Snodgrass et al. (1985, chapter 2) for further discussion.

5.3 Tasks which Require an Overt Judgement from the Listener

The listener's task must already have been considered when the stimuli are designed. Many widely used speech perception tasks require participants to listen to a stimulus, and make a judgement about it, which they then signal by pressing a button, or typing or writing a response. These types of experiments are based on the tenets of signal detection theory, and the descriptions here are simplified versions of those in Macmillan and Creelman's (2005) seminal text, extended by reference to other standard terminology when appropriate. The basic design types discussed below are distinguished by the following:

(1) How many stimuli are presented to the listener at any one time? Do they listen to a single stimulus and make a judgment, or do they hear two or more stimuli and compare them?

(2) How many different responses can be made? In button press tasks there is a closed-set of responses, as there are a fixed number of buttons to press (unless there is an 'other' button, but in that case you only know that the stimulus did not fit any of the expected categories). However, if listeners can say, or write any response, such as the word they heard, then the response set is open and only limited by the size of their vocabulary.

(3) How do the number of possible responses relate to the number of different stimuli? For example, if there are four unique stimuli there might be four unique responses, or only two possible responses and the experimenter is interested in how the four stimuli are divided among those responses.

In signal detection theory there are four basic design types, whose properties and their applications to speech perception studies we now outline. We describe typical designs but modifications (e.g. to the number/type of response) are quite common.

5.3.1 Detection
[One stimulus per trial (OSPT); 'go/no-go' response. Word-spotting; (phoneme/syllable)monitoring]

In detection experiments, participants hear a single stimulus in each trial. Their task is to respond only when they hear a particular target; otherwise they withhold their response. For example, in monitoring and word-spotting tasks, listeners hear words, pseudowords or sentences, and press a button when they hear a particular segment, syllable, word-within-a-word (arm in forearm) or other speech fragment. Similarly, mispronunciation detection tasks require listeners to indicate only when they hear a stimulus that has an incorrect pronunciation.

5.3.2 Recognition

[OSPT; 'yes/no' response. Lexical decision]

Recognition experiments likewise expose listeners to one stimulus at a time. However, unlike detection experiments, listeners choose between two responses on every trial. These designs are often called yes/no experiments, reflecting common labels for participants' response choices. In speech perception, the most common type of recognition experiment is lexical decision: listeners hear stimuli made up of words and pseudowords, and indicate whether each stimulus is a real word (yes) or not (no) in their language.

A slight variation to detection and recognition experiments are rating experiments. Listeners hear one stimulus at a time but can choose from more than two responses. Typically the response is a point on a rating scale. For example, they might rate the word-likeness of pseudowords, or how intelligible a speaker sounds.

5.3.3 Identification and Classification

[OSPT; equal or smaller number of responses, or open response. Phoneme labelling; word identification; intelligibility]

Classic identification experiments, where listeners hear only one stimulus at a time, generally offer listeners a choice from a large number of responses. Miller and Nicely (1951) played listeners multiple repetitions of 16 nonsense CV syllables in noise and asked them to choose which consonant they had heard from a choice of 16. Thus listeners had a 16-alternative forced choice from which they could respond, and, importantly, each stimulus had a different target response. An alternative is not to dictate the choices ('open response'). It has the advantage that the participant can record what he/she actually heard, and the disadvantage that the experimenter may have to decide how to classify different responses (e.g. are /k/ and /kl/ responses the same or different, when the stimuli are intended to be CV?). Open response is typically used when the stimuli are connected speech (e.g. sentences) whose intelligibility is being tested.

Classification experiments are similar to identification experiments, except that the number of responses is smaller than the number of stimuli, and thus the focus of interest is in how listeners 'sort' stimuli into the categories provided by the fixed responses. In speech perception, more common terms for this type of design are 'categorization' (see McQueen, 1996), and, confusingly, 'identification'. The classic example in speech perception is the so-called identification part of categorical perception experiments, whereby listeners hear synthesized sounds on a continuum between two sounds, such as [b] and [p] varying in VOT. For every sound they must classify it as [b] or [p] even though, physically, some of the stimuli are ambiguous. Designs with two choices are typical, but more choices are possible. For example, a three choice design is appropriate when formant transitions vary from /b/ through /w/ to /u/.

5.3.4 Comparison

[2 or more stimuli in a trial; usually forced choice response. Phoneme discrimination; any other overt comparison]

Finally, it is possible to present more than one stimulus at each trial, for listeners to compare directly. This contrasts with the three paradigms above, where the comparison is always with a standard held 'in the listener's head' rather than actually heard. Listeners hear two stimuli and might say if they are the same or different (normally called 'discrimination'), or which one of the two holds some property, such as being louder. Such same/different comparison/discrimination designs comprise the second part of the categorical perception experiments described above: listeners hear pairs of stimuli from the synthetic continuum and compare them. Results from these experiments can reveal how listeners judge stimuli that differ by the same amount acoustically but which either come from within or across a phoneme category boundary.

The number of stimuli presented in one trial can differ. This is indicated by letter names: the comparison stimulus to be judged is called 'X'; the standard against which it is compared is called 'A'; and if there is another standard, it is 'B'. Thus AX designs have only two stimuli per trial, whereas ABX designs present two different stimuli, A and B, and the task is to judge whether X is the same as A or B. To reduce short-term memory load of remembering A while hearing B, AXB designs are increasingly popular. In all these designs, it is usual to have equal numbers of 'same' and 'different' trials.

5.4 Procedures which Avoid Overt Listener Judgements

Sometimes asking a listener to make a judgement about stimuli is inadvisable or impossible. For example, young children, and people with certain types of clinical conditions, might not be able to make reliable judgements. In addition, making metalinguistic judgements is an unnatural task: we rarely in our daily lives have to classify a sound as [b] or [p], or overtly decide whether a particular word is real or not. Other tasks avoid these problems by eliciting responses in ways other than an overt judgement.

5.4.1 Repetition and Shadowing

Researchers in child language development have increasingly focused on pseudoword repetition (or non-word repetition as it is often known). The task requires listeners to repeat pseudowords manipulated for word-likeness and phonotactic probability so that the role of familiarity and the presence of a stored lexical representation can be assessed (Chiat & Roy, 2007). Shadowing tasks require the listener to repeat continuous speech while they hear it. Such experiments investigate if errors in the stimuli are repeated and how repetition can be disrupted by degraded, ungrammatical, or otherwise unpredictable speech. Shadowing is generally considered to be a fairly natural task (although 'speeded' shadowing, which can give more sensitive results, is demanding/tiring), and suitable for participants who are not able to read (Bates & Liu, 1996). Results from shadowing and repetition are necessarily affected by participants' speech *production* abilities, so are not indicative of perceptual behaviour alone (Munson et al., 2005).

5.4.2 Neuroimaging Procedures

Neuroimaging indicates brain activity. Positron Emission Tomography (PET) and Functional Magnetic Resonance Imaging (fMRI) measure blood flow in the brain, while ElectroEncephaloGraphy (EEG) and MagnetoEncephaloGraphy (MEG) measure electric currents and magnetic fields respectively. All inform about where and when neural activity occurs, but vary in their temporal and spatial resolution. PET and fMRI give better spatial information; EEG gives excellent temporal information but poor spatial resolution; MEG gives good temporal and spatial resolution. Cabeza and Kingstone (2006) describe PET and fMRI applications in language research. All four techniques offer dynamic information about brain function. Static speech perception data are less commonly collected, though Golestani et al. (2011) used Magnetic Resonance Imaging (MRI) to study structural plasticity among phoneticians. Brain imaging can be used with passive listening tasks which do not require overt judgement. Indeed, fMRI and MEG preclude movement, although the better studies include 'behavioural' (non-imaging) tasks such as identification and categorization, using the same stimuli. Passive and active tasks may give different results (Scott & Wise, 2004).

5.4.3 Eye-tracking Procedures

Eye-tracking allows researchers to see how perception unfolds over time, rather than giving a measure at a single point in time. In a 'visual world paradigm', listeners see pictures while hearing speech. They may simply listen (e.g. Kamide et al., 2003), but often, they mouse-click on the picture they hear described, from choices on the computer screen (e.g. Allopenna et al., 1998). Eye-gaze is measured using a camera attached to the head. Changes in gaze direction are involuntary and fast (about 200 ms), preceding any other response. Eye-tracking allows prediction to be assessed, and can be used with or without overt metalinguistic judgements such as lexical decision or sentence comprehension. Tanenhaus and Brown-Schmidt (2008) review eye-tracking across broad areas of speech perception; Gow and McMurray (2007) discuss assimilation.

5.5 Infant Testing Procedures

Methods of testing the speech perception abilities of babies, infants and non-human animals are reviewed by Werker et al. (1997) and Hawkins (1999c). Classical and operant conditioning paradigms are used. This section outlines two operant paradigms. Babies aged 1–4 months can learn that a strong (high-amplitude) suck on an 'electronic teat' produces a rewarding sound, for example, /ba/. Their sucking rate declines to a baseline when this sound becomes boring, then, on the next suck, the sound changes, perhaps to /da/. If they immediately suck more frequently, they are presumed to have detected the change (Floccia et al., 1997 discuss the underlying mechanisms). 6–10 month old infants (and sometimes non-human participants, for example, Ramus et al., 2000) need a different technique. In the conditioned head turn procedure, the same sound plays every few seconds, and participants learn to turn their head when they hear a different sound; correct responses are rewarded with interesting visual stimuli. Of many variants of these procedures, observing whether infants prefer to look at a face with the appropriate mouth shape for the current sound examines audio-visual understanding, and older infants can turn in different directions to indicate the type of stimulus heard.

6 Results – Dependent Variables

In this section we consider which aspects of participant response are measured and analysed and reported in the results section of a paper.

6.1 Response Time

As we have seen, many speech perception experiments ask listeners to make an overt judgment about stimuli by pressing a button. A common dependent variable is response time (RT), also known as reaction time, which is the time taken to press the button. In other types of task, RT can be the time taken to repeat a word, or the time taken for an infant to turn his or her head. However, RT is only used as a measure for fairly rapid responses, as there is a great deal of variation between participants when they have to think for a long time about their response. The assumption behind RT measurement is that a stimulus which requires more processing will result in a longer RT than a stimulus that needs less processing.

RT is typically only calculated for correct responses. It is normally measured in milliseconds, and because of the way responses are distributed, is sometimes mathematically manipulated (usually converting to logarithms) before statistical analysis. Luce (1991) gives a thorough description of a variety of considerations in RT experiments. RT measures are typically subject to speed-accuracy trade-offs. Listeners may be very quick to respond but make errors, or are rather slow and largely accurate. The degree of the speed-accuracy trade-off may be affected by the instructions given, particularly whether participants are required to respond quickly (see Rinkenauer et al., 2004 for a discussion of models and the locus of speed-accuracy trade-offs).

It is important to consider carefully where to begin measuring RT from. In the recognition of spoken words, for example, measuring from the end of the word will miss responses to words that have been recognized before their acoustic offset. However, measuring from word onset is also problematic as words will become unique from all other words in the lexicon at different points, and therefore the uniqueness point must be controlled for (see Goldinger, 1996 and references therein).

6.2 Accuracy (Correct Responses)

Button press and other types of responses are also analysed for accuracy – either the percentage of correct responses, or the number correct if the number of responses in each condition is the same. For example, in a comparison task, where listeners are asked to say if two stimuli are different, researchers might calculate the hit and miss rates. Hits are the number/percentage of physically different stimuli classified as 'different', while misses are the number/percentage of physically different stimuli classified as 'same'. Responses to 'same' stimuli are not always analysed, but sometimes false alarms, when 'same' stimuli are responded to as 'different', are examined. In fact hit and miss rates can be misleading on their own; they assume that, when a listener is unsure of the correct answer, they respond randomly. However, listeners might instead employ a strategy, such as always answering 'same' or 'different' if they are unsure. This problem, called bias, can be overcome by calculating d' (d-prime). D' is part of signal detection theory, and is the number of hits minus the number of false alarms, or, more accurately, the z-transforms of these quantities. Keating (2005) briefly discusses d' in speech research; Macmillan and Creelman (2005) provide more information.

6.3 Errors

The *number* of errors is taken into account in the calculation of accuracy, as we saw in our discussion of the d' calculation, but other, more qualitative, analyses of errors can also be used. Such analyses are typical when participants have an open set of items to choose from. In gating tasks, for example, the incorrect words suggested after each gate can be compared to indicate which features of the stimuli influenced listeners (Grosjean, 1980). In pseudoword repetition, segmental and prosodic errors can be compared to give further information on processing (see Marton, 2006.)

6.4 Confidence Ratings

After making any kind of overt response listeners can be asked to indicate how confident they are in their judgement. Confidence ratings usually use a 5- or 7-point scale (often called a Likert-type scale). Even if listeners are forced into making a categorical choice (such as labelling a stimulus as a particular phoneme or as a real word), the rating scale allows them to indicate that they are more or less sure of their choice. Confidence ratings are frequently used in gating paradigms to distinguish the point at which the listener is only guessing at the target word from the point when they are sure of their choice (this point is known as the Total Acceptance Point). The use of confidence ratings in some designs (such as comparison designs) may also allow for statistically interpretable results while exposing listeners to fewer trials (Strange & Hawles, 1971). Norman (2010) discusses some of the difficulties and controversies in analysing Likert-type data. However, when there are lots of responses to every stimulus, confidence ratings are usually unnecessary. In these cases participants who are less confident will also perform less consistently, and this can be calculated by comparing their responses to chance level (which is 50% when there are only two possible responses).

6.5 Brain Function

In establishing where and when neural activity occurs, neural activity during the task (be it active or passive listening) must be compared to a relevant baseline. Silence is an inappropriate baseline if we wish to distinguish perception of speech from perception of noise, and thus baseline stimuli are usually 'as complex as speech, but not engaging the lexical semantic system' (Scott & Wise, 2004, p. 31). Researchers have used temporally reversed speech, spectrally rotated speech, or foreign languages. McGettigan and Scott (2012) discuss issues of lateralization of speech processing, while Price (2012) gives a useful historical perspective in summarizing the various brain structures (such as the left temporal lobe, premotor and frontoparietal regions) implicated in speech perception.

In EEG research, the signals recorded from the brain are called event related potentials (ERPs), which are time-locked to the beginning of a stimulus and recorded as waves that show voltage change over time. Researchers are interested in the amplitude of the wave (an indication of the amount of processing), and the delay between stimulus onset and peak amplitude of a wave (an indication of the speed of processing). Negative (N) and positive (P) peaks are often named with a number to indicate their time of occurrence (in milliseconds) after stimulus onset. For example, the N400 is a typical dependent variable in many experiments. The amplitude of this negative peak, occurring around 400ms after stimulus onset, is sensitive to many of the stimulus factors discussed above, such as neighbourhood density and context (see Kutas & Ferdermeier, 2011 for a review).

6.6 Saccades and Fixations in Eye-gaze

Experiments which measure responses by eye-gaze typically assess two variables: the number of times the eye moves (saccades) to look at a particular referent, and the proportion of time that the eye is fixated on the referents (Huettig et al., 2011). 'Looks' are usually investigated before, during and after the occurrence of the sound(s) of interest, such as the locus of an assimilation. The status of time as a continuous variable requires statistics different from those used with more static measures (see Barr, 2008 for detailed discussion).

7 Conclusion

We have considered a number of factors that must be taken into account when designing and carrying out research in speech perception. Rather than describing individual paradigms, we have broken down tasks into sections relevant to writing up papers, because many of the issues are the same across very different paradigms. Even the newest paradigms share with classical paradigms many of the same issues in stimulus and task design, despite novel response formats and measurements.

3 Research Methods in Speech Production

Marija Tabain

Chapter Overview

1 Introduction

Speech researchers study articulation because it provides the crucial link between how speech is represented in the mind, and how it is produced in the acoustic signal. However, while the acoustic signal provides a complete dataset for the acoustic speech researcher (see Watt, this volume), *no single articulatory technique is able to provide the complete dataset for the speech articulation researcher.* As a result, when studying speech articulation, it is as important to be aware of what aspects of the system are not being studied, as it is to pay careful attention to the part of the system that is being studied. The various components of the system interact in many ways, and the patterns that are observed in any one part of the system may be influenced by another part of the system.

In this chapter, I will provide an overview of a selection of articulatory techniques that provide different views of the speech production system. I will then provide a little more detail on three techniques in particular: electropalatography (EPG), electromagnetic articulography (EMA) and ultrasound. These three techniques are quite popular for examining supralaryngeal articulation, and I will list the pros and cons of each technique. I will conclude with a discussion of certain issues that are common to all speech production studies.

2 An Overview of Speech Production Techniques

Speech is essentially a dynamic process – although it is useful to define targets for the individual speech sounds, the reality is that the articulators are in constant motion, as they transition from one target to the next. Moreover, since different articulators are involved for different sounds, there is necessarily an overlap between the various gestures that are used to achieve the various speech targets (see Harrington et al. this volume). This is a very important aspect of speech production which needs to be kept in mind when looking at articulatory data.

Since speech is essentially a dynamic process, one of the main distinctions between different articulatory techniques is whether they are static or dynamic. Dynamic techniques can capture aspects of speech movement. Static techniques, by contrast, can capture only a 'snapshot' of the articulation. Static techniques include static palatography (see Butcher, this volume) and imaging techniques such as computed tomography (CT) and magnetic resonance imaging (MRI) – see Stone (1999) for a brief overview of these imaging techniques. The main limitation of static techniques lies in the fact that, as mentioned above, speech is inherently dynamic. For MRI, for example, the speaker must maintain the articulators in the position of the target sound for several seconds while the image is produced (however, technology is advancing in this area so that MRI studies of continuous speech may be available in the near future); for static palatography, by contrast, the image that is captured of the contact between the tongue and the palate may in fact include the movement that is inherent to the production of the sound itself (e.g. the velar loop involved in the production of velar consonants – Perrier et al., 2003; or the forward movement of the tongue tip involved in the production of retroflexes – Tabain, 2009).

However, static speech production techniques are often used for very good reasons. In the case of static palatography, it is much cheaper and can be used with more speakers than EPG (discussed further below), since it does not require the same specialist and expensive equipment. In the case of CT and MRI, these techniques can provide excellent 3-dimensional (3D) images of the vocal tract and its articulators. Such images are crucial in detailed modelling studies which seek to map the relationship between speech articulation and speech acoustics, since they allow the researcher to estimate volumes and shapes of the various vocal tract cavities. Access to such machines requires collaboration with medical professionals, and although establishing such cross-disciplinary research links is a lengthy process, it can be very rewarding for all researchers concerned.

We turn now to dynamic techniques. There is one notable technique that provides very comprehensive data, but that is not used very often, and that is X-ray. A full X-ray image of the vocal tract can provide an excellent 2-dimensional (2D) image of speech articulation across time. However, this technique is rarely used for the simple reason that the health risks posed to the speaker far outweigh any benefit that speech science can obtain from the study (see below for some discussion of ethical issues). If any speech studies are carried out these days using X-ray data, the data is almost always archival.[1]

There are, of course, a vast number of other techniques available for studying speech production. Among these is *electromyography*, which is used to study muscle activity of the main articulators during speech (for an introduction, see Hardcastle, 1999). Electromyography for speech research can involve either surface electrodes or hook-wire electrodes: the latter are much more invasive and require medical supervision and anaesthetic. There are also various techniques which involve *naso-endoscopy*; although technically possible without medical supervision, it is recommended to have a physician present in order to administer an anaesthetic spray for the comfort of the speaker. Naso-endoscopy involves the insertion of a fine tube through the nostrils and the naso-pharyngeal port in order to study laryngeal function (it can also be used to study velo-pharyngeal function if it is not inserted through the velo-pharyngeal port). A miniature light source and camera are placed at the end of the special fibre-optic tube in order to view the movements of the vocal folds. In the situation where the vocal folds are vibrating (as opposed to producing a de-voicing gesture), the technique of *stroboscopy* is used in order to make the vocal fold movement appear slower (it does this by producing the pulsing of the light source only slightly out-of-phase with the rate of vocal fold vibration): this allows the speech researcher to view how the vocal folds open and close.

Other common dynamic techniques are far less invasive than the ones just mentioned. *Video* capture is often used by researchers interested in audio-visual speech, but is of use to other speech researchers as well: for example, if one camera is placed to the front, and the other to the side of the speaker, it is possible to estimate the extent of lip-opening and lip protrusion during speech for acoustic modelling studies. In this case, the articulators of interest may be marked: for example, the speaker's lips may be painted blue, in order to facilitate edge extraction from the images produced. A related technique is *Optotrak*: in this technique, markers (Light Emitting Diodes (LEDs)) are placed on the surface of the face and then tracked optically in 3D. This technique is very popular with audio-visual speech researchers in particular, because it provides very rich data for reconstruction and synthesis of speech movements.[2]

Two other techniques are very common in the phonetics lab, partly because of their ease of use. The first is *airflow* measurement. As the name suggests, this involves the measurement of airflow from the nasal and oral cavities. It may also involve the measurement of air pressure within the oral cavity (but not within the nasal cavity, since the speaker has no way of manipulating air pressure in this cavity!). Airflow is measured when the speaker places a special mask over their mouth – and, if nasal flow is being measured, another mask over their nose. The masks contain transducers which measure the flow, and the oral mask also contains a microphone to record the speech sound. If air pressure is being studied as well, a small tube is inserted into the oral cavity (in order to study the build-up of air pressure before a stop closure is released). Airflow and air pressure measurements are commonly used to examine various manners of articulation, such as stop versus nasal consonants, aspirated versus voiceless, ejectives and implosives, etc. They are also used in studies where the extent of nasal flow outside of nasal consonants is of concern – for example, to examine the extent of nasalization on adjacent vowels. However, one downside of airflow studies is that the presence of the mask has an important effect on the speech acoustics: the oral mask itself serves to lengthen the oral cavity in acoustic terms, and the main effect of this lengthening is that F1 is lowered in the acoustic signal. For this reason, detailed acoustic study combined with airflow measurements is usually problematic (see Zajac & Yates, 1997; Shadle, 2010).

The other common technique in phonetics laboratories is laryngography, or *electroglottography* (EGG). It is a relatively non-invasive technique used to examine laryngeal behaviour. In EGG, electrodes are placed on each side of the larynx (either one on each side, or two on each side if raising of the larynx is likely to be involved). A small electrical current is passed between the two electrodes, and the amount of resistance to the current is an indication of the degree of contact of the vocal folds. Unfortunately, due to the complex nature of vocal fold movement, EGG does not provide a good indication of the amount of glottal opening, which is much more accurately inferred from airflow measures or endoscopic measures. However, EGG is very useful for non-invasively inferring the quality of the vocal fold movement (i.e. breathy, modal, creaky – see Esling, this volume), since different qualities have different characteristic EGG pulse shapes – see Mooshammer (2010) for some discussion of EGG issues.

In a sense, the range of possible articulatory techniques is limited only by the imagination and inventiveness of the researcher. Phoneticians and other speech researchers have been trying various methods for examining speech for many centuries (for an introduction, see Fletcher, 1992; or watch the film *My Fair Lady*). I do not wish to give the impression that the techniques I mention here are all that is available to the researcher. As for any scientific study, the starting point should be the question: What do I want to know? Once this is clear, the researcher is free to imagine how best that question can be answered.

We turn now to an examination of three supra-laryngeal techniques in a little more detail.

2.1 EPG

EPG measures the contact between the tongue and the roof of the mouth. It is perhaps the best technique available for studying consonants produced with the tongue tip/blade or tongue body. The great advantage of EPG data is that it is comparatively easy to quantify and to interpret. The contact is registered by electrodes which are embedded in a very thin artificial palate that is custom made for each speaker (Hardcastle, 1972; Wrench, 2007). In the Reading EPG system[3] there are 62 electrodes: they are arranged into eight rows, with each row having eight electrodes except for the first row, which has six. The electrodes are connected by very thin wires, which are then grouped together in order to exit the oral cavity along the sides of the teeth. The wires are then connected to a special EPG 'key' (which in fact resembles a hair-comb); this key is then inserted into a special multiplexer unit (about the size of a book or video cassette), which the speaker wears around the neck. A special rod/handgrip is also connected to the multiplexer, and serves to complete the electrical circuit when the tongue touches a palate electrode: the speaker holds this rod during the recording (or alternatively, the rod is taped to the speaker's hand after a conductive ultrasound gel is applied between the rod and the hand – however, with the newer EPG systems, this rod/handgrip is not needed). Figure 3.1 shows a speaker ready to do an EPG recording, and a picture of an Articulate EPG palate and Figure 3.2 gives an example of EPG data presented as part of a published study.

The registering of tongue-palate contact relies on the fact that the human body can conduct electricity. The crucial aspect of tongue-palate contact for EPG is that the tongue is coated in saliva, which is able to conduct electricity.

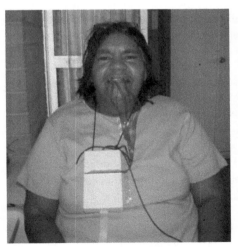
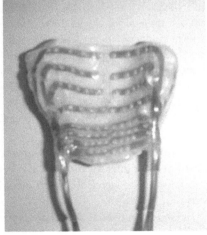

Figure 3.1 (a) a speaker prepared for an EPG recording, and (b) a picture of her EPG palate. The wires coming out of her mouth are from the EPG palate, and the white box is the multiplexer unit which is connected to the EPG machine

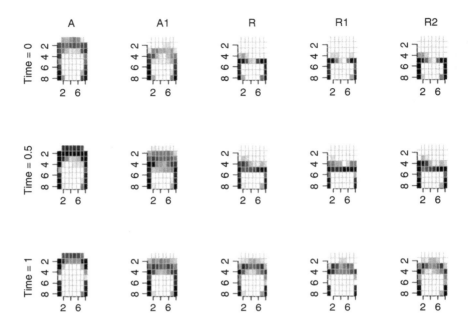

Figure 3.2 An example of data from a single speaker in an EPG study of Central Arrernte. These grey-scale palatograms show average contact patterns using the Reading EPG layout. For each palatogram, the hard-palate/soft-palate juncture is at the bottom of the palatogram (row 8), and the base of the teeth are at the top of the palatogram (row 1). Each of the eight rows has eight electrodes, except for the first row, which has only six. A darker shading of an electrode cell denotes more frequent contact of this electrode across the repetitions; a white cell denotes that this electrode was never contacted in any repetition of this apical category. Data are sampled at three points in time: consonant onset (time=0), consonant midpoint (time=0.5) and consonant offset (time=1). Note that due to mismatches in acoustic and EPG sampling, the endpoint was in fact sampled at 0.95. The columns of data list different types of apical consonants: A and A1 are different kinds of alveolar consonants, and R, R1 and R2 are different kinds of retroflex consonants. See Tabain (2009) for more explanation

Although the tough outside layer of skin offers a high resistance to the flow of electricity, the current used for EPG must not be too high. It is kept well below 1 milliamp, the level at which electrical flow is perceived as a faint tingling sensation.

EPG is often used in two main types of studies: (1) coarticulation (e.g. Gibbon & Nicolaidis, 1999; Recasens & Pallarès, 2001; Recasens & Espinosa, 2005), and (2) tongue modelling (e.g. Stone, 1991; Stone et al., 1992). In coarticulation studies, the production of a particular lingual consonant may be compared in different vowel contexts, usually [i] versus a low central vowel like [ɐ] (ideally), or front [a] or back [ɑ]. This gives an estimate of how resistant to coarticulation the consonant may be (for instance, [s] is highly resistant to any sort of vowel influence on the tongue, whereas velar consonants show a large amount of coarticulation along the front/back dimension). EPG is also useful in studies which look at coordination between the tongue tip and the tongue body – for example, in [kl] sequences. In tongue modelling studies, EPG is often used in combination with other techniques such as ultrasound, since it gives an excellent picture of tongue-palate contact patterns in both the sagittal (front-to-back) and coronal dimensions. It is also used in studies of complex lingual consonants, such as retroflexes and other coronal consonants in Australian languages, or fricatives in certain Slavic languages.

EPG data is easily divided into articulatory zones. Typically, rows 1 and 2 are considered (denti-) alveolar, rows 3 and 4 postalveolar, rows 5 to 7 palatal and row 8 velar. It is a very simple matter to simply sum the contact in each zone, or to find the front-most or back-most row of contact, in order to determine the place of articulation of the consonant. It is also possible to find the duration of the consonant closure (a closure is defined as any complete row of contact) – this can even be done for separate zones if a tongue tip consonant is temporally adjacent to a tongue body consonant (hence the common use of EPG in coarticulation studies).

Commonly used EPG measures are the centre of gravity measure, the anteriority index, the centrality index and the dorso-palatal index. The centre of gravity measure is a general purpose articulatory measure across the entire palate: it weights each more forward row incrementally more than the preceding row. This is done because there are finer articulatory distinctions in the front part of the palate. The anteriority index (Recasens & Pallarès, 2001) is similar to the centre of gravity measure, but is calculated only on the first five rows of the palate, with an exponentially higher weighting for each more forward row. The centrality index is similar to the anteriority index and the centre of gravity, except that it works on a lateral rather than a front-to-back dimension – it is most useful for studying groove width in fricatives. The dorso-palatal index is a simple sum of the electrodes contacted in the back three rows of the palate, and is useful for gauging the extent of tongue body raising.

2.1.1 Pros

- EPG provides both front-back and lateral coverage of consonants produced in the denti-alveolar, palatal and front velar regions.
- It provides data outside of the mid-sagittal plane. This is of immense benefit in the study of sounds such as fricatives and laterals, since it is possible to have an indication of the width of a groove for a fricative, and of the reduction in side contact for a lateral. It also means that it is possible to

have an indication of the bracing of the tongue against the lateral margins in the articulation of high vowels.

- EPG provides excellent information on the closure and release of lingual consonants – this is useful when the acoustic signal does not provide this information, for example, in the case of a stop consonant at the beginning or end of an utterance.
- EPG data is relatively easy to quantify – Byrd et al. (1995) and Hardcastle et al. (1991) provide excellent overviews of the main measures used in EPG research.
- The sample rate of 200 Hz (100 Hz in older systems) means that most speech movements can be captured (although trills and flaps may be problematic).
- The set-up time during the recording itself is negligible. Since the palate is custom-made for the speaker well ahead of time, it is possible to begin the recordings relatively quickly. This ensures that the speaker is not fatigued early into the recording process. This is an important factor when dealing with speakers who are not used to phonetics recordings.
- The head does not need to be stabilized, leading to a much more comfortable experience for the speaker than systems where stabilization is required (e.g. EMA – see below).

2.1.2 Cons

- EPG provides no information on consonants produced by the tongue back, tongue root or the lips.
- It provides no information on vowels, with the exception of some lateral contact for high front vowels.
- It provides no information on the velocity of the tongue movement as it contacts the palate (although technical research has aimed at providing this information).
- Older Reading palates provided very little information on dental and velar contact (this was less of a problem with the Kay and Rion palates, which were alternative EPG systems). However, the newer Articulate palate which interfaces with the Reading system addresses this concern to an extent, by placing the front row of electrodes a little further forward, and the back row of electrodes a little further back (see Wrench, 2007; Tabain, 2011).
- Very brief movements, such as trills and flaps, may not be well captured, especially if the sample rate is only 100 Hz.
- The beginning and end of an articulatory trajectory is not captured, only the point at which the tongue contacts the palate. This is of relevance for studies which are concerned with the relative phasing of speech gestures.

- Older style artificial palates require a significant adjustment time for the speaker – once inserted, the speech is audibly distorted, and it may take several hours for the speech to become normal. This is not a problem with the newer Articulate palate (Wrench, 2007).
- Each speaker must visit the dentist to have a plaster impression made of their upper palate and teeth. This impression is then sent to a specialist laboratory to have the EPG palate made. The total cost per speaker is several hundred dollars.

2.2 EMA

Electromagnetic midsagittal articulography (EMA, sometimes EMMA) tracks the movement of the tongue, lips and jaw.[4] EMA is an articulator flesh-point tracking technique, which means that particular points on the articulators are selected and tracked through time. In EMA, the selected points are tracked within an electromagnetic field.[5] This field is created by three emitter coils placed within a helmet that is worn by the speaker. The helmet also serves to stabilize the speaker's head, so that any movement of the articulators remains within the same Cartesian plane. Figure 3.3 shows a speaker prepared for a set of EMA recordings. He is using the Carstens system from Germany (the other main systems are the MIT system from the United States, and the Movetrack system from Sweden). Figure 3.4 gives an example of EMA data from a published study. Hoole and Nguyen (1999) provide some further information on EMA.

2.2.1 Pros

- EMA provides excellent information on the location of the selected articulator points at any given time.
- It provides excellent information on how the various supra-laryngeal gestures are coordinated in time.
- Compared to EPG, it provides excellent information on vowels.
- EMA also provides data on labial consonants.
- It provides better information on velar consonants than does EPG.
- EMA is an excellent technique for tracking jaw movement (note: the jaw sensor should ideally be placed on the lower gum, which, unlike the chin, is unaffected by muscles involved in lip movement).
- It is possible to have a good indication of the palate shape and its location in the electromagnetic field. An image of the palate shape is obtained by tracing an electrode along the midline of the roof of the mouth – this can either be done with the sensor attached to the tongue tip, or by a sensor placed on the (gloved) finger of the experimenter.

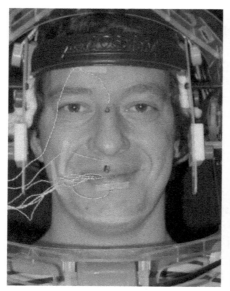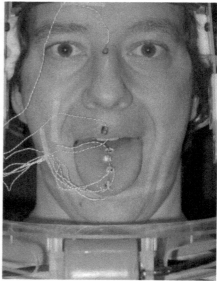

Figure 3.3 A speaker prepared for an EMA recording. He has four transducers attached to his tongue, one to his upper lip and one to his lower lip (at the vermillion borders) and one to his lower gums (as the jaw sensor). He also has transducers attached to the bridge of his nose, and to his upper gum: these serve as reference sensors, which in principle should not move during speech (the bridge sensor, however, is on skin which covers muscle, and so may move independently of the speech)

2.2.2 Cons

- EMA does not give direct information on the shape of the tongue. For some sounds (such as some vowels), the shape of the tongue can be inferred from the selected points. However, for many sounds, the tongue can assume a very complex shape that cannot be inferred from the position of the transducers (e.g. for sibilant fricatives).
- It does not provide information on pharyngeal articulations.
- EMA does not provide data outside of the midsagittal plane (i.e. no coronal sections). However, newer 3D systems are now available to provide such information, although they have as yet not been extensively used for this purpose.
- The technique is not at all portable.
- It requires a very high level of technical support, usually from a qualified engineer.
- Calibration, which should be conducted before each set of recordings, can be problematic and time-consuming.

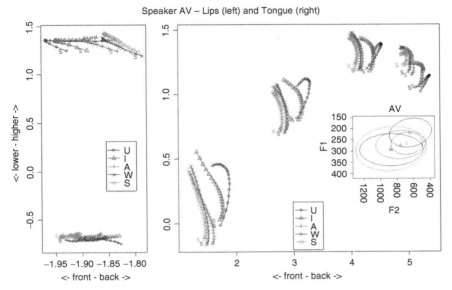

Speaker AV – Lips (left) and Tongue (right)

Figure 3.4 An example of data from a single speaker in an EMA study of French. Plots of averaged *Tongue* trajectories (right), and averaged *Upper and Lower Lip* trajectories (left) for the vowel /u/ at different prosodic boundaries (U = Utterance, I = Intonational phrase, A = Accentual phrase, W = Word, S = Syllable). All four tongue sensors are shown on the Tongue plots. Data are collapsed across consonant contexts and time-normalized for plotting purposes, with each trajectory showing 20 points equidistant in time. The beginning of each trajectory, marked 'S', is taken at the acoustic release of the /p/ in /apu #/, and the end of each trajectory is taken at the acoustic endpoint of the vowel. Note that /u/ at the Utterance boundary is followed by a pause, whereas at the other boundaries it may be followed by one of six different consonants. Units on both the x- and y-axes are in cm from the reference transducer. Note that the scales differ for the *Tongue* and *Lip* trajectory plots. Also shown are ellipses showing *F1 and F2* (in Hertz) for the /u/ vowel in each prosodic context. Data are sampled at the acoustic midpoint of the vowel. Only the mean values for each prosodic context are shown, with each ellipse containing 2.45 standard deviations around the mean. See Tabain and Perrier (2007) for more information

- Set-up time with the speaker before recording is lengthy, often around an hour.
- The speaker may become uncomfortable and headachy as a result of wearing the special helmet which holds the head steady within the electomagnetic field.
- Post-processing of the data is non-trivial. This includes rotation of the recorded data to the occlusal plane (= bite plane) of the speaker: this needs

to have been measured during the recording itself (this is usually done with the speaker biting onto a ruler containing two transducers along its length). It also includes subtraction of the reference transducers (usually placed on the bridge of the nose, and on the upper gum) from the active articulator transducers: this ensures that any movement of the head within the EM field during the recording is not misinterpreted as articulator movement. All signals must also be smoothed.

- EMA is prone to measurement error – transducers can be unreliable, especially when further away from the centre of the electromagnetic field; or, in the 2D-EMA system, whenever the articulators deviate from the midsagittal plane (which is quite often in the case of the tongue tip).

- Labelling of the data is also non-trivial. While automatic techniques are preferred (these usually involve finding landmarks in the first derivative of the signal), hand-labelling of the data may be necessary in exploratory studies where the exact nature of the movement is not yet clear.

2.3 Ultrasound

Ultrasound provides excellent information on speech sounds that involve complex tongue shapes because it can record multiple planes. It involves the use of special piezoelectric crystals which emit ultra-high frequency sound waves, and then measure the amplitude and delay of the sound waves which are reflected back. The sound wave reflection depends on the fact that different mediums have different sound transmission properties. Within the oral cavity, the main mediums are tissue, bone and air. The tongue is made up of tissue, and when the ultrasound wave travels through this tissue and reaches the air layer above, the sound wave is reflected back. This is due to an impedance mismatch between the two transmitting mediums, and the magnitude of the mismatch is represented by the brightness of the image at the point of reflection. Since tissue and air have very different sound transmitting properties, the edge of the tongue is often seen as a bright white line on ultrasound images. Stone (2005), and other articles in the same special issue, provide an excellent overview of ultrasound as used in speech research.

The most commonly used ultrasound these days is a real-time B-scan. This contains a row of identical piezoelectric crystals, all of which emit and receive sound waves. B-scan transducers contain between 64 and 500+ crystals. The crystals emit sound waves in sequence, rather than simultaneously, since if all crystals emitted at the same time, adjacent crystals would register reflected sound waves from each other, resulting in a very confusing image. Each crystal must wait for the reflected sound wave of the previous crystal to return before emitting its own sound wave, and as a result, the last crystal emits a sound wave at a considerable delay after the first crystal. This scan lag is usually about 30 ms: this means that, technically, one part of the tongue is imaged about 30 ms later than the opposite part of the tongue. As a result of the scan lag, the sample rate is usually 30 Hz (this includes some time for the computer to reconstruct the complete image). However, newer systems have sample rates of 100 Hz, as is the case with the Articulate Instruments ultrasound device.

Figure 3.5 shows a speaker ready for an ultrasound recording. The ultrasound transmitter is placed under the chin in such a way that the desired image of the tongue can be obtained (coronal or sagittal). The transmitter can be held by hand, or, as is shown here, it can be held in place by a stabilizing headset. Figure 3.6 shows an ultrasound image from a recording session: the tongue is at rest in this image.

2.3.1 Pros

- Ultrasound allows excellent imaging of both sagittal and coronal dimensions of the tongue.
- It can image the portion of the tongue which is in the pharyngeal region.
- As a result, excellent 3D images of the tongue can be reconstructed.[6]
- Ultrasound images sounds which have a reasonably flat or gently curved tongue shape quite well. This includes low vowels such as [a], and certain alveolar consonants.

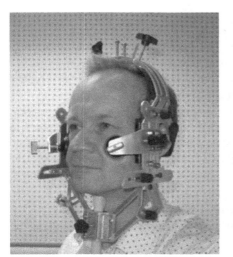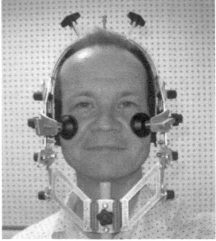

Figure 3.5 A speaker prepared for an ultrasound recording. The ultrasound probe is held in place underneath the chin by the head stabilizing helmet.
Images courtesy of Alan Wrench

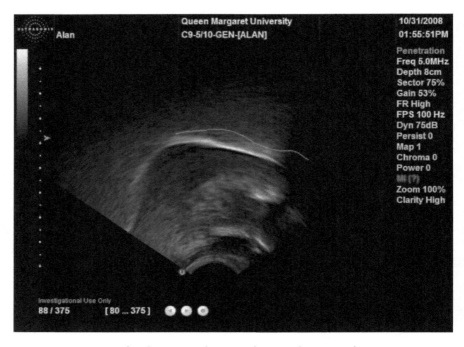

Figure 3.6 An example of an image from an ultrasound session. The tongue is at rest in this picture: it can be seen as a white line just below the palate, which is traced in green. Image courtesy of Alan Wrench

- It is possible to view the floor of the nasal cavity when the tongue contacts the velum (which is made up of tissue, like the tongue).
- It is also possible to have an indication of the palate shape by asking the subject to swallow (either a dry swallow, or a swallow of water).
- Ultrasound provides a much better image of the edge of the tongue than do other imaging techniques such as MRI and X-ray – however, extraction of this edge is not always trivial, although various software are available to facilitate the effort (see Stone, 2005).
- Ultrasound is, compared to EMA and EPG, relatively non-invasive (i.e. nothing is put inside the mouth).
- It can be used with children and with other special populations.
- Many ultrasound machines are portable and comparatively inexpensive.

2.3.2 Cons

- The sample rate of 30 Hz is quite low for many speech movements. This is particularly true for the tongue tip, which has velocities of up to 200 Hz.[7]

Although faster ultrasound rates are available (80–90 Hz), they are unable to scan as deeply as the slower rates, since the machine must wait for each sound wave to return before emitting the next sound wave.

- In general, fast sounds such as stops, clicks and taps involving any part of the tongue should be avoided.
- Often, ultrasound does not provide information on the tongue tip and the tongue root. This is due to the interfering presence of the mandible and hyoid bones (which have different sound transmitting properties to tissue and air), and also to the presence of air pockets (e.g. when the tongue tip is raised).
- The presence of air pockets is particularly noticed in coronal images, where the tongue may appear more narrow due to the presence of air pockets beneath the sides of the tongue. This is problematic because the tongue narrows quite often as part of the speech production process (e.g. to elevate the tongue body or to produce a lateral consonant) – as a result, true narrowing cannot be separated from the artefact of the imaging process.
- The issue of head stabilization is an important issue in ultrasound speech research, since there is no reference structure visible in the ultrasound image (the jaw and hyoid bone produce a shadow in the ultrasound image due to refraction of the sound waves, and appear black). Various solutions have been proposed to this problem – see Campbell et al. (2010) for a recent approach, and Stone (2005) and the papers in the same special issue. The solution in Figure 3.5 is the Articulate Instruments stabilization helmet.
- The presence of the ultrasound transducer beneath the chin interferes with jaw lowering. This is a problem for two reasons. First, the jaw works together with the tongue to achieve lingual speech sounds (this is particularly true of the tongue tip/blade). And secondly, as the jaw lowers, the presence of the ultrasound transducer causes the tongue tissue to compress. This problem can be partly resolved by the use of an acoustic stand-off – this is a special soft pad that allows the ultrasound waves to travel through unimpeded.
- When the ultrasound transducer is held against the underside of the chin by hand, it can easily move around during recording. This is particularly noticeable early on in recording when the ultrasound gel has just been applied (the gel serves to increase contact between the skin and the ultrasound transducer).
- Speakers vary greatly in the quality of images they produce for ultrasound. This means that it is highly desirable to test speakers before doing a full set of recordings. As a result, ultrasound may not be a useful technique where special populations are involved (e.g. minority language

speakers, or speakers with pathologies). In general, smaller speakers (i.e. women and children) tend to produce better images than bigger speakers (i.e. men); younger speakers tend to produce better images than older speakers; and thinner speakers tend to produce better images than larger speakers. The reasons for these trends are not completely clear, but may be related to levels of fat in the tongue (fat is known to scatter sound-waves in tissue) and levels of moisture in the mouth (a dry mouth does not reflect sound waves as well – it is believed that moisture coats the tongue surface, making it more smooth and reflective). However, these tendencies are not absolutes, and it would be unwise to exclude larger, older men, for example, from any study.

- The ultrasound image often contains speckle noise. This results from the scattering of soundwaves from targets smaller than the wavelength of the sound (usually less than 1 mm), and causes problems for automatic edge extraction.

- Sound is reflected best when the impedance mismatch is perpendicular to the sound wave emitted by the ultrasound transducer. This means that tongue edges which are parallel to the direction of ultrasound travel are not well imaged. In particular, sounds which involve a steep slope in the tongue, such as [i] and the velar consonants, are not imaged as well as other sounds.

Sometimes, EMA is used together with ultrasound or EPG to provide a more complete picture of the speech articulation. Although such data are very useful, there are certain practical problems which must be kept in mind. First of all, the level of speaker discomfort is increased when the number of measurement devices is increased. This may have the extra, undesired side effect of interfering with the speaker's natural speech production patterns. Second of all, the transducers placed on the tongue for the EMA machine interfere with both EPG and ultrasound measures: in the case of EPG, they prevent certain parts of the tongue from contacting the EPG palate, and in the case of ultrasound, they leave a 'comet tail' (a localized reverberation artefact) on the image, which may interfere with automatic edge detection algorithms.

3 Some General Concerns for Speech Production Studies

One concern with any articulatory study is that the *data should be carefully synchronized with the acoustic signal*. It is rare that an articulatory study can be conducted in complete ignorance of the acoustic signal, and it is quite common, especially with newer techniques, for careful consideration to be given to the issue of synchronization. At the very least, the researcher should conduct a visual verification of a sample recording before beginning any full data collection. For EPG, a simple sequence of stop-vowel syllables provides a good indication of the articulatory-acoustic alignment, since the moment of articulatory stop release corresponds very well with a burst which follows a period of silence in the acoustic signal. Unfortunately, modern laptop computers (especially PCs) usually do not have good sound cards, and it is often necessary to purchase an external USB sound card for any experiments that are to be conducted outside of the laboratory (a sound card designed for professional musicians is a good choice).

Speech production studies differ from acoustic studies in several ways, but perhaps the most important is that *speakers differ in their articulatory strategies far more than they differ in their acoustic output*. This is due to the fact that the same acoustic output can be achieved via different articulatory strategies, and also to the fact that different speakers have different oral morphologies (at the most basic level, for example, relative oral vs. pharyngeal cavity size is different for male and female speakers). As a result, each speaker must be treated separately in the data analysis stage, even if the speakers are later pooled. This process is very time-consuming, and consequently, speech production studies have fewer speakers than speech acoustics studies – typically four to five speakers, depending on the demands and invasiveness of the technique, and also on the language being studied (with fewer speakers understandable for studies of special populations). It should also be noted that the technical issues involved in setting up a speech production experiment are non-trivial (familiarizing oneself with the hardware and the software involved, ensuring that they are working properly, etc.).

This brings us to another important issue with regard to speech production studies, and that is the issue of *ethics*. In most countries, research institutions are required to have a board or committee that approves research proposals as being ethical. Speech production studies may appear problematic for such committees, because they are often invasive for the speaker (i.e. they involve contact between the speaker and some foreign object, such as a transducer or paste, and this contact is often on the inside of the body, namely, inside the mouth); and they may involve a small degree of discomfort to the speaker. The fear is that the object with which the speaker comes into contact may transfer disease, or cause other health problems for the speaker; and that the discomfort experienced by the speaker may be too great or too traumatic.

Before embarking on a speech production study, the novice researcher should make every effort to observe the technique being used by another researcher experienced in that technique, and preferably in a real data collection situation (being the speaker subject of one such study is an excellent way to learn). This way, the researcher new to the technique can observe the hygiene protocols that are used (and which are usually not at all onerous or difficult to set up), as well as the problems that arise in gathering the data. The researcher should also carefully read peer-reviewed journal papers that use the technique in order to appreciate finer details of the methodology. Finally, it is also very useful to look carefully at equipment manufacturers' websites, which often provide handy hints for using the techniques, references to published papers that use the techniques and various other pieces of information of reassuring interest for institutional ethics committees (e.g. the therapeutic or clinical uses of a particular technique, such as is the case with EPG). With all of this experience and information at hand, it is usually not difficult to convince an institutional ethics committee that the potential discomfort and health risks to the speaker subject are minimal, and that the speaker's time will be well spent in advancing the knowledge base of speech science.

In sum, speech articulation provides many challenges to the researcher. However, the knowledge of speech production that is acquired in overcoming these challenges forms part of the reward when novel and useful speech data are gathered. Such data further our understanding of how humans are able to produce meaningful communication.

Notes

1. In addition, it is difficult to automatically detect edges from X-ray images for the purposes of speech studies, and as a result, the most usual method for examining areas of interest involves manual segmentation.
2. I am also ignoring fMRI here, which allows the researcher to examine speech production from a neurological point of view.
3. www.articulateinstruments.com/
4. It is also possible to track movements of the velum, but most speakers are not able to tolerate the placement of transducers in this part of the oral cavity.
5. X-ray microbeam is a technique which is essentially comparable to EMA in terms of the data it produces. The main difference is that a special X-ray beam is used to track the flesh-points, rather than an electromagnetic field (Westbury, 1994).
6. See examples at www.speech.umaryland.edu.
7. Since the tip/blade usually occupies about 1/3 of the ultrasound image, the scan lag is usually around 8–10 ms for this articulator, with about 20–30 ms gap between scans.

4 Research Methods in Phonetic Fieldwork

Andrew Butcher

1 Introduction

Despite the old anecdote about Daniel Jones taking 'only his ears' on a phonetic field trip (Ladefoged, 1997, p. 141), there is a long tradition of phoneticians lugging equipment over great distances to record speakers in remote locations. The first field recordings of speakers of 'exotic' languages were made by anthropologist-linguists not long after the invention of the phonograph. John Peabody Harrington was one early adopter of the new technology and (with over a million pages of phonetic transcription to his name) probably the first 'real' phonetician to make audio recordings of speech in the field (Glenn, 1991). With the advent of the aluminium disc in the mid-1930s,

Harrington is said to have paid a neighbour's son to manhandle his 65 kg. 'portable' recording machine up and down mountains and across valleys by means of rope bridges. The introduction of magnetic tape recording after the Second World War initially meant little reduction in weight. It was the production of high quality portable reel-to-reel decks in the 1960s which brought the first real improvement in the fieldworker's lot. But even up to the 1980s, as Peter Ladefoged recounts, 'before we had laptop computers and pocket-sized tape recorders, a travelling phonetics lab was heavy and bulky. . . . All told, my equipment topped 80 pounds [36 kg], without considering notebooks and clothes' (Ladefoged, 2003, p. 55). The 1980s saw the introduction of small audio cassette recorders of relatively high quality and the following decade the arrival of portable digital audio tape (DAT) recorders, offering the possibility of true professional-quality field recordings. Ten years later fully digital solid-state recorders are a reality: small and light with no moving parts and with ever-expanding recording capacity in digital uncompressed format. Phoneticians are now able to collect data in the field which is of comparable quality to that recorded in the laboratory.

There are several useful guides available to the novice fieldworker. Ladefoged (1997, 2003) is undoubtedly the foremost of these, but sections of Newman and Ratliff (2001), Crowley (2007), Bowern (2008), Chelliah and de Reuse (2011) and Thieburger (2012) are also relevant to phoneticians. Bear in mind, however, that modern phonetic fieldwork differs in a number of ways from traditional linguistic fieldwork. The linguist may spend many months or perhaps even years in a community, sitting day after day with a consultant, painstakingly working through semantic fields and grammatical paradigms, and then poring over field notes every evening in order to prepare questions for the following day. The phonetician, on the other hand, may well spend 90 per cent of his time waiting around for consultants to become available or to decide that they can spare some time to do phonetic work (especially if that work involves the introduction of foreign objects or substances into the mouth or the insertion of tubes into the nose). The remaining 10 per cent of the time will undoubtedly be filled with frenetic and intense activity, during the course of which enough data may be recorded to keep us busy for the next couple of years; but phonetic fieldwork can be very much a waiting game. One should always take sufficient reading matter on a phonetic field trip. According to my linguist colleagues, I am typically to be found on field trips in what they refer to as 'The Fieldwork Position': lying on my back with a book in my hand. Most of what follows is necessarily based on my own experience of working in remote areas of Australia with speakers of Aboriginal languages over the past 20 years. I hope, however, that much of this will be relevant to phonetic fieldworkers in similar situations in other parts of the world.

2 Planning

Planning must begin many months before the intended trip. If you are going to another country, you will usually need a valid passport and you may also need a visa. If you are intending to work on indigenous-held land, you will need various permits and, wherever you are going, you will need ethics approval. The application procedures differ from country to country and indeed from institution to institution, but seem everywhere to have become more complex and more demanding in recent years, especially where indigenous people are involved. In the United States of America, researchers must first apply to their local institutional review board (IRB), who must review and approve all federally supported research involving human subjects. Britain's Integrated Research Application System and Australia's electronic National Ethics Application Form (Australian Government – NH&MRC, 2010) both represent attempts to centralize the ethics application process, but until these systems are accepted as completely replacing all the existing lower levels of approval, they remain an additional superimposed procedure. Unfortunately, those who make decisions about the ethics of your research, however well-intentioned, will rarely be experienced fieldworkers themselves and almost never members of the community concerned. This means that you must be prepared for the ethics approval process to be frustrating, burdensome and of questionable relevance to your work. Since patience is an essential quality for any fieldworker, you might as well start practising it as early in the process as possible.

Equally important (and much more rewarding) are the preparations for travelling to and staying in a community, linking up with the right people and ensuring that they are able and willing to work with you during the time that you are there. It is in my view essential for the first trip and extremely useful for any subsequent trips to a community to have a 'go-between'. This means someone with local knowledge and who is known and respected by the locals. This might be a local school teacher, missionary or bible translator. Ideally it will be a linguist who has been working on the language for some time. Such a person will not only know all the right people and be familiar with the politics of the community but will, if you are lucky, already have worked out the phonology of the language and will be able to discuss the issues that they think are particularly worthy of phonetic investigation. Be aware that these will not necessarily be the same issues that a phonetician would identify, but it is usually a good idea to go along with them, not just as a reciprocation of good will, but also because they may well turn out to be right!

The timing of your field trip may be crucial. Many field locations are subject to seasonal weather constraints. Large parts of northern Australia may become inaccessible by road during the wet season from November to March, for example. Of course many remote communities have airstrips, so this may not be a problem. Listen to the advice of your contact person. If they are a linguist, they may tell you that the wet season is in fact the best time of the year to do language work, as local people are confined to the immediate area and have time on their hands. This may be true, but remember that it is difficult to produce a decent sound recording or conduct a viable perception experiment with the noise of monsoonal rain drumming on a corrugated iron roof. The other major consideration is the occurrence of ceremonies and other community events. Insofar as these can be predicted, short trips should be planned so as not to coincide with such events, as the entire community may be 'otherwise engaged' for days on end. Funerals, of course, cannot be predicted and unfortunately are all too frequent in indigenous communities, where health status and life expectancy are usually way below those of the mainstream population. On longer trips, on the other hand, ceremonial events, if public, may provide an opportunity to witness and even participate in the cultural life of the community and to strengthen the bonds between you and your indigenous co-workers.

3 Preparation

Your contact person may be able to provide you with accommodation or, if not, to advise you on the best options. In some situations, accommodation may be available for visitors, in which case, it is obviously advisable to book ahead. More likely, you will need to fend for yourself and provide your own bed, either under the stars or in any available room. Thus a 'swag' is part of the equipment of most language researchers in Australia – a weather-proof canvas bag, lined with a thin foam mattress and (depending on the climate) a couple of cotton sheets, a sleeping bag, or numerous blankets. In northern Australia, where for most of the year you may well wish to sleep on top of your swag rather than within it, this is normally supplemented with a 'mozzie dome' – basically a mosquito net stretched over a couple of fibreglass hoops (see Figure 4.1). This is essential for excluding not only mosquitoes – which, in Australia at least, are carriers of an increasing number of debilitating and potentially fatal diseases – but also a host of larger unwanted creepy-crawlies, some of which may give you a nasty bite. While on the topic of bugs and diseases, be sure to seek advice from your own doctor (or health department website) as to what inoculations are recommended for the area you will be visiting. Make sure that jabs you have had in the past are up to date. You may have to think about this at least six months before your trip, since some inoculations cannot be taken together, while others may require a course of shots over an extended period of time.

In choosing your wardrobe, consider not only the climatic conditions but also cultural factors. In hot climates wear a hat, and always go for thin, loose fitting, all-enveloping garments, rather than short and skimpy ones. If you are

Figure 4.1 Swag and mozzie dome ready for phonetician to adopt 'The Fieldwork Position'. Mumeka outstation, Arnhem Land, Northern Territory. Photo: Christel Butcher

female, make sure you are aware which parts of your body need to be covered – it may not always be what you expect. In some parts of Australia, for example, it is not considered appropriate for a woman to wear trousers, so long skirts are the rule.

Transport is another important consideration. In some situations air or water transport are the only options, but wherever possible, it is a huge advantage to be able to drive to your destination in your own vehicle. This enables you to be more flexible with your equipment (i.e. take more of it) and to get around more easily once you are in the community. The latter is crucial for a variety of reasons: you can transport your equipment to your co-worker's house or you can transport your co-workers to where you have your equipment set up. Most importantly you can repay people 'in kind' by transporting them to other places they want to go and helping them with tasks such as gathering firewood and hunting for food. Most likely you will be hiring a vehicle, either from your home institution or from a commercial firm. In remote areas such as central and northern Australia a four-wheel drive is essential. Rather than a station wagon, a more community-friendly option is a dual cab pick-up, which has a lockable and weatherproof cab, while leaving plenty of room in the tray for large amounts of firewood, a couple of dead kangaroos or a surprisingly large (and illegal) number of live human beings.

As a phonetician, the way you work will be dictated to a certain extent by the availability of mains electricity. Audio recording without mains power is usually not a problem, as long as you make sure that you have a plentiful supply of batteries. However, most other pieces of equipment will need a mains supply, if only for recharging. Take a 20 m extension lead and a four-way power board (power strip). If you are going to work in a community without mains power, you will need a power inverter, which will provide 240 (or 110) Volt ac power from a car battery. Your four-wheel drive vehicle may be equipped with an auxiliary battery, in which case it can be recharged when driving around. If not, consider a 100 Amp deep cycle gel battery, which can be recharged from a solar panel – a 2 × 60 Watt array is normally sufficient. On no account rely on a single battery for powering your equipment AND starting your car! A petrol-powered generator is also a possibility, but check availability of fuel. In your vehicle, do not forget to pack a powerful torch (flashlight), a Swiss-army knife, matches and a large roll of gaffer tape (duct tape).Take a basic first aid kit with you, which, apart from the usual sticking plasters (adhesive bandages), disinfectant and analgesics, should also include SPF 30+ sunscreen, insect repellent and aluminium sulphate cream for bite and sting relief. If you are planning to do anything more than straightforward audio recording (e.g. palatography, aerodynamic measurement, perceptual experiments), it is a good idea to take a large bottle of strong antiseptic or disinfectant. This should be used for cleaning equipment such as mirrors, masks, keyboards and headphones.

4 Starting Work

The main function of your contact person is to introduce you to the people who really matter – the members of the community who are interested in their language and keen to have it recorded and preserved. Be aware that ideas and attitudes about this may not coincide with what is taken for granted by white, middle-class, Western academics. For most indigenous peoples language is inextricably interwoven with culture and knowledge. It is viewed as a constant and unchanging entity which is owned by the community and whose custodianship is entrusted to certain elders of that community. Consequently those who are regarded by the community (and perhaps the linguist) as the 'best speakers' may not necessarily be the best speakers for the purposes of phonetic research. They may be breathless, toothless, lacking in volume, with slurred articulation and a poor understanding of the nature of the task. It may well be appropriate to spend some time making recordings of such speakers, however, in terms of your relationship with the community, before discreetly seeking out the younger, clearer speakers you will undoubtedly need, especially for tasks such as palatography and aerodynamic recording. Bear in mind also that older speakers are often the last living source of some interesting and important phonetic feature of the language which has been lost by younger generations. In Australia, for example, older speakers of Yindjibarndi in the Pilbara have a unique dental approximant phoneme/ð̪/, which speakers younger than 40 no longer have. Similarly, only older speakers of Mparntwe Arrernte in Alice Springs retain the velar fricative /ɣ/, and there are probably no speakers of Gulf country languages such as Yanyuwa or Djingulu left alive today who pronounce the fronted velar /ḵ/ sound that I was still able to record over 20 years ago (Butcher & Tabain, 2004).

In most countries nowadays, co-workers will expect a cash payment, so it is important to establish appropriate rates of pay for the area you will be in and the type of work you will be asking your participants to do. In most cases you will need to state these rates in your grant and ethics applications. It is always best, if possible, to take an appropriate amount of cash with you in the appropriate denominations. If you want to pay somebody $20, it is no use presenting them with a $50 note. The act of handing over the money, by the way, may be somewhat fraught with cross-cultural issues. On the one hand, it is usually appropriate from the participant's point of view that this be done unobtrusively and almost casually; Australian indigenous culture is not unique in recognizing kinship obligations which may require the recipient to share his earnings immediately with various family members. He may not wish it to be generally known that he is currently in possession of a fairly large amount of cash. On the other hand, the researcher will normally require a receipt to be signed, so that he may be reimbursed by his institution, so it is best to choose a private moment and hand over the cash in an envelope, together with a completed receipt for immediate signature. Over and above this purely business transaction, your developing relationship with the community will hopefully lead to opportunities for repayment in kind, in the form of transport (see above) or food, for example. Children in particular appreciate small gifts, but it is advisable to check with school staff first. Certainly sweets and lollies are to be avoided, but there is a wide variety of things, such as coloured pencils, erasers, stick-on jewellery, small toys and joke-shop items, which are normally considered appropriate.

5 Basic Equipment

The centrepiece of your equipment nowadays will certainly be a laptop computer. Obviously you should choose the fastest processor, the biggest memory, the largest hard drive and the longest battery life your budget will allow, but for fieldwork, there are two other important requirements: lightness and robustness. Unfortunately these two variables seem to be pretty much inversely proportional, but it is worth considering a 'fully ruggedized' [sic] laptop that is built to military standards. These machines are designed for outdoor use and rough treatment, including resistance to extreme temperatures, humidity and dust. They come with a range of features such as armoured casing, dust seals on ports, screen and keyboard, an extra bright screen and solid-state hard drives. The ones we currently use weigh around 4 kg. If you wish to take a printer and a scanner with you, these items are also available nowadays in highly portable form – there are even 'ruggedized' versions! More specialized phonetic kit, such as electropalato-graphy (EPG) and aerodynamic equipment, is not, of course built to such stand-ards. So, whether you travel by road or air or boat, storage of your equipment is something that needs careful thought and preparation. The best option, if your budget allows, is to use the dustproof, heatproof and waterproof polypropylene cases that take their name from a certain water bird with a large beak.

But this is not the only kind of storage you will require: you will also need some means of storing the vast amounts of data you will be acquiring. I like to have two backup copies of all my data – preferably, kept in different places. Our current practice is to use portable external hard drives – once again it is worth getting a 'rugged' version of these – but, if internet access is available (and fast enough), cloud storage is the best way to back up your data. If you are going to be away from internet access for some time, it may be worth invest-ing in satellite-based communication equipment, although with overall costs in Australia currently between $2,000 and $4,000 and data rates at 2.4–2.8 Kbps, this is not an attractive option at the time of writing. Nevertheless, the days of lugging eminently losable and damageable tapes and discs around with us are almost gone.

6 Audio Recording

Only ten years ago I would undoubtedly have been writing about the pleasures and pitfalls of using a portable DAT recorder in the field. Currently I would not recommend anything other than a digital solid-state recorder, but by the time you read this we may all be going into the field armed only with a mobile phone. You could of course record directly on to your computer, but the sound card is unlikely to be of the best quality and the microphone input will undoubtedly be only a 3.5 mm jack (tip-ring-sleeve (TRS)). And there really is no need to com-promise: today's solid-state flash memory recorders are small in size, have large recording capacity and no moving parts. Most make use of standard Secure Digital (SD) memory cards, which can be slotted into your laptop for quick and easy backup. Make sure that the device will record in an uncompressed format (preferably one with embedded metadata, such as Broadcast Wave Format) with at least 16-bit resolution at a 44.1 kHz sample rate. Yes, you only need 22 kHz for phonetic analysis, but most archives require 44.1 kHz and in the United States of America funding bodies may even insist upon it. Most palm-sized models will come with built-in microphones but, even though mechanical noise from the recorder is a thing of the past, frequency response is often an issue and most researchers will want to use external microphones. Ideally your recorder should have balanced XLR microphone connections with +48 Volt phantom power, (otherwise you will need pre-amps and extra cables for use with condenser microphones). As far as the microphones themselves go, the more durable the better – they may well weigh more than the recorder (and be just as expensive). It is probably best to avoid condenser microphones in tropical environments, as they are more sensitive to humidity. The most important characteristic the microphone should possess is as flat a frequency response as possible through-out its range, which should be from 50 Hz minimum up to at least 20 kHz. As far as directionality is concerned, a cardioid or supercardioid pattern is best. In the field situation, achieving a reasonable signal-to-noise ratio can be a chal-lenge. Choose the quietest available environment. This may well be outdoors, away from buildings, people, vehicles and diesel generators – I have made some really good recordings in dry creek beds. Wind noise will be the greatest enemy here, so windshields for microphones are essential. With indoor recording, on the other hand, the most important consideration is reducing background noise and echo, which is best achieved by minimizing the mouth-to-microphone dis-tance. If noisy situations are unavoidable (recording children in a schoolroom, for example) a head-mounted microphone is best, positioned approximately five cm from the lips and slightly to the side; it has the additional advantage that kids think it is 'cool' to wear. For adults, a lapel microphone may be more appropri-ate, but, at 20 cm from the lips, it needs a quieter environment. Free standing microphones should be 10–15 cm from the lips and are best mounted on a shock mount fixed to a boom arm which can be clamped to a table. It is vital to do a 'dry run' to rehearse the speaker and to set the recording level. The gain should be set so as to capture the loudest signal level without causing distortion (clip-ping). Use headphones to monitor your recording and pay particular attention to the presence of '50 Hz hum' (60 Hz in the United States) resulting from inter-ference from the power supply. This can be eliminated by running the equip-ment on battery power, but if the problem persists, you may need to invest in a 'hum eliminator' (otherwise known as a galvanic isolation transformer).

7 Audiovisual Recording

Much greater attention is being paid nowadays to the role of visual parameters in speech. Consequently a digital camcorder is now an almost indispensible fieldwork companion, which can be used for a range of purposes, from taking still pictures to give to co-workers as souvenirs (one reason for taking a printer with you) – to videoing an entire recording session. Nowadays camcorders are also, of course, very small and available in 'ruggedized', waterproof (and therefore dustproof) versions. For good-quality video the minimum requirements would be a 3-CMOS image sensor and 'full HD' (i.e. 1080/30p or 60i) recording capability. However, there are other issues to consider, especially if you are intending to use the camera in conjunction with audio recording. There is no doubt that the day is fast approaching when we will be able to capture synchronous high-quality audio and video on the same low-cost device. At the time of writing, however, there are three choices:

(1) good quality video and good quality audio: use two separate devices – a semi-professional (i.e. $ 3,000+) camcorder and a SMPTE time code-capable audio recorder, which will allow you to synchronize with the video recording.

(2) good quality video with compressed audio: use the above camcorder as your only recording device – it should have XLR audio inputs and *optional* automatic gain control (otherwise it will turn up the volume as soon as the speaker pauses).

(3) good quality (uncompressed) audio and basic video: use a so-called hand-held (or 'handy') video recorder. At the time of writing there is only one such recorder on the market. It records audio in WAV format at up to 24-bit resolution and 96 kHz sampling rate and video in MPEG-4 SP format, with 640 × 480 resolution, at a frame rate of 30 fps and a fixed-focus lens. I have no personal experience of using such a device in the field, but it may well be a very good option for phonetic fieldwork.

At the risk of sounding like your mother: make sure that you take all the necessary connecting cables, adapters, chargers and plenty of batteries. If you are going to be the sole researcher out bush for any length of time, seriously consider taking two audio recorders, and perhaps even two laptops. And make sure you have copies of essential manuals and procedures, especially if you will be without internet access.

8 Speech Material

So now you are ready to begin recording, but what is your speaker going to say? You will, of course, have meticulously prepared the speech material that you wish your co-worker to record, preferably in collaboration with the local linguist, or at least with the help of a dictionary of the language. I am a firm believer in beginning with a phonologically balanced list of citation forms. Such a list should not be longer than about 200–50 forms and should contain examples of all of the consonants and all of the vowels (and, where relevant, all of the tones) of the language, ideally in all possible segmental and structural contexts.

As a rule of thumb, I would aim to have each consonant represented in the context of a high front, a high back and a low vowel in word-initial, word-final and intervocalic positions, plus any interesting cluster combinations. The recording will run more smoothly if you go through the list with the speaker beforehand. There are bound to be words which are unknown (obsolete, different dialect), vulgar or taboo – Australian Aboriginal culture, for example, forbids the uttering of a recently deceased person's name *or any word resembling it phonologically*. For the recording itself ask the speaker to repeat each word three or four times and get them to repeat again if they stumble or if some external noise interferes with the recording. Putting words in the middle of a carrier sentence will ensure that there are no unwanted phrase-final phenomena, especially on the final repetition. If the speaker is literate, they can read the list at their own speed; if not, you will need to give prompts, either using the English translation or, as a last resort, the word itself in the language.

The next stage is to record some connected speech. Literate speakers may read a text, such as a story from a schoolbook. Non-literate speakers might tell a story of their own. Be aware, however, that many cultures will have a storytelling mode of speech, which may well have phonetic characteristics that differ from everyday speech, prosodically and even segmentally. Finally, it is essential to have recordings of natural conversation, especially if you are interested in connected speech phenomena. This may require a different recording set up: participants (who should be well-known to each other) will need to face each other, with either a stereo microphone between them, or each wearing their own lapel microphone. It is important to have such texts orthographically transcribed by a native speaker, preferably the recordees themselves, as this is an almost indispensable aid to phonetic transcription and subsequent segmentation. Having obtained a representative sample of the language, there will no doubt be specific issues which warrant closer attention, such as: 'What is the phonetic nature of the contrast between phonemes X and Y?' or 'Is the allophony of phoneme Z the same as that found for comparable sounds in other languages?' Questions like this may require the development of more focused speech material and the use of techniques other than acoustic analysis, as described below.

9 Static Palatography

Direct palatography is still carried out using much the same method as that described by Dart (1991), Butcher (1995) and Ladefoged (1997), but I would recommend any fieldworker contemplating this technique for the first time to read the definitive guide by Anderson (2008). The inventory of essential items probably does not need to be quite as long as she suggests, but if you take this as a starting point, you will not overlook anything! Essentially you paint a black 'contrast medium' on to the speaker's tongue, ask them to pronounce the sound you are interested in, and photograph the resulting 'wipe-off' of the medium on the roof of the mouth. It is good practice to demonstrate the technique on yourself before invading your co-workers' oral space (try to get a group of potential collaborators together, rather than demonstrating to each one separately). The core item of equipment will be either a commercially available dental camera or your all-purpose camcorder with a couple of custom-made attachments: (1) a mount fixed under the camera, into which slots a full arch occlusal dental mirror (chromium- or titanium-plated steel) at a 45° (upward) angle. This avoids the problem of variable angular distortion caused by hand-held mirrors – you will need at least two (big and small); (2) some means of illumination – preferably a light emitting diode (LED) ring light around the lens (see Figure 4.2).

To paint the contrast medium on to the speaker's tongue (or palate) you will need to make up a mixture of medicinal activated charcoal powder (obtainable from pharmacies) and cooking oil and you will need some cheap paint brushes

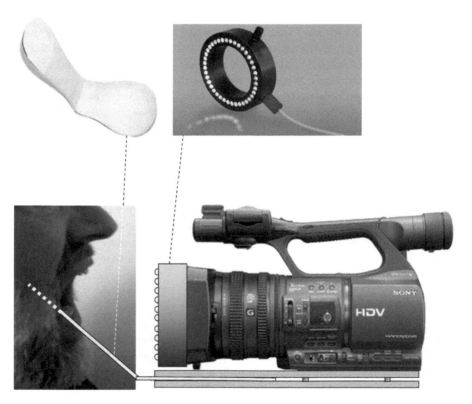

Figure 4.2 Set-up for recording palatograms: camcorder with LED ring light and custom-built mount holding 45° full arch occlusal dental mirror

about 10 mm in width. I would also recommend the use of disposable latex gloves (for the researcher) and a towel, an overall or thin plastic sheet and paper towels (for the speaker). The process should preferably be carried out in the proximity of a sink, wash basin or other water source.

As always, the choice of speech material is critical. With each palatogram there must be no interference from any other articulations beside the one under investigation. This essentially means that any other consonants in the word can only be bilabial, and carrier phrases are normally out of the question. It is also vital that the speaker does not allow the tongue to contact the palate following the pronunciation of the word. Once a successful 'deposit' has been obtained, the palate can be photographed (or a short video taken) by inserting the mirror into the mouth over the tongue, so that a satisfactory image is reflected back to the camera lens (see Figure 4.3). Your camera will almost certainly have a zoom lens, so be sure to use the same focal length for all your palatograms.

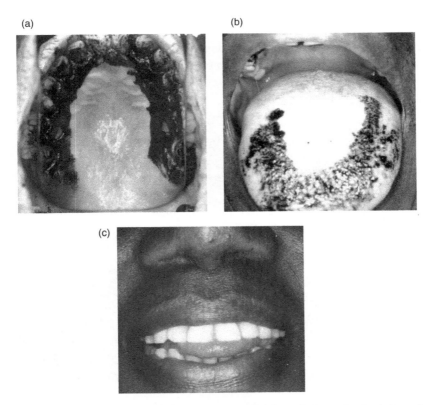

Figure 4.3 (a) Palatogram, (b) linguagram and (c) frontal view of articulation of dental stop in the Mparntwe Arrernte word *atheme* /ɐ̯ʈəmə/ (= 'to grind'); speaker: Margaret-Mary Turner-Neale, OAM. Photos: Andy Butcher

Linguagrams are made by coating the hard palate with the contrast medium and either photographing the tongue within the mouth, by inverting the mirror, or taking a frontal shot with the tongue protruded. In this case it is useful to have an anterior extension piece made up which can fit into the mirror slot on the camera and rest against the speaker's chin. This will ensure that all your linguagrams are to the same scale and is also useful for photographing or videoing the lips (see Figure 4.3).

In order to get the maximum information out of a palatogram, it is essential to take an impression of the speaker's palate. You should practice this procedure on a friend or family member until you have perfected it. You will need a full arch maxillary impression tray (again at least one large and one small) and a supply of dental alginate (both available from dental supply companies). The alginate powder is mixed with water, loaded on to the impression tray, inserted into the speaker's mouth and pressed upwards on to the palate and upper teeth. It may be necessary to do this with great speed, as the alginate sets much faster than the advertised 2 minutes and 15 seconds when the ambient temperature is above 45°C.

Once set and removed from the tray, the impression is sliced in half in the midsagittal plane, using a scalpel, and a profile of the palate traced on to paper.

(a)   (b)

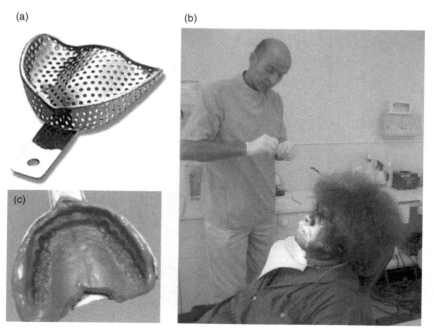

(c)

Figure 4.4 Making a good impression: (a) maxillary impression tray, (b) waiting for the alginate to set and (c) the end result. Photo: Bruce Birch

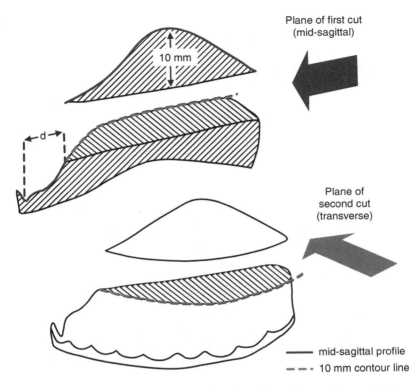

Plane of first cut
(mid-sagittal)

10 mm

d

Plane of
second cut
(transverse)

——— mid-sagittal profile
— — · 10 mm contour line

Figure 4.5 Making the cuts. How to slice the alginate impression to obtain a midsagittal profile and a 10 mm contour line

This is used to draw midsagittal diagrams of the speaker's palate. A line parallel to the plane of the upper teeth is then drawn on the cut surface of each half of the impression, 10 mm below the highest point of the palatal arch, and each half is sliced through in the transverse plane at this line. The two halves of the impression above this line are then put together again and used to trace the 10 mm contour line (see Figure 4.5). The distance from the tips of the upper incisors to the contour line is measured and used to transfer the 10 mm line to subsequent prints or tracings of the palatograms. Anderson (2008) describes some useful ways of quantifying and categorizing contact patterns.

10 Electropalatography (EPG)

The main drawback of static palatography is, of course, that it does not capture the time-course of the articulation. For this we must turn to EPG. The technique of EPG and its uses are described elsewhere by Tabain (this volume – see also

Tabain et al., 2011) and I shall not repeat the details here. Suffice it to say that modern EPG systems are light enough to be transported into the field, although they do need to be carefully packed and will require a constant AC power supply (see Figure 4.6). The Articulate Instruments system allows for the display of prompts in the form of large font text and also pictures – a particularly useful feature when working with speakers whose literacy levels are not high (see Figure 4.7). Take a small file and a pair of pliers with you and be prepared to play dental technician. You may need to modify an ill-fitting electropalate or adjust a retaining clip.

(a)

(b)

Figure 4.6 (a) EPG system with laryngograph, 'rugged' laptop and all peripherals. (b) Recording EPG data in the Warlpiri language with speaker Bess Nungarayi Price in Alice Springs (inset: electropalate). Photos: Andy Butcher

(a) Kamakmarddardda-no ngayime?

Marrekyiyimemarddardda-no, Nuddayiyimen bard-no.

(b) Kamakbard-no ngayime?

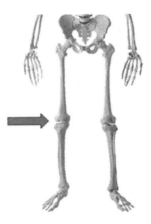

Marrekyiyime bard-no, Nuddayiyimenmarddardda-no.

Figure 4.7 Prompts used in an EPG study of consonant clusters in the
Kune ([kʊˈnɛ]) language:
(a) Prompt: 'Is it OK to say "knee"?' Response: 'Don't say "knee", say "collar bone"'.
(b) Prompt: 'Is it OK to say "collar bone?"' Response: 'Don't say "collar bone", say
"knee"'.

The main drawbacks of EPG as a fieldwork technique are that it restricts the
researcher to a small number of speakers and requires a great deal of painstak-
ing and expensive preparation before the field trip begins. The recording of data
is the culmination of a long and rather expensive process involving repeated
contact with the speakers, and in order to make this worthwhile, they must
be consistently available for further recording. EPG above all is a technique

best employed with speakers who you have already worked with (using other techniques) in the past and who can be relied upon to work with you again in the future.

11 Other Data Acquisition Techniques

The remaining measurement techniques are covered in varying degrees of detail by Tabain (this volume), so again I will confine myself to commenting on some issues relating to their use in the field. Most of these techniques will be based on a multichannel speech data acquisition system. These systems are now commercially available, rather than having to be custom built in the work-shop, as in the past.

11.1 Measuring Air Flow and Pressure

Aerodynamic data are particularly useful for investigating obstruent voicing contrasts (see, for example, Stoakes et al., 2006), for verifying the direction of airflow (egressive or ingressive) (see, for example, Butcher, 2004) and for deter-mining the degree and timing of nasalization (see, for example, Butcher, 1999; Butcher & Loakes, 2008; Demolin, 2011). Volume velocity of the air flow during speech is normally registered by means of a device known as a pneumotacho-graph. Oral and nasal airflow are best recorded via separate airtight masks in order to eliminate the risk of leakage between the two channels. As the air exits the mask, the pressure drop across a nylon gauze screen is registered by a vari-able reluctance differential pressure transducer. A miniature electret microphone is normally mounted in the oral mask to record the audio signal from the mouth. This is a relatively low-quality (11 or 22 kHz) signal which is used as an aid to subsequent segmentation of the airflow signals and for duration measurements, such as vowel length and voice onset time. One of the main bugbears of pneu-motachography is air leakage from the mask; this tends to happen with the oral mask in people with wide faces or receding chins and with the nasal mask in people with wide noses. You may need to check and adjust the mask after each utterance is recorded.

Intraoral pressure is measured during bilabial articulations by placing a plastic catheter between the lips, inserted through the mask and connected to a third transducer. Theoretically pressure can also be measured during lingual articulations by inserting the catheter through the nose and into the pharynx (Ladefoged, 2003, pp. 57–8), but I have never attempted to persuade a co-worker that this would be a fun thing to do.

Calibration is important, particularly where differences in climate and altitude are likely to produce changes in output. The intraoral pressure transducer can be calibrated in the laboratory using the u-tube device generally supplied by the manufacturer and the calibration can be simply re-checked in the field from time to time, using a ruler and a glass of water (Ladefoged, 2003, p. 61). Calibration of the airflow transducers involves using a rotameter, a much heavier piece of equipment, and can really only be done in the laboratory before and after a field trip (Ladefoged, 2003, pp. 61ff). As opposed to the transducers available in the 1970s and 1980s, we find that with modern systems there is normally very little variation, with only occasional drifting of the zero line.

11.2 Electrolaryngography (ELG)

The laryngograph is another device which is light enough to use in the field and can be used with the multichannel data acquisition system (see Figure 4.6). Laryngography measures the degree of vocal fold contact over time. As well as producing an excellent signal for deriving a fundamental frequency contour, the technique is useful for investigating subtle differences in the timing of vocal fold vibration and distinguishing phonation types such as breathiness and glottalization, although waveforms must always be interpreted with care (see Titze, 1990).

A particularly useful derivative is the open quotient – the proportion of the glottal cycle that falls between the point of maximum contact (normally the peak) and the end of the minimum contact phase (normally the flat trough). A large open quotient is found during breathy or lax voice, while a small open quotient is found in tense, creaky or laryngealized voice (see, for example, Brunelle et al., 2010). Laryngography is also a useful way of looking at glottal stops and glottalized consonants, which are commonly accompanied by a single sharp rise in the signal (see, for example, Stoakes et al., 2007). This is a non-invasive technique, but once again the physical characteristics of the speaker may need to be taken into account. Small larynges embedded in chubby necks are not good laryngography material – in other words, it is best to choose scrawny adult male speakers for this type of work.

11.3 Ultrasound

Similar caveats apply to working with ultrasound – in this case skinny younger women seem to produce the best images (see Tabain, this volume). I have no personal experience of using ultrasound in the field, but a number of excellent portable systems are now available (some of which are battery-powered) with sample rates up to 124 Hz (see Miller & Finch, 2011). As well as tracking the time course of overall tongue shape, ultrasound enables the observation of parts of the vocal tract other techniques cannot reach, especially tongue root and pharynx wall, as well as non-sagittal lingual measures such as lateral release and tongue grooving (see, for example, Gick, 2002). The trade-off for this is that the tongue tip (and epiglottis) are difficult to observe because of shadows from neighbouring cavities.

The main challenge with ultrasound in the field is stabilization of the position of the transducer relative to the speaker's head. Current practice in the lab is to use a stabilization headset. This is cumbersome (and somewhat daunting) but not heavy and probably could be used in the field. Gick (2002) proposes a method whereby the transducer is held in position by the speaker, with a small laser pointer attached to it. This projects an image of cross-hairs onto a 10 cm square target facing the speaker and they are instructed to keep the cross-hairs upright and within this target area during recording. There is no stabilization for the head, however, other than a convenient wall.

12 Perceptual Experiments

Fieldwork on speech perception does not have a long history. For obvious reasons, it has generally been limited to the behavioural type – that is, subjects are presented with stimuli and asked to make conscious decisions about them. Clearly, meaningful research questions can only be developed once knowledge of the (articulatory and acoustic) phonetics and phonology of the language is sufficiently advanced. The topic of research in speech perception is dealt with at length by Knight and Hawkins (this volume), so again I will confine myself to commenting on specific issues relating to the fieldwork context (see also Brunelle, 2011). Probably the most important advice is: keep it short and simple. There are two reasons for this: (1) you will probably be working with participants who are less than fully literate in the language, are unused to the task and may indeed have difficulty comprehending what it is about and why you would want them to do it; (2) you will probably be working in less than ideal conditions, as regards noise and other distractions (see Figure 4.8a). So use tasks such as identification (yes/no, forced choice labelling) or simpler forms of discrimination (AX, ABX, oddball). Anderson (2000, pp. 149–56) gives an excellent account of a simple identification task carried out in the field.

A screening test is essential to get your participants used to the stimuli and establish that they can do the task. You cannot assume that 'white western' concepts of privacy and quietness will prevail in the culture you are working in. Always use closed (circumaural) headphones in the quietest place you can find. Use pictures to reinforce the stimuli – make the task as much like a computer game as possible. Figure 4.8b shows an example from a four-way

(a)

(b)

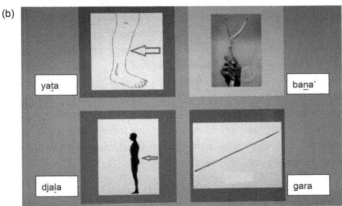

Figure 4.8 (a) Hywel Stoakes conducting a perception experiment in the Djambarrpuyŋu language with Peter Dätjiŋ (and family!) at Galiwin'ku on Elcho Island, Northern Territory. Photo: Andy Butcher. (b) Pictures used as response options in the above study. Listeners heard one of /ˈaʈa/, /ˈaɳa/, /ˈaɭa/ or /ˈaɻa/ and had to respond by pressing the appropriate key for /ˈjaʈa/('calf'), /ˈbaɳaʔ/ ('forked stick'), /ˈdaɭa/ ('coccyx') or /ˈgaɻa/ ('spear')

forced choice labelling task to test manner discrimination in the Australian language Djambarrpuyŋu. A good laptop is probably sufficient for stimulus presentation, especially if an oral response is all that is required. We have been using a 55 cm (21½ inch) screen for perceptual experiments in the field (see Figure 4.8a), although it has the disadvantage of weighing 6.0 kg. This is used in conjunction with an old keyboard with response keys painted in bright colours. Natural stimuli are probably best, but, where appropriate, you might want to use gating or masking. There are some excellent commercially available software packages for presentation of the stimuli. These take care of most aspects, including inter-stimulus intervals, randomizing, blocking and adding masking noise, all of which can be done in the field (make sure that your license is still current). Perceptual research in the field may shed light on questions of neutralization, syllabification, phoneme boundaries and the relative importance of acoustic cues.

13 Epilogue

A summer's day sometime in the twenty-first century: amid the bustle of the City of London shuttleport a group of linguists and phoneticians is about to depart for a field trip. They have spent the previous five years filling out the electronic intergalactic ethics application form and obtaining permits from 387 indigenous planetary land councils. Now they are about to board the research vessel *UKSS Ladefoged*, bound for the planet !Xgarkk. Among them is a familiar figure in a weather-beaten leather jacket: the world's leading phonetician is looking forward to several months of audio-visual recording, airflow measurement, EPG, EMA, EEG and ultrasound recordings with some of the last remaining speakers of Wngi'h. 'Professor Jones', calls an eager young science reporter, 'What equipment are you taking with you?' As she reaches the departure gate, Daniella turns and smiles deprecatingly from under her trademark wide-brimmed bush hat. 'Only these', she replies, pointing to her twin earlobe-mounted multimedia multichannel wireless data acquisition devices.

5 Research Methods in Speech Acoustics

Dominic Watt

1 Introduction

In around 20 years the acoustic analysis of speech has gone from being a pursuit viable only for laboratories with generous equipment budgets and technical support to one available to anybody with a personal computer. For most applications it is now no longer necessary to have dedicated, and expensive, hardware (e.g. the Kay Elemetrics *CSL*), although high-quality external sound cards are still recommended in favour of those built into PCs and laptops. General purpose software packages like Sensimetrics *SpeechStation2* are still available for sale, but *Praat*, the program that is now the industry standard for acoustic analysis of speech, is freely downloadable, runs on multiple platforms and has considerably more functionality and flexibility than rival software packages. Its programmers make updated releases available every few months, and it is customizable owing to the accompanying scripting language and the provision of add-ons for specific applications, such as *Akustyk* (http://bartus.org/akustyk) for vowel analysis and plotting.

Other freeware packages for performing acoustic speech analysis are *WaveSurfer, Speech Analyzer* (Windows only), *Speech Filing System* and its pared-down counterpart program *WASP, Sonogram Visible Speech* and *STx*. Most are superior to *Praat* in terms of the user-friendliness and intuitiveness of the interface, but because there is considerable variation in the algorithms used in each for pitch extraction, formant tracking and the like, the results they produce are not necessarily identical even where the same recording is being analyzed

(Harrison, 2011). When reporting results, researchers must therefore always specify what version of what package was used to collect the data.

The researcher may be fortunate enough to be analyzing recordings made under his or her own guidance using the best quality equipment available, but in many cases the material to be analyzed has not been recorded in optimal conditions. The recording may not have been made in a quiet or otherwise controlled environment. This is often the case with recordings made in the field, or anywhere outside the laboratory. The quality of microphones and sound recorders used for recording speech is highly variable, and the technical properties of the resulting recording vary in line with factors such as the type of microphone used (the recorder's built-in microphone versus an external omni-directional boundary microphone connected to a pre-amplifier, say) and its frequency response characteristics. The flatter the frequency response spectrum the more faithful to the original signal the sound recording will be.

The sampling rate and bit-depth settings of the recorder, the choice of recording in stereo versus mono formats, and file format chosen (PCM .wav versus a compressed 'lossy' format such as .mp3, for example), will also determine the quality of the recorded signal, and consequently the types of acoustic analyses that can be performed on it. Advice on best practice in this area can be found in Cieri (2010), Plichta (2010) or Butcher (this volume).

It must be remembered that converting an analogue signal into digital format involves processing of different sorts at the intervening stages, and that the resultant sound file is only one of a limitless number of possible ways of representing the original signal. It is worth stressing that spectrograms of the kind illustrated in this chapter and elsewhere in this volume are quite indirect representations of the input signal. The Fourier analysis of the signal necessary to produce a spectrogram results in a representation approximating the psycho-perceptual properties of that signal as if it were being processed by the inner ear of humans, so is not a direct acoustic representation per se (Studdert-Kennedy & Whalen, 1999). After all, spectrograms may be computed so as to foreground frequency-domain information (as in narrow-band spectrograms in which the harmonics of the fundamental frequency are clearly visible) or to highlight time-domain information (as in wide-band spectrograms in which individual glottal pulses and formant resonances become visible; Figure 5.1 shows examples).

2 Making Measurements

The remainder of this chapter is devoted to a discussion of key parameters that may be measured when investigating aspects of the acoustic properties of speech. These parameters are duration, frequency and intensity.

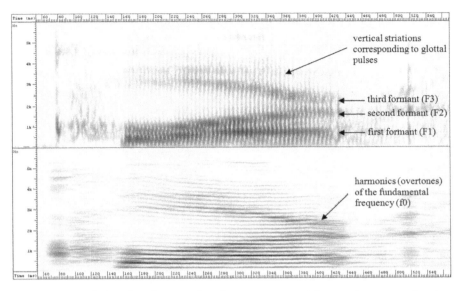

Figure 5.1 Wide-band and narrow-band spectrograms of the word *court*, spoken by a young woman from Eyemouth, Scotland

2.1 Duration

Measuring duration is generally a straightforward matter, in that – unlike in the frequency domain – no decomposition of the signal is necessary before measurements can be made. Older sources often express durational measurements using centisecond (cs, that is, 0.01s) units because they had to be made from paper printouts, but contemporary programs can show durations with extreme, indeed superfluous, accuracy. It is sufficient for almost all purposes to express durations in milliseconds (ms, that is, 0.001s).

Using so-called interval tiers in signal annotation 'TextGrids', *Praat* allows the user to segment and label the file in such a way that the durations of selected intervals, and other relevant associated information, can be logged semi-automatically. This is particularly convenient when making large numbers of duration measurements. Figure 5.2 shows an example of an annotated file, in which a recording of the word *purse* has been subdivided into sections: the post-release aspiration phase of the initial /p/, the vowel, and the final fricative. The duration of the /p/ aspiration is shown as 0.030s (i.e. 30ms) at the top and bottom of the display. This period between the release of a plosive and the start of voicing for the following vowel – the plosive's Voice Onset Time (VOT) – is one of the most commonly cited durational measurements, and because it is known that the human perceptual system is sensitive to absolute VOT values

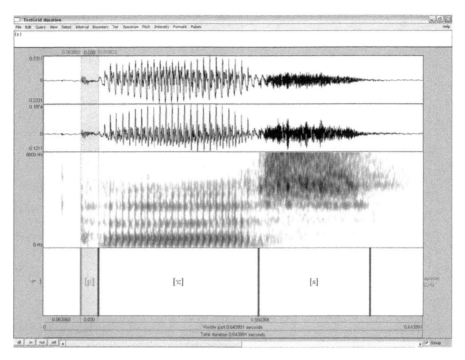

Figure 5.2 Stereo waveform and wide-band spectrogram of the word *purse*, with segmented and annotated *Praat* TextGrid below. The duration of the VOT portion of the initial /p/ is 30ms

as well as relative ones (e.g. Kuhl & Miller, 1978), VOT durations are generally reported in the literature in their original ms units without any rescaling.

Where the relative durations of segmental phenomena are at issue, as for example in the study of vowel-length contrasts (e.g. Myers, 2005; Myers & Hansen, 2005), it may be appropriate to normalize the durations, for example, using duration ratios or percentages. In a study of the durational properties of vowels and consonants in the English spoken in the border region between England and Scotland, Watt et al. (2010a) demonstrated correlations between raw VOT measurements for /p t k/ and vowel durations in phonological contexts that predict length alternations resulting from the operation of the Scottish Vowel Length Rule (SVLR; see also Docherty et al., 2011). The SVLR specifies that vowels in Scottish English will be phonetically longer where they precede voiced fricatives, /r/, or a pause than in other contexts. It has been found in studies of Scottish English (e.g. Scobbie et al., 1999) that the vowels /i u ai/ are more strongly and consistently affected by the SVLR than other vowels, so the identity of the vowel in question must also be taken into account (see also Watt & Yurkova, 2007).

The durations of pairs of SVLR and non-SVLR vowels are best expressed in terms of the ratio of the shorter vowel to the longer one of each pair. For example, while the duration of /e/ in the word *mace* for a speaker of Scottish English might be 204ms, that of the same speaker's vowel in *maze* could be 292ms, yielding a shorter : longer ratio of 1 : 1.43. This is more than simply the Voicing Effect (VE) described by Chen (1970), as the two lengthening effects operate on Scottish English vowels simultaneously. That is, the VE predicts that the duration of the vowel of *made* will be somewhat longer than that of *mate*, but because the SVLR is sensitive to the manner of articulation as well as the voicing of a following consonant, it triggers an appreciably greater lengthening of /e/ in the word *maze* relative to the vowel in *mace* than would be brought about by the VE alone. In accents in which the SVLR operates consistently, one would expect to find large differences between the duration ratios for vowels before voiceless and voiced consonants. In VE-only accents, which are the norm outside Scotland, one would expect to find only small differences, if any, between these ratios.

Durational properties of consonants can be handled in similar ways. For example, Cohn et al.'s (1999) study of gemination of plosive, fricative and approximant consonants in three Indonesian languages presents absolute and ratio values for the durations of intervocalic stop closures. They found that geminate voiced plosives exhibit the longest singleton : geminate ratios of all the segment types they tested, and that for the voiceless plosives the singleton-geminate contrast is implemented in all three languages solely by closure duration (post-release VOT is not any longer for geminates than for singleton plosives). There is a trading relation, however, between the durations of vowels preceding medial singleton and geminate consonants, in that vowels before geminates are significantly shorter than those before singletons. Cohn et al. suggest that speakers of these languages adjust the relative durations of adjacent segments according to a timing model based upon the syllable.

In much the same way, the durations of syllables themselves, and their relationship with higher-order units such as the foot, are frequently the subject of investigation by researchers interested in speech rate and rhythm. Speech rate (or 'tempo') is calculated by counting the number of words or syllables uttered per minute, or syllables per second. Articulation rate (AR) is a related metric based on speech productions from which any pauses and hesitation markers have been removed, such that the focus is more specifically upon the linguistic content of utterances. Jacewicz et al. (2009) show that AR in two US English accents – one northern, one southern – is significantly different, with the speakers of the northern (Wisconsin) accent talking faster than those with the southern (North Carolina) accent. Younger speakers had higher AR values than older ones in both accents when reading sentences aloud, and men spoke somewhat faster than did women.

Related to speech and articulation rate is the rhythmicity of utterances, the principal acoustic correlate of which is the relative durations of syllables (see further Astruc, this volume). The neat subdivision of languages into 'stress-timed' or 'syllable-timed' categories, a dichotomy commonly attributed to Pike (1945) but proposed considerably earlier than this by the British phonetician Arthur Lloyd James (Michael Ashby, p.c.), has been shown to be excessively simplistic (Roach, 1982). Instead, a cline exists between languages exhibiting more of the properties associated with stress timing (including non-durational features such as the phonotactic complexity of syllables, syllable weight and vowel centralization in unstressed syllables), and languages for which a greater tendency towards syllable isochrony is in evidence, alongside other cues such as a lack of vowel reduction and relatively simple syllable structures (Dauer, 1983, 1987; Ramus et al., 1999; Arvaniti, 2009).

Using a variety of metrics it has been possible to quantify the timing characteristics of various languages and dialects objectively (e.g. Grabe & Low, 2002). However, Nolan and Asu (2009) believe that attempts to portray the rhythmical properties of languages in terms of their location along a unidimensional continuum with stress-timing versus syllable-timing at its poles are flawed. Rather, they believe stress-timing and syllable-timing are not mutually exclusive, and that languages may have both stress-timed and syllable-timed properties simultaneously. New rhythm metrics and refinements to existing ones have more recently been proposed by researchers such as Dellwo (2006) and White and Mattys (2007), and consensus is increasing on which metrics are the most valid and reliable (Wiget et al., 2010; Knight, 2011). It has been argued that an over-reliance on timing measurements has hindered an adequate understanding of rhythm, however (e.g. Cummins, 2003, 2009; Arvaniti, 2009), and that we should give fuller consideration to the perceptual underpinnings of rhythm if we are to make progress in this area of phonetics.

While it was stated earlier that making durational measurements is generally comparatively simple – one can easily derive highly accurate temporal values just by placing cursors on a waveform or spectrogram – it should not be forgotten that our decisions about where to draw boundaries between phonetic and phonological units are grounded in theoretical considerations and are not necessarily motivated by evidence of discontinuities in the acoustic domain. If one is interested in measuring the durations of syllables for the purposes of calculating the Pairwise Variability Index (PVI) of an utterance, for instance, one must come to a set of working principles concerning how to treat ambisyllabic consonants. Measuring the durations of individual segments in consonant clusters can be very difficult if adjacent segments are heavily coarticulated, and the nucleus and glide portions of diphthongs can be impossible to demarcate from one another in any objective way. Vocalic consonants such as the liquids [ɹ] and [l] and the glides [j] and [w] can prove particularly troublesome where they occur adjacent to vowels, owing to their close acoustic similarity to vowels. In some cases, such as the V[ɹ] sequence in a rhotic production of *bird*, the best compromise may actually be to measure the duration of the sequence as though it were one unit, because what is heard as V[ɹ] may be a unitary /r/-coloured vowel rather than a sequence of two discrete articulations. Turk et al. (2006) give very useful advice on the identification of 'acoustic landmarks' in the speech stream, and how these can be used to formulate consistent segmentation criteria.

Other phenomena which involve the measurement of duration include the so-called rise time of fricatives versus affricates. Rise time is the period which elapses between the initiation of a fricative and the point at which it reaches maximum amplitude. In fricatives it has been found to be typically longer than in the fricative portion of a homorganic affricate. For example, the rise time of [ʃ] in *watch out* is expected to be shorter than that of [ʃ] in *what shout*, though it appears that the absolute duration of the fricative is at least as important perceptually as the rise time (Kluender & Walsh, 1992; Mitani et al., 2006).

The durations of formant transitions from consonantal occlusions into or out of vowels are also important cues to consonant identity. Manipulation of the length of the transition from a voiced bilabial consonant can change the listener's percept of [w] into [b] (Liberman et al., 1956; Miller & Liberman, 1979). It should of course be remembered that perception of this phenomenon, as is true also of the others mentioned above, is to a significant degree dependent upon speech rate. An increase in speech rate may result in compression of articulations, or a reduction of their magnitude or precision. Failure to reach articulatory targets in this way is known as *undershoot* (Lindblom, 1963), which is thought to be a factor underlying processes of diachronic change. Hypoarticulated speech may lead the listener to perceptually misclassify sounds in ways not intended by the talker: for example, velar plosives may be misperceived as bilabial ones, and vice versa (see, for example, Ohala, 1981; Blevins, 2007).

2.2 Frequency

A second key acoustic property of speech sounds is frequency, measured in Hertz (Hz) units, which supplanted the older, but equivalent, 'cycles per second' (cps). Frequency in its strict definition is the rate at which an acoustic event is repeated, which means that it does not make sense to talk about the frequency of 'one-off' events such as transients (clicking and popping noises, stop release bursts and the like) and non-repeating random noise such as that found in fricatives. All the same, we can specify that the stop burst of the velar plosive [k] might feature a concentration of energy at 2 kiloHertz (kHz), and that the low-frequency cut-off is at approximately 1.3kHz for an [s]. Probably the most commonly measured quantities in the frequency domain are fundamental frequency (F0), which corresponds to the rate of vibration of the vocal folds and gives rise to the perception of pitch (see Astruc, this volume), and the frequencies of the formants of voiced sounds, particularly vowels and other vocoid sounds. These are dealt with in turn below.

Variation in fundamental frequency is used for various communicative purposes. The lexical tone contrasts found in a very large number of the world's languages (including Mandarin Chinese, Cantonese, Thai, Yoruba, Zulu and thousands of others) are sometimes implemented using rather subtle differences in F0. Khouw and Ciocca (2007) provide F0 data for the six tones of Hong Kong Cantonese, which are assigned numbers reflecting the F0 level (high, mid and low) and whether the tone is a level tone or a contour tone (falling or rising). Thus, for example, tone 55 is 'high level', tone 25 is 'low rising' and tone 21 is 'low falling'. Using four sets of words which illustrate each of the six contrastive tones (e.g. si_{55} 'poem', si_{25} 'history', si_{33} 'try', si_{21} 'time', si_{23} 'city' and si_{22} 'surname'), spoken by 10 male and female speakers, Khouw and Ciocca determine that although some tones are extremely similar with respect to the trajectory of F0, as can be seen for tones 25 and 23, or tones 33 and 22, in Figure 5.3 the perception of tone contrasts seems to depend on the frequency of F0 in the final quarter of the tone-bearing vowel.

Related to lexical tone is pitch accent, which operates over subsets of polysyllabic words in languages such as Japanese, Norwegian and Swedish. In eastern dialects of Norwegian *fjæra* 'the feather' is distinct from *fjæra* 'low tide' in that the first features a rising pitch contour that contrasts with the fall-rise contour of the second; see van Dommelen and Nilsen (2002). Syllable stress, and hence word and phrasal stress patterns, in many languages also depend on F0, marked changes in which may cue prominence, typically in combination with differences in duration and intensity.

If the dynamic aspects of F0 are of interest it may be sufficient for investigative purposes to generate an F0 contour track or 'pitch track' for visual inspection so as to ascertain whether perceptual judgements of F0 movements are borne out by the instrumental data, or to compare the tonal or intonational properties of utterances with one another. Where a quantitative investigation is called for, it is a simple matter in *Praat* to export the F0 data to a separate file, and to handle the values as time-series data. Normalization of the figures with respect to time, which can be achieved by converting raw durational values into percentages, may be necessary if utterances are of varying lengths. The F0 values shown in Figure 5.3 have been sampled at fixed positions within the vowels of the target syllables so as to eliminate these durational differences. It should of course be remembered that where the duration of a pitch-bearing unit is very short the time available to execute F0 movements is constrained. In such cases one may find that F0 contours are truncated or compressed (Grabe et al., 2000).

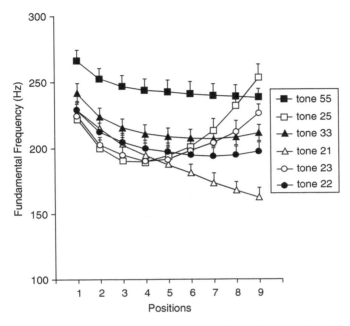

Figure 5.3 Mean fundamental frequency (Hz) values for 10 male and female speakers' productions of the six lexical tones of Hong Kong Cantonese at 9 time-normalized positions. Gender was found not to have a significant effect on F0, so the values for men and women are collapsed. Error bars represent 1 standard error. From Khouw and Ciocca (2007, 109)

Because the sound waves emitted by the vocal tract are complex, they feature additional periodic properties besides F0. Formants are amplitude peaks in the acoustic spectrum which result from the excitation of particular vocal-tract resonances brought about by the vibration of the vocal folds setting the column of air inside the pharyngeal, oral and nasal cavities in motion. They are responsible for differences in vowel quality, among other things, and correlate with the position of the tongue in the oral cavity, and the degree of jaw opening and lip rounding involved in the articulation. Formants are visible in wide-band spectrograms (as in the upper pane of Figure 5.1) as dark, approximately horizontal bars, or as peaks in the spectral envelope, as per those shown for the vowel [i:] in Figure 5.4. The individual harmonics, which are integral multiples of F0, are visible in the right-hand pane.

By and large, it is only the lowest two or three formants that are measured in phonetic research. It is conventional to represent the frequencies of F1 and F2 graphically by plotting their values on xy scattergrams with the axes arranged in such a way that the configuration of points on the F1~F2 plane resembles

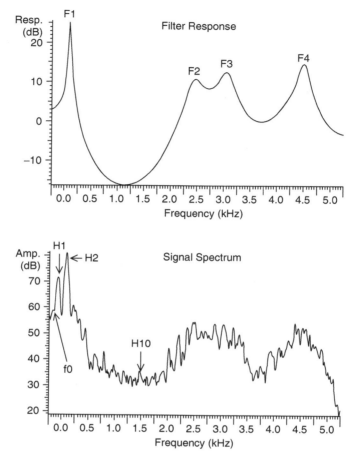

Figure 5.4 Filter response (LPC) and signal (output) spectra of the vowel [iː] in the word *feet*, spoken by an 82-year-old woman from Carlisle, England. The four lowest-frequency formants (F1–F4) are marked on the filter response spectrum, at left. An approximately similar overall spectral shape, as well as the individual harmonics of F0, are evident in the signal spectrum, at right. F0 and the first, second and tenth harmonics (H1, H2, H10) are labelled

the traditional vowel quadrilateral, as for example that in Figure 5.5. Although there is more to vowel quality than just the frequencies of the lowest two formants, it is very much easier to appreciate vowel productions as manifestations of a system of qualitative oppositions when they are presented in this format. The points in Figure 5.6 represent F1 and F2 values for monophthong vowels produced by a middle-aged speaker from Galway, Ireland. The proximity of some of the points, which are labelled using Wells's lexical set keywords

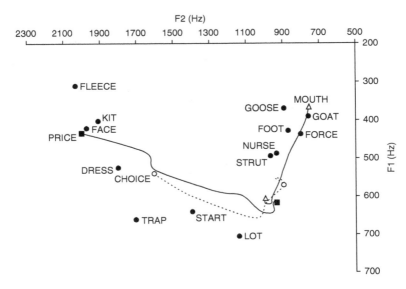

Figure 5.5 Scatter plot of F1 and F2 values for 13 monophthong and 3 diphthong vowels produced by a speaker of Irish English (Hughes et al., 2012)

(Wells, 1982), reflects the auditory similarity of the vowels in question. NURSE and STRUT, for example, share a quality that might be transcribed as [ʌ], while the vowels of the GOOSE and GOAT sets are impressionistically very similar to one another, as are those of the FOOT and FORCE sets. Owing to its relatively high F2, the speaker's START vowel is much fronter than his LOT vowel, bearing out the auditory values for these vowels of [aː] and [ɑ] respectively.

Three-dimensional vowel plots which incorporate F3 values on the z axis are also found in the literature from time to time (e.g. Schwartz et al., 2005), but more common are formant plots which capture the dynamic (time-domain) properties of vowels by presenting the data as formant 'trajectories'. This is particularly useful when representing diphthongs, which can be plotted as connected pairs of points corresponding to the nucleus and the glide, or as formant tracks as per those shown in Figure 5.5 for the PRICE, CHOICE and MOUTH vowels. These are based on F1 and F2 values measured for each vowel at 10 per cent intervals, connected by a smoothed line and labelled at the endpoint. It can be seen that the PRICE and CHOICE vowels follow a similar trajectory, in keeping with the perceived similarity of these diphthongs in Irish English, but they are nonetheless distinct in that CHOICE has a closer onset and a more open glide than does PRICE.

Depending on the level of acoustic detail sought, it may be worthwhile to measure formant values at multiple points in all vowels, not just diphthongs. Monophthong vowels are in many cases acoustically diphthongal, and vice

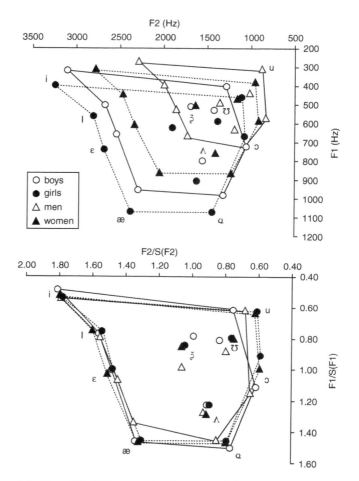

Figure 5.6 Mean F1~F2 frequencies for monophthong vowels spoken by 76 American English-speaking men, women and children. Left pane = values in Hz; right pane = normalized values using the modified Watt and Fabricius (mW+F) method (Fabricius et al., 2009; Watt & Fabricius, 2011)

versa, and capturing the dynamic nature of vowels in this way gives a fuller picture of the vowel's quality than does taking a single pair of observations of the F1 and F2 values at a single slice through a vowel, which is normally at its temporal midpoint, or the point of maximal formant displacement. The paths taken between the onset and offset of diphthongs and (phonological) monophthongs have furthermore been found to be of forensic relevance, in that, while for a given accent the start and end points of vowels may be essentially the same for different speakers, the curves described by individual formants between these points may be characteristic of individual speakers (Cawley & French, this volume). McDougall (2004) and Morrison (2009) have modelled these trajectories for F1–F3 using polynomial equations to approximate the curves involved, and have attained impressively high same-speaker recognition rates in speaker-matching experiments.

Formant frequency values given in published sources have typically been measured from the speech of adult males, in large part because it is in gener- ally easier to do so, owing to the relationship between the spacing of harmonics and formant bandwidth. Because of sex differences in vocal tract length, form- ant frequencies for equivalent vowels are correspondingly higher in women's speech than in that of men. It is not feasible, therefore, to compare men's and women's vowel productions directly, and for the same reason children's vowels with those of adults. Normalization of formant frequencies to correct, as far as possible, for these differences should be carried out, although because there are numerous ways of doing so (as described next) it can be difficult to decide which of the available methods is most suitable for the data at hand.

Conversion of Hertz measurements into one or other of the psychoperceptual scales available goes some way towards correcting for vocal tract length-related differences. These psychoperceptual scales, as the name implies, are intended to replicate the non-linear mapping between the Hz scale and the frequency response characteristics of the human inner ear, which treats doublings of fre- quency as perceptually equivalent, as per the musical octave. As listeners we are thus considerably more sensitive to a change in frequency of a given size low down in the frequency spectrum than we are to a change of the same size higher up. The Equivalent Rectangular Bandwidth (ERB) scale (Moore & Glasberg, 1983) is considered to model this relationship most accurately, although the longer-established Bark and mel scales (Beranek, 1949; Traunmüller, 1990) con- tinue to be frequently used. Converting from Hz to ERB only has the effect of compressing higher frequencies relative to low ones; however, while this brings the vowel spaces of speakers with shorter vocal tracts (women and children) more closely into agreement with those of male speakers, it does not eliminate the mismatch as fully as is possible using 'true' normalization methods. Methods of the latter sort seek to minimize talker differences by applying transforms that are based on formant values from the same speaker (speaker-intrinsic) ver- sus different speakers (speaker-extrinsic), and/or from the same vowel versus multiple vowels (vowel-intrinsic vs. vowel-extrinsic). A third criterion distin- guishing normalization algorithms from each other concerns whether, when normalizing values for formant n, one uses values for the same formant only (formant-intrinsic methods) versus multiple formants (formant-extrinsic).

Several surveys that evaluate the pros and cons of the different available methods have been published in recent decades (Disner, 1980; Adank et al., 2004; Fabricius et al., 2009; Flynn & Foulkes, 2011; Kohn & Farrington, 2012), and normalization tools are built into packages such as *Praat*, *Akustyk* or *Plotnik* (a dedicated vowel plotting program for Mac OS authored by the sociophonetician William Labov). The vowel plotting and normalization interface NORM (Thomas & Kendall, 2007), implemented using the R programming language, generates normalized data using a variety of algorithms and will produce exportable scatter plots of the results. Among the methods built into NORM are two permutations of the routine developed by Watt and Fabricius (2002), which on measures such as the increase in the area of intersection of pairs of mismatched vowel spaces performs as well or better than the majority of the other routines tested (Fabricius et al., 2009; Flynn & Foulkes, 2011). Figure 5.6 shows an example of the improvement in mapping that can be made for four vowel spaces after one of these methods has been applied. It is also an advantage if the shape of each polygon is not warped too much by normalization. In the present case, the angles of the lines connecting the peripheral vowel means in the two plots do not differ greatly, indicating that the normalization process has not removed much of the information contained in the original Hz data other than the unwanted differences resulting from speaker sex and age.

It is usually assumed that normalization of formant values for same-sex adult speakers is unnecessary, but in some cases it may be worthwhile. There can, after all, be substantial differences in vocal tract length, and consequently formant frequencies for equivalent vowels, between speakers of the same sex. Before carrying out any transformation of data the researcher should first inspect them carefully, a task which is made easier by plotting them. Watt et al. (2010b) make suggestions for effective ways of visualizing vowel formant data before and after normalization.

Investigation of the acoustic properties of consonants is more complex than is the case for vowels, because of differences among consonants produced using different airstream mechanisms, the greater range of places and manners of articulation involved and the fact that consonants are characterized by a greater number of combinations of acoustic events than vowels are (e.g. a voiced fricative combines periodic noise with aperiodic noise; a plosive consonant is a sequence of identifiable changes in airflow; etc.). In a chapter of this length it is not feasible to attempt a detailed account of the research methods used in the analysis of consonants; for more detailed treatments, readers might instead like to consult Fry (1976), Ladefoged and Maddieson (1996), Ladefoged (2003), or Harrington (2010a, b), Johnson (2011).

Formant data for the most vowel-like of the consonants (glides such as [j], [w] and [ɥ]) can be handled in the same way as those measured from vowels, although it may be more difficult to make the measurements in the first place owing to the relatively short durations of these consonants compared to those of vowels, and the formant transitions that occur from glides into adjacent vowels and vice versa.

Liquid consonants – the lateral and rhotic approximants – present comparable difficulties. We must take into account the acoustic consequences of the changes in cavity shape produced for the articulation of lateral consonants, and for rhotics by movements of the tongue tip/blade and or the dorsum/root, and, potentially, also the lips. Identifying acoustic properties that are common to members of the class of rhotics has been notoriously difficult (Lindau, 1985; Magnuson, 2007), which is unsurprising given that the class can be said to subsume everything from labial approximants such as [ʋ] (e.g. in varieties of British English; Foulkes & Docherty, 2000; Knight et al., 2007) to uvular trills and fricatives [ʀ ʁ] (Ladefoged & Maddieson, 1996). Alveolar laterals are cross-linguistically the most common lateral type, and in many accents of English are realized as 'clear' and 'dark' allophones. The principal distinction between these is the relative spacing of F1 and F2: in the clear variant F1 is low and F2 high, while in the dark one F1 is higher and F2 lower than for the clear form. It should be noted that some analyses argue for clear and dark variants of /r/ too. Work on the acoustic effects of secondary articulations on the English liquids – those giving rise to 'clear' and 'dark' variants of /r/ and /l/ in different accents – has been carried out by Carter and Local (2007), while West (2000) and Heid and Hawkins (2000) have investigated the spreading of liquid resonances across longer domains, in some cases up to five syllables upstream of the /r/ or /l/ in question. Detailed accounts of the acoustic techniques recommended for the analysis of liquids are given in Lehiste (1964), Nolan (1983), Barry (1997), Plug and Ogden (2003), Lawson et al. (2010) or Simonet (2010).

In nasals the measurement of formants is especially problematic, given that the coupling of the oral/pharyngeal and nasal cavities results in the attenuation of acoustic energy at a broad range of frequencies. One can expect there to be a prominent first formant at approximately 300Hz, but given the low amplitudes of the higher formants and the relatively broad formant bandwidths found in nasals, obtaining accurate formant values is troublesome. Owing to the complex branching shape of the cavities involved, interference of resonances can result in cancelling out of acoustic energy at certain frequencies in nasals. These gaps are known as 'zeroes' or anti-formants, and their frequencies are cues to place of articulation: the further forward the oral closure, the lower the frequency of the anti-formant (Kurowski & Blumstein, 1987).

(Oral) plosive consonants can be thought of as sequences of three phases: an approach phase, a hold phase and a release phase. The state of the glottis is also relevant, where plosives are distinguished by voicing (see the discussion of VOT earlier in the chapter). The sequence of phases is best illustrated in the case of intervocalic plosives. In the approach phase, the active articulator approaches the passive articulator, then makes contact with it. If a complete closure is made between the articulators, airflow passing between them will cease. This is the hold phase. Voicing may persist from the preceding vowel throughout this phase, but will only last as long as transglottal airflow can be maintained. Again, this is dependent upon place of articulation, because a closure further forward allows airflow to be sustained for longer before the subglottal and supraglottal pressures are equalized. Lastly, the active and passive articulators are separated. In voiceless plosives, the air pressure that has built up behind the occlusion can be substantially higher than that in front of it, so the pent-up body of air is released forcefully and noisily. It may be some time before voicing for the vowel following the plosive release can resume, and the presence of post-aspiration (as seen in Figure 5.7 below) may prolong this phase further, such that VOT values exceeding 100ms are not uncommon.

Figure 5.7 shows this sequence as it is reflected in the pressure waveform and spectrogram of the word *daughter*, where for the medial /t/ the tongue tip starts to be raised towards the alveolar ridge at the left-hand boundary of segment (a), marking the onset of the approach phase. There is an abrupt diminution of amplitude visible in both the waveform and the spectrogram at this

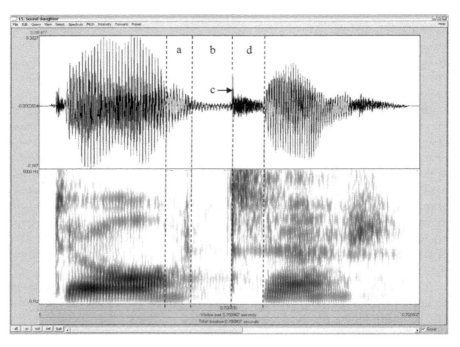

Figure 5.7 Waveform and spectrogram of *daughter*, spoken by a 61 year old woman from Gretna, Scotland. Phases of the intervocalic /t/ are segmented and labelled: a = approach phase; b = hold phase; c = release burst transient; d = release phase (post-aspiration)

point, and a deflection of the formants; there is a momentary period of friction just before the onset of the closure phase (b) as the active and passive articulators make contact. There is generally much more variation in the articulation of intervocalic and word-final plosives with respect to the timing of articulatory gestures than textbook accounts of the phonetics of English would lead one to believe (see, for example, Jones & Llamas, 2008; Jones & McDougall, 2009).

In Figure 5.7 there is some voicing present in the hold phase (b), which is released at point (c), resulting in a sharp spike or 'transient' across the frequency spectrum. Segment (d) is the release phase, which is occupied here by a period of voiceless post-aspiration friction that ceases on the resumption of voicing at the right-hand boundary of segment (d). Formant transitions may be visible between the plosive release and the vowel that follows it.

For utterance-initial voiceless plosives the approach and hold phases may be completely silent, so observing the duration and frequency properties of either is not possible. The cues to place of articulation in cases of this kind lie in the spectral properties of the release burst and CV formant transitions (Cooper et al., 1952; Stevens & Blumstein, 1978; Li et al., 2010). Utterance-initial voiced plosives are prevoiced in many languages, and so periodicity may be visible in the waveform in advance of the release burst. The measurement of VOT in prevoiced plosives is anchored on the release burst, such that VOT values are expressed as negative numbers. VOT values for prevoiced plosives tend to be distributed bimodally, because for plosives with longer VOTs there is often a cessation of voicing prior to the release, owing to the fact that transglottal air-flow cannot be maintained as long as the hold phase persists. Prevoicing of shorter durations can, by contrast, be maintained until the plosive release. This leaves a gap in the distribution between long-lead and short-lead VOT tokens (see, for example, Docherty, 1992).

Various approaches to the acoustic description of fricative consonants exist. Principal among these are *spectral moments* (e.g. Forrest et al., 1988; Jongman et al., 2000) and *Discrete Cosine Transform* (DCT) analyses (Nossair & Zahorian, 1991; Watson & Harrington, 1999). Spectral moments are statistics describing different aspects of the distribution of energy in a spectrum. *Praat* will generate the first four spectral moments – *spectral centre of gravity, standard deviation, skewness, kurtosis* – for a recorded sample via simple commands that can readily be built into a script. The centre of gravity (abbreviated COG) is a measure of the average amplitude of frequency components in the spectrum, indicating where the energy is predominantly located, while the standard deviation quantifies how far individual frequencies deviate from the COG. Skewness is a measure of the shape of the spectrum on either side of the COG – a high skewness index being a sign of asymmetry – while the kurtosis measure indicates how far the shape of the spectrum deviates from a Gaussian (normal distribution) curve, and is commonly thought of as the 'peakedness' in the spectrum.

Taken together, these quantities may provide a useful means of distinguishing between strident and non-strident fricatives, and/or between fricatives with different places of articulation (Tomiak, 1990; Shadle et al., 1991; Jongman et al., 2000; Gordon et al., 2002).

DCT analysis decomposes the complex signal into a set of cosine waves, and then treats the amplitudes of these waves as coefficients, the first three of which correspond to the *mean*, the *slope* and the *curvature* of the signal. Praat can create so-called *Mel Frequency Cepstral Coefficients* (MFCCs) from sound files, by first converting the frequencies from Hertz into mel units (Beranek, 1949), and then converting the mel values into MFCCs. MFCCs are directly comparable to DCT coefficients. Although they are more frequently used for signal processing applications such as speech recognition than they are for laboratory phonetics of the type that is likely to be of most interest to readers of this book, these analysis methods provide the researcher with additional ways of characterizing the similarities and differences between fricative spectra, and indeed they could be applied equally effectively to noise associated with plosive consonants.

Other measures that are useful for the analysis of spectral shape in fricatives include *peak frequency* (the frequency at which the maximum amplitude in the spectrum is attained), *peak amplitude* (the amplitude of that frequency component) and *front slope* (the slope of a line connecting the amplitude peak to a fixed lower-frequency point). Stuart-Smith (2007) chooses 500Hz as this point in her analysis of spectral properties of Glaswegian /s/. *Low-frequency cut-off* and *range* (frequency range within a fixed intensity band, for example, 12 deciBels (dB) from the major spectral peak, as per Jones & Llamas, 2008) are also useful parameters, as are formant transitions, duration and other intensity measurements (Gordon et al., 2002).

Measuring acoustic intensity in absolute terms is generally impractical, because unless one is using speech recordings made under optimal conditions – which would involve the use of a soundproofed room with a microphone at a fixed distance from the speaker's mouth – the reference intensity to be used as a baseline against which to express the sound pressure level (SPL) of a given sound cannot be established with certainty. Comparing utterances produced by the same speaker at different times, or by different speakers, is therefore also often problematic. Use of a headset microphone, the capsule of which can be positioned at the same distance from the mouth across different subjects, may assist in helping to control one source of variation in intensity. Ultimately, however, the researcher may have to express intensity measurements in relative terms. An example of how this might be done for the analysis of the intensity of plosive bursts is given by Vicenik (2010), who expresses the intensity in dB of the burst portion of the release phase of Georgian plosives by subtracting the maximum intensity in the burst from the maximum intensity of the following vowel (see also Stoel-Gammon et al., 1994).

Finally, should one wish to analyse phonation type (voice quality) using acoustic measures there are a variety of parameters associated with changes in phonatory setting. Intensity is one; breathy and creaky phonation are generally marked by lower intensities than other phonation types. Another relevant parameter is fundamental frequency, including its *periodicity*, which is quantified using a measure called 'jitter', values for which are highest in creaky voice. Variations in formant frequencies and duration have also been found to be associated with changes in voice quality. The parameter known as *spectral tilt* – the slope defined by the dropoff in the intensity in the spectrum as frequency rises – is a reliable indicator of voice quality. The relative amplitudes of F0 and its harmonics, particularly those low in the frequency spectrum (the second harmonic, and those harmonics closest to the first and second formants), appear to correlate with modal, creaky and breathy phonation. The spectral tilt for a creaky voiced vowel is defined by a shallower negative slope than for the same vowel produced with breathy voice. For details of techniques for making measurements of voice quality see Ladefoged et al., 1988; Kirk et al., 1993; Gobl & Ní Chasaide, 2010; Kreiman & Gerratt, 2011; Esling, this volume).

3 Conclusion

This chapter has touched on some of the key investigative techniques available to researchers in speech acoustics, but there are many others which, owing to space limitations, cannot be discussed here. Existing methods and technologies are constantly being refined and new ones are regularly developed, so although many of the techniques researchers apply to speech data are long established, the battery of analytical methods is always expanding. The fact that so many of these methods can now be automated means that large bodies of data are easier to gather than ever before, especially given the freely available nature of *Praat* and other powerful and readily customizable software packages. High-quality solid-state recording technology is now cheap by any standard, and even very large digital sound files can be handled with ease. Excellent reference works, demonstrations of the principles of acoustics, downloadable databases of recordings, data files and labour-saving internet tools are all available online, supported by online communities of researchers who are willing to help less-experienced colleagues to design and execute experiments, to make reliable and accurate measurements and to analyze and interpret the data their investigations produce. The researcher is encouraged to make full use of these resources, and to contribute to them if he or she feels capable of doing so.

6 Speech Perception Development

Valerie Hazan

1 Introduction

Understanding how infants develop the ability to hear and produce speech is one of the most exciting challenges of speech science research. Speech is one of the most complex codes imaginable: it is complex in its structure, supremely variable in its acoustic-phonetic manifestation due to within- and across-speaker differences at all levels of production and also highly irregular in its spontaneous form. Consider the number of grammatical irregularities in a typical snippet of spontaneous speech: '*the- like we went to estate agents and they were really unhelpful we were just like they were like you can have this one it's seven hundred pounds a week we were like oh* !'. In spite of this highly complex input, most infants acquire speech without difficulty and within a surprisingly short time frame. Infants have to overcome multiple hurdles to achieve this: with a meaningless speech stream as input, they have to learn to segment words and link them to a specific meaning, and also have to learn which sound and word combinations are allowable in their language.

Research on speech development has moved in leaps and bounds since the seminal work by Eimas in the early 1970s which launched wide-scale experimental investigations of speech perception in infants. Most importantly, the field has moved on from merely examining *what* infants can perceive to considering *how* learning might be achieved. Current studies are searching for strategies and mechanisms that may account for the learning of phonetic categories, lexical items and phonological and grammatical rules of the language from the speech stream without prior knowledge. In this chapter, I will consider the current state of knowledge as regards infants' abilities at birth, the development of phonetic discrimination and word segmentation and early word learning. I will also consider the interrelation between speech development at the phonetic level and the development of higher levels of language processing. One important outcome of the most recent research in this area is the realization that speech sound development cannot be considered in isolation from other aspects of language such as word segmentation, lexical and syntactic acquisition and from the social environment within which learning is taking place.

2 In the Beginning . . .

The field of infant perception research truly began with the development of reliable techniques for investigating infants' discrimination of speech sounds. In 1971, Peter Eimas first presented speech discrimination data for very young infants collected using the high amplitude sucking paradigm (Eimas et al., 1971). This behavioural technique, suitable for use with even week-old infants, involved presenting a sound (e.g. the syllable /ba/) repeatedly to the infant to ensure habituation and then presenting a novel sound in order to see whether the sound change could be detected. The behavioural measure used was the infant's sucking rate on a dummy connected to a computer, with higher rates of sucking following the switch in the stimulus presented denoting perception of sound change. In this study, Eimas and colleagues presented pairs of syllables (e.g. /ba/ and /pa/) varying in the Voice Onset Time (VOT) of the initial plosive; the 20 ms difference in VOT either marked a phonemic distinction in English (e.g. comparison between a token with VOT=20 ms, which is an instance of /ba/ vs. one with VOT=40 ms, an instance of /pa/) or was within a phonemic category (e.g. tokens with VOT=40 ms and VOT=60 ms, two variants of /pa/). The surprising finding was that infants reacted to the distinction that was phonemic (i.e. VOT= 20 ms vs. VOT=40 ms) but not to the within-category distinction (e.g. VOT=40 ms vs. VOT=60 ms). This early work, and subsequent studies showing sensitivity to a wide range of other phonetic contrasts using high amplitude sucking or the later-developed head turn paradigm, were taken as support for the view that infants had an innate ability to perceive all sound distinctions of all languages. Another seminal paper published some 10 years later (Werker & Tees, 1983) presented a further surprising finding. In this work, Werker and Tees presented infants with phonetic distinctions from a language that they had never been exposed to. Six-month old infants were able to hear these non-native distinctions but they could no longer do so when presented the same contrasts a few months later, before the age of one. This early work on infant perception development therefore suggested the following picture: infants are born with an (innate?) ability to hear all sounds of all languages; within the second half of their first year, this 'universal' perception is shaped through exposure to the sounds of the infant's native language and becomes language-specific, with a maintenance and even attunement (Kuhl et al., 2006) to the sounds of their own language and loss of sensitivity to non-native phonemic contrasts.

Problems soon emerged with these early theories. First, studies with animals showed that species as varied as chinchillas, Japanese quail, bonobo monkeys and rats could discriminate speech sounds in very similar ways to young infants, thus suggesting that this early discrimination had more to do with the capabilities of the auditory system than some innate ability to perceive speech sounds (for a review, see Lotto et al., 1997). Second, studies showed that certain phonetic distinctions, such as some fricative contrasts, could not be discriminated by the very young infants (e.g. Eilers & Minifie, 1975), thus putting paid to the view of universal early speech discrimination abilities; finally, it was shown that certain non-native distinctions could still be discriminated by infants past the age at which they supposedly attuned to language-specific distinctions (e.g. perception of Zulu clicks by 12–14 month olds, as shown by Best et al., 1988).

In the last 20 years, the focus has moved on from *what* infants can hear to *how* they decode the speech stream. This implies getting a better sense of infants' auditory and other abilities in this crucial first year of life, and then investigating potential learning mechanisms that could be used to gradually extract patterns and regularities from the speech stream.

3 Infants' Early Auditory Processing Abilities

Eimas's interpretation of his findings assumed that infants were born as 'blank slates' and that any phonetic discrimination ability in the first few days after birth would have to be due to an innate knowledge of phonetic distinctions, presumably linked to a speech mode of perception (Eimas et al., 1971). However, the inner ear is fully formed and functioning by 28 weeks gestation age and there is evidence that foetuses can hear at least certain aspects of speech sounds in the womb, even though the perception of these sounds is distorted due to the effect of sound conduction through amniotic fluid and maternal tissues; 'external' speech sounds are also masked by sounds from within the mother's body, such as that of blood rushing through the umbilical chord (Smith et al., 2003). Even though many aspects of the foetus's auditory processing are immature, there is evidence, through the measurement of the foetus's heart rate for example (James, 2009), that, while still in the womb, infants can discriminate many aspects of sounds. They discriminate sounds varying in frequency (e.g. Hepper & Shahidullah, 1994), speech tokens produced by different voices (Lecanuet et al., 1993), show preference for a rhyming story that is read regularly to them even when read by a different speaker (DeCasper et al., 1994) and, even more surprisingly, can discriminate two words varying in syllable order, such as 'babi' from 'biba' (Shahidullah & Hepper, 1994). Exposure to certain sounds while still in the womb can also be reflected in the infant's response to the same sounds soon after birth. For example, deCasper and Spence (1986) showed that infants, when tested after birth, showed preference for a story that was read to them regularly while they were still in the womb, even if read by a different speaker. Infants also showed preference for their mother's voice over other female voices soon after birth (deCasper & Fifer, 1980). By the time infants are born, they have therefore already learnt something about the sounds of their language.

In considering how an infant may be able to begin the process of discovering regularities in the speech stream, it is important to review their auditory processing abilities in the first year of life (for a detailed review, see Saffran et al., 2006). Indeed, in order to be able to discriminate between speech sounds, infants need to be able to decode variations in the acoustic patterns that mark phonetic contrasts, typically involving changes in frequency, intensity and in the duration of sounds. Even though the inner ear is mature by the time of birth, it appears that sound conduction in the outer and middle ear is less efficient in newborn infants (Keefe et al., 1993), and that the auditory nervous system is also not fully mature, so auditory perception is not yet 'adult-like'. Neonates show good frequency resolution for low-frequency sounds but frequency resolution for high-frequency sounds only reaches maturity around the age of six months (e.g. Schneider et al., 1990), which might help explain why very young infants are less able to discriminate fricative contrasts. Infants show good abilities to perceive pitch distinctions in complex non-speech signals (Montgomery & Clarkson, 1997). Duration discrimination appears to be immature in young infants (Morrongiello & Trehub, 1987) and intensity discrimination shows development throughout the first 3–4 years of life (Nozza & Henson, 1999). In order to decode speech sounds, infants also need to be able to selectively attend to speech, that is, to segregate speech sounds from background noise or other conversations. This ability is not as robust in infants as in older children or adults. In the first year of life, the overall picture, in terms of auditory processing, is therefore of a system that is still developing and that shows a bias towards the processing of low frequency components of speech but that has a sufficient degree of acuity to be able to distinguish many of the important distinctions in speech.

4 Infants' Sensitivity to Different Aspects of Speech in the First Few Months of Life

Before infants can start extracting regularities out of the speech stream, they need to be sensitive to those aspects that will help them with this decoding process. As infants live in a world filled with sound (music, environmental sounds), a preference for speech over other sounds would seem like a useful attribute. This seems to be present at an early stage of development: infants aged 2 to 4 months show preference for speech over non-speech sounds of similar complexity (Vouloumanos & Werker, 2004, 2007). Second, it would be helpful for infants to be particularly attuned to the speech directed at them, as child-directed speech (CDS) provides clearer input than adult-directed speech, as discussed below. Indeed, very young infants show an early preference for child-directed rather than adult-directed speech (Cooper & Aslin, 1994). Another prerequisite for pattern decoding is sensitivity to the rhythmic patterns of the language, as these will help with word segmentation, as discussed below. This sensitivity to rhythmic patterns seems to be particularly well developed in young infants. Mehler et al. (1988) showed that, soon after birth, neonates could distinguish languages from different rhythm classes. This ability cannot merely be explained by exposure to the rhythmic patterns of their own language as infants were also able to discriminate between two unknown languages from different rhythmic classes (Mehler & Christophe, 1995). In order to recognize regularities in speech, an ability to distinguish words differing in their sylla-ble structure also seems important. Indeed, neonates can distinguish between bi- and tri-syllabic words (Bijeljac-Babic et al., 1993). Infants also appear to be sensitive to at least some within-category variations. Pegg and Werker (1997) showed that 6–8 month infants could distinguish between different instances of /t/ for example. This is important if they are to develop sensitivities to allo-phonic variations in the signal. In summary, within the first few months of life, infants are well-equipped for developing strategies to extract regularities out of the speech stream that is directed to them.

5 At what Age are Infants Able to Extract Regularities from the Speech Stream?

One of the greatest challenges that infants face in decoding speech is that the speech stream that they hear is continuous, without any acoustic segmentation between words. Research has showed that only 9 per cent of maternal utterances directed to their infant (aged between 9 and 15 months) were isolated words (Brent & Siskind, 2001). Despite this lack of segmentation, in an extensive series of studies, Juzscyk and colleagues were the first to show evidence that even very young infants were able to recognize recurring patterns in the speech stream (for a detailed review of Jusczyk's contributions to the field, see Gerken & Aslin, 2005). In a seminal study, Jusczyk and Aslin (1995) showed that, after being exposed to passages of fluent speech in which a number of target words (such as 'dog' and 'cup') appeared, 7.5 month-olds showed a greater listening time to these keywords when played in isolation to the infants together with some novel words. The infants did not show longer listening times to 'incorrect' versions of the words (such as 'tog' for 'dog') showing that they had accurate acoustic-phonetic representations for the items that they recognized. By 9 months, infants also show evidence of having learnt that only certain sound combinations are allowable in their language, and that these combinations may be position specific (i.e. they have learnt the phonotactic rules of their language), but six-month-olds do not (Jusczyk et al., 1993). Frequent phonotactic structures were preferred by infants aged nine months over infrequent structures (Jusczyk et al., 1994). Infants also show evidence of being sensitive to higher-level prosodic units: seven-month-olds listened longer to speech with pauses at clause boundaries than pauses clause medially (Jusczyk et al., 1993).

6 What Learning Mechanisms might Infants be Using?

If claiming that the ability to decode speech is not innate, it is necessary to identify learning mechanisms that infants could use to extract regularities from the speech stream despite the high degree of variability of the input that they receive. The most plausible explanation is a form of statistical learning, that is, that infants learn something about the rules of language from tracking the rate of co-occurrences of specific patterns, or from accumulating patterns of distributions of different sounds, for example. Statistical learning has been shown to be a plausible learning mechanism both for the learning of phonetic categories of the language and of higher-level language units (for a review, see Graf Estes, 2009).

6.1 Phonetic Regularities – Acquisition of Phonological Categories

Maye et al. (2002) were the first to show experimentally that distribution statistics of the input material provided to an infant could influence the learning of category structure at the phonetic level. In their experiments with six- to eight-month-olds, they first familiarized the infants with stimuli signalling a novel phonetic contrast (a [da]-[ta] continuum varying in amount of prevoicing). One group of infants was exposed to tokens from a unimodal distribution, where stimuli from the middle of the continuum occurred more frequently, while another group of infants was exposed to tokens from a bimodal distribution, in which stimuli at both endpoints of the continuum occurred more frequently. A bimodal distribution is of course akin to the highly variable input that infants hear in real speech, with 'clear' instances of each phoneme more often heard, and other tokens being more variable and less distinct. In the test phase of the experiment, only those infants exposed to a bimodal distribution could discriminate the novel contrast, thus showing that infants were sensitive to the frequency distribution of the sounds that they hear. Maye et al., (2002) thus suggested a mechanism that could be used by infants to determine the phonetic categories of their language from the variable acoustic input that they are exposed to from birth.

6.2 Other Evidence of Statistical Learning

Statistical learning has also been shown to plausibly explain the learning of higher-level units of language. Jennifer Saffran made a key contribution to this work by designing a test paradigm that could be used to investigate these learning mechanisms (Saffran & Theissen, 2003). Saffran and her colleagues used an artificial language so that they could control the recurrence of different levels of patterning in the speech stream. This speech stream was presented to the infants in chunks of around two minutes in which a set of syllables were produced using synthesized speech with all prosodic cues removed and no pauses to indicate word or clause boundaries (e.g. *BIDAKUpadotigolabuBIDAKU . . .*). They then tested the infants by presenting trisyllables that were either recurring 'words' (e.g. *bidaku*) in the input or 'non-words' (e.g. syllable combinations that only co-occurred in the speech stream infrequently, for example, *labubi*). Through manipulations of the recurring patterns in the input, Saffran and colleagues showed that infants were able to extract information from the statistical properties of the speech input. There are two possible mechanisms that could be used for this purpose. Either they are simply tracking the frequency of occurrence of the trisyllabic 'words' in the two-minute stream of speech, or they are tracking the probability of co-occurrence of pairs of syllables. Saffran (2003) provides a nice example of how co-occurrence probabilities could be used. In the phrase 'pretty baby', the transitional probability across pre- and –ty is .8 in that in 80 per cent of the occurrences that infants hear the syllable 'pre', it is followed by 'ty'. The transitional probability of 'ty' followed by 'ba' is much lower (.003), probably leading infants to estimate that 'pretty' is a more likely word than 'tyba'. Aslin et al. (1998) gave support for the co-occurrence probability explanation by showing that infants prefer listening to the 'words' even when the 'word' and 'non-word' items presented in the test were matched for syllable frequency of occurrence in the speech stream. Infants are also sensitive to non-statistical regularities in the input, and can extract rules that they can apply to new materials. For example, Marcus et al. (1999) exposed infants to 3-syllable sentences (e.g. as ABA pattern as in *ga ti ga, li fa li*) in a familiarization phase. In the test phase, they presented the infants with novel 'sentences' that followed or violated the pattern: *wo fe wo* (ABA) versus *wo fe fe* (ABB). Infants showed preference for 'regular' (ABA) sentences showing that they had learnt the recurring pattern and applied it to new syllables.

One criticism of this type of work concerns its ecological validity. To what extent does short exposure to synthesized (hence, simplified) speech in a highly simplified artificial language reflect what processes the infant might be using when faced with more naturalistic speech, characterized by much greater variability and complexity? To date, most studies exploring this statistical learning mechanism in infants have been based on highly constrained learning environments: the infant is first exposed to an artificial language containing certain regularities, and then tested to ascertain whether these patterns have been learnt (Saffran & Theissen, 2003). Showing that infants can learn from a highly constrained input does not in itself provide any evidence that this is the strategy that infants are using in language acquisition, as researchers in the field are keen to stress (Saffran et al., 2006), but it is a key step to showing that such a mechanism is feasible and that an innate mechanism does not need to be invoked. Pelucchi et al. (2009) set out to address this issue by exposing eight-month-old infants to a natural speech stream in an unknown language (Italian, in this case) to see if they could show evidence of sensitivity to transitional probabilities in this complex speech stream. They replicated the results obtained with an artificial language, and also showed evidence that infants were tracking probability of co-occurrence of syllables rather than merely tracking frequencies of occurrence of syllables.

Although plausible mechanisms have been presented to explain how infants might be learning regularities from a variable input, Saffran et al., (2006) suggest that there remains a 'chicken and egg' conundrum: to use words for word segmentation, infants must have learnt something about the correlations between sounds and word boundaries, but how do they achieve this initial segmentation? It has been suggested that this might be achieved by learning highly frequent words early, which can then help with the subsequent task of word segmentation (Thiessen & Saffran, 2003). For example, words that are frequently presented in isolation to young infants could help begin the task of segmentation when then heard in the speech stream (Brent & Siskind, 2001). This hypothesis is supported by evidence that infants aged six months could learn a novel word that, in familiarization, followed a known high-frequency word (e.g. their name or 'mommy') but not when it followed a less frequent name. Another strategy that infants may use in early word segmentation is to use their knowledge of function words (i.e. words such as 'the', 'a', 'his', 'her', 'at') to segment novel input. Infants show an early sensitivity to the acoustic and phonological cues that distinguish function from content words, cues that are magnified in infant-directed speech (Shi et al., 2006). Function words are indeed typically unstressed monosyllables. This distinction between function and content words appears indeed to be due to acoustic or phonological patterns rather than mere exposure as, by six months, infants prefer to listen to content words rather than function words, even in an unfamiliar language (Shi & Werker, 2001). At 11 months, infants cannot distinguish between real function words (e.g. 'the', 'his') and nonsense function words which are phonetically similar (e.g. 'kuh', 'ris'), but 13 month olds do so, indicating that detailed recognition of function words is established by the end of the first year. (Shi et al., 2006). This is likely to assist further learning of new content words during the second year of life.

7 What do we Know about the Role of the Input?

If infants learn the sound categories and rules of their language through some kind of statistical analysis of the speech that they hear, then it would be informative to know more about the quantity and characteristics of the speech input that infants are exposed to in the crucial first 12 to 18 months of life. It has long been recognized that infant-directed speech (IDS) shows enhanced acoustic-phonetic characteristics relative to adult-directed speech (e.g. Fernald, 1989; Fernald & Mazzie, 1991; Kuhl et al., 1997).

Recent work on the characteristics of IDS has shown that the acoustic enhancements that adults make are attuned to the child's stage of development. For example, tone enhancements were reduced in Mandarin *child*-directed speech relative to *infant*-directed speech (Liu et al., 2009) and enhancements in fricative contrasts between /s/ and /ʃ/ were found at an age where infants were actively learning language, that is, in IDS directed to 12- to 14-month-olds but not for speech directed to four-month-olds (Cristià, 2010). The recent availability of more extensive corpora (e.g. the study by Cristià involved 32 caregivers) is also beginning to give greater opportunity to look at individual variation in the degree of phonetic enhancement seen in IDS. For example, Cristià found that out of 32 caregivers, only 19 clearly showed the pattern of enhancement and in fact six showed an opposite pattern.

Does this individual variation in caregivers' IDS influence learning? A study on the interrelation between the input provided to the infant and speech learning has indeed shown the impact of this individual variation. For example, the size of the vowel space in the IDS produced by the principal caregiver has some bearing on the child's later performance in a phonetic discrimination task (Liu et al., 2003). Other evidence for the impact of IDS on learning comes from work suggesting that the exaggerated prosodic patterns that occur in CDS are particularly important for learning: when they are absent, as in the CDS of depressed mothers (Kaplan et al., 2002) or fathers (Kaplan et al., 2007), children are less effective at learning in controlled tasks (e.g. learning a voice-face association) although they are effective when 'normal' CDS is used. A striking finding is therefore that, far from being a barrier to learning, as was first thought, variation in the acoustic-phonetic characteristics of speech has been shown to be beneficial. In learning-type tasks, adding variation in talker gender and affect in the familiarization phase of the task can lead to infants performing better at the word segmentation task (Houston & Jusczyk, 2000). It is well known that providing within-category variation in phonetic training studies with adults leads to more robust learning of novel categories (e.g. Logan et al., 1991). It now also seems that within- and across-speaker variability in speech production aids infants in the learning of their native phonetic categories.

Another aspect of the relation between input and learning that has been gaining prominence is the contribution of social interaction to learning. The role of social interaction was highlighted in a study that compared the impact of exposure to a novel language (Mandarin Chinese) on learning by American infants aged nine months (Kuhl et al., 2003). Infants who were exposed to Mandarin Chinese via interactions with a Chinese speaker during naturalistic play in a series of 'training' sessions maintained sensitivity to a phonetic contrast that occurs in Mandarin Chinese but not in English, while infants exposed to the same Mandarin Chinese speech input but via a television screen or audiotape did not. Attention scores showed that infants exposed to the recorded materials attended significantly less than infants exposed to live speakers suggesting an important role for social interaction in maintaining strong attention to the speech input and motivating learning. Joint visual attention to the object being named may also help with the learning and word segmentation process (e.g. Morales et al., 2000).

Research on the relation between caregiver input and speech development in the infant is dependent on corpora tracking the interactions between caregiver and infant during crucial stages of development. There have of course been corpora of adult-child interactions for decades, going back to Brown's famous early corpus of child-adult interactions for three children (Brown, 1973) and other similar corpora made available to the research community through the CHILDES database (MacWhinney, 2000). Many corpora include a very limited sample of the infant's speech exposure although corpora involving a substantially greater amount of transcribed speech and more caregiver-infant pairs are becoming available (e.g. Brent & Siskind, 2001). The availability of these more sizeable corpora permits the type of analysis carried out by Swingley, using the Brent and Siskind corpus, which examined the frequency of occurrence of words directed at infants; they also examined which subset of words occurred with high frequency and were therefore candidates for being early acquired by the infants (Swingley, 2009). However, these corpora still only include snapshots of the child's speech exposure, with recordings made at regular intervals over a period of a few weeks or months. Here again, some fascinating developments are being facilitated by advances in speech technology and computational modelling and analysis tools. The most ambitious of these projects is without doubt the Speechome project by Deb Roy and his colleagues at the MIT Media lab (Roy, 2009). In order to trace the evolution of the early words produced by a child to the many contexts in which he heard instances of this word, Roy set out to record the great majority of the input that a single child (his first son) would be exposed to in the first three years of life. This was done by having 14 cameras installed in his own home that recorded all of the interactions in the home between his son and principal caregivers; these captured about 80 per cent of the child's waking hours (Roy, 2009). The technical challenge has been to analyse and extract patterns of learning emanating from these interactions given the sheer scale of the data collected (approximately 90,000 hours of video and 140,000 hours of audio recordings between birth and the age of three). The full analysis of this data will take many years but already informative is the estimate of the quantity of speech (both child- and adult-directed) heard and produced by the child between the ages of nine and 24 months. For the days fully transcribed over that period, the mean number of words a day that the child was exposed to was 23,055 words (giving an estimated 10 million words of child- and adult-directed speech heard over a 16-month period). A previous study of speech recordings by 78 mothers had estimated a lower daily word exposure of around 11,300 words (Gilkerson & Richards, 2007). An interesting analysis carried out on the CDS collected in a subset of the Speechome corpus addressed the degree to which adults attune their speech to the particular stage of speech development of the infant. Roy and colleagues found some evidence that caregivers fine-tune the characteristics of words that they produce (in terms of utterance length) according to whether the word is being produced by the child (Roy et al., 2009).

8 Moving onto Linking Sound Patterns to Meanings. How does this Skill Interact with Phonetic Perception?

Towards the end of the first year of life, infants are able to associate some highly frequent words with their referent. In experiments using known words and objects, infants aged between 14 and 20 months were sensitive to mispronunciations in one of the words (e.g. *vaby* rather than *baby*), thus showing sensitivity to phonetic detail (Swingley & Aslin, 2000, 2002). Werker and her colleagues have extensively used the 'Switch' experimental design to investigate the ability to associate new word forms with objects; using this technique, they obtained some intriguing results regarding the relation between word learning and sensitivity to phonetic detail. Indeed, 14-month-olds were able to learn the association between two nonsense words and two objects but failed at the task when the two nonsense words were phonetically similar (e.g. /bi/ and /di/), even though they were able to discriminate the same two nonsense words in tasks that did not involve associative learning (Stager & Werker, 1997). However, this problem is short-lived as 17- to 20-month-olds succeed at this task (Werker et al., 2002). The fact that infants are sensitive to phonetic detail for novel words in discrimination tasks but not when an associative-learning task is involved suggests that this temporary loss of sensitivity to phonetic detail may be due to attentional resource limitations at early stages of word learning. These types of studies illustrate the complex interrelation between phonetic, phonological, syntactic and lexical acquisition.

9 Future Directions

Enormous progress has been made in our understanding of the early stages of the perceptual acquisition of speech sounds. The development of appropriate behavioural techniques, initially for investigating the discrimination of speech sounds by infants, and more recently for evaluating statistical learning processes has done much to advance the field. As for research in adult speech perception, the increasing use of non-invasive neuroimaging techniques with excellent temporal and spatial resolution, such as magnetoencephalography (MEG), to measure brain activity in infants in response to speech input is likely to lead to further major breakthroughs in our understanding of speech development (see Smith, and Knight and Hawkins, this volume). More specifically, these techniques can be used to delve further into the processes involved in early statistical learning, by revealing, for example, what memory traces are present of the regularities that the infant extracts from the speech stream (Huotilainen et al., 2008). Further progress in our understanding of speech development is also likely to come from the type of detailed investigations of the relation between the specific speech input that the infant receives and their pattern of speech development made possible thanks to large-scale longitudinal corpora such as those emerging from the Human Speechome Project (Roy, 2009).

7 Voice and Phonation

John Esling

1 Initiation Mechanisms

Two essential processes underlie the production of speech: *initiation* and *phonation*. Initiation refers to the source of power for generating speech sounds. This process is also referred to as airstream mechanism – that is, the mechanisms by which an airstream is generated. Phonation usually refers specifically to the production of voice at the glottal opening through the larynx. Phonation type is a broad classification scheme that incorporates the various types of voice, or vocal qualities, that can be produced by the combined operations of the larynx and identified by the turbulence (noise) or by the vibratory patterns (periodic waves) that can be heard. These qualities are generated as the airstream passes through the larynx and is modified by the strictures and movements of the multiple valves within the larynx.

Phonation is normally associated with speech in which air is coming from the lungs, up through the larynx – the result of 'pulmonic' initiation. The majority of speech sounds are produced with pulmonic initiation of the airstream. There are traditionally three types of initiation: *pulmonic, glottalic* and *lingual* (Catford, 1968, 2001). Lingual initiation has usually been called 'velaric' because it is the back of the tongue that forms closure with the back of the palate, but 'lingual' implies that the tongue is the principal participant without specifying whether the lingual closure is velar or uvular. Glottalic initiation accounts for sounds produced when the glottis (the opening through the larynx, between the vocal folds) is either closed or actively descending while open.

The airstream can either flow out through the vocal tract or inwards into or through the vocal tract. The most common form of speech production is *pulmonic egressive*, where the airstream is pulmonic, coming from the lungs, and flowing outwards, or egressing, through the vocal tract. In the chart of the International Phonetic Association (IPA), the majority of symbols representing the various possible sounds of speech are pulmonic consonants, and these are all taken to be egressive under normal circumstances. This also applies to the vowels, which are normally understood to be egressive. Pulmonic sounds, however, can also be produced ingressively; that is, the airstream can be drawn into the lungs as the various articulatory stricture gestures are performed. This combination of initiatory and articulatory manoeuvres can be performed most easily on vowel sounds, since vocalic articulations are the most open strictures, and the airstream is relatively free to move out or in without being impeded. The quality of the sound of ingressive airflow is nonetheless quite different – generating more and unusual friction because the articulators are naturally shaped to function most efficiently on outward-flowing air rather than on inward-flowing air. This applies to the outwards (upwards) orientation of the vocal folds, and particularly to the protective supraglottic structures within the larynx, as well as to the tongue and other oral articulators. Many consonantal sounds are much more difficult to produce using inward-flowing air, for example, trills and many fricatives. The auditory/acoustic quality of *pulmonic ingressive* sounds can be quite different from their pulmonic egressive counterparts, due to aerodynamic constraints and the inefficiency of the resonating chambers.

Sounds produced glottalically can be either egressive or ingressive. The initiator is within the larynx – specifically the state of the glottis during the articulatory production of the sound. *Glottalic egressive* sounds are produced with the glottis closed – in effect with a glottal stop – and with an oral articulatory stricture while the larynx pumps upwards, compressing the air in the vocal tract, before the oral stricture point is released explosively. These non-pulmonic consonants are identified on the IPA chart as ejectives. They are most commonly stops, but also affricates or fricatives. *Glottalic ingressive* sounds are typically produced with voicing at the glottis and with an oral articulatory closure while the larynx pumps downwards, momentarily increasing the size of the resonating chamber before release of the oral stricture point. These non-pulmonic consonants are identified on the IPA chart as implosives. If the vocal folds at the glottis are vibrating to generate voicing while the larynx pumps downwards, the sounds are voiced glottalic ingressive (voiced implosives). If the state of the glottis is open for breath while the larynx pumps downwards, the sounds are voiceless glottalic ingressive (voiceless implosives).

Lingually initiated sounds are produced with a closure in the rear part of the oral vocal tract, during which the forward parts of the tongue or the lips can be compressed against opposing articulatory surfaces and then rapidly pulled away to generate suction. These are the *lingual ingressive* sounds known as clicks. It is also possible to use the tongue or lips to expel air during rear-lingual closure, producing *lingual egressive* sounds where the air is 'squeezed out' by the articulators; however, sounds produced in this way are rare and not common as speech sounds.

To summarize, pulmonic egressive sounds dominate the chart of the IPA (IPA, 1999). Pulmonic ingressive sounds are rare in linguistic usage but are more common in paralinguistic expression. Glottalic ingressive (implosive) and glottalic egressive (ejective) sounds are found in many languages of the world. Lingual ingressive sounds (clicks) are found in only some of the languages of the world and are also used in paralinguistic expression; but lingual egressive sounds are more likely to occur paralinguistically or extralinguistically than in linguistic usage.

2 Basic States of the Larynx

The larynx is the most important instrument in driving articulatory mechanisms. Between the lungs and the oral vocal tract, the larynx is the critical valve or set of valves for controlling the airstream (Negus, 1949; Edmondson & Esling, 2006). It is the site of voicing (of the vibrating vocal folds) in the most common pulmonic egressive speech sounds, and it is the site of opening of the glottal space between the vocal folds for the commonly occurring voiceless fricative sounds, produced with the glottal state of breath. Stops constitute the top row of the IPA chart and are characterized primarily by the coordination of their oral stricture onset and release with the timing of opening, closing or voicing at the glottis within the laryngeal mechanism. This delicate coordination of timing between these two different locations in the vocal tract is one of the most fundamental components in the production of speech sounds for use in human language. It is for this reason that the definitions of what have been called 'states of the glottis' are important. Because the larynx is a complex and multifaceted mechanism, and the glottis is the opening at only the lowest level of this mechanism, these configurational changes are more comprehensively referred to as 'states of the larynx'. Some of these 'states' are not only static but describe dynamic phonation types. The most basic examples of this dichotomy are the classic states of 'breath' and 'voice', where breath is not only identified as a glottal shape (of the separated vocal folds) but also represents voiceless airflow through the glottis, and where voice is not only identified as a glottal shape (of the adducted, approximated vocal folds) but also represents voiced airflow through the glottis. The dichotomy reflects two different media of observation. In the case of states, it is the visual medium that is the primary descriptor; while in the case of phonation types, it is the aural medium that is the primary descriptor. This observational dichotomy can also reflect a time component: visual states can be captured relatively quickly in a single image, while phonation generally requires a period of time or a sequence in time for its auditory quality to be detected. A set of basic states of the larynx and their associated phonation types will be presented, with Figure 7.1 as a reference point.

Two examples of nil phonation – basic states of the stopped larynx – are *epiglottal stop* and *glottal stop*. Epiglottal stop is presented first because it is the most fundamental of strictures. It is the vocal tract stricture used earliest by human infants and which, it can be argued, is the stricture point at which infants first acquire the ability to produce a consonantal sound in combination with the vowels of crying (Benner et al., 2007). Epiglottal stop is the essential reflexive mechanism of full protective closure of the airway (Figure 7.2). Its anatomical role is critical in the gag reflex, in coughing, clearing the throat or swallowing.

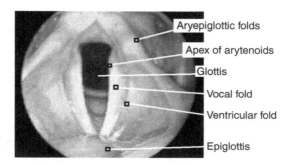

Figure 7.1 The breath state of the larynx. The vocal folds are widely abducted

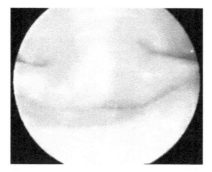

Figure 7.2 Epiglottal stop. The structures of the larynx are completely obscured by the protective closure

Its label is epiglottal because the passive articulator against which stricture occurs is the epiglottis; the active articulator being the aryepiglottic folds along the upper borders of the epilaryngeal tube above the glottis (Esling, 1999). Although it is a stop, in which the aryepiglottic folds, the epilaryngeal tube and the vocal folds are all sealed shut, it has implications for voice in that the voice qualities that occur around it are all constricted; that is, like the epiglottal stop itself, they are a function of the compressed laryngeal constrictor mechanism. So while phonation is nil during the closure phase of an epiglottal stop, the types of phonation that occur in the transitions into or out of an epiglottal stop have a distinct and predictably constricted quality (Esling et al., 2005).

Glottal stop is a closure of the airway that has been termed reduced protective closure (Gauffin, 1977), that is, compared to epiglottal stop. Its production is acquired by infants in their first few months, once the dangers of choking are reconciled and somewhat finer muscular control has developed (Esling, 2009). During the stop itself, phonation is nil, but neighbouring vowels are not greatly affected in quality, even though a slight degree of laryngeal constriction (compression) is necessary to narrow the epilaryngeal tube and to cause the ventricular folds to press down on the vocal folds, inhibiting their vibration (Figure 7.3). It is important in the static state of glottal stop that the ventricular folds (immediately above the vocal folds) appear adducted, at least partially obscuring and impinging on the vocal folds from the anterior end of the glottis.

The two most basic, contrasting states of an unstopped larynx are *breath* and *voice* (Catford & Esling, 2006). Breath is the characteristic open (abducted) state of vocal fold positioning (Figure 7.1), while voice is the characteristic adducted (brought-together) state of the vocal folds (Figure 7.4). Breath is the most straightforward, least complex laryngeal posture to achieve voicelessness short of closing off the glottal opening altogether. Its phonation type can be described as 'breath phonation'. Voice is the most straightforward laryngeal posture for voicing. Its phonation type can be described as 'modal voice'. These two states are at the heart of the voiceless/voiced distinction that pervades the IPA chart

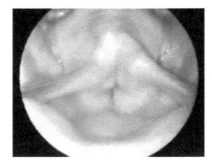

Figure 7.3 Glottal stop. The vocal folds are tightly adducted

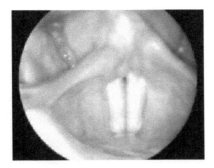

Figure 7.4 The voice state of the larynx. The vocal folds are lightly adducted

(Esling, 2010). Most voiceless airflow adopts the efficient state of breath. This is particularly true of voiceless vowels, approximants, fricatives, taps/flaps, trills or nasals. If the glottis is too widely open, no noisy turbulence is produced, which would be one case of 'nil phonation'; and the wide opening would slow down the rapid functioning of the articulators. Voiced airflow is assumed to be most efficient when the simple state of voice is adopted, although it is not known whether most speakers of most languages actually use modal voice in preference to other possible phonation types.

The state of an adducted glottis in preparation for voicing is *prephonation*, which is another instance of 'nil phonation'. In prephonation, the arytenoid cartilages of the larynx are adducted, but there is not yet any airflow to make the vocal folds vibrate (Figure 7.5). Some voiceless consonants, namely the plosives (stops), realize voicelessness with prephonation rather than breath. Since they interrupt the airstream to a significant degree (hence their location at the top of the IPA chart), voiceless stops have a different laryngeal posture during their oral closure phase. Voiceless unaspirated stops shift from prephonation to voice immediately when the oral closure opens and a following vowel

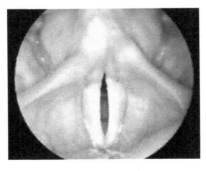

Figure 7.5 The pre-phonation state of the larynx

115

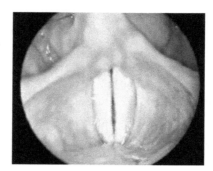

Figure 7.6 Falsetto

begins. Voiceless aspirated stops shift from prephonation to breath when the oral closure opens, and then to voice as the following vowel begins. This intricate sequencing of the timing of oral and laryngeal events takes about a year for an infant to master. Prephonation can also characterize the onset of a (voiced) vowel, as it usually does in English, from which the name prephonation is derived.

Two modifications to modal voicing by means of the pitch-control mechanism yield the two opposing states and phonation types: *falsetto* and *creaky voice*. For falsetto, the vocal folds are stretched longitudinally, while the epilaryngeal tube remains open, as for modal voice. Adductive tension is required, to bring the vocal processes of the arytenoids together, achieving the state of prephonation before airflow is applied to induce phonation by means of the Bernoulli effect, as occurs for voicing in general. Airflow between the vocal folds (and indeed between other paired structures within the larynx) causes a vacuum to occur between structures, drawing them together before they are again blown apart in the airstream (van den Berg, 1968; Catford, 1977). A certain amount of medial compression is required to tension the vocal folds and to create the thin edges necessary for low-amplitude, high-pitched (rapid) vibrations. The tense, thin vocal folds vibrate only along a short distance, near their posterior ends. As such, this creates a shape that is recognized as a traditional state of the glottis, with tensioning components that are basically limited to their effect on the vocal folds proper (Figure 7.6). To lower pitch, an opposing mechanism is used, and its effect is potentially more complex and not limited to the vocal folds alone. Creaky voice – so-called because of its low-pitched (slow) pulses – is, like glottal stop and epiglottal stop and whisper (below), a function of the laryngeal constrictor mechanism. That is, the means of achieving low pitch and the means of achieving laryngeal closure are part of the same mechanism. In creaky voice, the aryepiglottic folds are brought upwards and forwards, nearly closing off the airway but with enough space for the shortened, bunched and loose vocal folds to be visible beneath the tightened sphincter (Figure 7.7). The

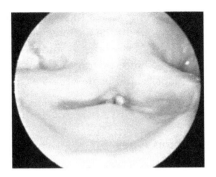

Figure 7.7 Creaky voice (vocal fry)

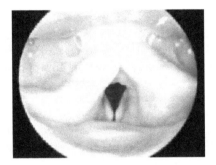

Figure 7.8 The whisper state of the larynx

resulting vibration is a slow and undulating pattern due to the thickness of the vocal folds, which has also been called 'vocal fry' (Hollien et al., 1966; Hollien & Michel, 1968; Hollien, 1971). The bottom-to-top motion of the vocal folds, referred to as a vertical phase difference, is a characteristic of phonation in this constricted mode and does not play a role in falsetto. The ventricular folds and the aryepiglottic folds do not contribute to the vibration during clear examples of glottal creaky voice. However, because of the compressed laryngeal constrictor, the potential for additional vertical components to enter into the vibratory cycle, especially with enhanced aerodynamic flow, is increased. These possibilities will be outlined below as complex forms of harsh phonation.

When progressively greater laryngeal constriction is applied to the basic state of breath, the voiceless airflow is channelled into an ever narrower epilaryngeal tube, between the forward- and upward-pinching aryepiglottic folds and the tubercle of the epiglottis, creating greater turbulence and more noise, resulting in whispery phonation. The state of *whisper* differs from the state of breath not so much at the glottis but in the positioning of the aryepiglottic constrictor mechanism above the glottis – disengaged and open for breath – actively engaged and compressed for whisper, usually with a raising of the larynx (Figure 7.8). To close off the airflow completely from the state of whisper, the next logical posture of stoppage would be an epiglottal stop rather than glottal stop, due to the advanced degree of constriction already present in whisper. The state of whisper could be described as a combination of breath plus constriction (Esling, 1996).

3 More Complex Phonation Types

The two states of breath and voice, which at the most simple level oppose each other in function, can combine, forming the complex phonation type known as *breathy voice* (Catford, 1964; Laver, 1980). This is possible because there are two clearly defined regions at the glottis: the so-called cartilaginous glottis, between the arytenoid cartilages at the back, and the so-called ligamental glottis, between the vocal fold tissues at the front. At the back, the cartilages can remain apart (abducted), allowing air to flow through as in breath, while at the front, the vocal folds can be brought together (adducted) enough to induce periodic vibration as in voice (Figure 7.9). The volume of airflow is greater than in modal voice and the mode of vibration less efficient.

Whisper can also combine with voice to produce *whispery voice*. As with breath and whisper, the difference between breathy voice and whispery voice is in the degree of engagement of the laryngeal constrictor mechanism controlling the size of the tube above the glottis (Esling, 2005). At the glottis, breathy voice and whispery voice demonstrate the same components: an open passage for airflow at the back of the glottis and vibrating vocal folds at the front. In whispery voice, however, the aryepiglottic constrictor mechanism above the glottis is actively engaged and compressed, usually with a raising of the larynx (Figure 7.10). This posture can be easily identified from its shape as a static state as well as auditorily from its quality as a phonation type. The state of

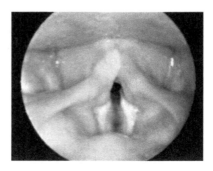

Figure 7.9 Breathy voice

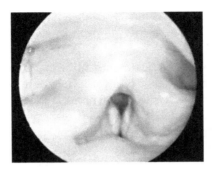

Figure 7.10 Whispery voice (contrast with Figure 7.8. whisper)

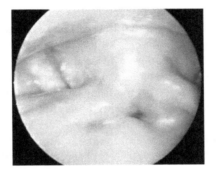

Figure 7.11 Harsh voice (mid-pitch)

whispery voice could be described as a combination of breath plus voice plus constriction.

The effect of laryngeal constriction, as mentioned above, adds a vertical dimension to the modification of the airstream that is not present when the epilaryngeal tube is wide open (Esling & Moisik, 2011). Increasing airflow during whisper, and pressing the constrictor even tighter, adds greater noise to the signal emanating from the larynx and also increases the likelihood that the structures above the glottis (within the epilaryngeal tube) will begin to vibrate, usually irregularly given the asymmetry of the aryepiglottic structures, producing a harsh whisper. These articulatory adjustments in the upper larynx can also affect voiced sounds (i.e., when the vocal folds are also vibrating), and they will also be labelled as forms of harsh phonation (Esling & Edmondson, 2002). When the vocal folds are vibrating, and a gap is maintained posteriorly in the glottis to permit the flow of breath, and the epilaryngeal tube is narrowed to create noise, and constriction and airflow are great enough to induce waves of movement vertically through the pressed structures of the constrictor, the resulting phonation is a harsh whispery voice. Without the posterior opening in the glottis but with voicing at the glottis, the resulting phonation would be *harsh voice* (Figure 7.11).

Due to the complexity of adjustments in the supraglottic structures when the constrictor is engaged, harsh types of phonation can have many forms. One way to categorize these types of harshness is to relate them to the mechanism for pitch change. As noted above with respect to creakiness versus falsetto, creaky phonation is produced when the constrictor engages. In this same mode, at low pitch, when the aryepiglottic folds are tightly approximated to the tubercle of the epiglottis, there is a higher probability, especially when constriction or aerodynamic flow is increased, that the aryepiglottic folds themselves will begin to vibrate. Variations in the vertical dimension along which turbulence and vibrations are produced make the auditory quality of harsh phonation quite variable, but the action of the aryepiglottic folds adds a distinctive periodicity to the signal that can be referred to as harsh voice at low pitch or harsh voice with aryepiglottic trilling (Moisik et al., 2010). Many approximated structures can be seen to be moving in Figure 7.11. Lowering pitch predisposes the right aryepiglottic fold to vibrate relative to the bas of the epiglottis. Trilling of the aryepiglottic folds can be voiceless (occurring without glottal vibration) or voiced (occurring with glottal vibration). Voiced aryepiglottic trilling is the compound phonatory effect known as growling, and it occurs as a speech form in several language families and at various levels of phonological representation. Voiceless aryepiglottic trilling also occurs as a way of realizing speech forms.

It is perhaps an oversimplification to identify harsh voice at mid pitch as a single phonatory entity, but it is a useful canonical category. It resembles creaky voice in posture, with enhanced compression, inducing greater irregularities in the speech signal due to the effects of the impeding tissues from the vocal folds up through the pursed epilaryngeal tube. These aperiodic acoustic effects, and perhaps variations in loudness, are generally what is associated with harsh (sometimes termed rough or hoarse) phonation. One other effect that can occur in the context of this constricted posture, and which is not necessarily a common speech sound or a category appearing in general phonetic taxonomies for speech, is diplophonic phonation or the effect known as ventricular phonation. It occurs when the vocal folds and their immediately superior ventricular folds combine in a double-pulsed vibration. Its quality is distinct from that of aryepiglottic trilling, and it is perhaps less common as a speech sound than as a persistent characteristic long-term voice quality.

An interesting laryngeal configuration results when the laryngeal constrictor mechanism (the aryepiglottic sphincter) is engaged at the same time as the mechanism for increasing pitch (the cricothyroid mechanism for longitudinal stretching). Their combined effect produces an isometric tension (shortening vs. lengthening) in which the vocal folds are no longer covered by the aryepiglottic sphincter but are stretched and tight, very much as they are during falsetto. Still, unlike falsetto, the constrictor is exerting force to keep the airway closed. The resulting configuration resembles the state of glottal stop, except that the ventricular folds do not impinge as much on the glottis, and the vocal folds are able to move more freely when aerodynamic forces are applied. The auditory quality of phonation under such conditions has been called strained, tense or pressed. Articulatorily, the tension arises from the effort to close down the airway, and the unique quality of straining arises from the longitudinal adjustment of the pitch-increasing mechanism to expose and stretch the vocal folds, at the same time removing other supra-glottic structures from the path of the airstream. If the aryepiglottic sphincter acted alone without the longitudinal stretching component, looser vocal fold vibration or sympathetic vibration of other impinging structures above the glottis would result. If only the cricothyroid mechanism acted on the vocal folds, pitch would rise without any impeding closure tension, as it does in falsetto. The two mechanisms normally perform opposite functions when they act on the vocal folds alone, but together, they create a uniquely efficient tensioning system that allows strict reduction of the airway at the same time as allowing controlled voicing to occur. This is largely because they recruit the action of the supraglottic constrictor while also invoking the longitudinal tension and medial compression used in high-pitched phonation. This is the laryngeal control system used by weightlifters and other athletes to retain air in the lungs, under pressure and in order to oppose muscular exertion by the arms, while releasing small amounts of air with a steady voicing stream at strategic moments. Under such conditions, not a lot of breath is released, since the glottis is not allowed to abduct, and voiceless sounds generally give way to voiced sounds.

4 The Relationship of Initiation to Phonation

Most speech sounds of the languages of the world are produced on a pulmo-nic egressive airstream. Vowel sounds are particularly likely to be produced with outgoing lung air. There are, however, instances where vowels and even consonants, in certain paralinguistic circumstances, will be produced with a pulmonic ingressive airstream. Sounds produced with a glottalic egressive, glottalic ingressive or lingual ingressive airstream are generally consonants of short duration, interspersed within a stream of pulmonic egressive air. In terms of speed of production, glottalic egressive sounds (ejectives) can be produced as quickly as it takes to make a glottal stop or an epiglottal stop. They may be produced more quickly than the timing required for a pulmonic egressive aspirated stop. The main component of both is a fine coordination of the opening and closing movements of the laryngeal and the oral articulators. Glottalic ingressive (implosive) stops may take no longer to produce than a pulmonic egressive voiced stop. Laryngeal-oral timing is again the key, stops and affricates (stop plus fricative) being the principal speech sounds that coordinate the stopping of airflow between the oral vocal tract and the larynx. Lingual ingressive sounds (clicks) can combine readily with simultaneous pulmonic egressive (or ingressive) airflow, since the oral vocal tract is closed off at the back by the tongue during the production of the click, allowing pulmonic air to flow freely out (or in) through the velo-pharyngeal port and the nasal tract.

The various phonation types outlined above contrast most effectively on a pulmonic egressive airstream, particularly on vowel sounds. In a manner of speaking, languages may 'choose' where in the phonological system phonation will be used for making sound-meaning contrasts. The most commonly occurring phonological contrast is the breath-voice distinction, defining the many voiceless-voiced consonant pairs in the IPA chart. The type of voicing can also distinguish voiced consonants from each other. For example, a modal-voiced stop can contrast with a breathy-voiced stop and with a creaky-voiced stop or with a stop with other phonatory qualities. Vowels, as syllable nuclei, generally longer in duration than consonants, are able to carry many phonatory contrasts. In many languages of the world, they carry phonatory and pitch information, yielding languages with tone contrasts, register contrasts or tonal register contrasts. Breathy-voiced (or whispery-voiced), creaky-voiced and various kinds of harsh-voiced syllables can combine with a range of pitch targets to produce phonological systems with tone along one dimension and phonatory register along another. Even so, laryngeal phonation is only one component of the types of contrast that can occur on syllables. Pharyngeal resonance qualities and oral/nasal qualities can also add to the matrix of contrasting syllable categories.

The types of phonation characteristic of a particular language, indicative of certain linguistic communities, or those that are used for paralinguistic purposes can also vary (Esling & Edmondson, 2011). Although the presence of different types of initiation can be indicative of a particular language, for example, some languages have many clicks, or ejectives, while some have none; phonation is a ready carrier of fine-grained differences. At the individual level, forensic speaker identification can probe deeply into the characteristics that make a given individual's voice recognizable. Different languages also exploit the voice quality component of accent, with some preferring a more open (breathier) quality and others preferring a tighter (harsh/constricted) quality. The ways in which the phonatory aspects of the voice interact with the phonological level of contrasting sound categories and the socially indexical level of voice quality is an especially rich boundary of phonetic variation.

5 Appendix: Examples

5.1 Laryngeal Constriction

The quality of phonation produced in the context of laryngeal constriction (e.g. in the neighbourhood of a glottal stop) can be called laryngealized, which may be more harsh than creaky; or the quality of voicing in the context of laryngeal constriction (e.g. in the neighbourhood of an epiglottal stop) can be called raised larynx voice or pharyngealized voice, depending perceptually primarily on whether the pitch at which it is produced is high or low.

5.2 Glottal Stop

This is a relatively rapid manoeuvre, which occurs before initial vowels of words in German or in emphatic prosodic contexts in English. It also occurs medially in several dialects of English as a reflex of the /t/ phoneme, for example, 'water', 'bottle'. Language varieties that have epiglottal stop in their inventory also inevitably have glottal stop as a phoneme. Many languages have a series of consonants that are glottalized as a secondary articulation, for example, preglottalized or postglottalized sonorants, such as [ʔn], [nʔ], or [ʔw], [wʔ]. Glottal stop can also be realized phonetically as merely laryngealization on a vowel (creaky voice or harsh voice), but this should not be confused phonetically with the stopping of airflow for an appreciable period of time. Glottalization signifies the presence of glottal stop in the articulation; while laryngealization signifies a slightly constricted phonation type such as creaky voice or harsh voice during a sound that is a continuant.

5.3 Epiglottal Stop

At the beginning of life (for infants), this is the wholly reflexive manoeuvre that shuts the airway. The sound produced before and after the stop is distinctive in its constricted nature, reflecting the small volumes of the pharyngeal resonators. The burst on its release is also distinctive, because the articulator is complex and massive compared to other closures in the vocal tract. The sounds of aryepiglottic closure can be recognized when a person gags or chokes or vomits, which are still reflexive instances of the use of the closure.

5.4 Falsetto

Many singers use falsetto for high-pitch effect: Lou Christie, Frankie Valli, the Bee Gees.

5.5 Creaky Voice

It is often observed that young persons, in English and in other languages, and especially in female speech, are increasingly using creaky voice as a speaking style. Germanic languages, such as Swedish, often use laryngealization as a preferred vocal style or long-term 'voice quality setting'.

5.6 Breath and Whisper

Airflow without voicing induces friction in the vocal tract. An opening in the glottis creates the conditions for voiceless airflow. A very large opening, on exhalation, produces a sound at the far 'breath' end of the 'noise' continuum, for example, as in exhaling during yawning. Slightly less opening, but still with an unconstricted larynx, produces the classic phonetic sound of breath, as heard in voiceless fricatives. Further laryngeal narrowing (by constricting the epila-ryngeal tube) produces even greater friction at the intense end of the 'noise' continuum and is called phonetic whisper.

5.7 Breathy Voice

This has also been called 'sexy voice'; but 'heavy breathing' is more complex – having alternations between pulmonic egressive and ingressive airflow and a whispery-voice component with voiceless aryepiglottic trilling constituting a harshness effect. An [h] fricative is an example of breath (at the glottis), while a voiced [ɦ] is actually breathy-voiced.

5.8 Whispery Voice

The breathy-voiced stop series of most Indic languages (the so-called voiced aspirates) involves a laryngeal accompaniment in the sequence of stop production that could range phonetically from breathy voiced to whispery voiced, depending on the language.

5.9 Harsh Voice

Harshness can be realized in several ways, especially combined with pitch effects. At low pitch, an example of aryepiglottic trilling is the singing of Louis Armstrong. A consistent example of harsh voice in a wide pitch range is Rod Stewart. Harshness with constriction and high pitch can be found in one type of 'rikimi' voice quality in Japanese.

8 Prosody

Lluisa Astruc

1 Introduction

Prosody covers all aspects of stress, rhythm, phrasing and intonation in speech.[1] Some important prosodic distinctions are conveyed in writing using commas, colons, semi-colons and other punctuation marks:

(1)
    a) Politicians can't talk, honestly.
    b) Politicians can't talk honestly.

In (1a), the adverb *honestly* is separated by a prosodic break (represented by a comma in writing) which indicates that this adverb is a sentential adverb modifying the whole sentence and its meaning is equivalent to 'in my honest opinion'. In (1b), *honestly* is a manner adverb modifying the verb; its meaning is '[to talk] with honesty'. Parenthetical comments and restrictive relative clauses are generally both set aside by prosodic breaks and uttered with a faster tempo. Changes in rhythm, phrasing and intonation can thus convey syntactic and semantic information.

Another function of prosody is structuring the phonology. The units of phonology, from the segment up to the utterance, are organized into a prosodic hierarchy (see Table 8.1); segments form syllables, syllables form feet (a foot is a strong syllable and one or more weak syllables; for example, *water* has a strong and a weak syllable), feet can be combined to form multisyllabic words (*watermelon* has two feet with a strong and a weak syllable each) and words

Table 8.1 The elements of the prosodic structure

Intonational phrase (IP)	IP						
Phonological phrase (PhP)	PhP				PhP		
Prosodic word (PW)	PW		PW		PW		
Foot (Ft)	Ft		Ft		Ft		Ft
Syllable (σ)	σ	σ	σ	σ	σ	σ	σ

Table 8.2 The phonetic aspects of stress, rhythm and intonation

Prosodic subsystems	Main acoustic parameters		
Stress	Duration	Intensity	Pitch
Rhythm	Duration	Intensity	Pitch
Intonation			Pitch

form different types of phrases. This hierarchical ordering of prosodic elements is known as the prosodic structure and is part of the phonology of a language (e.g. Selkirk, 1978; Nespor & Vogel, 1986).

In the speech signal, prosodic distinctions are conveyed by a set of acoustic parameters: duration, intensity and pitch. The combination of these parameters is perceived as stress, rhythm and intonation, which are the main subsystems of prosody. We see above (in Table 8.2) the relationship between the main acoustic parameters and the prosodic subsystems of stress, rhythm and intonation.

We see that whereas all three acoustic parameters are used to convey stress and rhythm (since the perception of rhythm relies on the alternation of stressed and unstressed syllables), only one parameter (pitch) is used for intonation. In practice, however, duration, intensity and pitch are used in all the prosodic subsystems and it becomes a very difficult task to tease apart their respective contribution.

In the next sections we will examine each parameter in detail, with reference to the acoustic properties that can be identified in the speech signal.

2 Acoustic Parameters of Prosody

Prosody is characterized by (1) the duration of speech sounds; (2) the intensity of speech sounds; and for voiced sounds, (3) pitch, which corresponds to the fundamental frequency of vibration of the vocal folds. The situation is somewhat more complicated by the fact that the same acoustic parameters that characterize prosody are also used in other speech (and non-speech) sounds. One complication, for example, is that segments have their own *intrinsic duration, intensity* and *pitch*, and these interact with prosody. For example, because of the way they are articulated, some sounds are intrinsically longer than others, for example, open vowels such as [a] are longer than other vowels because they require a more prolonged opening movement of the jaw (see House & Fairbanks, 1953 and Peterson & Lehiste, 1960, in English; Lindblom, 1967, in Swedish; see a summary of early studies in Lehiste, 1977, and a discussion in Fletcher, 2010, pp. 558ff). Segments also have a specific intensity, as a result of having been articulated with different degrees of pulmonic force and constriction. For instance, a close vowel such as [i] has less intensity than the mid-vowel [e] and this in turn less than the open vowel [a]. And the same holds for pitch; segments have intrinsic frequencies which in turn interact with sentence-level pitch patterns (see a review of early studies on intrinsic intensity and pitch in Möbius, 2003; a study of intrinsic pitch in Whalen & Levitt, 1995; and a discussion in Harrington, 2010b, pp. 86ff).

These segmental differences in duration, intensity and pitch are not part of prosody, but they affect prosody. When designing test materials for an experiment, the researcher has to control for these differences by using the same segmental context or by balancing the number of open and close vowels. In this way, an increase in the duration, intensity or pitch of a segment or syllable due to prosody can be distinguished from the variation inherent to segments.

2.1 Duration

Duration is normally expressed in milliseconds (ms) and can be measured fairly easily. The only difficulty lies in deciding the start and end points of segments and syllables, for example, whether to include or not the burst of plosive consonants or what part of the vocalic transitions to label as the start or end of a vowel (see Peterson & Lehiste, 1960; Watt, this volume). However, measuring duration with too much precision can be unnecessary or even misleading, since there is a limit (called the 'just noticeable difference', JND) to the durational differences that the human ear can perceive. Extensive research since the late 1940s has shown this limit to be between 10 and 40 ms, depending on the type of sound and how loud this is in relation to the background noise (see Lehiste, 1977, pp. 10–17).

The duration of segments is determined by a combination of intrinsic and contextual factors, such as position in the syllable, word and utterance, often with cumulative effects. It is well attested across languages that segments in multisyllabic words tend to be shorter than in monosyllabic words. This is called *polysyllabic shortening*. Klatt (1973) used word pairs such as *smooth* and *smoothest* and found that the stressed vowel of disyllables was 103 to 131 ms shorter than that of monosyllables.

More recently, White and Turk (2010) measured monosyllables, disyllables and trisyllables (*cap, captain, captaincy; juice, produce, reproduce*) controlling for position of the target vowel in the word and in the sentence because segments at the end of words and phrases are much longer than in any other position. They also controlled for the interaction with pitch, using accented and unaccented words (that is, words with and without pitch prominence; see Section 3.3 below) since it is known that syllables made prominent by pitch are longer. They found substantial shortening of the target vowel in monosyllables compared to disyllables (*cap* to *captain*) and also when a further syllable was added to form trisyllables (*captain* to *captaincy*), in the accented condition but not in the unaccented condition. An explanation for this is that unaccented words are already much shorter than accented words and they cannot be reduced any further.

2.2 Intensity

Intensity refers to the acoustic effects of sound pressure calculated as the pressure per unit area and is one of the most commonly used measures of sound energy in speech research. Intensity must be measured in relation to frequency because the higher the frequency, the louder the sound is perceived to be. Loudness is the perceptual correlate of intensity and is measured in decibels (dB) using a logarithmic scale set in relation to a reference value, which is generally the threshold of human hearing for a sound with a frequency of 1,000 Hz.

Root Mean Square (RMS) is used to calculate the overall intensity over a section of speech. This method involves taking values, squaring them, averaging them and taking the final square root (squaring and taking the square root is done to avoid negative values). The method can be applied to the calculation of the intensity over a segment, syllable or word.

Another measure of intensity which has been developed more recently is spectral balance (or spectral tilt). This refers to the distribution of energy in the spectrum; syllables which have more energy in the upper bands than in the lower bands are perceived to be louder. Spectral balance is thus measured as the difference in energy between the upper and the lower frequency bands at some local point, which is generally the peak of intensity of a formant in a vowel (for more information, see, for example, Stevens, 1998).

2.3 Pitch

Pitch is determined by the by the rate of vibration of the vocal folds, which produces a set of harmonic frequencies superimposed upon a fundamental frequency (known as 'f-zero', and abbreviated as F0). Although, strictly speaking, pitch and fundamental frequency refer to different aspects of the same phenomenon (the first is an acoustic parameter, the second its perceptual correlate), both terms tend to be used interchangeably in the literature (e.g. Ladd, 2008) and they will not be differentiated here. Each movement of the vocal folds creates an amplitude peak in the speech waveform which is repeated periodically; a faster rate of vibration produces a perception of higher pitch. Physiological differences such as those between men, women and children have an effect on pitch. The shorter and the more tense the vocal folds are, the faster they vibrate, producing a perceptual impression of high pitch whereas longer and slacker folds vibrate more slowly and produce a perception of low pitch. We find similar effects in string instruments. For instance, when playing a guitar a string is pressed against a fret to allow different lengths of the string to vibrate – the longer the length of string vibrating, the lower-pitched the sound.

Pitch is generally measured in hertz (Hz). One hertz is defined as one cycle per second. For instance, 22 amplitude peaks, each corresponding to a cycle of vocal fold vibration, in a 100 ms interval correspond to a pitch of 220 Hz per second. Although the relationship between pitch and the vibration of the vocal folds is relatively simple, measuring pitch is not straightforward. The measurement of pitch presents several problems: (1) interference of the intrinsic pitch of segments (as stated previously, high vowels as [e] or [i] have a higher pitch than the rest); (2) effects of surrounding consonants (voiceless consonants interrupt the pitch trace and produce a perturbation at their onset); (3) end of word and utterance effects; and (4) voice source effects (e.g. creaky voice, see Esling, this volume). All these potential problems have to be taken into account when designing experimental materials. For optimal results, test words should be maximally voiced; *lemony* (fully voiced and with two syllables between the stress and the end of the word) is preferable to *coke*, for instance.

Another complicating factor is human perception: pitch differences at the low frequencies of the scale are much more noticeable than differences at the higher frequencies. This poses a problem when comparing the pitch of individuals with very different pitch ranges (e.g. comparing adult with child, or male with female). t' Hart et al. (1990, pp. 23ff) have advocated the use of psychoacoustic scales such as the semitone scale, a logarithmic scale borrowed from music, because these resemble human perception. The semitone scale captures the perceptual similarity between a pitch movement from 100 Hz to 150 Hz in a male voice and what would be an equivalent movement in a female voice of 170 Hz to 270 Hz. When measured in semitones, in both cases the change would be 7.02 semitones, whereas if measured in hertz it would be 50 Hz in one case and 90 Hz in the other (t' Hart et al., 1990).

Further evidence is furnished by Nolan (2003) who compared hertz, semitones and another two scales. He asked participants to imitate a male and a female voice reading two sentences ('We were relying on a milliner – A milliner!?') in three different pitch contours, neutral, compressed and expanded. The pitch spans of the original and the imitated contours were measured in each of the four scales and compared. The results showed that the semitones gave the best fit.

3 Prosodic Subsystems: Stress, Rhythm and Intonation

As stated in the Introduction, duration, intensity and pitch combine with each other to create the perception of stress, rhythm and intonation. Now that we have covered the acoustic basis of prosody, we will turn to examine each of these three prosodic subsystems in detail.

3.1 Stress

Word-level (or lexical) stress is the degree of relative prominence of a syllable in relation to others in the same word and makes use of all three acoustic parameters. Accentuation (or sentence-stress) refers to the degree of prominence of a word in relation to others in the sentence and will be described in the next section, but we need to mention it here because it interacts with word-level stress.

Words with stress on the last syllable (*giRAFFE*; upper case marks stress) are called *oxytones*, those with stress on the penultimate syllable (*PANther*) are called *paroxytones*, and trisyllabic words with stress on the antepenultimate syllable (*Elephant*) are called *proparoxytones*. Words with stress on syllables before the antepenultimate (e.g. *CATerpillar*) do not have a specific name and are rather rare in most languages.

Before discussing the phonetic features of stress in detail, we will comment briefly on the typological distinction between *pitch-accent* and *stress-accent* languages. Pitch-accent languages use a limited set of pitch patterns to signal lexical distinctions. Japanese, Norwegian and Swedish, are among the several languages in the world that use pitch in this way. Swedish, for instance, has two pitch patterns which differentiate about 500 pairs of words, such as *anden* 'the duck' and *anden* 'the spirit' (illustrated in Figure 8.1).

Stress-accent languages, on the other hand, are languages such as English, Spanish and French, which use duration and intensity in addition to pitch to convey lexical stress. English has words such as *OBject* and *obJECT* where stress has a contrastive (often morphological) function. Stress-languages can have *free*

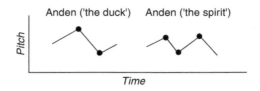

Figure 8.1 Schematic diagram showing the difference in pitch accent between Swedish *anden* 'the duck' and *anden* 'the spirit'

stress such as English or Spanish or *fixed stress* such as French, where stress always falls on the last syllable in the word.

It is generally accepted that the main acoustic correlates of stress are the pitch changes that occur in the vicinity of the most prominent syllable in a word, together with the longer duration and increased intensity of the syllable, as was shown in Fry's pioneering studies (Fry, 1955, 1958). Much research has investigated the relative order of contribution of each acoustic parameter to the perception of stress and whether the ranking of the acoustic parameters is language-specific or universal (see review in van Heuven and Sluijter, 1996: 255ff; Cutler, 2005: 270ff). Fry (1955, 1958) proposed that there were three main acoustic parameters which were ranked in the order: pitch, duration and intensity. Lieberman (1960) examined 16 English noun-verb pairs (e.g. *REbel* and *reBEL*) which were read by 16 speakers and, in contrast with Fry's results, he found that intensity was a stronger cue than duration and consequently ranked the parameters in a different order: pitch, intensity and duration.

The divergence in relation to the role of duration may have been a methodological artefact, since Lieberman's experiment did not control for the position of the syllable in the word and sentence or for the presence of accentuation (see Section 3.3 below). Accentuation refers to the use of pitch to make a syllable or word prominent in the sentence. Most lexical words in a sentence are accented, that is, they carry a pitch movement in the vicinity of the stressed syllable. Additionally, the most prominent word in a sentence is said to be focalized and is longer and with a more noticeable pitch movement. Work by Huss (1978) and by Sluijter and collaborators (Sluijter & van Heuven, 1996; Sluijter et al., 1997) has been among the first to examine the acoustic and perceptual correlates of stress without the confounding effects of accentuation and focalization. Sluijter and van Heuven (1996) used a design in which Dutch minimal stress pairs such as *KAnon* and *kaNON* (which correspond to the English homophones 'canon' and 'cannon' respectively) were embedded in an accented and in a non-accented context, as shown in 2a and 2b below:

(2)

   a) The word *kanon* is accented (accent in upper case; stress marked by '
before the stressed syllable in *kanon*).

     i) *Wil je 'KANON zeggen (en niet liedje).* 'Will you say CANON (rather
than song)'.

     ii) *Wil je KA'NON zeggen (en niet geweer).* 'Will you say CANNON
(rather than rifle)'.

   b) The word *kanon* is unaccented (accent in upper case; stress marked by '
before the stressed syllable in *kanon*).

     i) *Wil je 'kanon ZEGGEN (en niet opschrijven).* 'Will you SAY canon
(rather than writing it down)'.

     ii) *Wil je ka'non ZEGGEN (en niet opschrijven).* 'Will you SAY cannon
(rather than writing it down)'.

Sluijter and van Heuven measured five parameters in total. In addition to pitch, duration and intensity, they measured spectral balance and vocalic reduction. Vocalic reduction is the degree of centralization of a vowel and is usually measured as the difference between the first and the second formant. They found that duration and spectral balance were the strongest correlates of stress and these results were soon replicated in American and British English and in other languages and were also confirmed by perceptual experiments. Intensity rise time, that is the relative steepness of the rise in intensity, is a correlate of stress which has been used in psychoacoustic studies (e.g. Goswami et al., 2010). Lehto (1969) measured the correlates of stress (intensity, pitch and duration) in relation to different phases in the intensity curve (primary phase, beat phase, after-phase and final phase). She argued that the combination of duration and intensity during the beat phase (intensity rise time) was the strongest correlate of stress in English.

One question that arises is whether the ranking of the acoustic parameters is language-specific or universal. The *Functional Load Hypothesis* (e.g. Berinstein, 1979; Remijsen, 2001) proposes that if a language uses any one of these acoustic parameters for other phonological uses, then this parameter will have to play a lesser role in stress. Thus, in a language that uses duration to distinguish between phonemes, duration will be a less important cue to stress, while in a tone language such as Mandarin pitch will be of less importance. Some studies have found support for the Functional Load Hypothesis (e.g. Potisuk et al., 1996 in Thai; Levi, 2005 in Turkish), whereas others have failed to do so (Berinstein, 1979; Rozelle, 1997 in Aleut). Berinstein (1979) investigated the role of duration in the production and perception of stress in K'ekchi, a language with phonemic use of duration, English, with a more limited use, and Spanish, where duration is not used at all. A perceptual experiment in which duration was manipulated in four steps and participants were asked to judge whether the syllable was stressed or not showed mixed results. On the one hand, and in line with the Functional Load Hypothesis, K'ekchi listeners did not perform well at all. However, Spanish listeners performed worse than the English, a result which was difficult to explain. Rozelle's study of Aleut, a language with the same phonemic use of duration as K'ekchi, showed that duration was used both to mark stress and to differentiate between phonemes.

In summary, over the last decades, most research has investigated the relative ranking of the main acoustic parameters of stress and whether this ranking is universal or not. Although these questions are not totally answered, these lines of research have yielded some useful insights into the typology of stress and into the interdependencies between stress and intonation.

3.2 Rhythm

As defined by Crystal (1985), rhythm refers to the perceived regularity of prominent speech units, which can be a succession of patterns of stressed and unstressed syllables (as in English), long and short syllables (as in Latin) or accented and unaccented syllable (as in Modern Greek), or indeed some combination of these. Nursery rhymes, poetry and oratory prose furnish examples of maximally regular rhythmic patterns. The rhythm of other forms of speech is much less predictable as it depends on the organization of words and sentences and also on the personal style of the speaker (some speakers are much more sensitive to rhythm than others).

Rhythmic patterns arise from the regular repetition of sequences of stressed syllables (S, strong) and unstressed syllables (W, weak). An example of strong-weak (SW) metrical pattern is the nursery rhyme *Insy winsy spider*, with a SW metrical pattern. The first line of *Jack and Jill*, another nursery rhyme, displays a strong-weak-strong (SWS) metrical pattern. These sequences of stressed and unstressed syllables are called feet. The most common ones have names: SW, trochee; WS, iamb; WWS, anapest; WSW, amphibrach.

Early studies (e.g. Pike, 1945; Abercrombie, 1967) observed that languages tended to maintain roughly equal intervals between prosodic units; some would maintain equal duration between stressed syllables (stress-timed) while reducing the intervening unstressed syllables whereas others maintained roughly equal durations between syllable onsets. This is known as the Isochrony Hypothesis and has led to the typological classification into 'syllable-timed' languages such as Spanish and French and 'stress-timed' languages such as English and Dutch.

Empirical research, however, has failed to find evidence for the Isochrony Hypothesis. The duration of interstress intervals in English appears to vary in direct proportion to the number of syllables (Bolinger, 1965 and Roach, 1982, among others). Bolinger (1965) found that syllable type and position within the utterance affected the duration of interstress intervals. Roach (1982) examined the six languages previously analyzed by Abercrombie (1967), three of them stress-timed (French, Telugu and Yoruba) and three syllable-timed (English, Russian and Arabic) and found that foot duration showed more variability in the 'stress-timed' than in the 'syllable-timed' languages, which was counter-intuitive. Roach (1982) concluded that distinctions between linguistic rhythm classes were subjective, and for a while, rhythm was considered a perceptual 'illusion' with no measurable acoustic correlates at all. Fortunately, the quest for the linguistic basis of rhythm continued. Dauer (1983) noticed that a number of properties such as syllable structure (the variety and complexity of syllables), differences in the correlates of stress (see previous section) and vowel reduction, co-occurred with the distinction between stress-timed and syllable-timed languages. She argued that such properties largely determine the perceptual prominence of stressed syllables in relation to other syllables and that differences in the perception of rhythm between languages arise from distinct combinations of these properties, especially syllable structure and vowel reduction (Dauer, 1987). 'Stress-timed' languages like English have a greater number of syllables with complex codas and onsets, and also tend to reduce unstressed vowels both in duration and in quality. Languages such as Spanish, a typical 'syllable-timed' language, have a larger number of open syllables and no vowel reduction.

The next wave of studies aimed at developing appropriate quantitative measures for rhythm. Such studies fall into two types: those that searched for perceptual centres (P-centres) (e.g. Morton et al., 1976; Scott, 1998) and those that measured the duration of vowels and consonants (Ramus et al., 1999; Low et al., 2000; Grabe & Low, 2002).

The concept of perceptual centre (P-centre) is linked to the early Isochrony Hypothesis. Morton et al. (1976) defined the P-centre as the hypothetical specific moment at which a rhythmically relevant brief event (generally shorter than 1.5 seconds) is perceived to occur. The rhythmically relevant part of a syllable, the P-centre, is located near the syllable onset but its exact location will depend on the segmental composition of the syllable. In syllables with long onsets ('me') the P-centre will be located later than in syllables with short onsets ('bee'). Several models of P-centres have been developed, often with problematic comparability and reliability (see comparison and review in Villing, 2010), and it is fair to say that durational approaches seem to offer more promise.

Durational metrics aim at quantifying the rhythmic differences between languages by measuring the duration of intervals of vowels and consonants directly from the speech signal, without any reference to syllables, words or higher prosodic units. For instance, *next Thursday* will have, depending on the pronunciation, these vocalic and consonantal intervals: /n/-/e/-/ksθ/-/ɜː/-/zd/-/eɪ/.

One of the most widely used metric indices, the Pairwise Variability Index (PVI) (Low et al., 2000; Grabe & Low, 2002), requires the measurement of the difference in the duration of each successive pair of consonantal and vocalic intervals (in the example, /n/ and/e/, /ksθ/ and /ɜː/, /zd/ and /eɪ/) which is divided by the duration of the pair in order to normalize speaker variations. Grabe and Low applied the PVI to 18 languages and concluded that stress-timed and syllable-timed languages do not fall into two separate classes but rather form a continuum with languages such as English and Spanish at the extremes and Catalan, Greek, Luxembourgish and Japanese in the middle (Grabe & Low, 2002).

Ramus et al. (1999) developed and tested several durational metrics, among them the proportion of vocalic interval (%V) and the variability of vocalic and consonantal intervals (expressed as standard deviations, ΔC and ΔV). A whole range of metric indices has been added in recent years to the ones described here, as for instance, rate-normalized versions of Ramus' ΔC and ΔV, VarcoC and VarcoV respectively; see Dellwo (2006), and Ferragne and Pellegrino (2004). See a comparison in White and Mattys (2007) and Knight (2011). Applying these metrics, they found that stressed-timed languages (e.g. English, Dutch) were set apart from syllable-timed ones (e.g. Italian, Spanish) by a number of properties, from vowel reduction to durational contrasts, but syllable structure appeared to be the more reliable of them all. Stress-timed languages had a lower proportion of vowels and these were more variable.

Although most research since Ramus et al. (1999) has taken the view that the perceived rhythmic differences between languages derive from phonological properties such as syllable structure, the proponents of the so-called phrasal approach emphasize the need to take into account durational effects across syllables, words and sentences – across the whole prosodic hierarchy. White and Mattys (2007) found that accentual lengthening, word-initial lengthening and phrase-final lengthening contributed to the perception of rhythm in English. White et al. (2009) found similar effects for northern and southern Italian. Similar results were also found by Prieto et al. (2012), with 27 English, Catalan and Spanish female participants.

In summary, the use of duration to convey rhythm is strongly influenced by the language-specific phonological properties such as the variety and composition of syllables. Languages with a large proportion of vowels, and with less variability in the duration of vowels, form a separate group from languages with fewer vowels and more variability in duration. However, sentence-level properties such as the distribution of prosodic boundaries also have strong effects on rhythm. Such findings call for extreme caution when designing experimental materials, since the number and type of syllables, semantic content and the position of pitch accents and prosodic breaks need to be controlled.

3.3 Intonation

We will use the term intonation in a narrow sense[2] to refer to the use of prosodic features, especially pitch, to convey differences in meaning at the sentence level and above such as these:

(3)
  a) She is a rocket scientist?
  b) (Yes) She is a rocket scientist.
  c) (Really?) She is a rocket scientist?!

(4)
  a) MARY won the lottery (not Anna).
  b) Mary WON the lottery (she didn't lose).
  c) Mary won the LOTTERY (not the raffle).

(5)
  a) The neighbour has planted black tulips and roses (both are black).
  b) The neighbour has planted black tulips // and roses (the roses can be any colour).

Intonation is used to convey functional distinctions such as those between a question (3a) and a statement (3b) and pragmatic distinctions such as those between a neutral question (3a) and an incredulous or surprised question (3c). Intonation is also used to signal which word is the most prominent in the sentence, as we see in (4). In (4a) *Mary* stands out in contrast to *Anna*; in (4b) *win* contrasts with *lose*; and in (4c) *lottery* contrasts with *raffle*. The prominent words in all three sentences are said to receive *narrow focus*. Narrow focus is also used when answering a partial question ('Who did win the lottery?' 'MARY won the lottery'). The sentence in (4c) can also be a reply to a broad question such as 'What happened . . .?' ('Do you know what happened today? Mary won the LOTTERY'), in which case it is said to be in *broad focus* (see Cruttenden, 1997, pp. 73ff for a description of the functions of intonation, including focalization). Finally, last but not least, as shown in (5) another important function of intonation is that of grouping constituents into separate phrases.

The main typological distinction in intonation is that between *tone languages* (for instance, Chinese and Vietnamese) and *intonational languages* (English and French). All languages use intonation to convey sentence-level meaning, but in addition, tone languages also use pitch for lexical distinctions. However, recent typological work has cast doubts on the existence of a clear-cut distinction between tone and intonational languages. Indeed, there seem to be many languages that fall in some intermediate category between 'pure' tone languages such as Chinese and 'pure' intonational languages such as English, thus calling for a finer-grained classification. For instance, Mandarin Chinese, can be considered a mixed tone language, as it has both lexical pitch and stress (e.g. Jun, 2005, see review of typological work in Zerbian et al., 2009).

Intonation is difficult to analyse and to transcribe. Pitch accents are notably fluid and tend to move around because of pragmatic factors, as in (4), or change their shape because of segmental factors (see Section 2.3), or because of the position of the stressed syllable in the word. Figure 8.2 shows an example of how the same low-high-low pitch movement changes in different Spanish phrases:

One of the most widely used methods for analysing intonation is the autosegmental metrical framework (AM) and its specific notational method called Tones and Breaks Indices (ToBI). This method was developed in the 1980s extending early work on African tone languages to intonational languages (Pierrehumbert, 1980; Gussenhoven, 2005; Ladd, 2008). From the work on tone languages comes the concept of tones being autonomous from segments (hence 'autosegmental'). The AM framework has been applied to many languages and has become popular because of its facility for cross-linguistic comparisons. According to the AM approach the intonational system of a language involves an inventory of *pitch accents* and *boundary tones*, and a set of phonetic rules for mapping these. Pitch accents are tonal events associated (aligned) with the stressed syllables. The most prominent pitch accent, which is usually also the final one in a sentence, is called the 'nuclear' accent and all other accents that precede it are called 'prenuclear'. Boundary tones are aligned with the end of phrases.

Most of the empirical research in intonation has investigated the properties of the scaling and alignment of pitch accents and boundary tones. It was observed that speakers show remarkable regularity in their pitch scaling. For instance, the pitch of the low point at the end of a statement tends to vary little for any given speaker (Liberman & Pierrehumbert, 1980) even in spontaneous speech (Boyce & Menn, 1979, in six American English parent-child dialogues; Anderson & Cooper, 1986, comparing read spontaneous and read speech). The

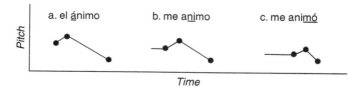

Figure 8.2 A schematic diagram showing the same low-high-low pitch movement over time in three different Spanish phrases

work in Central Swedish by Bruce (1977) provided evidence of the regularities in the timing of tones. Bruce found that that the precise alignment of the peak was the most reliable correlate of word accent in Swedish.

Throughout the 1990s, intonationalists have continued to seek evidence of the relative invariance of tonal targets in different languages (Arvaniti & Ladd, 1995; Arvaniti et al., 1998; Ladd et al., 2000). Further research, however, seems to suggest that the alignment of tones and segments may differ according to the absolute duration of the nuclear syllable and of the nuclear word (Ladd et al., 2009, for Southern British English and Scottish English). This alignment is also influenced by the proximity to the boundaries of prosodic constituents (syllable, word, intonational phrase) and by the speech rate (Dutch: Rietveld & Gussenhoven, 1995; Pisa and Bari Italian: Gili-Fivela & Savino, 2003; English: van Santen & Hirschberg, 1994; French: Welby & Loevenbruck, 2005; Spanish: Prieto & Torreira, 2007, among others). For a summary of tonal alignment research see Ladd, 2008, pp. 172ff.

4 Conclusion

Prosody is complex – stress, rhythm and intonation are not separate systems; on the contrary, they interact with each other. Furthermore, all sub-systems make overlapping use of the same acoustic parameters and these in turn are affected by the intrinsic acoustic characteristics of segments (for instance, pitch is as a property of segments, of stressed syllables and of accented syllables). When designing an experiment, it is of paramount importance to control the interactions of these factors in order to ensure that we are measuring what we set out to measure.

Notes

1. Prosody has also been referred to as suprasegmentals, suprasegmental features and nonsegmental features.
2. This is a definition in line with Ladd (2008). A wider definition of intonation such as Gussenhoven's (e.g. 2004, chapters 4 and 5) would also include non-linguistic components such as the expressions of emotions and psychological or cognitive states.

9 Phonetic Universals and Phonetic Variation

Mark J. Jones

1 Introduction

The aim of this chapter is to present an overview of universal patterns in phonetics and sources of phonetic variation. In some ways, the universalist approach is something of an anachronism in these relativistic times, when the focus is more on differences than on similarities. The idea that there might be such things as phonetic universals is rooted in the biological and physical bases of speech itself. Rather than meaning patterns which always occur, the term universal is used here to mean patterns which can be expected, as a result of the properties of the human vocal tract and aerodynamics. Although supraseg-mental universals undoubtedly occur (Xu & Sun, 2002; Xu, 2009), this chapter focuses on segmental effects. Despite the predictions of phonetic theory, some patterns may not occur where expected. These unexpected deviations are of vital interest because they lead phoneticians to evaluate what they know and how they know it, and to consider why speakers do what they do. Systematic variability may be traced to different sources. The focus on phonetic variation in this chapter rules out the kind of categorical changes seen in traditional phonological alternations or sociolinguistic variables, but the status of pho-netic categories is discussed as the basis for comparisons across languages.

Variation within categories is also an inevitable consequence of using quantitative techniques, so variation in measured speech data cannot be taken at face value. Understanding the significance of variation, particularly whether or not it reflects direct speaker choices, requires a proper consideration of the role of universalist (i.e. physical-biological) mechanisms.

2 The Nature of Phonetic Universals

Phonetic universals arise from the physical-biological basis of speech. As physical behaviour taking place in time and space, speech is subject to the same laws as throwing a ball or running. Speech also involves structures present in more or less the same arrangement within all typical adult humans. Given the universality of the laws of physics and the shared structures of the human vocal tract, it would be unsurprising if the physical characteristics of speech were not broadly comparable across speakers (see Maddieson, 1997). If this were not the case, phonetic analysis across speakers would be impossible. But the details of speech do differ across speakers and also across languages. It seems that speakers are capable of circumventing some universalist pressures in various ways, so that any utterance displays a complex mixture of universal human, individual and language-specific patterns. Some of these patterns are obviously learned and might involve suppressing universalist tendencies, some come for 'free', because they occur as a by-product of other effects which the speaker does intend, and some patterns are language-specific augmentations or exaggerations of universalist patterns. Distinguishing which patterns are characteristics of a speaker's speech target and which patterns are peripheral and due to the physical implementation of that target is not easy. With the increase in interest in exemplar or episodic memory approaches to speech variation in perception (e.g. Port, 2007), there is a tendency to view speech production as drawing on relatively detailed targets (Pierrehumbert, 2001, 2002; Kirchner et al., 2010). One danger of an extreme version of this approach is that surface patterns are interpreted as direct and perfect implementations of stored representations, and any deviant contribution due to physical factors in implementation is minimized. The broad aim of this chapter is not to disregard the possibility of detailed representations, but to emphasize the fundamentally physical basis of speech and to call for caution in interpreting any and all phonetic variation as being planned by the speaker on some level.

The first section below sets out the objects of crosslinguistic comparison. There follows a section which discusses some universalist patterns, and then a section discussing systematic sources of phonetic variation. The chapter closes with an overview and a consideration of some implications of universal patterns and systematic sources of variability for speech analysis.

3 Crosslinguistic Comparisons

This section discusses what objects can be used as the basis of comparisons across languages. In historical linguistics, cognate forms from ancestral languages might be used. In sociolinguistics, cognates are also generally used in the form of variables which are historically or functionally linked across (related) varieties. Neither of these units work in phonetic comparisons of unrelated languages. The basic object of crosslinguistic comparison is the phone or segment, as characterized by the International Phonetic Alphabet (IPA; see Esling, 2010). The terms phone and segment are often used interchangeably, as here. Phones are categories used to classify speech sounds which are defined in broad articulatory-aerodynamic terms. As phones are primarily defined with reference to the shared structures of the human vocal tract, the categories can in theory be identified across speakers. The categorization of individual phones is not, however, problem-free. Categories are defined broadly with respect to an idealized 'average' human vocal tract. Individual vocal tracts obviously differ. Normally, phones are not identified directly from static representations of articulatory states, but indirectly and impressionistically, so that the articulations themselves are not seen. Then there is the dynamism of speech itself, which almost seems designed to obscure any underlying units. Difficulty alone should not dissuade us from accepting the phone as a valid unit; electrons are/were hardly easy to detect, either. Neither is the obvious dynamism of speech a valid counterargument – the Earth does not appear spherical to an observer on the ground, after all, so first (and even second) impressions may be deceptive.

With sufficient training, phones can be identified readily enough, as numerous descriptions of the segmental phonetics of many languages testify, and phones can even be seen as more than simply a convenient fiction, if wider sources of evidence are consulted than the superficial hurly-burly of speech and the non-local distribution of perceptual cues (e.g. segmental loci of coarticulation, dissimilatory sound change, onset vs. nucleus in consonant-vowel (CV) languages, segmental morphology in Hebrew, etc.). There is not sufficient space here to examine these issues in detail, except to say that given that phones are composed of various articulatory subcomponents (e.g. jaw, tongue, velum), all of which have different masses, neuromuscular control regimes and starting points in connected speech, the idea that phones should or even could be realized like distinct morse code elements or piano notes is implausible (for more discussion on this, see Laver, 1994). The phone is relatively broadly defined. Categories like phones are defined on the basis of a few shared classificatory characteristics: [p] is a voiceless unaspirated bilabial plosive, [a] is an open front unrounded vowel. In the same way that the term 'human' can be applied to individuals sharing certain criterial features but varying in non-criterial characteristics, so too no two instances of [p] need be the same in all respects.

Phonemes should not be used for crosslinguistic comparison (see Pierrehumbert et al., 2000), for two reasons. First, most (all?) phonology textbooks start by defining phonemes as classes of systematically related contextual variants (allophones), which are opposed to other phonemes on the basis of lexical contrasts. These systematic contextual and lexically contrastive relationships are discovered by examination of a single language's lexicon, that is, phonemes are by their very nature lexicon-specific, and therefore language-specific. But most current phonology textbooks then go on to discuss phonemes as bundles of Distinctive Features, phonological units which are hypothesized to have at least some basis in phonetics. This view of phonemes defines them phonetically, at least by proxy, via the possible existence of Distinctive Features. Under this view, the phoneme is not abstract and language-specific at all, but vaguely concrete and much like a phone in some respects. Given this Jekyll-and-Hyde whiff which hangs around phonemes, it would seem safest to ignore them for crosslinguistic comparison. When these Distinctive Feature-style 'phone-phonemes' are compared crosslinguistically, they are often compared within similar contexts and must be interpreted first as allophones anyway. So the phone is an uncontroversial unit of crosslinguistic comparison (see also Huckvale, this volume).

Another valid comparison is what might be called 'contrastive position' or 'point within a system', for example, the formant frequencies of the most peripheral high front vowel. This is essentially what is explored in Bradlow (1995), who uses acoustic analysis to quantify an impressionistically perceptible difference in the vowels of American English and Spanish (her aim is to investigate the effects of vowel inventory size on the dispersion of contrasts through phonetic space, see below). Contrastive positions might be defined in terms of Distinctive Features. For example, Jongman et al. (1985) investigate whether [coronal] plosives in specific languages are more likely to be dental or alveolar, and many studies of contrastive [voice] in obstruents could also be seen in this light (Keating 1984; Petrova et al., 2006).

Having identified what to compare, the next section discusses some implications of universals.

4 Investigating Phonetic Universals

The physical basis of speech and the shared properties of the human vocal tract allow us to make various hypotheses about the realizations of phones and phone sequences, even without any actual speech data. For example, if a constriction prevents pulmonic egressive airflow, pressure in the vocal tract will rise, and if the velum is lowered to allow acoustic coupling between oral and nasal cavities during a vowel, antiformants can be expected in the output spectrum. These hypotheses are one source of information on universals. Other universals are identified as patterns exhibited across languages, and potential universals can be identified across relatively small samples. Even the most extensive crosslinguistic surveys of phonetics and phonology (e.g. Maddieson, 1984) fail to cover more than about 10 per cent of human languages, not least because we do not have descriptions of all languages or their dialects. But if the same pattern is observed across several unrelated and geographically diffuse languages, there is a good chance that the pattern is a universal (see Ohala, 2003, etc. for a similar and related approach to sound change). Some patterns which occur in speech may therefore be present for 'free', rather than intentionally executed by the speaker in a controlled way.

To give one example of a 'free' pattern of variation, the release of a voiceless (denti)alveolar plosive typically involves some oral frication as the articulators come apart. This frication is particularly extensive before an [i]-type vowel (Hall et al., 2006) because the high jaw and tongue position provide good conditions for turbulent airflow. This universalist pressure to have oral frication before [i] means that finding a [tsi] like sequence would not, on its own, be a good candidate for diagnosing whether a language is developing affricated plosives. If some speakers of the language occasionally had [tsa], however, this would indicate more support for affrication, because release-related frication should not be very extensive before an [a]-type vowel.

There are undoubtedly universal constraints on suprasegmental features too (e.g. Xu, & Sun, 2002; Xu, 2009), but the focus here is on segmental aspects of speech. Segmentally oriented phonetic universals may also arise in the auditory domain because of hard-wired responses to the acoustic signal (e.g. Pisoni, 1977, on the minimum discriminability of temporal events and Voice Onset Time (VOT); Kluender et al., 1988, on voice-related vowel duration), and in many cases whether a pattern has a physical-biological origin or an auditory-perceptual origin may not be certain. Uncertainty surrounds the mechanism underlying the widespread phenomenon of intrinsic F0, in which high vowels have a higher F0 than low vowels, other things being equal (Whalen & Levitt, 1995), because the physiological hypothesis usually suggested – that of the tongue pulling upwards on the hyoid bone for the high vowels and thus tensing the vocal folds – is not always supported by evidence from experimental results (Takano et al., 2006).

Solé has advocated the use of speech-rate data to examine the extent to which certain phonetic patterns are actively controlled by speakers (Solé, 1992, 2007; Solé & Ohala, 2012). Nasal airflow in vowels due to velic lowering for a following nasal consonant maintains a proportional duration across speech rates in American English, suggesting a planned timing pattern, whereas in Spanish, nasal airflow always occupies approximately the same duration across speech rates, suggesting a biomechanical effect (Solé, 1992; see also Cohn, 1993).

Unaspirated plosives across languages show a relatively constant pattern across speech rates, suggesting an aerodynamic explanation for voice onset, but voiceless aspirated plosives show proportional timing in English and Thai (Solé, 2007). High vowels tend to be shorter than low vowels, but Solé and Ohala (2012) show that the effects are controlled across speech rates in American English and Catalan, but vary mechanically in Japanese. Hoole et al. (2012) present similar data on release trajectories of velar plosives and intrinsic F0.

Using experimental data of this kind across languages, it is possible to identify what phonetic aspects are under active speaker control.

5 Sources of Phonetic Variation

If the basic vocal tract architecture is shared across humans and is subject to the same physical laws whenever speech occurs, why do phones vary in their phonetic details across languages? The idea that variation exists for essentially random (i.e. unrecoverable) reasons must be kept in mind, but the circular observation that, for example, French and English realizations of the same phone differ because one is French and one is English is unrevealing. Statements like this prevent further questions being asked; arguably the opposite of what scientific study of natural phenomena should be about. Randomess should only be accepted once other systematic sources of variation have been evaluated and excluded.

This section details some causes of systematic phonetic variation across speakers and languages, including a brief discussion of the way that the basic vocal tract architecture is less uniform across races than is implied by the mid-saggital sections presented in textbooks, as well as consideration of long-term variations in air pressure due to altitude. Obviously, any statement about the phonetic patterns of a given language requires generalizations based, usually, on averages calculated over repeated instances of phones in specific contexts in the speech of individual speakers of that language. We should be aware at the outset that no two repetitions of the same phone are ever the same, even by one speaker in one context (see above), and that segmental and prosodic context, speech rate, morphology, etc., all the factors normally controlled for in laboratory experiments, in fact, must be broadly comparable to get a solid basis for a generalization. This section does not cover temporary sources of variation such as elicitation method, speaker posture, menstruation (Wadnerkar et al., 2006), illness, fatigue, intoxication, position of the phone in the breath cycle (Hoit et al., 1993), etc., or of speaker-specific individual differences (see Nolan & Oh, 1996; Nolan, 1997). Also not discussed are lexical effects such as neighbourhood density and lexical frequency (e.g. Scarborough, 2010), or contextual predictability (e.g. Fowler & Housum, 1987; Clopper & Pierrehumbert, 2008); these can all be viewed as changes along a hypoarticulated-hyperarticulated continuum (Lindblom, 1990; and see Cho et al., 2011). All the factors listed above can create measurable phonetic variation and need to be considered or controlled for when interpreting speech data (for excellent overviews of these issues, see chapters in this volume by Tabain, Harrington et al., Knight & Hawkins and Smith).

Speaker sex and age are usually also controlled for in sampling, if possible; these factors may influence biological sources of variation across languages and so they are discussed in more detail below. This subsection deliberately avoids discussion of speakers intentionally creating phonetic patterns for a particular linguistic or socioindexical purpose; these issues are treated in the discussion.

The first section discusses language-specific sources of variation. The second section discusses biological-physical sources of variation.

5.1 Language-specific Variation

There are three main sources of language-specific phonetic variation: systemic constraints, articulatory setting and phonetic fossils.

5.1.1 Systemic or Contrastive Effects

Languages have different phonological systems; they vary in which phonetic contrasts they utilize and how phones are related as systematic variants. These differences can impose different contrastive pressures on phones, and lead to what I have called here 'systemic effects'. For example, the West African language Ewe contrasts two acoustically similar fricatives: bilabial [ɸ] with labiodental [f], as in the words [éɸá] 'he polished' and [éfá] 'he was cold' (Ladefoged, 1968, p. 53). English also exhibits the phone [f], but there is no contrast with [ɸ]. We might reasonably expect that Ewe speakers do their best to keep [ɸ] and [f] distinct, whereas English speakers face no such pressure. Utman and Blumstein (1994) found that Ewe [f] has a higher amplitude of frication than English [f], presumably as a way of maintaining or maximizing the contrast. This idea – that contrasts are dispersed in phonetic space – is perhaps most familiar from studies of vowels (e.g. Liljencrants & Lindblom, 1972) but it also applies to the more obviously multidimensional contrasts seen between consonants.

Other instances of systemic effects with consonants appear in the F2 polarization of liquids in varieties of English, (Carter & Local, 2007), and in place-related differences in fricatives (e.g. Boersma & Hamann, 2008). Lavoie (2002) notes that variation between velar fricatives and plosives is less common in Spanish (which contrasts [x] and [k]) than in American English (which does not). Similarly, Ortega-Llebaría (2004) finds that variation between bilabial fricatives and plosives is less common in English than in Spanish, perhaps because

English has a contrastive [v] which would be similar to a bilabial fricative [β]; tellingly, both languages exhibit the same degree of variation between voiced velar plosives and fricatives, and [ɣ] is not contrastive in either language.

Connell (2002) shows that intrinsic F0 appears to be more constrained in tone languages, not just with low tones, and despite its status as a universal, intrinsic F0 may be suppressed entirely in Mambila, another tone language, for reasons which are unclear. Size of tonal inventory itself does not seem to be a factor, but the nature of the tonal contrasts might be. There could conceivably be a physiological basis for this: Brosnahan, 1961, pp. 80–1 reports that the cricothyroid muscle may be composed of a single muscle in most indigenous Southern Africans, but as two separate muscles in Caucasians and East Asians (Japanese). Until we know more about the mechanisms behind intrinsic F0 and tone production, patterns like this remain difficult to interpret fully. In another case, Van Hoof and Verhoeven (2011) consider the reduced range of intrinsic F0 in Arabic dialects, which have few vowel contrasts, compared with Dutch, which has a large set of vowel contrasts. Here, intrinsic F0 seems to be being augmented to enhance the vowel contrasts of Dutch, especially the low vowels (Van Hoof & Verhoeven, 2011, p. 174; see also Traunmüller, 1981). Future work with languages having smaller vowel inventories could indicate what the 'basic' level of intrinsic F0 is, and to what extent languages co-opt it into their systems of vowel contrast.

Systemic effects on both vowels and consonants play a role in shaping language-specific phonetic variation. Existing contrasts seem able to suppress some patterns of variation, and when a new contrast emerges, systemic effects act to reorganize the system in phonetic space.

5.1.2 Articulatory Setting

One source of phonetic differences across languages may be the default posture of the vocal tract, or (long-term) articulatory setting (Honikman, 1964). The idea of a 'neutral' configuration of the vocal tract is a common one, but impressionistic analyses, now supported by instrumental studies, have indicated that speakers of different languages vary in what is the default or neutral position of the speech organs (Esling, 1978; Stuart-Smith, 1999). Imaging studies (Gick, 2002; Gick et al., 2004) have shown that North American English is characterized by an articulatory setting different from the setting for Canadian French, and within each language male and female speakers also differ (see below on sex differences). Explanations for some segmental patterns may reside in articulatory settings, for example, frication of plosives in Liverpool English could be promoted by the high jaw articulatory setting, although what conditions articulatory setting is itself a mystery. Articulatory setting may also arise as a kind of global systemic effect, if it relates to the average position of the articulators based on type or token frequency (Honikman, 1964; see also French & Stevens, this volume).

5.1.3 Phonetic Fossils

Phonetic fossils can also be seen as a kind of systemic constraint, but they are mentioned last because evidence for them is (so far) limited, and they must be appealed to with caution. The idea is that current patterns of variation might reflect older, fossilized dispersion effects, effects which are no longer required since the system of contrasts has changed. Ladefoged (1984) suggests that some differences in F1 in similar vowel phones in Yoruba and Italian could be due to a 'phonetic fossil' effect of lost vowel contrasts. The dialectal differences in liquid polarization reported in Carter and Local (2007) may owe something to phonetic fossils: Tyneside English is shown to have a liquid polarization pattern of lower F2 in (current) approximant /r/ than in /l/, unlike Leeds English which has the reverse pattern: a higher F2 in /r/ than in /l/. Historically, Tyneside English had a uvular trill (Wells, 1982, p. 374), a sound which seems to show a relatively low F2 (Engstrand et al., 2007). Perhaps the low F2 in Tyneside approximant /r/ occurs because older [ʀ] had a relatively low F2. Phonetic fossils are viable within exemplar approaches to speech representations because phonetic detail is stored (for an overview see Port, 2007). Phonetic fossils may motivate some apparently inexplicable patterns of phonetic variation, but there is a danger that phonetic fossils may be resorted to in the absence of firm evidence. Unless a pattern is attested in related languages or historical records and independent phonetic principles support dispersion, phonetic fossils should not be considered.

5.2 Physical-biological Factors

Three main sources of physical-biological factors on phonetic variation are discussed: biological differences (race, sex, age), altitude effects and cultural effects. As stated above, phones depend on their universal applicability on the shared structures of the human vocal tract, and there is no doubt that in its broad outlines, the human vocal tract is similar across individuals. Individual differences occur, just as they do in the shape and arrangement of features in the human face, but the basic layout is the same. That said, there are systematic variations in vocal tract features across the sexes and across racial groups. There are also changes which take place as speakers age. These differences can impose structure and systematicity on human phonetic variation (see also French & Stevens, this volume).

5.2.1 Race/Ethnicity

Craniofacial differences are apparent across races/ethnic[1] groups (Farkas et al., 2005), and as the face is a forward extension of the vocal tract which includes the lips and nostrils, racial/ethnic differences in vocal tract morphology can be expected. The extent of racial differences on speech production is largely unknown, but some data do exist. Ryalls et al. (1997) report VOT differences between groups labelled 'white' and 'black', with a sex effect also in evidence. These effects could be explained by observations in Hsu et al. (2005, citing also Lee et al., 1997) who present cephalometric data for males and females showing that there are significant differences in some measures such as pharyngeal diameter (Posterior Airway Space) across populations labelled 'South-east Asians', 'Blacks', 'Whites' and 'Hispanics' (Hsu et al., 2005, p. 240). The possibility of language-specific articulatory settings was not controlled for (see above), so it is not certain that these measures reflect purely racial effects, but these observations would predict differences in duration of passive devoicing across the racial groups studied. More speculatively, Ladefoged (1984) suggests that some of the differences in F2 frequencies between Italian and Yoruba could be due to differences in labial profile, and differences in vocal tract musculature have been noted (Brosnahan, 1961, pp. 76–85). Differences in dentition are known to have phonetic effects (e.g. Guay et al., 1978), and while culture may have an effect on dentition (e.g. Brace, 1986), there may are also be genetic factors involved; Proffit (1975) reports greater dental protrusion in Australian Aborigines than in North American Caucasians, and Soh et al. (2005) report that certain malocclusion types differ across (South) East Asians, South Asians (Indians) and Caucasians. Although not necessarily related to racial groups (but see Proffit, 1975), palate shape and height may also have an effect on speech variability (Hiki & Itoh, 1986; Brunner et al., 2009).

5.2.2 Sex

Sex differences between adult males and adult females are perhaps the most well-known biological differences between speakers. As well as an average difference in vocal tract length, there are also differences in proportion; adult males have proportionally larger pharynges than adult females as shown by Fitch and Giedd (1999) in developmental data from an Magnetic Resonance Imaging (MRI) study. Differences in vocal tract sizes and proportions are commonly considered in relation to normalization of vowel formant frequencies (e.g. Adank et al., 2004), but they may also have an effect on vocal tract dynamics (Simpson, 2001, 2002). Differences in pharyngeal volume may explain male-female differences in devoicing of obstruents (e.g. Verhoeven et al., 2011). There are also differences in larynx morphology (Titze, 1989). All these factors presumably underlie not only well-known differences in F0, but also VOT patterns between sexes (Koenig, 2000; Robb et al., 2005; but see Morris et al., 2008).

Sex and race may conspire to create systematic differences. Specifically, the work done on Caucasian vocal tracts by Fitch and Giedd (1999) may not apply to other races. Xue and Hao (2006) present data on both body size and vocal tract dimensions for white Americans, African Americans and Chinese subjects.

Figure 9.1 shows how ratios in body size are relatively constant across the sexes for all three groups, but the ratios for vocal tract sizes differ. While male

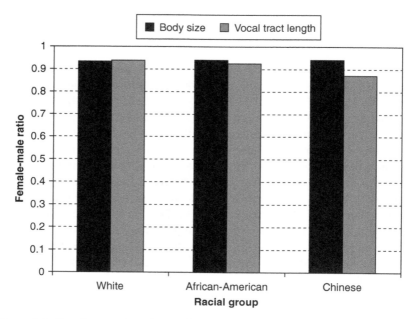

Figure 9.1 Female to male ratios (male = 1) for body size (dark bars) and physical vocal tract length (grey bars) across three racial groups: White Americans, African Americans and Chinese (data from Xue & Hao 2006)

and female Caucasians have almost equal ratios for body-size and vocal tract length, male-female relationships for body size and vocal tract length may vary across races. Chinese females, in particular, have much shorter vocal tracts relative to Chinese males than might be expected given data on male-female relationships in other races. These differences could result in systematic phonetic differences across the sexes. Just where the universal aspect of the human vocal tract might be expected to be felt most – in generating what might be called the *universal uniformity of human hypospeech* (see, for example, Lindblom 1990) – there is likely to be the considerable impact from subtle, but systematic, sex and race differences in vocal tract morphology.

5.2.3 Age
The effects of age are also evident in the growth of the vocal tract (see Fitch & Giedd, 1999), but also in the way that structures and motor control change after puberty and continue to change (e.g. Lee et al., 1999; Xue & Hao, 2003; Torre & Barlow, 2009). The effects here are varied, and involve changes in formant structure, VOT and F0, as well as respiratory effects (see Awan, 2006). Age also affects posture, and so there may be indirect effects on respiratory control (Beck, 2010). Shorter utterances would result in more plosives being produced

towards the end of a breath cycle, with subsequent effects on VOT (Hoit et al., 1993).

5.2.4 Altitude

Languages are spoken in different settings around the world, and as speech is primarily an aerodynamic activity, differences in altitude could potentially have long-term impacts on speech patterns (e.g. Catford, 1997). At sea-level (0 m), atmospheric pressure is around 1,040 cm H_2O, and lung volume must decrease by around 0.19 per cent to maintain voicing. Sana'a in the Yemen is one of the highest cities in the world at around 2,100 m, Quito in Ecuador is even higher at around 2,700 m and La Paz in Bolivia is between 3,000–4,000 m (water boils at 88°C). At the altitude for Sana'a, average atmospheric pressure would be around 802 cm H_2O, in Quito around 744 cm H_2O and in La Paz maximally around 715 cm H_2O. Above sea-level a greater reduction in lung volume is required to create the pressure differential because atmospheric pressure is lower. Estimated reductions in lung volume must be 0.25 per cent in Sana'a, 0.27 per cent in Quito and 0.28 per cent in La Paz; 25 per cent, 35 per cent and 40 per cent greater reductions in lung volume than at sea-level, respectively.[2] Recordings made at different altitudes will show atmospheric pressure effects, and languages spoken at different altitudes may change over time to reflect long-term, average aerodynamic effects on voicing (Catford, 1997). Cho and Ladefoged (1999) compare VOT patterns for Yapese, spoken just above sea-level, with Navajo, (now) spoken at around 1,500 m; any differences could be environmental adaptations, or if the recordings were made in the same environment rather than in the speech community itself, speakers may be adapting 'online' to radically different aerodynamic conditions.

5.2.5 Cultural Body Modifications

Finally, cultural habits may have an effect on the speech apparatus. Cultural practices may involve deliberate changes to the articulators, as in tongue-piercing (Kovacs and Finan, 2006), tongue-splitting (Bressman, 2006) or the insertion of lip-plates (Yigezu, 2002). These practices may be limited to, or more common in, some social groups (Laumann & Derick, 2006) and may provide systematic patterns of variation. Dentition could be affected by cultural practices (Brace, 1986), so that differences could even extend to different classes (e.g. references in Infante, 1975). As angle class II malocclusion also known (somewhat incorrectly) as 'overbite' probably has a 'labiodentalizing' effect on speech posture, it is tempting to consider whether the increase in incidence of so-called labiodental /r/ in British English (Foulkes & Docherty, 2001) can be linked to dentition changes due to increasing affluence in some socio-economic groups. Dentition could account for at least some of the differences in /r/ realizations between British English speaking twins reported in Nolan and Oh (1996).

6 Discussion

This chapter has argued that as speech is physical-biological behaviour subject to the laws of physics and the constraints of shared human vocal tract structures, phonetic universals are to be expected. Paradoxically, as the term *speech science* becomes more widespread as an umbrella term, research in phonetics and related areas is more and more concerned with the linguistic and cognitive aspects of communication, and less and less with the physical and biological basis of speech itself, continuing a trend noted by Ladefoged (1997). Research into the communicative and cognitive aspects of spoken language use is providing fascinating insights into how speakers interact (see chapter by Simpson and by Smith, this volume), but the physical basis of speech should not be forgotten. Attempts to explain speech patterns in purely cognitive terms cannot succeed. If speech production and perception act both as sources of variation for and selection pressures on sound change, creating trends in phonology-phonetic typology, then it is clear that long-term systems of contrast and ephemeral acts of communication are often at odds. Segmentation of the speech stream is not made easier by common phenomena like the simple phonotactics of CV structures, non-peripheral lexical stress and 'resyllabification' of final consonants (when these do occur).

The phone rather than the phoneme was argued briefly to be the object of crosslinguistic comparison, with contrastive positions or the realizations of Distinctive Features also being possible objects of comparison, usually also related to phones. When seen from a mathematical-phonological perspective, phonetic variation is considerable, but when a biological-phonetic stance is taken, variation is expected. If all the possible influences are taken into account, it is perhaps more surprising that phonetic variation is so constrained that similar patterns arise crosslinguistically as often as they do (Blevins, 2008; Hyman, 2008). Similarly, uncontrolled speech is predictably subject to multiple sources of variation. The fact that laboratory speech can be so uniform is nothing less than amazing in the face of the aerodynamic and physical factors acting on it, all the more so if speech targets are computed 'at random' over phonetically detailed exemplars (Pierrehumbert, 2001, 2002; Kirchner et al., 2010; see also Ernestus, 2012).

Just as with colour categorization, there may be more of a universalist flavour to crosslinguistic uses of phonetic possibilities than is commonly assumed (Pierrehumbert et al., 2000, p. 284). The role of universalist factors such as the racial and population genetics of iris colour, iris size and macular pigmentation (Woo & Lee, 2002; Dain et al., 2004), as well as biogeographical effects of latitude, habitat and sunlight exposure (Reimchen, 1987; Laeng et al., 2007) may nudge crosslinguistic colour perception in particular directions (Bornstein, 1973). It would not be surprising if similar pressures were found in phonetics due to differences in, for example, vocal tract dimensions, articulator musculature or altitude (see also Ladd et al., 2008). Combined with systemic pressures to facilitate contrast, much variation could be non-random. The universal uniformity of hypospeech may be given subtle twists by sex and race differences.

Universals can help to explain and add perspectives to patterns seen in speech data, as well as typological patterns (Ohala, 1983) and patterns seen in hypospeech (Barry & Andreeva, 2001; see also Maddieson, 1997). The chapter presented an overview of some of the sources of systematic variation which can be identified, focusing mainly on language-specific factors such as systemic constraints, articulatory setting and phonetic fossils, as well as physical-biological effects such as race, sex, age, altitude and culture. Not all investigations of systemic constraints have shown the expected results; Manuel (1990) did not find the expected pattern of vowel-to-vowel coarticulation in Shona, and Bradlow (1995) did not find greater dispersion in the larger American English than in the smaller Spanish vowel inventory. Manuel's data could be explained in terms of the actual vowel qualities found, as she herself notes, or the existence of 'phonetic fossils' (Ladefoged, 1984); sound changes to the vowel system may have left trace patterns of variation. In the case of Bradlow, the results could be partially due to a pharyngeal articulatory setting (reported for Canadian English in Gick et al., 2004), which would have the effect of raising F1 and lowering F2, reducing the spread of the vowel space. Similarly, differences in coarticulation such as those noted for Amharic and Navajo [ʃ] in Ladefoged (1984) could be systemic in origin: Navajo has a larger inventory of fricative contrasts (McDonough & Ladefoged, 1993) than Amharic (Hayward & Hayward, 1999). This is not to say that effects which are essentially random do not occur, for example, articulatory setting itself may be something which is hard to explain fully, but considerable evidence exists to suggest that at least some crosslinguistic differences are non-random. As some patterns can be explained, phoneticians need to consider all possibilities before admitting defeat in the search for a systematic explanation.

This chapter has been concerned with phonetic sources of variability, not with sound change itself, and it has not dealt with the kind of traditional categorical phenomena seen in the sociolinguistic transmission and adoption of variables across social groups. In recent times, a discipline calling itself 'sociophonetics' has arisen which uses instrumental phonetic techniques to investigate patterns of variability (e.g. Foulkes et al., 2010; Di Paolo & Yaeger-Dror, 2011; Thomas, 2011). This discipline is, in my opinion, still positioning itself between a methodological update of sociolinguistics (i.e. sociolinguistics with spectrograms), and something more phonetic which considers the mechanisms for and origins of variability, as well as correlations with social groups. Traditional sociolinguistics considers the spread of a pre-existing variable, not how the phonetic characteristics of that variable come into being. This view persists in some valuable recent additions to the sociophonetic canon. In their

The Bloomsbury Companion to Phonetics

study of sexual orientation on vowel production, Pierrehumbert et al. (2004) take it as read that targets already exist for lesbian, bisexual and gay (LBG) speech. Their study, quite legitimately, does not concern itself with where the LBG target forms might come from, but for sociophonetics as a discipline, questions about origins do matter. Can speakers spontaneously create variation to serve a particular function, or do they adapt what is already there (its existence remaining to be explained in a more phonetic way)? The problems in acquiring a native-like accent in a second language suggest that even if speech patterns are not completely inflexible, radical adaptations are severely constrained, and crosslinguistic studies do not show as much categorical phonetic variation as we might expect if speakers really did have free rein to generate completely new phonetic patterns and hybridize old ones. Too much teleology is unwelcome in the search for explanations because it stops us asking questions.

As phones are subject to so many influences – in addition, it must be emphasized, to subsegmental implementation errors and measurement errors – the status of phonetic variation must be carefully considered before it can be judged to be 'intentional', or part of a speaker's target. Work done by Solé and Ohala (2012), among others, has shown that careful experimental studies can indicate whether an effect is controlled by the speaker or not. Importantly, such research cuts both ways: widespread patterns do arise in vocal tract constraints, but the size of the 'default' patterns cannot be estimated without further experimentation. This work shows that over time, universalist tendencies can become systematized and augmented, such as intrinsic F0 or vowel height duration effects, and indeed, the absence of any sociolinguistic patterns (to the best of my knowledge) in which men consistently have higher F0 than women suggests that variation evolves from lawful phonetic mutations. More detailed instrumental analyses place variation under the spotlight, and exemplar models incorporate phonetic detail into representations. The challenge for phoneticians is to combine an understanding of universalist and language-specific pressures in accounting for variation.

Notes

1. The term race is problematic in biology and anthropology, but seems established in areas like forensic osteology which are most appropriate to phonetics. As the term ethnicity may refer to a social construct, race is probably to be preferred.
2. These calculations are for illustrative purposes and assume that speakers do not actively modify vocal fold tension or other speech parameters, and that the temperature, humidity and density of the air is constant (which cannot be the case). They also assume that the two cm H_2O pressure differential is required to overcome constant elastic tension forces in the vocal folds, and that the air mass above the vocal folds is not a factor. In practice, altitude will have very complex effects.

10 Spontaneous Speech

Adrian P. Simpson

Chapter Overview

---

1 Introduction

Spontaneous speech is unscripted speech planned and produced by a speaker in real time in response to immediate needs. The most common form of spontaneous speech is conversation, and it is this form of spontaneous speech which represents the 'most natural, the most frequent, and the most widespread occurrences of spoken language' (Abercrombie, 1965, p. 3). By contrast, spoken prose, that is, reading texts out loud, only plays a significant role in particular professionals, for example, acting, newsreading, etc. More than 70 years ago Firth made the following comment about conversation: 'Neither linguists nor psychologists have begun the study of conversation, but it is here we shall find the key to a better understanding of what language really is and how it works' (Firth, 1935, p. 71).

However, it took several decades before phoneticians began to take this statement seriously. Halliday's (1967) description of intonation patterns in British English or Hurford's (1968a, b, 1969, 1970) detailed phonetic analysis of Cockney English are early examples of conversations providing data for phonetic analysis.

Given the ubiquity of spontaneous speech and the early recognition by a prominent linguist such as Firth of the significance of the study of conversation, it may seem somewhat surprising that even today investigations in many areas of phonetic research analyse spoken language which has been elicited from subjects reading texts out loud. There are two main reasons for this practice. The first is the lack of controllability. The ability to make reliable statistical statements generally requires a robust experimental design providing repeated tokens of the same expression being produced in the same context, for example, 'Say WORD again' (see, for example, Tabain, and Knight & Hawkins, this volume). By contrast, naturally occurring conversations never produce comparability of this type. The other reason, which has perhaps lost some credibility in recent years, is the contention that conversation is too complicated or messy (Lass, 1984, p. 294) to be analysed in its own right. Indeed, some analysts still insist that the patterns of read speech are representative of the patterns found in the conversation, obviating the need for collecting it.[1]

In this chapter, we will look at spontaneous speech from different perspectives. We will examine the methods that have been used to elicit spontaneous speech, the patterns that characterize it setting it apart from other types of speech such as spoken prose and we will take a critical look at some of the explanations that have been proposed to account for the patterns.

2 Eliciting Spontaneous Speech and Spontaneous Speech Databases

Although we are literally surrounded by spontaneous speech every day of our lives, collecting it in an ethically sound fashion, that is, not making illicit recordings, while at the same time maintaining naturalness and spontaneity can be difficult. Analysts have come up with different methods of collecting spontaneous speech, often consciously sacrificing one aspect in favour of another.

One common source of material for studies examining phonetic aspects of conversational structure is from telephone calls, recorded either with the prior consent of the speakers or else in the public domain, for example, radio phone-ins. In the CALLHOME corpora (e.g. Canavan et al., 1997) which contain telephone conversations from speakers of American English, German, Mandarin Chinese, Arabic, Japanese and Spanish, subjects were able to make a free 30-minute telephone call with a friend or relative in return for having the call recorded. The analysis of voice quality in Finnish talk-in-interaction by Ogden (2001) is an example of material taken from radio phone-ins. An analyst using telephone material is accepting poor auditory quality in return for a high degree of naturalness. It should be added, however, that one of the main aims of many larger databases, such as the CALLHOME corpora, is not to carry out phonetic analysis, but rather to train automatic speech recognizers on telephone quality speech.

In an attempt to counteract the lack of comparability and repetition, researchers have come up with different techniques to maintain spontaneity

Table 10.1 Selection of corpora containing different types of spontaneous speech from different languages

Corpus	Language	URL
Buckeye Corpus	American English	www.buckeyecorpus.osu.edu/
IViE Corpus	British & Irish English	www.phon.ox.ac.uk/IViE/
CLIPS	Italian	www.clips.unina.it/
AVIP-API	Italian	www.parlaritaliano.it/parlare/visualizza_prog.php?idp=59
CORP-ORAL	Portuguese	www.iltec.pt/spock/
BEA	Hungarian	www.nytud.hu/adatb/bea/index.html

(not naturalness) while at the same time retaining some control over the content. Levelt (1983, 1989) elicited spontaneous monologues to study speech planning by requiring subjects to describe the path through a network of coloured shapes, for example, brown square, blue circle. The 'map task' (Anderson et al., 1991) is still a commonly used scenario for the controlled elicitation of spontaneous dialogues and has been successfully used to record spontaneous data from a number of languages. Two subjects each receive a simple map containing a number of landmarks. The maps differ, however. One contains a path around the landmarks which one subject must then describe to the other. The subjects also notice during the ensuing dialogue that there are slight differences in the landmarks present on each map. Names of locations on the map are often specially constructed to elicit patterns such as place assimilation in consonants, for example, 'yacht club', 'telephone box'. Both the network of shapes and the 'map task' elicit spontaneous speech with structures and content that are repeated across different recordings, thus providing a degree of repetition and comparability. However, the artificiality of the recording set-up and the control imposed by the material have led some analysts studying the phonetic organization of conversation to question these techniques and, as a consequence, also the validity of the conversational material they produce (Local, 2003a, p. 117).

Another common method of eliciting unscripted spontaneous speech from a speaker is to have the analyst acting as an interviewer guiding the subject to talk about different subjects. Examples of corpora elicited using this method are the *Buckeye Corpus* (Pitt et al., 2005) of American English and the *Hungarian Spontaneous Speech Corpus BEA* (Gósy & Horváth, 2010).

Recent years have seen the collection of spontaneous speech corpora in a number of languages using different amounts of control over the elicitation process. Although many databases have to be purchased, several databases are free following simple registration or can be accessed directly. Table 10.1 contains a small selection of free databases illustrating some of the languages available.

3 Phonetic Patterns of Spontaneous Speech

We only have to listen carefully to a few utterances extracted from a conversation to confirm that there are a number of differences between the pronunciation of a word in spontaneous speech and the pronunciation of the same word spoken in isolation. In this section we will describe some of these patterns illustrating them with concrete conversational extracts from data the reader can access her/himself.

A common way of describing the patterns in spontaneous speech is to compare the phonetic shape of a spontaneous token of a word with its phonetic shape when spoken in isolation, also known as the citation form. Although intuitively appealing, this method is not unproblematic and I will return to some of the theoretical problems below. However, for the time being, as a descriptive point of departure for describing some of the phenomena found in spontaneous speech it will suffice.

Many of the phonetic patterns found in spontaneous speech are described as consonant or vowel reduction. In other words, in comparison with the phonetic shape of the citation form, the phonetic shapes of the spontaneous speech token are somehow reduced. A reduced vowel can have a shorter duration and be produced with a tongue position that is less peripheral in the vowel space than the form spoken in isolation. A reduced consonant can also be shorter than its citation form counterpart. A reduction of tongue movement for a consonant can give rise to a different manner of articulation. So, for instance, if the top and bottom lip do not make sufficient contact to bring about the complete closure for a bilabial plosive [b], then a bilabial fricative [β] or an approximant will be the result.

The most extreme form of reduction is *elision*: a vowel or consonant in the citation form is no longer present in a spontaneous speech token. In Germanic languages such as English or German that have relatively complex syllable structures, alveolar/dental plosives in a syllable coda containing more than one consonant are particularly subject to elision. Unsurprisingly, it is vowels in unstressed syllables which are most likely to be elided. In some cases, the elision of a vowel can lead to the loss of a syllable. However, if the syllable contains a sonorant consonant such as a nasal or a lateral approximant, syllabicity may be carried by the consonant.

Several examples of consonant elision are contained in a conversational extract taken from the IViE corpus (Grabe et al., 2001) shown in Figure 10.1. The extract has been segmented and labelled to indicate the lexical and phonetic content of the extract. A first approximation at the citation form phonetics of this extract would be [ɪtsɪmɪdʒdʒʌstwɛntʌp]. As we can see, the transcription of the spectrogram differs significantly at various points from the citation form representation. There is no alveolar plosive in 'its'. Instead of a post-alveolar affricate

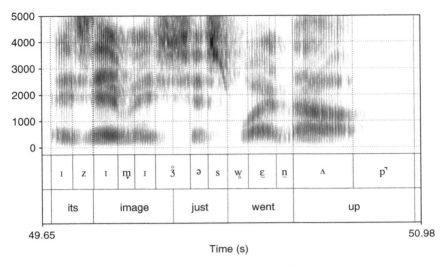

Figure 10.1 Spectrogram and aligned transcription of the excerpt *its image just went up* from the IViE corpus (f4cma.wav)

at the offset of 'image' and the onset of 'just' there is just a stretch of unvoiced post-alveolar friction. And there is no alveolar plosive at the end of 'just'.

Elision is often seen as the most extreme type of *lenition* or weakening. Lenition refers to a range of consonantal reduction patterns in which some aspect of the articulation or the voicing of a consonant in the spontaneous speech form of a word appears weaker than it is in the corresponding citation form.

One of the most common lenition patterns is described under *fricativization* or *spirantization*. Instead of the stricture of complete closure of the plosive found in the citation form, the spontaneous speech token has a stricture of close or open approximation, in other words a fricative or approximant. Whether we find a fricative or approximant depends on a number of factors involving stricture size, amount of airflow and place of articulation. So, for instance, incomplete closure of the lips for a voiced bilabial plosive in the citation form is most likely to result in an approximant. This is because the relatively weak airflow combined with stricture at the lips that offers no downstream obstacle to the airflow provide poor conditions for making the airflow turbulent. By contrast, the open glottis and the upper teeth acting as an obstacle to the airflow just behind the stricture in a fricativized alveolar voiceless plosive in a word such as *butter* create ideal conditions for a strong fricative. Fricativization or spirantization of plosives is commonly found intervocalically, both within but also across word boundaries. The final stage of this type of weakening, before elision, may take the form of a change in vowel quality. For instance, in German, a possible realization of the conjunction *aber* 'but' ([ʔaːbɐ] in isolation) is as a triphthong

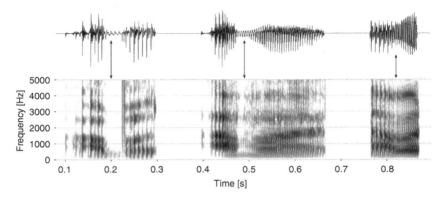

Figure 10.2 Sound pressure waves and spectrograms of three tokens of the German conjunction *aber* from the Kiel Corpus of Spontaneous Speech (g373a008, g414a008, g252a008). The arrows indicate the approximate location of the bilabial stricture

with frictionless approximation of the lips between the vowels of the first and second syllables. Figure 10.2 shows three tokens of the word *aber* from the *Kiel Corpus of Spontaneous Speech* (IPDS 1995–7). The arrows indicate the location of the intervocalic bilabial stricture. In the first token energy is only present in the lower part of the spectrum, in other words the speaker produced a voiced bilabial plosive. In the second token, a clear formant structure is present throughout the bilabial stricture, but the sound pressure wave shows marked attenuation, indicating that a relatively narrow bilabial stricture has been attained. The downward movement of all formants towards the middle of the stretch shown in the third token also indicate that the lips are approximated, but, by contrast to the second token, the attenuation of the sound pressure wave during this approximation is much less than it was in the second token, suggesting a sound sequence perhaps best described as a triphthong.

A further case of articulatory lenition is *debuccalization*. This refers to the loss of the oral, articulatory component of an obstruent, leaving behind only the glottal component. A frequent pronunciation of the phrase *I think is* [aɪhɪŋk] or [aɪfɪŋk]. In other words, the oral gesture – apico-dental stricture of close approximation – is absent and only the glottal opening gesture remains, giving rise to a glottal fricative, which in turn may still be voiced, that is, [aɪɦɪŋk].

Lenition affects not only the oral component of an obstruent, but can also affect the state of the glottis. Voicing or sonorization refers to the voicing of an obstruent, which in the citation form is voiceless, and occurs in a voiced environment, for example, intervocalically.

Flapping / tapping[2] represents the lenition of both the oral, articulatory as well as the glottal, phonatory component. An intervocalic apical plosive [t, d] in a citation form pronunciation is a voiced tap in the spontaneous speech form. This combines *voicing* with the reduction of a stop gesture to the ballistic gesture of a tap. For example, we might find a voiced tap intervocalically in *what I* [wɒraɪ].

Vowel reduction can take a number of shapes. Reduction can involve a reduction in vowel duration in an otherwise long vowel, the vowel quality found in the spontaneous speech form can be less peripheral (closer to the centre of the vowel space) than the corresponding vowel in the citation form and an otherwise rounded vowel can become less rounded or completely unrounded. In English several grammatical items, such as determiners, pronouns, prepositions have established reduced forms, more commonly known as weak forms, for example, *to* has the weak forms [tʊ] and [tə] depending on the following syllable beginning with a vowel or a consonant, respectively. Lists of the strong and weak forms in English are an indispensable part of any introduction to English phonetics (e.g. Gimson, 1975, pp. 261ff).

Fortition is the opposite of lenition and describes articulatory or phonatory strengthening of consonants. Glottal closure accompanying the oral closure of a plosive in syllable final position in certain varieties of English has often been treated as a glottal 'reinforcement' of a stop and, hence, as a form of fortition (see Lodge, 1984 for examples of this from a number of varieties of English). Likewise, the devoicing of a voiced fricative in an unexpected position, such as the voiced environment between two vowels, may also be treated as fortition.

4 Non-linear Patterns

Although the instances of reduction we have looked at so far may seem fairly straightforward, it is less easy to see exactly how some of the patterns in spontaneous speech relate to the citation form phonetics, or more accurately, how much and in what way the phonetic correlates of the different phonological units are involved. Figures 10.1 and 10.3 contain examples which can only be reasonably interpreted if we assume that the phonetic correlates of two or more phonological elements are in complete or partial temporal overlap. Consider first the stretches of creaky voice in 'went' in Figure 10.1 and 'get this' in Figure 10.3. When you listen to these stretches you will have little trouble recognizing the words 'went' or 'get' and, what's more, also acknowledging that each has a 't' at the end. However, phonetically speaking they do not. In both cases the phonetic correlate of /t/ is a stretch of creaky voice which overlaps the vocalic portion of 'get' and 'went' as well as the dental approximant at the beginning of 'that' and the nasal of 'went'. The phonetic shape of the pronoun 'you' in Figure 10.3 is a further example. The weak form of 'you' as [jə] is well-known as it has even found its way into written English in forms such as 'gotcha', but in Figure 10.3 'you' is realized as nothing more than a close front spread vowel [j], which can be interpreted as being the frontness and palatality of [j] blending with syllabicity.

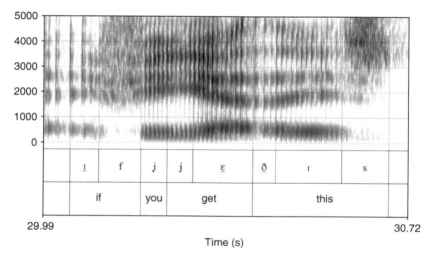

Figure 10.3 Spectrogram and aligned transcription of the excerpt *if you get this* from the IViE corpus (f1cma.wav)

An example of patterns extending over two or more syllables is described in Simpson (1992, 2001, 2006). Unsurprisingly, spontaneous Suffolk English exhibits many of the patterns of lenition already described. However, Simpson found for one female speaker of Suffolk English that an apparently disparate array of lenition types (tapping, fricativization, etc.) was in fact part of a larger pattern which involves a restriction on the occurrence of glottalization in two or more adjacent syllables. So, for instance, words such as *look, keep, put*, can have final glottalization with or without an oral consonantal stricture: [ki:ʔ(p), gɛʔ, lʊʔ(k)]. However, when followed by the pronoun *it* or the preposition *at*, glottalization is absent. Instead, we find an oral stricture of complete closure or close approximation which is either voiced or voiceless, for example, *keep it, get it, look it* [ki:ɸəʔ, gɛɾəʔ, lʊxəʔ]. Simpson called this the *glottal piece* and showed that this pattern can extend at least up to three syllables, for example, *look at it* [lʊgæːɾəʔ], where only the final *it* closes with glottalization.

Brown (1981) and Shockey (2003) contain a large number of examples of the patterns of reduction found in spontaneous speech. Kohler and Simpson (2001) contains a number of papers illustrating phonetic patterns in spontaneous speech from a number of mainly Indo-European languages.

5 Explaining the Patterns

Describing the phonetic patterns of spontaneous speech is one step. Explaining why the patterns are the way they are is a more complex problem, in other words, what reasons do speakers have for producing different phonetic shapes for the same lexical item?

The first explanation often offered for reduction is in terms of *ease of articulation*. Reductions represent a decrease in the amount of time and effort that a speaker puts into articulation. However, ease of articulation itself puts no limits on when and how a speaker can reduce. The H and H theory proposed in Lindblom (1983, 1990) sees ease of articulation as one factor shaping the phonetic output of a speaker. 'H and H' describes two ends of a speaker's articulatory continuum, between careful, slow, maximally clear hyperarticulation and fast, reduced hypoarticulation. Just like other animals, human beings strive to minimize energy consumption by optimizing the movements needed for a particular activity. Lindblom sees this as being as relevant for articulatory movements during speech as it is for the whole body movements of a horse cantering or galloping. Speakers can optimize speech movements either by reducing the size of individual movements, or even by getting rid of them altogether. The patterns described above (apart from fortition) can all be seen as examples of such optimizing reductions. So, for instance, if we reduce the size of a gesture for a bilabial plosive so that the lips no longer close completely, the result is a bilabial fricative or approximant. Likewise the pronunciation of the relative pronoun *that* with a central mid-vowel quality [ðət] rather than a more open quality [ðat] can be seen as a reduction in the size of the vowel gesture. However, merely stating that the size and number of articulatory gestures can be reduced puts no limits on the amount of reduction. The H and H theory sees an utterance as being the product of a speaker optimizing his speech movements to minimize energy consumption (*system-oriented*), while at the same producing a phonetic signal which can be understood (*output-oriented*) given the communicative situation. Each utterance, then, is the result of a compromise between these two opposing forces (system- and output-orientation) at work in every communicative situation, as well as at different places within individual utterances. In each communicative situation a speaker makes assumptions about the linguistic and extralinguistic knowledge shared with the other interlocutors. Different communicative situations put different demands on speakers and hearers and offer widely differing opportunities for clarifying misunderstandings. And within individual utterances there are large differences in predicting what is coming next. Consider the probability of correctly predicting the word *nine* in the sentences *The next word is . . .* and *A stitch in time saves . . .* (Lindblom, 1990, p. 405, from Lieberman, 1963). In the first sentence, *nine* is unpredictable and the hearer must rely exclusively on the signal, that is, phonetic information to decode the word. By contrast, a speaker of English familiar with the saying will be predicting *nine* probably from shortly after *stitch* has been interpreted, and the phonetics has little contribution to make.

Concrete examples of different communicative situations will make the different factors influencing system- and output-orientation clearer. First, consider a conversation between two people who grew up in the same village and have been good friends for 30 years. There will be a great deal of overlap in the linguistic and extralinguistic knowledge they share. In the context of a conversation between them, any misunderstandings which occur can be clarified immediately. The H and H theory would predict that such interlocutors can be maximally system-oriented, producing speech at the hypoarticulated end of the continuum. At the other extreme, a radio or television presenter attempting to convey complex news content is talking to an audience varying widely in linguistic background. More importantly, any misunderstandings cannot be directly clarified. H and H theory would predict that a newsreader can be maximally output-oriented, producing careful, slow hyperarticulated speech.

An important conclusion to draw from H and H theory is that although it offers an explanation for reduction, it does not predict that spontaneous speech itself should be more reduced than, say, a more formal speech style, such as newsreading. In fact, analysts have as yet been unable to show that many of those patterns described as reductions do actually represent a reduction in articulatory effort. This is simply because it is still not possible to measure directly the amount of effort or energy that goes into the short and small muscular contractions producing a single sound. Instead, analysts rely on calculations made in computer models which attempt to simulate articulatory movements (e.g. Browman & Goldstein, 1989; Kirchner, 1998). While it has been possible to show that certain reduced sounds require less effort within such models, one common lenition type in which a stop becomes a fricative raises problems (Simpson, 2001, 2007). Essentially, there are two fricatives which can arise from a plosive. In the first, the articulatory target is a plosive, but temporal constraints might mean that movement towards the plosive is curtailed and complete closure between the articulators is not made. This fricative will also be shorter than a plosive would have been and the reduced articulation will be correctly modelled. Consider, however, how to model the second type of fricative. The second fricative is one which has become established and can no longer be treated as a reduced plosive, although it may alternate with plosive allophones. A prevalent example of such an alternation in Southern Standard British English (SSBE) is the range of allophones of /t/, which for some speakers is a strongly affricated plosive at syllable onset and coda, but an apical fricative intervocalically. Figure 10.4 shows two tokens of the word *fourteen*. In the token on the left *four'teen*, the arrow points to an affricated plosive, whereas in a token of *'fourteen* on the right, we can see that there is only a period of frication between the two vowels. There is no evidence, such as duration or alternation with a plosive in the same context, that the speaker intends anything other than a fricative in such contexts. Ironically, such a fricative, although possibly the product of a reduction originally, can be shown to require more effort than the corresponding plosive because the fricative

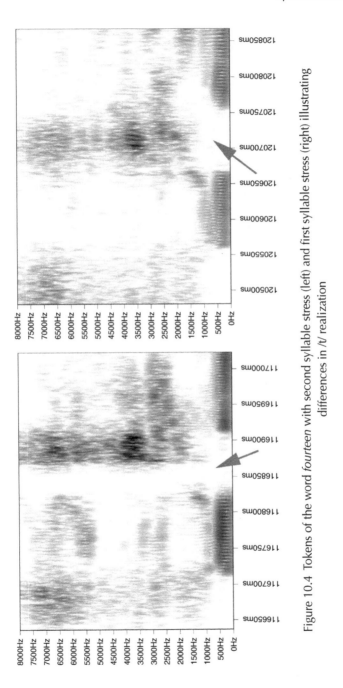

Figure 10.4 Tokens of the word *fourteen* with second syllable stress (left) and first syllable stress (right) illustrating differences in /t/ realization

stricture of close approximation requires more careful articulatory control to create and maintain a narrow stricture.

A further approach to accounting for reduction, related to H and H theory, is usage-based (e.g. Bybee, 2001; Pierrehumbert, 2001). Put simply, a usage-based model predicts that a word will be more subject to reductions such as lenition, assimilation, deletion, etc. than another word if it is used more frequently. Bybee (2001, pp. 41ff), citing an earlier experiment (Hooper, 1976), describes differences in the phonetic shape of the words *every*, *memory* and *mammary*. She shows that tokens of a frequently used word such as *every* are always disyllabic [ɛvɹi], whereas a less frequent item, such as *mammary* is always realized trisyllabically: [maməɹi]. Between these two extremes are tokens of a word like *memory* – less frequent than *every*, more frequent than *mammary* – being realized both di- and trisyllabically: [mɛmɹi, mɛmᵊɹi]. A usage-based model also predicts that a single speaker using a particular word more frequently than others will produce them more reduced. The director of the British Museum in London, Neil MacGregor, narrating the BBC Radio 4 series *A History of the World* is a good example of this. Unsurprisingly, tokens of the adjective *British* are very frequent for this speaker and accordingly are subject to strong reduction sound monosyllabic: [bɹɪʒʃ] (the two fricative symbols represent portion fricative starting voiced then becoming voiceless).

6 Phonetic Organization of Conversation

In the previous sections I have described a number of phonetic patterns which are commonly found in spontaneous speech. However, these patterns do not define spontaneous speech to the exclusion of speech from other linguistic activities and it is possible to find many of the patterns of reduction described above in spoken prose, such as the text read out by radio and television journalists. But there are a number of phonetic patterns which characterize speech that is produced in real time in response to immediate communicative needs, and set it apart from other types of speech.

At first sight, a conversation between two people might just seem to be a simple exchange of utterances: first one person talks, then the other. However, studies over the last 30 years, mainly on different varieties of English, but also on other languages, such as German, Finnish and Japanese, have shown that speakers employ a number of phonetic devices to organize different aspects of a conversation. The study of the phonetics of talk-in-interaction has become an established and independent area of phonetic research (e.g. Local et al., 1986; Local & Walker, 2005). Talk-in-interaction combines detailed auditory and acoustic phonetic analysis with the type of conversational analysis that originated in sociology in the 1960s (Sacks et al., 1974; Sacks, 1992).

Here is a small selection of the interactional functions that participants in a conversation have been found to carry out using phonetic means:

(1) Signal to other participants that you are completing your turn at talk.
(2) Continue to talk although a turn may look as though it is grammatically finished.
(3) Compete for a turn, in other words two people trying to talk at once.
(4) Hold the floor (prevent others from talking) although you are not actually saying anything yourself.
(5) Repair mistakes – sometimes you will notice that something has come out wrong or you want to reformulate.
(6) Search for the next word – when you start talking you may not have planned everything you want to say and may have to stall and search for a word.

Many of the phonetic means used to signal these different interactional functions are generally classified as prosodic or suprasegmental: pitch, loudness, voice quality, tempo, length, vowel quality. Let us consider a couple of these functions beginning with the first: turn-completion. Intuitively, one may think that a turn at talk is completed by producing something which is grammatically complete, for example, the end of a sentence, and stopping talking. And in many cases, this is certainly the case. However, it has been shown that a number of phonetic features can accompany turn-completion: decreasing tempo, reduction in volume, breathy or creaky voice quality of voiced segments and the centralization of vowel quality (e.g. Local & Kelly, 1986; Local et al., 1986). But how do we know that these features are actually fulfilling an interactional function? The main way this is done is to look at the way participants in a conversation behave. In this case, a speaker producing this bundle of features invariably stops talking, but, perhaps more importantly, another speaker will begin his/her turn immediately after the other speaker has stopped. In fact, turn transition may be produced with a slight overlap. In other words, an incoming speaker may begin a new turn a few syllables before the other has completed his/her turn. The overlap is of particular interest because it seems to indicate that the first speaker is signalling that the end is near, before s/he is finished, and also that the other participant is making use of this information.

This interpretation is supported by the recurrence of systematic bundles of phonetic events at other places in conversations. We have just described some of the patterns that occur when a turn is completed. But what happens when a speaker reaches a point in his/her turn that is syntactically complete, but s/he wants to continue with his/her turn, that is, s/he wants to signal that this is not a point where s/he would like someone else to begin a turn? Perhaps not unsurprisingly, a speaker will not slow down, become quieter, etc., but instead 'rush through' (this is the technical term) a major syntactic boundary (e.g. between two sentences) increasing tempo and without pausing (Walker, 2003) as well as failing to produce certain segmental patterns that would be present turn-finally, such as aspirated plosive release.

Interviews between politicians and journalists often provide good examples of what happens when two speakers compete for the next turn at talk. Figure 10.5 shows the sound pressure wave of an excerpt from an interview between the former British prime minister Gordon Brown and the moderator of BBC Radio 4's *Woman's Hour* Jane Garvey. The two arrows indicate points in the dialogue at which both participants compete for the turn to talk. At such points, speakers become louder, pitch goes up and tempo increases. While it is not possible to see changes in pitch or tempo in the sound pressure wave, the abrupt change in amplitude of the sound pressure wave is a direct consequence of an increase in loudness. However, as soon as one of the speakers has 'won', there is a return to normal pitch, tempo and loudness levels.

One early study illustrating the phonetic intricacy of turn-holding and turn-completion is Local and Kelly (1986). In a non-phonetic analysis, Jefferson (1983) showed that conjunctions, such as *but, and,* etc. seemed to mark possible points of turn transition, or lack of transition. Local and Kelly were able to show that there were systematic differences in the phonetic shape of the conjunction prior to a pause, but crucially, that the pause itself was articulated differently. Some pauses began with a closed glottis and ended with the release of the glottal closure, and it was this type of pause that was least likely to correlate with turn transition, in other words the pausing speaker wanted to continue his/her turn and the other participants, by usually not talking, seemed to be attending to this feature.

Finally, another feature which sets spontaneous speech apart from read speech is dysfluencies. The complex task of planning and producing speech

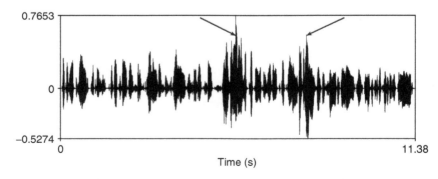

Figure 10.5 Sound-pressure wave of an excerpt from an interview between the former British prime minister Gordon Brown and a presenter of BBC Radio 4's *Woman's Hour*

subject to immediate demands means that spontaneous speech contains many dysfluencies. A speaker may have problems finding the right lexical item or discover while monitoring his/her own speech output that a mistake has been made, ranging from the wrong choice of word to a prosodic error such as false placement of a word accent (Levelt, 1983). Speakers have different strategies for signalling such problems. Lexical search problems can be signalled in English and other languages with a hesitation particle comprising a vowel or a vowel-nasal sequence. Often indicated in written English with *uh* or *uhm*, the range of vowel qualities used is both language- and speaker-specific (Levelt, 1989; Pätzold & Simpson, 1995; Shriberg, 2001). Another way of indicating lexical search difficulties is by lengthening a vowel or consonant directly prior to a pause (Shriberg, 2001). Here, too, it has become clear that the ways in which participants in a conversation deal with dysfluencies is orderly.

Two very good collections of studies illustrating the phonetic patterns associated with different interactional functions from a range of different languages are Couper-Kuhlen and Selting (1996) and Couper-Kuhlen and Ford (2004).

7 Conclusion

This chapter has examined some of the phonetic patterns of spontaneous speech. We have seen that although a number of segmental patterns of reduction are very common in spontaneous speech they by no means define spontaneous speech to the exclusion of other types of speech such as spoken prose. Only when we look at the way speakers employ different phonetic means to organize the most common form of spontaneous speech, conversation, do patterns occur which are exclusive to spontaneous speech.

Notes

1. 'The comparison of the alignment of the F0 minimum in the dialog speech from the Map Task with the results of Study I gives us no reason to think that the read speech data from Study I are phonetically unrepresentative of what happens in natural interaction. On the contrary, it lends plausibility to the assumption that read speech can be used as a source of evidence in experimental work that addresses phonological and phonetic questions. Indeed, it suggests that it makes practical sense to study the phonetic and phonological issues on the basis of controlled speech materials, rather than recording natural conversations and hoping for the occurrence of appropriate utterances' (Lickley et al., 2005, p. 179).
2. Often tapping and flapping are used as interchangeable equivalents. However, strictly speaking a flap describes a transitory gesture of the tongue tip or the bottom lip which begins in one place and comes to rest in another. So, for instance, [ɽ] describes a retroflex flap: starting from somewhere behind the alveolar ridge, the tongue tip makes passing contact with the roof of the mouth somewhere between the front of the hard palate and the alveolar ridge before coming to rest on the floor of the mouth.

11 Clinical Phonetics

*Tom Starr-Marshall, Susanna Martin
and Rachael-Anne Knight*

---

1 Introduction

Clinical phonetics is the study of the sounds of non-typical speech, and their comparison with those found in normal speech. Thus it covers the speech of both children and adults and includes a wide range of speech disorders, both developmental and acquired. The preponderance of speech work, however, is carried out in paediatric settings, so child speech disorders will be our focus here. In the clinical setting, knowledge of phonetics (and phonology) is crucial for the assessment of clients, for classification and diagnosis and for choice of intervention.

2 Assessment

The main aim of assessment is to discover if a client has a speech difficulty and, if so, the nature of that difficulty, so that an appropriate programme of remedial intervention can be devised.

When assessing speech, clinicians have many choices, including whether to use perceptual or instrumental methods. Perceptual methods of assessment are most typically used (certainly in relation to child speech), and involve clinicians using their own perception (i.e. hearing and vision) to make judgements about an individual's speech such as which sounds are produced and the degree of intelligibility (Kent, 1996). Opinion is divided on the use of instrumental assessments in general clinical work. However, electropalatography is regularly used at centres which specialize in Childhood Apraxia of Speech. Laryngography, stroboscopy and programmes for voice analysis are used by voice specialists and other imaging techniques are often used where a physiological speech difficulty, such as cleft palate, exists. The use of sound spectography is often discussed in the research literature but is more rarely used in clinical practice (Howard & Heselwood, 2011). Electromyography and electropalatography (Ball, 1993, pp. 101–8) may occasionally be used in a therapeutic context, but are more common in research-based settings. Use of ultrasound is in its relative infancy in the speech clinic, particularly in the United Kingdom, but studies in North America have found positive outcomes (Bacsfalvi & Bernhardt, 2011).

Clinicians will typically use perceptual methods of assessment for their relative ease and portability (there is no need to carry any machinery) (Kent, 1996). Indeed, even where techniques of instrumental investigation are available (in general they are not widely found) perceptual judgements are still integral to assessment; they cannot be excluded. It is these perceptual methods that are our focus here, although these can be supplemented with instrumental techniques and followed up by acoustic analysis if a good quality recording is taken at the time of assessment. As recording equipment becomes relatively inexpensive and as the availability of instrumental methods increases, it is hoped that both will become more commonly used over time.

2.1 The Speech Sample

Before analysis a sample of speech must be collected. Both Dodd (2005) and Bowen (2009) recommend sampling single words from a speaker's vocabulary. The 'confrontation naming test', in which a clinician shows a picture of an object to a child and asks them to name it, is possibly the most common method of doing this, and occurs frequently in formal speech and language therapy assessments. In principle a good naming test samples all the sounds of the native language in all possible syllable/word positions, to take account of coarticulatory variability, since the client's productions may be affected by the phonetic environment. It is good practice to include words of different lengths and with different stress patterns, and to include a number of repetitions to check for consistency. A full assessment would also include some test of prosody, including intonation, voice quality and rhythm. In practice many of these considerations are negated by time and resource constraints. Typically only consonants are sampled, as these are understood to be more prone to disruption. Usually only three (word initial, word medial and word final) or four (where word medial is divided into syllable initial within word, and syllable final within word) word positions are assessed, and prosody is not tested (but see Peppe & McCann, 2003, for a dedicated test of prosody). Still, even leaving out a number of variables, the logical possibilities for English number into the low hundreds, and Grunwell (1985) recommends that a speech sample contain around 200–50 words. In practice the attention levels of young children can prove restrictive in obtaining such a large sample size. Consequently the sample sizes of many published assessments range between 30–50 words, for example, the Developmental Evaluation of Articulation and Phonology (DEAP) (Dodd et al., 2002) and the South Tyneside Assessment of Phonology (STAP) (Armstrong & Ainley, 1992). An initial sample of about 50 words may also serve to point to areas of phonological and articulatory difficulty (and conversely competence), which require more thorough investigation, and which can be specifically targeted with further data collection.

In addition it is important to gain a conversational speech sample so the two samples can be compared, and to ascertain intelligibility in both single words and in general conversation. One significant challenge arises in speech samples where the target word is unknown: for very unintelligible speech, one may not know how the speaker's production differs from the target. The speech then only becomes of use for phonetic/articulatory assessment. However, the clinician may use action pictures as stimuli for the conversational sample and thus have some control of word content.

2.2 The Role of Transcription in Assessment

The raw data taken from the confrontation naming assessment and conversation sample need to be recorded so they can be analysed. Ultimately this is done by transcribing the speech either live at the time of assessment, or later from an audio recording. Each method has its advantages and drawbacks. For example, live transcription is efficient and makes good use of the transcriber's time, but may be difficult to accomplish at any level of detail while managing other aspects of the assessment. Transcription from an audio recording gives the transcriber time to focus on transcription and listen several times to each item. However, it will not allow access to visual details which may give useful information regarding a speaker's lip shape (Kent, 1996), and the very act of repetition may change the transcriptions given (Shriberg et al., 1984; Munson & Brinkman, 2004; Knight, 2010), as, indeed, may the visual details (Stephens & Daniloff, 1977; Nelson & Hodge, 2000; Starr-Marshall, 2010).

It is important to remember at this point that transcription is not a direct translation from one medium to another but merely an abstract representation of the original meaning (Müller & Damico, 2002). Nevertheless, the transcriber's aim is to use perception to interpret the articulations used by the client in producing particular sounds. Therefore, 'a transcription made from analytic listening is a record of what the transcriber heard couched in terms of how phonetic theory explains the articulatory cause of that auditory effect' (Howard & Heselwood, 2002, p. 388). The need to differentiate reliably between which exact phonetic gesture is being made is especially pertinent when considering the covert contrasts which are produced by some speakers with a speech disorder. A covert contrast exists where two words, while sounding homophonous, are clearly different as far as the speaker is concerned, and may contain minimal phonetic differences, which are, however, insufficient to indicate an easily discernible contrast (e.g. Hewlett, 1988). In other words, the speaker is producing distinct phonetic sounds, which are, however, hard to distinguish, and which are therefore judged to be the same. When assessing disordered speech this is very important as it has phonological implications; the child is marking a difference in phonological categories by producing distinct phonetic sounds, albeit narrowly different.

When seeing a client for the first time, the clinician should use a detailed impressionistic transcription, making use of any symbols from the International Phonetic Alphabet (IPA) and its extensions (ExtIPA). Much of the literature (e.g. Shriberg & Lof, 1991; Howard & Heselwood, 2002; Ball, 2008) recommends that transcription is at the highest level of detail to give the best impression of the characteristics of an individual's speech. However, several studies have suggested that narrow transcription causes lower agreement among transcribers (e.g. Amorosa et al., 1985; Pye et al., 1988; Shriberg & Lof, 1991) which may suggest that narrow transcription, while being sensitive, may not be reliable enough to consistently identify patterns in the speech being analysed. It should be added that impressionistic transcription is difficult, especially of disordered child speech, and is critically reliant on the transcriber's levels of skill.

It is also important to remember that transcription involves 'selective interpretations' in that transcription cannot usefully aim to describe fully or adequately all the details of speech; 'even if this were possible . . . such a document would be too detailed to use effectively and efficiently' (Müller & Damico, 2002, pp. 301–2). In general, the more selective a transcript, the more potentially useful it may be to the reader (Ochs, 1979). The transcriber must, therefore, select only those aspects of speech they deem to be the most relevant to their purpose and so, after making a preliminary analysis of the client's speech, and coming to an understanding of their phonological system, an experienced clinician might move quite quickly to using a phonemic transcription. However, it seems that many clinicians feel under-confident about any transcription at all (Windsor, 2011), and begin by using a transcription which is a phonemic interpretation, 'normalized' to fit the target phonology. This practice leads readily to an inaccurate representation of the client's output.

3 Analysis Types

For the assessment of child speech, Stoel-Gammon (1988) recommends that both independent and relational analyses are conducted, and this is the normal practice in clinic. Independent analyses give an insight into the child's unique system and relational analyses (typically a distributional analysis and an analysis of any error patterns present) give normative comparisons in relation to an appropriate adult target (taking into account, for example, the variety of the language spoken in the child's environment). Relational Analyses may also include a calculation of token-to-token consistency (which contributes to differential diagnosis) and a measurement such as Percentage Consonants Correct (PCC) and Percentage Vowels Correct (PVC) (e.g. Shriberg et al., 1997) (which are useful for charting severity and progress). Preston et al. (2011) discuss issues of validity and reliability surrounding these and similar measures.

3.1 Phonetic Inventory

Typically the first step in analysis is to construct a phonetic inventory. This includes all the sounds that are produced, regardless of their relationship to target, or whether they are part of the typical inventory of the target variety. The clinician will organize an inventory along similar lines to the IPA chart, with logical groupings of voice, place and manner. A review of the inventory will then illustrate the productive capabilities of the client, and suggest particular areas for attention in the relational analyses. For example, if a child shows no evidence of producing voiced fricatives, this might suggest inability to produce voicing and friction simultaneously, and that loss of contrast might result. The results of the inventory will also provide useful information for devising therapy. For example, if a child can produce plosives only in certain positions, diagnosis and intervention strategies will not be the same as for a child who has no plosives in the inventory.

3.2 Distributional Analysis

A relational analysis typically begins with a distributional analysis. Here a child's productions are shown against the phonemes of the target adult accent in different positions (three or four, as described above). In the analysis, the production of each target sound in each position is noted. For the novice this can seem somewhat challenging, but the clinician will generally proceed through the data sound by sound, and word by word, rather than searching for examples of each phoneme in each position. For example, if the first word in the sample is 'cat', the clinician will note the realization of /k/ in initial position, and then the realization of /t/ in final position, before moving onto the sounds of the next word. If a phoneme in a certain position is realized in different ways in the sample this should also be included in the analysis, and it should also be noted if the target is not realized at all. Clusters should be treated in their entirety, so, for example, the analysis of 'spider' would begin by noting the realization of /sp/ in word initial position.

From this analysis the clinician can begin to identify where the child is losing contrastivity. For example, if a child consistently produces both /k/ and /t/ as [tʰ] in initial position, then the words 'can' and 'tan' will be produced in the same way: words that are a minimal pair for an adult will be homophones for the child, and thus a phonemic contrast has been lost. Such loss of contrast will contribute greatly to a child's unintelligibility, and will often be the focus of remediation in therapy.

3.3 Error Patterns

The next step in distributional analysis is generally to describe how each erroneous production differs from the adult target. Errors are often 'described in terms of patterns or phonological processes' (Bowen, 2009, p. 58). However, it should be noted that the term 'process' originally refers to Stampe's (1979) assertion that phonology is based on a set of universal phonological processes or rules which interact with one another. Clinicians may still use the term 'processes' without accepting this assertion, but instead to organize their analytical thinking. Thus, many clinicians prefer the term 'error patterns'. Error patterns can be categorized in to two groups: syllable error patterns (errors that affect the syllabic structure of the target words) or substitution error patterns (errors involving substituting one sound for another) (Bernthal & Bankson, 1988). Syllable error patterns describe different types of insertions and deletions of syllables into or from the adult form of a word. 'Syllable processes can be divided into eight subcategories: final consonant deletion, weak syllable deletion, reduplication, consonant cluster reduction, assimilation, epenthesis, metathesis and coalescence' (Dodd, 2005, p. 31). Substitution error patterns describe how articulation differs from the norm in terms of the features of: voice, place and manner of articulation. Substitution error patterns can also be classified into eight subcategories: velar fronting (e.g. /k/ →[t] 'cat' → 'tat'), backing (e.g. /t/ →[k] 'tea' → 'key', stopping (e.g. /s/ →[t] 'sea' → 'tea'), gliding of liquids (e.g. /ɹ/ →[w] 'red' → 'wed'), affrication (e.g. /ʃ/ →[tʃ] 'shop' → 'chop'), deaffrication (e.g. /tʃ/ →[t] 'chop' → 'top'), vocalization (e.g. /l/ →[ʊ] /lɪtəl/→[lɪtʊ]) and voicing (e.g. /p/ →[b] 'pea' → 'bee') (Stoel-Gammon & Dunn, 1985; Bernthal & Bankson, 1988; Dodd, 1995. See Grunwell (1987) for a detailed list).

3.4 Formal Assessments of Speech

Formal tests for speech published in the United Kingdom include the DEAP (Dodd et al., 2002) and the STAP (Armstrong & Ainley, 1992). Joffe and Pring (2008) surveyed the assessments that clinicians use and found that STAP was one of the most popular. However, it is likely that the DEAP may have grown in popularity since the survey was completed (Pring, personal communication). The design of such tests is basically the same as the steps in analysis described above, and all will typically include a phonetic inventory, distributional analysis and error pattern analysis in some form, possibly with instructions for producing PPC or PCC metrics. An advantage of published tests is that much of the work is done for the clinician, as pictures to name will be provided, and record sheets are available for analysing the data. In addition, an important advantage is that some of the published assessments are standardized so the performance of an individual can be compared to that of a wider population. Clinicians may opt to use only selective parts of such tests, or to design their own as described above. Of course when dealing with a language (or variety) for which such tests have not been published, the latter is the only option, and therefore it is essential that clinicians understand the first principles on which published tests are based.

4 Diagnosis

4.1 Diagnosis from a Speech Assessment

The information from the independent and relational analyses is used as part of the differential diagnosis of speech difficulties. First the results of the phonetic inventory and error pattern analysis are compared with normative data from children of different age groups. For typically developing children, the phonetic inventory becomes gradually more complete and complex over the course of the first five or so years of life. There are commonalities in the earlier and later acquired sounds, that is, in which order, and at what age, sounds are added to a child's repertoire, though there is also considerable variability. The generality of order and age of acquisition is reported in the research literature (see McLeod & Bleile, 2003 for a useful summary), and is often available in some form in formal assessments of speech. In addition, clinicians are trained to recognize what is normal in terms of children's phonological and articulatory competence. They can match the information from the analyses both to the published norms and to their own knowledge of child speech acquisition to estimate whether speech is age appropriate, and to ascertain the nature of any diversions from the target age.

4.2 Other Knowledge needed for Differential Diagnosis

A diagnosis cannot be completed from the speech sample alone. To the speech analyses the clinician will need to add other aspects of assessment to differentially diagnose the nature of the speech difficulty, which will then inform the selection of intervention type. Many of these additional tests are used to differentiate the psycholinguistic underpinnings of the speech difficulty. The Stackhouse and Wells (1997) model may be used to identify more precisely which psycholinguistic operation the child is finding difficult. This can be to differentiate input and output difficulties or may indicate other levels of disruption, such as impaired auditory processing or impaired phonological representations. This psycholinguistic profiling is achieved through the plethora of tests suggested by Pascoe et al. (2006); for example, testing a child's ability to discriminate non-words or real words can indicate whether there is a difficulty in phonological recognition or phonological representation. Two crucial factors are whether sounds can be produced in isolation (stimulability) and whether the child can discriminate between the sounds which they are having difficulty producing.

The clinician will also need to know whether the errors produced are consistent; inconsistency can indicate particular diagnoses. Inconsistency in this case refers to token-to-token inconsistency, that is, whether the child's production of a single target word is different for each attempt at production, for example, the target /pɪg/ is first produced as [pɪd] next as [bɪg] then as [pɪg]. Inconsistency can be an indicator of inconsistent phonological disorder and Childhood Apraxia of Speech (CAS) (sometimes, however, it indicates that a speech difficulty is resolving).

Another element that may contribute to differential diagnosis is a motor examination, such as the diadokinetic rate. This is simply the rate at which a speaker can repeat the sounds [p], [t] and [k] in sequence, which is usually performed as a game where a child repeats 'pat-a-cake' as fast as possible. Errors or a slow rate (when a child can produce these sounds in isolation or in words) can be an indicator of motor speech difficulties such as CAS. The clinician will also need to observe any additional speech behaviours such as articulatory effort or groping, which may be an indication of motor speech difficulties or dysarthria. An oral examination may inform the differential diagnosis of a speech disorder that is physical in nature such as cleft palate. Any marked degree of cleft is likely to have been identified early and referral to the speech clinic will be accompanied by information regarding surgical and /or feeding intervention, but other anatomical anomalies, such as ankyloglossia (tongue tie) or mis-proportioned oral structures may also contribute to speech difficulties. Extralinguistic factors need to be considered, such as general learning ability, attention and listening, psychosocial impact of the disorder, motivation for intervention and so forth.

5 Categorizing Disordered Speech

As above we will focus on the categorization of disordered speech in children, due to more speech work being carried out in paediatric settings. Children with disordered speech are 'far from being a homogenous group' (Dodd, 2005, p. 2), and we have discussed above how details of the speech, and other aspects of the client's presentation may inform differential diagnosis. There is no universally agreed classification system for child speech disorders (see Waring & Knight, 2013), but the two most widely used are the Dodd (1995, 2005) and Shriberg (2006) systems. In adult speech there is, perhaps, greater clarity in the classification of motor speech disorders. Any close scrutiny of these is, however, beyond the scope of this chapter (but see Duffy, 2005).

Dodd (1995) differentiates speech sound disorders by linguistic symptomatology. Articulation Disorder is an impaired ability to pronounce specific phones. Phonological Delay is exhibited when the error patterns found are those which occur during normal development but which are typical of younger children. For Consistent Phonological Disorder the use of some non-developmental error patterns are found but used consistently. Inconsistent Phonological Disorder is revealed in a child's phonological system which shows at least 40 per cent variability (on a token to token basis). Dodd (2005) adds a fifth category of CAS which is a controversial label but is broadly considered to be 'a childhood motor speech disorder' (Dodd, 2005, p. 71)

Shriberg and colleagues have a long history in the classification of speech sound disorders. Shriberg (2006) proposes seven putative subtypes for disordered speech in children based on inherited and environmental risk factors:

Speech Delay – Genetic
Speech Delay – Otitis Media with Effusion
Speech Delay – Developmental Psychosocial Involvement
Speech Delay – Apraxia of Speech
Speech Delay – Dysarthria
Speech Errors – Sibilants
Speech Errors – Rhotics

If we combine these two approaches to classification, as shown in Table 11.1 we reach a clinically useful compromise in which we can define the categories by the nature of their presentation, only broadly categorizing cause, rather than stipulating a particular aetiology, as Shriberg (2006) does.

It should be noted that the categories are not represented equally in children with Speech Sound Disorder. In particular, the vast majority of children seen in clinics will fall into the phonological group. It is still unclear if and how

Table 11.1 Combined classification of speech disorders.
Adapted from Bowen (2011)

Type	Description
Physiological in nature	a physical abnormality (e.g. Cleft lip, velo-pharyngeal, incompetence, etc.).
Phonetic in nature	difficulty executing singular movements without a physiological difficulty (e.g. Articulation disorder).
Phonological in nature	difficulty sequencing the psychological representations of sounds (e.g. phonological delay/disorders).
Motoric in nature	difficulty planning or sequencing speech movements (e.g. Childhood Apraxia of Speech/ Developmental Verbal Dyspraxia).
Neuro-Muscular in nature	difficulty executing speech movements (e.g. any of the dysarthrias)

children in this group can be differentiated, and whether this subtype is in need of further refinement (Waring & Knight, 2013).

The subtype of motoric disorders is currently receiving much attention in speech and language therapy. Impairments in praxis (CAS in the United States of America and Developmental Verbal Dyspraxia (DVD) in the United Kingdom) have long been considered subtypes of Speech Sound Disorder but have until recently lacked a specific definition or set of characteristics (RCSLT, 2011). DVD is used to describe 'a condition where a child has difficulty in making and co-ordinating the precise movements which are used in the production of spoken language although there is no damage to muscles or nerves' (Ripley et al., 1997). The core impairments of DVD that differ from other types of Speech Sound Disorder are defined by ASHA (2007) as:

Inconsistent errors on consonants and vowels in repeated productions of syllables or words

Lengthened and disrupted co-articulatory transitions between sounds and syllables

Inappropriate prosody, especially in the realization of lexical or phrasal stress

Ozanne (2005) suggests that DVD should be considered as a symptom cluster involving elements of three output levels: phonological planning, phonetic planning and speech-motor programme implementation, in the absence of neuromuscular damage. However, it is differentiated from dysarthrias whose impairment lies at the level of motor execution (Caruso & Strand, 1999).

An additional approach to classification is one in which speech disorders are subtyped as 'input' difficulties which refer to any hearing impairment or impaired discrimination between speech sounds, and 'output' difficulties which refer to an impaired ability to formulate speech sounds or sequences of speech sounds (Stackhouse & Wells, 1997). It is increasingly popular to extend this approach using the 'Psycholinguistic Framework' of Stackhouse and Wells (1997), which was mentioned above in the light of additional tests needed for diagnosis. The approach identifies where there are breakdowns in the speech chain. In their model Stackhouse and Wells divide the speech chain into the following functions:

Peripheral auditory processing which refers to general auditory ability, not specifically related to speech.

Speech/non-speech discrimination which is a pre-linguistic level of recognising that what is heard is speech rather than non-speech sounds and noises.

Phonological recognition which describes the level at which a listener recognizes the language heard as familiar as compared to a language that is not. The listener is using knowledge about language-specific structures and will recognize, for example, that /blɪk/ is a possible English word but /bnɪk/ is not.

Phonetic discrimination which is the recognition of phonetic distinctions that are new to the listener, and is used in early stages in language learning as a child begins to learn which segments are contrastive. It is also used in second-language learning when unfamiliar segments are heard.

Phonological representations which contain enough information for a heard word to be recognized as distinct from other similar-sounding words (e.g. /tæp/ vs. /kæp/; /kæp/ vs. /kæt/).

Motor programmes which are a series of stored gestural targets (or articulatory instructions) for the production of known words.

Motor programming which is a facility to create new motor programmes. It is conceived as a store of phonological units that are selected and assembled into new combinations so that new productions of words can be articulated.

Motor planning which assembles the gestural targets (articulatory instructions) into the correct sequence in real time, taking into account the context, for example, assimilations and the appropriate intonation for a question form.

Motor execution which refers to the peripheral production of speech at the level of the vocal tract.

The Stackhouse and Well's model is extremely useful for identifying the processes underlying speech difficulties, which in turn has implications for the intervention. It should be noted, however, that the model pays little attention to the child's inventory and error patterns (Broomfield & Dodd, 2004), and does not consider factors outside the speech processing chain. Thus, a full and complete diagnosis requires information regarding the speech assessment itself, and details of underlying psycholinguistic processing.

6 Intervention

6.1 Target Selection

The clinician will use all the information gained in assessment to set target sounds or error patterns on which to focus intervention, and to decide on which type of intervention to use. Where only one sound is mis-articulated or only one error pattern present, decision making is straightforward. However, where there are many errors the clinician must decide which to prioritize.

There are many approaches to creating a hierarchy of errors for target setting. Bowen (2009, pp. 282–6) identifies 16 selection criteria, and the interpretation of many of these differ in traditional and more modern approaches. One of the main differences in approach to the target selection decision-making process depends on whether the clinician adheres to the more traditional approach where the focus is on the learnability of a sound, or more recent approaches which focus on phonological restructuring. For example, traditionally clinicians would first target sounds that occur early in the inventories of typically developing children, as these sounds were thought to be easier to learn. In this approach, a problem with an early developing sound like [b] would be targeted before a problem with a late developing sound like [ʃ], all other things being equal. However, more recent work (Bowen, 2009 cites Gierut et al., 1996) has suggested that targeting first those sounds that are usually acquired late will lead to generalization and thus restructuring of the phonological system. In a similar fashion there are traditional and modern approaches to target selection in relation to whether or not sounds are stimulable, and whether sounds differ in terms of one or many features. Nevertheless, the choice between traditional and modern approaches to target selection is not cut and dried. Bowen is careful to stress that any of the 16 criteria she identifies might be considered by clinicians depending on the individual profile of the child at any particular time. Many of the approaches await further evidence before one can be definitively chosen over another.

6.2 Intervention Approaches

Having decided which sounds or error patterns to prioritize the clinician needs to decide which intervention approach best suits the presentation of the individual child. The choice of intervention approach may be dependent on the subtype, error type and the target selection criteria chosen. For example, if the root of the difficulty is phonological, then the approach to remediation will be different from that taken for a child with a disorder of motoric origin. Bowen (2009) highlights two general differences in approach dependent on the underlying psycholinguistic origin of the disorder (phonological disorders being located either in phonological recognition or phonological representation and motoric disorders being located in either motor programme, motor planning or motor execution), differentiating between general intervention principles for phonological disorders and motor speech disorders.

The principles of phonological intervention are based on the systematic nature of phonology and are characterized by conceptual activities rather than motor activities which have generalization as their ultimate goal, promoting intelligibility (Bowen, 2011). The principles of motoric intervention are based on the principles of motor learning and are characterized by motor activities rather than conceptual activities which have habituation and then automaticity as their ultimate goal, promoting intelligibility (Bowen, 2011).

There are numerous published intervention approaches some of which are designed to focus on different subtypes of speech disorder and some of which can be used in conjunction so that they complement each other, for example, using auditory input type activities as well as working on production to focus on both ends of the speech processing chain. Williams et al. (2010) split each of these therapy approaches into categories of planning, programming or execution and whether they target speech perception, phonological awareness or speech production. However, Joffe and Pring (2008) found that one of the most popularly used approaches to intervention was an eclectic one where clinicians pick and choose the specific parts of different interventions that they feel best suit the specific presentation of each individual child.

The goal of any intervention is intelligible speech and /or functional communication. Sometimes the child may make little progress and, therefore, speech may be deemed as not functioning for communication. In such cases alternative means of communication, for example, communication books or voice output devices, must be introduced (ASHA Admission/Discharge Guidelines, 2004; RCSLT Communicating Quality 3, 2006; Baker, 2010).

There are several factors which govern the end of clinical intervention. The child may be fully intelligible or may have lost motivation to improve further. There may no longer be any psychosocial impact, either on the child or the family (ASHA Admission/Discharge Guidelines, 2004; Baker, 2010). Any residual difficulties may have ceased to interfere with education. However, the child may still be seen for other difficulties or in some cases monitored over time (Communicating Quality 3, 2006). Finally, if the child has ceased to progress, a period without therapy may be indicated, after which a review will be indicated to reassess the need for further targeted intervention.

12 Forensic Speech Science

Peter French and Louisa Stevens

Chapter Overview

---

1 Introduction

Forensic Speech Science (FSS) – or Forensic Phonetics as it is sometimes known – is undoubtedly the most vigorous growth point in Applied Linguistics. Currently, in the United Kingdom alone, we would estimate that experts in this field are called upon to analyse recordings or provide other advice in around 500 cases per year. The majority of these cases concern forensic speaker comparison, which is the main focus of this chapter. However, before we introduce the current principal approaches to the speaker comparison task and explain the major areas of divergent thinking and contention, we shall provide an outline of other sub-areas of FSS concerned with recording analysis, namely speech content analysis and speaker profiling.[1] The reader seeking more comprehensive information about these sub-areas is directed to Jessen (2008) in addition to the specific studies referenced in each section.

2 Speech Content Analysis

Speech Content Analysis involves the examination of audio recordings to determine what was said. It has become customary to differentiate two types of task, depending on the breadth of focus and the level of detail involved. At a very broad and general level, it may involve the phonetician listening to a recording on high quality replay equipment, perhaps partially and occasionally aided by speech analysis software, in an attempt to produce a detailed and comprehensive transcript of conversation. At a more localized level, it may involve very intensive, detailed and comparative acoustic analyses of speech segments and syllables in order to resolve narrowly focused disputes of lexical content. The former task is conventionally referred to as *transcription* and the latter as *questioned* or *disputed utterance analysis* (French, 1990). In fact, the two tasks occupy two ends of a generality-specificity continuum, and are not qualitatively distinct.

2.1 General Transcription

Normally, expert advice on issues of speech content is only sought where a recording is poor quality or otherwise problematic; for example, it reflects a foreign or non-standard accent unfamiliar to the instructing party. Legal personnel (often victims of the 'CSI effect' (Schweitzer & Saks, 2007), frequently consider speech 'enhancement', that is, sound processing, as their first option. However, the improvements achieved to speech intelligibility are often limited (Hilkhuysen & Huckvale, 2010a, b; Loizou & Kim, 2011) with the consequence that FSS practitioners are required to prepare a transcript. Indeed, the prevailing view, expressed by Fraser (2003), is that problematic recordings should only be transcribed by speech experts:

> . . . transcription of difficult material must be done by someone who understands the likely errors in their perception, and can be critical of their own perceptions, so as to consider a wider range of options, and judge the level of confidence to assign to any interpretation. Such knowledge is only gained through considerable study of linguistics phonetics and psycholinguistics. (Fraser, 2003, p. 221)

A main source of potential misperceptions and transcription errors is the 'priming' effect of context and background information, as well as interpretations suggested by instructing parties. Faced with inadequacies in the acoustic information encoded in the recording signal, the listener attempts – albeit unconsciously – to reconstruct missing acoustic cues by reference to such 'higher order' information and 'map' the inadequate information that is present onto words and phrases that might conceivably provide a rough fit. Constant awareness of priming effects, and an appropriately parsimonious approach to what might safely be included in a transcript, are prerequisite to the task (see Fraser et al., 2011 for a dramatic experimental demonstration of the power of priming). Further safeguards in place at the authors' laboratory involve an iterative approach to the task over multiple drafts and the involvement of more than one analyst. For relatively clear speech, which we are seldom asked to transcribe, one works on a transcription time to recording time ratio of c. 8:1; for the very worst material the ratio may be near 180:1.

2.2 Questioned/Disputed Utterance Analysis

Where a very specific section of a recording is in dispute, often a highly contentious single word or short utterance, very detailed phonetic and acoustic analysis is required. In some cases there might be available a body of undisputed and clear reference speech from the speaker, either within the same recording or in another recording. Unclear or ambiguous vowel or consonant segments in the questioned material can be compared both auditorily and acoustically with realizations of candidate sounds in the reference speech and where there are two competing interpretations, tokens relevant to both can be extracted for comparison. Studies of questioned/disputed utterance cases may be found in French (1990), French and Harrison (2006) and Innes (2011).

3 Speaker Profiling

Speaker profiling involves the analysis of a recording in order to derive as much information as possible about the speaker (Foulkes & French, 2001). It is typically undertaken where someone has been recorded committing or confessing to a crime, and where a suspect has not yet been identified. A list of questions a forensic speech scientist might realistically address in assembling a profile, together with those regarded as lying outside the expertise of a phonetician or unsupportable by reference to established knowledge and research appears in French and Harrison (2006). Realistic, addressable questions include regional, social and ethnic influences, which may be researched and confirmed by reference to published studies (see, for example, contributions to edited collections by Foulkes & Docherty (1999), Llamas & Watt (2010), Beal et al. (2012) and Hughes et al. (2012)); and/or by recording of reference material for comparison from potential candidate populations. The value of obtaining judgements from native speakers within relevant populations is argued in Nolan (2011, 2012) and underscored in a case report on the profiling of a famous criminal hoaxer (the 'Yorkshire Ripper Hoaxer') by Ellis (1994) and French et al. (2006).

Caution is urged in formulating conclusions with respect to ethnic minority and foreign language influences in recordings. There are no necessary homological relationships between the presence/absence of features and speaker identity. High, (near) native level competence in L2 English speakers and poor or brief recordings may mean that L1 interference is absent or not observable. Also, members of ethnic groups whose first (and sometimes only) language is English, such as second or third generation British Asians, very often exhibit 'residual' L1 features in their speech from, for example, Punjabi or Bangla as cultural identity markers. Further, recent studies show an emergence of 'multi-ethnic' varieties in areas of high contact, such that features previously associated exclusively with minority groups are now present in other sections of the community (Hirson et al., 2003; Cheshire et al., 2008).

A specific application of speaker profiling, known as Language Analysis for the Determination of Origin of Asylum Seekers (LADO), is used in many countries to assist immigration authorities with determining the nationality of asylum seekers. The practices and methodologies used continue to be surrounded by controversy – particularly in relation to whether this work should be carried out by linguists, native speakers or a combination of both. The reader is directed to Zwaan et al. (2010) for an overview of recent developments.

In compiling a profile, forensic speech scientists might also interrogate a recording for the presence of speech impediments or voice pathologies (extreme hypernasality from cleft palate, dysphonia from cysts on the vocal folds, stammer, etc.). This work is properly undertaken in consultation with clinical colleagues. From an investigative viewpoint the importance is that the speaker may have been subject to clinical attention and his/her condition noted in medical records.

Speaker age lies only marginally within the range of addressable profiling questions. Longitudinal studies provide a range of interesting voice parameters on which changes occur in predictable ways. For example, age-related and maturational pitch and phonatory changes for women and men are documented in Hollien and Shipp (1972), Wilcox and Horii (1980), de Pinto and Hollien, (1982), Russell et al. (1995) and Harrington et al. (2007). Pitch and phonation features from a voice which is being profiled are of limited assistance in determining age, as they can only be interpreted relative to earlier data from the same speaker, and this data is not available. And perceptual studies have shown some substantial discrepancies between chronological age and perceived age (Shipp et al., 1992; Braun, 1996).

With regard to questions that cannot realistically be addressed, studies have shown that there is no close correlation between speech features and physical characteristics such as weight and height (van Dommelen & Moxness, 1995; Greisbach, 1999; Gonzalez, 2004; Rendall et al., 2005) or the psychological characteristics of a speaker, including stress and deception. Indeed, no reliable acoustic index of speaker stress is retrievable from speech (Kirchhübel et al., 2011). While in recent years there has been a great deal of public interest in 'voice stress analyzers', which claim to analyse microtremors in the voice associated with lying and deception, empirical testing has shown that these systems perform at chance level (Eriksson & Lacerda, 2007). Members of the International Association for Forensic Phonetics and Acoustics (IAFPA) are bound by a clause in its Code of Conduct prohibiting members from providing profiles of speakers' psychological states or estimates of sincerity.

4 Forensic Speaker Comparison

Together, speech content determination (transcription and questioned/disputed utterance analysis) and speaker profiling make up around 30 per cent of cases undertaken annually by the forensic speech and audio laboratory in which the authors are based. The majority of the laboratory's work (c. 70%) involves forensic speaker comparison, that is, the comparison of a voice in a criminal recording with that of a known suspect, the purpose being to assist the courts with determining identity or non-identity of criminals and defendants.

5 Methods of Analysis

There are five basic approaches to the forensic speaker comparison task (Gold & French, 2011a, b):

(1) auditory phonetic analysis only (AuPA), that is, analytic listening and comparison of segmental and suprasegmental features;
(2) acoustic phonetic analysis only (AcPA);
(3) auditory phonetic *cum* acoustic phonetic analysis (AuPA+AcPA);
(4) analysis by automatic speaker recognition system (ASR);
(5) analysis by automatic speaker recognition system with human assistance (HASR).

(1)–(3) are highly labour intensive and reliant on the skills of the individual analyst. (4) is person-independent and requires minimum analyst input. (5) may involve more or less input, depending on the nature of the 'human assistance' given to the system. The latter might range from cursory holistic listening to more detailed analyses of the types entailed in (1)–(3). We return to this point later in the chapter.

A recent survey of forensic speaker comparison practices involving 47 analysts based in 13 countries (Gold & French, 2011a, b) found the most prevalent approach to be the combined AuPA+AcPA method (35 respondents; 75%) with HASR coming second (8 respondents; 17%) and the AuPA and AcPA approaches trailing well behind (respectively, 3 respondents and 1 respondent).

No respondent in the survey reported in Gold and French used ASR alone. However, it has subsequently come to light that two non-surveyed laboratories do so, and also that speaker comparison results from one ASR system[2] alone have been used in evidence in courts in 21 different countries (Moreno, p.c.).

From involvement in the field, it seems clear to us that AuPA and AcPA are moribund. It is also clear that the use of ASR systems is rapidly gaining ground. We regard such systems potentially as making a valuable contribution to the reliability of speaker comparison outcomes. However, there are strong grounds for considering them as a supplement to, rather than a replacement for, the AuPA+AcPA approach. The reasons for taking this view are both theoretical and pragmatic. It is worth considering them in a little detail.

5.1 Automatic Speaker Recognition Systems

ASR systems work by taking a known (suspect) recording, performing complex mathematical transformations on it and reducing it to a statistical model based on mel frequency cepstrum coefficients (MFCCs). The recording of the questioned voice (the criminal recording) is similarly processed and a set of features is extracted. The system then compares the extracted features with the statistical model of the suspect's voice and produces a measure of similarity/ difference (distance) between the two. In order to determine whether the measure is indicative of their having come from the same or different speakers, the extracted features are also compared with a set of statistical models from a reference population of other speakers held within the system.

The systems have some strong advantages. One is their objectivity. Although analyst decisions are required, for example, over the editing of samples to be processed by the system, they are relatively analysis independent and minimize the extent to which individual interpretation enters into the analytic process. Linked to this are the possibilities they provide for replicability of results. Any analyst processing the same material with the same system and using the same settings will produce exactly the same results. Another advantage is their speed of operation. One comparison may take upwards of 15 hours to perform using the AuPA+AcPA approach. However, with an ASR system it is possible to compare many samples in a matter of minutes. This means that the systems are readily testable. One can subject them to multiple trials in order to establish their error rates. This may be a legal requirement for those working in the United States of America where a Supreme Court ruling specifies that a known and suitably small error rate should be established for any method used to produce expert evidence for judicial purposes, for example, *Daubert* versus *Merrell Dow Pharmaceuticals, Inc.* (509 US 579 (*1993*)). A further benefit is that the output of certain leading systems is a likelihood ratio (LR) in the form of a number. The number specifies the likelihood of finding the evidence if the recordings were from the same speaker over the likelihood of finding it if they were from different speakers (see below for further explanation). Results expressed in terms of LRs are seen as the desirable and logically correct output of forensic analyses of all types (Robertson & Vignaux, 1995; Evett, 1998).

Notwithstanding the clear advantages of ASR technology, there are limits on its performance. The performance error rates established for ASR systems are very low when working with good quality recordings (French et al., 2009). However, with real forensic recordings the error rates can be very much higher unless one takes a discriminating approach vis-à-vis the technical adequacy (sound quality and duration) of material one is prepared to accept for analysis, and also an extremely rigorous approach to the preparatory editing of samples. Such editing would involve careful removal of all extraneous noises and non-speech sounds such as coughs, leaving only a continuous stream of speech. In a study involving 767 recordings from 'dead' cases carried out in the authors' laboratory, 80 per cent of the recordings, which they had processed using the AuPA+AcPA approach, would have needed to be either rejected or scrupulously re-edited before being suitable for ASR system analysis (Harrison & French, 2010). However, even with optimum recordings and further technical development of systems, we take the view that they could never be infallible. Our main reason for assuming this position concerns the voice 'dimension' that ASRs measure. Although the relationships between MFCCs and the features of speech that phoneticians examine and describe are far from fully understood,[3] MFCCs are most closely related to supralaryngeal vocal tract resonances arising from the geometry of the individual cavities (hypopharynx, oropharynx, oral and nasal cavities, etc.) and 'articulatory settings' (Honikman, 1964; see also Jones, this volume). However, studies of vocal tract anatomy repeatedly report little variation across individuals *within* gender, age and racial groups (see Xue et al., 2011). One recent study by Xue and Hao (2006), for example, examined 60 male speakers equally divided across 3 groups: White American, African American and Chinese. Using acoustic reflection technology, length (in cms) for vocal tracts overall and for their pharyngeal and oral sub-components were calculated as shown in Table 12.1.

The relatively low standard deviations that are repeatedly shown by studies of this kind indicate a strong degree of convergence across same sex speakers within ethnic groups. A consequence of having only small inter-speaker vocal tract variation is that it restricts the range of variation in acoustic output found across populations. Given that ASR systems work exclusively on analysis of this output, it leads to a performance limitation that is unlikely to be surmounted simply by further technical development of ASR software.[4]

Further, the problem caused by small inter-speaker variation in dimensions is exacerbated by the plasticity of the vocal tract (Nolan, 1983). Vocal tract

Table 12.1 Means and SDs of vocal tract parameters for male speakers across racial groups (Key: OL oral length; PL pharyngeal length; TL total vocal tract length; Adapted from Xue & Hao, 2006)

	White American		African American		Chinese	
	Mean	SD	Mean	SD	Mean	SD
OL (cm)	7.78	0.86	7.78	0.82	8.17	0.62
PL (cm)	9.07	1.00	9.31	0.84	8.99	1.33
TL (cm)	16.85	0.54	17.09	1.07	17.16	1.03

boundaries and surfaces, being soft tissue masses, are not static, but moveable. Furthermore, at an individual speaker level, at least some of the tissues – for example the velum, areas of the tongue and the walls of the nasopharynx – may become swollen through illness, through smoking or ingestion of certain intoxicants. Thus, a speaker does not have a fixed and stable set of dimensions, but the dimensions and proportions of sub-components of the vocal tract are subject to transitory changes – with, obviously, attendant changes in the acoustic characteristics of speech output.

At a group level, any individual's congenital 'default' settings are likely to be varied through social and linguistic socialization towards ethnic, social-class and regional norms. Sociophonetic research on variation in English indicates that accents cannot comprehensively be described solely in terms of consonant and vowel pronunciation practices, but may be characterized by voice quality settings too. The latter involve both laryngeal features (e.g. creakiness, breathiness) also supralaryngeal settings (e.g. pharyngeal expansion/constriction, fronted/backed tongue body orientation). In other words, speakers of an accent converge in adopting, unconsciously and involuntarily, positions and orientations of vocal tract component parts. Trudgill (1974) found that working-class Norwich speech is characterized by raised larynx (which shortens the overall tract length), lowered tongue body (which enlarges the oral cavity generally) and vocal tract tension and nasalization. Knowles (1978) records the Merseyside accent as having backed and raised tongue body (which narrows the rear portion of the oral cavity), constriction of the pharynx (reduction of its width) and closed jaw and denasality. The observations of Trudgill and of Knowles are based on general impressions rather than systematic, scheme-based analysis of voice quality. Other studies, however, provide descriptions based on quantified data deriving from the application of the Edinburgh Vocal Profile Analysis (VPA) scheme (Laver, 1980); Laver et al., 1981. For example, Esling's (1978) study of Edinburgh speech found that lower class speakers from the city were characterized by, inter alia, raised larynx, pharyngeal constriction and protruded jaw settings. Stuart-Smith (1999) working in Glasgow found working-class speech to be characterized by raised and backed tongue body (which reduces the oral cavity overall, but particularly the rear portion) and open jaw. Stevens and French (2012) applied a modified version of the VPA to 100 young male (18–25 years) speakers of Standard Southern British English (SSBE)[5] and reported that the speech of more than 80 per cent of the group was characterized by fronted tongue body, advanced tongue tip and sibilance.

Convergence across speakers of the same or similar varieties can be very strong. In a study of voice quality in a group of 16 female speakers of Scots English carried out by Mackenzie Beck (1988), 17 of the 120 speaker pairs were 'vocal twins', that is, they had overall (laryngeal and supralaryngeal) vocal profiles that were the same to within one scalar degree on a seven point scale. In the SSBE study, Stevens and French (2012) reported a range of figures for the occurrence of twin pairs within the group of 100. These range from a minimum of 2 to a maximum of 29 twin pairs, depending on how 'twin' is defined.

At a group level, then, one sees a measure of convergence across speakers of particular language varieties in terms of the vocal tract settings they adopt (see also Jones, this volume).

Irrespective of the technical quality of forensic recordings, the above considerations are in themselves sufficient grounds for rejecting the use of the ASR system as a stand-alone method for forensic speaker comparison. In our view, the proper use of an ASR system is as one component within a more comprehensive testing scheme, as represented in an AuPA+AcPA approach described below. This may be seen as a variant of HASR. However, the major element of the analytic process here rests with the human analysis, that is, the 'H' components. Crucially, many of the human components relate to speech habits and/or socially learned speech and language behaviours rather than acoustic reflexes of vocal tract anatomy.

5.2 Auditory Phonetic cum Acoustic Approach

The AuPA+AcPA approach seeks to exploit the componentiality of speech. Within it, the speech signal is conceptualized in terms of a number of separable components, each of which can be analysed and documented for comparison across the questioned and known recordings. The components are found at both the segmental and suprasegmental levels of phonetic description (French et al., 2010; Foulkes & French, 2012). They include:

5.2.1 Suprasegmental Features
Voice quality. A thorough analysis of voice quality should always be undertaken. This may be carried out using a version of the Laver Vocal Profile Analysis scheme (Laver, 1980; Laver et al., 1981). The scheme distinguishes phonation features (e.g. creaky voice, tremor), laryngeal and vocal tract muscular tension

(e.g. tense larynx, lax vocal tract) and vocal tract settings (e.g. nasalization, pharyngeal constriction, fronted lingual body orientation). There are around 38 individual settings and features to be considered, and a score may be assigned to each in terms of six scalar degrees. Formal training in the use of the scheme allows for the systematic examination and comparison of voice quality, and is considered to be a very powerful resource in the forensic speaker comparison task. It compels the analyst to deconstruct the otherwise holistic impression of voice quality into its component parts. Although the VPA scheme has an auditory basis, instrumental corroboration of many auditory impressions is possible. For example, judgements concerning creaky and harsh voice can be corroborated by reference to spectrographic representations of glottal pulses. Judgements concerning breathy voice can be corroborated by showing decreased harmonics to noise ratio, increased formant bandwidth generally and/or strengthening of the spectrum at the lower frequencies and in the area of the third formant. Impressions of strong nasalization may be verified by the presence of a low frequency formant running through phonologically non-nasal voiced segments; and the frontness or backness of tongue body orientation may be grounded in scatter plots representing the distribution in vowel space of first versus second formant values obtained for the peripheral vowels.

Intonation. Patterns of intonation may be analysed and notated using conventions from one or another of the established notation systems (see, O'Connor & Arnold, 1973; Ladd, 2008). Aspects of intonation that practitioners might find relevant to comparisons include tone unit boundary divisions, tonicity (nuclear syllable placement), tonality (tone selection) and head and tail organization (Gold & French 2011a, b). Again, judgements are normally made on an auditory basis but can, where necessary, be corroborated by, for example, reference to fundamental frequency (F0) curves.

General voice pitch. This may be measured as average (mean) and variation (standard deviation) in fundamental frequency (F0) using acoustic analysis software. Although the testing is instrumental in nature, judgment must be exercised in the selection of material for comparison that is similar in, for example, level of speaker animation and emotional tone.

Speed of speech/rate of delivery. Calculations are made of either speaking rate, based on the 'raw' speech sample including pauses and disfluencies, or articulation rate based on samples from which pauses and disfluencies have been edited out (Künzel, 1997). Measurements may be with respect to either the average number of phonological syllables per second (the syllable that would be expected to occur in citation forms of the words), or the average number of phonetic syllables (those that actually occur).

Rhythmical features. Useful considerations include the degree to which the speech tends towards stress-timing or syllable-timing and lengthening/shortening of stressed syllables in comparison with their relative canonical durations.

5.2.2 Segmental Components

Consonantal features that figure in the speaker comparison examinations include energy loci of plosive bursts and fricatives, durations of liquids, nasals and fricatives in specific phonological environments, voice onset time of plosives and presence/absence of (pre-)voicing in lenis plosives.

Vowel features figure prominently in most examinations. They may include the auditory quality of vowels, acoustic patterns such as formant configurations, formant centre frequencies, densities and bandwidths. They may also involve formant frequency averaging in respect of multiple instances of the same vowel phonemes and the computer generation and comparison of 'vowel space' scattergrams based on the lowest two formant values.

Connected speech processes. Although intricately bound up with rhythm and tempo, practices vary across individuals with respect to similitude, assimilation and elision.

5.2.3 Higher-Level and Non-Linguistic Features

Attention is also given to higher-level linguistic features. These may be situated at the levels of morphology, lexico-syntax or discourse organization (e.g. discourse markers 'like', 'you know', 'innit'). Non-linguistic features may include voice and speech pathologies, disfluencies, throat-clearing and tongue clicking habits (Gold, 2012), audible breathing and patterns of both filled and silent pausing.

6 Considering Findings and Expressing Conclusions

All speaker comparisons reveal differences and similarities between the known and questioned samples, even where the same speaker is involved. These must be interpreted against the analyst's experience-based knowledge and against information from research studies concerning the factors that may affect the component in question. With regard to F0, for example, a rise is to be expected for the same person speaking in noisy versus quiet conditions (Summer et al., 1988; Junqua, 1996; French, 1998) or over the telephone versus face-to-face (Hirson et al., 1994). First formant values are known to be upshifted as an artefact of the bandwidth limitation of the telephone channel (Künzel, 2001; Bryne & Foulkes, 2004). The impression of denasality in voice quality may also be heightened by telephonic transmission (Stevens & French, 2012). The significance of similarities must be assessed against the distributions and patterns found in relevant background populations, as similarities shared with large numbers of speakers have limited significance compared with those which are sparsely distributed or uncommon. In respect of certain – limited – components, population statistics are available for reference (see Enderby & Phillipp, 1986 for incidence of stammering; Hudson et al., 2007, for F0 statistics). More generally, normative descriptions of language varieties available in conspectus overviews (Hughes et al., 2012; Wells, 1982, vols 1–3) and edited collections containing sociophonetic studies (Beal et al., 2012; Britain, 2007; Foulkes & Docherty, 1999; Llamas & Watt, 2010) may serve as a backcloth against which speaker comparison findings may be evaluated.

The transformation of findings into conclusions is presently a controversial issue both within forensic science generally and FSS in particular. Until recently, the framework used almost universally within FSS was a classical, or 'frequentist', probability scale. Owing to a lack of population statistics concerning most components in the analysis, the conclusion was usually expressed in terms of a verbal, rather than percentage, probability of the likelihood of identity between the suspect and criminal speaker. Terms from such scales are, for instance, 'very likely to be the same speaker', 'fairly probably the same speaker'. Expression of conclusions in these terms, however, has recently been heavily criticized (Rose, 2002; French & Harrison, 2007; Morrison, 2009). Critics have pointed out that this type of framework embeds logical and legal flaws. They point out, inter alia, that, just because the suspect and criminal share speech features, it does not follow that they are likely to be the same person. Given that there may well be speakers other than the suspect who share the features found in the criminal's voice, then, on the basis of the voice findings alone, it is no more likely for the suspect to be the criminal speaker than it is for any of the other speakers who share the profile. This framework for presenting conclusions is said to commit the *prosecutor's fallacy* and overestimate the weight of the evidence in favour of the prosecution.

A major alternative to the classical probability framework is the Bayesian Likelihood Ratio (LR) approach. This avoids the logical and legal flaws attached to the classical probability framework. It turns the tables – rather than asking how likely it is that the suspect spoke the criminal sample, it involves an assessment or determination of the likelihood of finding the evidence arising from the comparison if the criminal and suspect samples were from the same speaker, over the likelihood of finding that same evidence if the samples were from different speakers.

LRs may be expressed as numbers using the following formulation:

$$\frac{\text{probability of evidence given same speaker hypothesis}}{\text{probability of evidence given different speaker hypothesis}} = \frac{P(E\,|\,H_{SS})}{P(E\,|\,H_{DS})}$$

For example, if the probability of finding the evidence given the same speaker hypothesis is 1 and the probability of finding it given the different speaker hypothesis is 0.05, then $1 \div 0.05 = 20$. In other words, the evidence found is 20 times more likely to have occurred if the same speaker, rather than different speaker hypothesis is correct.

With certain ASR systems, a numerical LR is the default output of comparisons. Within the componential AuPA+AcPA approach espoused here, a conclusion in the form of a numerical likelihood ratio is impossible, the reason being that population statistics for many of the component features examined simply do not exist. Further, given the large number of parameters examined and that many of the features are accent specific, with the high degree of geographical, social and ethnic differentiation found in countries like the United Kingdom, it would be impossible to amass them. Even if it were possible, their shelf-life would be limited owing to the ever-changing nature of speech and language use.

While remaining within the LR conclusion framework, an alternative to expressing the outcome numerically involves using impressionistic verbal LRs. Thus, one could say, for example, that the evidence found was 'moderately more likely' or 'very much more likely' if the criminal and suspect were the same speaker than if they were different speakers. The authors are in the process of adopting this approach.

It has been argued that forensic science is currently undergoing a 'paradigm shift' from the frequentist to the Bayesian LR approach (Morrison, 2009). The figures arising from the Gold and French (2011) survey do indicate a movement in that direction, in that some 11 per cent of the 47 experts/labs taking part expressed their conclusions in terms of a numerical LR[6] and 8 per cent as a verbal LR. However, the frequentist approach to conclusions still remains in ascendance (38%), with what some would regard as a transitional approach, known as the 'UK Position Statement' framework (French & Harrison, 2007),[7] which overcomes some but not all of the problems associated with the frequentist position, coming a close second (35%). Somewhat worryingly, given the absence of any known uniquely identifying voice parameter, 5 per cent (two) of those surveyed expressed conclusions as categorical statements of identification.

The outcomes of forensic speaker comparisons can seldom, if ever, be definitive, and whatever framework is used for expressing conclusions, due caution must be exercised. The IAFPA has, as a clause in its Code of Practice, the requirement that 'members should make clear, both in their reports and in giving evidence in court, the limitations of forensic phonetic and acoustic analysis' (www.iafpa.net/code.htm). It is usual for reports to contain a standard caveat along the following lines:

> The evidence from forensic speaker comparison tests is not comparable to fingerprints and it is recognised that there could be people in the population who are indistinguishable in respect of voice and speech patterns.

However, the methods allow one to arrive at an opinion, which can be supported by reference to phonetic and acoustic features of the material examined. Where such evidence is relied on in a criminal prosecution, it should be used in conjunction with other evidence. (JP French Associates report template)

No known miscarriage of justice has ever arisen from the use of the componential AuPA+AcPA approach, despite there being an estimated 500 cases processed using this method each year in the United Kingdom alone.[8]

7 Conclusion

In this chapter we have attempted to provide an overview of some of the main tasks undertaken by practitioners of FSS. Our main focus has been on the task most often carried out, forensic speaker comparison. In describing this, we have sought to introduce the reader to current areas of development and controversy with regard to methodology and the formulation of conclusions. In order to provide the highest quality of evidence to the judicial system, one must keep practices under continuing critical review and be willing to embrace beneficial advances in technology and thinking. An openness to change, together with a rigorous and comprehensive approach to testing and an appropriately cautious approach to the drawing of conclusions, are essential in preserving the integrity and maintaining the probative value of evidence from this developing field of speech science.

Notes

1. In addition to the analysis of recorded speech, FSS practitioners are occasionally asked to assist with assembling voice line-ups, that is, the auditory equivalent of visual identification parades, and to undertake evaluations of the reliability of earwitness identifications by lay witnesses. A summary of the issues associated with these areas can be found in (Rose, 2002).
2. The system is Batvox, produced by the Madrid based company Agnitio.
3. However, see Darch et al. (2005) on the relationship of MFCCs to formants.
4. It should be further borne in mind that we are not attempting to map directly individual variations in the surfaces of the vocal tracts themselves – an exercise that might well produce unique individual biometrics – but are doing so in a highly indirect way by taking measures of their acoustic outputs.
5. These are represented the in the Cambridge University DyViS corpus – see Nolan et al. (2009).
6. Those using numerical LRs all used the HASR methodology.
7. Within this framework, conclusions are expressed in terms of a two-part decision. The first part involves stating whether the known and questioned samples are compatible,

or *consistent*, with having been produced by the same speaker. If samples are found to be consistent, a decision is then made regarding how unusual, or *distinctive*, the combination of features common to the samples is considered to be.

8. In addition to pointing out the limitations of the evidence the analyst must also exercise caution against assigning individual weighting to potentially overlapping and highly interdependent components of the analysis. Apposite examples include supralaryngeal voice quality settings, formant distributions and the outputs of ASR systems.

13 Phonetic Pedagogy

Patricia Ashby and Michael Ashby

1 Introduction

Phonetics and pedagogy intersect in a number of distinct ways, partly because phonetics is a broad interdisciplinary field, and partly because it is both a discipline in its own right and a tool applied in the teaching of other subjects. This chapter offers a categorization of the various phonetics-pedagogy intersections, mainly according to the purposes each is required to serve.

Modern phonetics began to take shape around 1850 at the three-way meeting of biomedical science (at first, mainly physiology), physical science (in the early days, chiefly acoustics) and linguistic science (at the time dominated by a comparative-historical paradigm; see Heselwood Hassan & Jones, this volume). Each of those areas has subsequently undergone extensive diversification and development, with the result that the total field of phonetics is now very wide. Some idea of the interdisciplinary range of contemporary phonetics can be gathered from the present volume.

Though phonetics is thus in one sense a very large field, the number of teachers and researchers working within that field worldwide is relatively small. Hardcastle and Laver (1997, p. 1) point out that attendance at the four-yearly International Congress of Phonetic Sciences (ICPhS) is of the order of 1,000, and this is probably a fair indication of the size of the international research community. Given this small constituency, it is perhaps unsurprising that there is relatively little established work in phonetic pedagogy. There is, for example, no journal of phonetics education, nor even one which regularly gives space to pedagogical matters, and seemingly only one regular conference, the biennial Phonetics Teaching and Learning Conference (PTLC).[1] This is in marked contrast to the situation in numerous other disciplines – taking at random, for example, anthropology, music, physics, veterinary science – where it is not uncommon to find several high-profile journals devoted exclusively to educational matters, and series of international conferences. Similarly, there have been few surveys of phonetic pedagogy. The ICPhS has generally included papers on pedagogical topics,[2] but numerous as these papers are, relatively few of them deal with the teaching and learning of core phonetics; as the titles of special sessions and themes indicate, the focus is commonly on second or foreign language pronunciation and perception, and the practical pedagogical implications (if any) concern the teaching of pronunciation rather than of phonetics itself. Similar emphases are apparent in the papers submitted to the PTLC. In fact, it is hardly too much to assert that 'phonetic pedagogy' is widely taken to mean principally the teaching of pronunciation rather than the teaching of phonetics.

Certainly the numbers of those for whom phonetics is a tool must be far greater than of those concerned with phonetics as a discipline in its own right. It is instructive to examine the memberships of some relevant professional organizations. Teachers of English to Speakers of Other Languages (TESOL), a global association which oversees professional expertise in the second-language teaching of English claims 12,866 members at the time of writing, while the International Association of Teachers of English as a Foreign Language (IATEFL) claims more than 3,000 members across hundred countries. The Royal College of Speech and Language Therapists (RCSLT), the professional body for speech and language therapy in the United Kingdom) currently gives its membership as upwards of 14,000. It is plain that, even if only a half of the professionals who make up these memberships are imagined as having some measure of phonetic training, they must outnumber by an order of magnitude those trained and working within the discipline of phonetics proper.

2 Kinds of Phonetic Pedagogy .

A first necessary distinction is between the teaching *of* phonetics, taught and assessed as a discipline in its own right, and phonetics used as a tool *in* the teaching of the pronunciation of a second or foreign language. In the first of these, the aim is to give students a lasting insight into phonetic theory and description, and skills of general applicability. In the second, the aim is solely to facilitate the acquisition of skill in the perception and production of speech in the target language, this being the only outcome that will be assessed; once the required level is achieved, the temporary assistance from applied phonetics can be jettisoned, or indeed forgotten.

Each of the two categories just identified in turn invites a two-way subdivision. Taking first pure phonetics, we note that it may be *chosen* as the main focus of study, as it is for example by the relatively small numbers of students who undertake master's courses in phonetics, or instead it may be a *required* or *imposed* component of a type of programme with a primary focus elsewhere, such as courses in speech and language pathology and therapy.

Turning to applied phonetics, we note that phonetics may be used in two ways in pronunciation teaching. It may either be *implicit* – that is, kept behind the scenes (e.g. to inform the development of training methods and assessments) – or it may be in some measure *explicitly* introduced to students (for instance, using terminology, diagrams or phonetic symbols), with the possible result that students are not only helped towards their pronunciation goals, but are also likely to retain a degree of independent phonetic insight.

It may be worth clearing up a possible misunderstanding concerning the term 'applied'. We quite properly speak of the 'application' of phonetics within fields such as speech and language pathology and therapy. But phonetics is not applied as a tool in the training of speech and language therapists in the way that it may be so applied in the training of those learning a foreign language – that is, it is not employed as a method of reaching some other goal. On the contrary, a specific knowledge and competence in phonetics is stipulated as one of the component skills required for the profession, and a candidate hoping to enter the profession will have to satisfy examiners in tests of essentially pure phonetics. Hence the kind of phonetic teaching which arises in this connection is that relating to *pure* phonetics, but for those who have been *required* to undertake it.

Plainly there will be various possible mixtures and overlaps, but taken together, the distinctions just outlined suggest a basic four-way classification of types of phonetic pedagogy: (1) pure elective, (2) pure obligatory, (3) applied implicit and (4) applied explicit. These divisions necessarily affect the content and delivery of phonetics programmes.

2.1 The Teaching *of* Phonetics – Pure Elective

Any treatment of the teaching of phonetics ought to be able to consider the contexts in which teaching is undertaken, the programmes and syllabuses followed, the methods, materials and assessments employed and the validation of standards. There appears, however, to be no contemporary survey of any scope on which generalizations could be based. A review of European provision in phonetics, spoken language engineering and speech and language therapy, with indications of future directions, was made in the late 1990s (Bloothooft et al., 1997, 1998), though of course both that review and the proposals which were based upon it are now considerably dated. It is fair to assume that phonetics teaching generally takes place in a higher education context, and is linked to the award of degrees or diplomas. But there is much local variation in syllabus, assessment and type of award, with no single professional body validating content or awards, either nationally or internationally.[3]

Within this variation, the largest shared element in phonetic teaching worldwide must come from available coursebooks and online materials. The model for an introduction to the field has been set for more than a generation by Peter Ladefoged's outstanding *Course in Phonetics*, blending lucid exposition, original fieldwork observations, superb diagrams, detailed exercises and freely shared resources. Five editions appeared during the author's lifetime, the sixth being posthumously revised and augmented by K. Johnson (Ladefoged & Johnson, 2011).

Perhaps it is the very lack of syllabus standardization, and a perceived need to adapt materials to local requirements, which have prompted a surprisingly large number of other introductory texts. One may note Ball and Rahilly (1999), Carr (1999), Ashby (2005), Ashby and Maidment (2005), Davenport and Hannahs (2005), Hewlett and Beck (2006), Singh and Singh (2006), Clark et al. (2007), Collins and Mees (2008), Lodge (2009), Ogden (2009), Reetz and Jongman (2009), Roach (2009) and Ashby (2011) (in several cases these are second or later editions of established works).

Recent editions of Ladefoged's *Course* have been accompanied by a CD of speech examples, most of which are also accessible online, and many of the other introductions just cited are supported in similar ways. Leaving aside materials assembled to illustrate a particular course-text, the internet also hosts an enormous variety of open resources relating to phonetic symbols and transcription, speech production and perception, practical phonetics training and audio samples of particular languages.[4]

The main changes in pure phonetics teaching over the last 20 years or so are certainly those resulting from enormous growth in available resources, many of them freely shared, and rapid developments in the ease and speed with which information of all kinds – images, text, audio – can be processed, stored and exchanged (Mompeán et al., 2011). Parallel changes have of course affected all other academic disciplines, but the impact within phonetics has perhaps been greater than in many others. Phonetics teaching has always been quick to adopt multimedia enhancements of teaching materials (Daniel Jones's recordings of the Cardinal Vowels, for example, first appeared in 1917).

The changes just referred to have affected not only the delivery of phonetics teaching, but have also altered conceptions of the organization of the subject, and hence the curriculum. Divisions such as those among articulatory, auditory and acoustic or experimental phonetics date from the days when symbols and diagrams would be sketched on the lecture-room chalkboard, recordings of exotic languages consulted in the listening cubicles of the language lab and spectrograms made laboriously under supervision in a designated phonetics laboratory. When all of those activities can be carried out on the same laptop computer, the logic of the divisions between them becomes questionable. Vassière (2003) may have been the first to write of bringing the phonetics laboratory into the classroom, though no doubt the same possibilities were perceived around the same time by many phonetics teachers. Ashby et al. (2005) showed how the seemingly disparate activities of the phonetics practical class and the phonetics laboratory could be brought together by live on-the-spot analyses of the teacher's and students' productions, using radio microphones in an interactive class. Drawing on the whole range of available technologies, from Unicode phonetic fonts to Virtual Learning Environments, Ashby et al. (2008) were able to mount a complete e-learning distance course in phonetics, with 'lectures', ear-training exercises, formative assessments and feedback and a final examination (for a summary, see Ashby, 2008).

Programmes devoted to the teaching *of* phonetics thus have a great deal in common, and have seized similar opportunities for development. The main point of difference among such programmes concerns the importance (if any) attached to the training of practical skills in sound identification and production. Pioneers such as Henry Sweet (1845–1912) and Eduard Sievers (1850–1932) took it as axiomatic that a high degree of practical training was essential, an emphasis that was continued by Daniel Jones (1881–1967), and his pupils and successors such as David Abercrombie (1909–92) and J. C. Catford (1917–2009); see especially Catford (2001). Most recently, the companion website to Ashby (2011) seeks to continue this tradition.

By the mid-1990s a decline in the extent and status of practical phonetics training was well under way, even in Britain where it had been strongest. Bloothooft et al. reported that

> Training in the production of sounds of the world languages was offered as an obligatory part of the curriculum in about 40% of the institutes. A further third of respondents did not put great importance on these skills within their curricula. About a quarter of respondents offered no training in these skills. (1997, p. 18)

At around the same time, in a letter to the *Journal of Phonetics* occasioned by the death of David Abercrombie, Ladefoged (1997, p. 90) comments on the changing situation and reports how he had shamed 'leading participants' at a recent ICPhS by demonstrating in an impromptu practical phonetics test that they 'were unable to perform clicks and ejectives in words'.[5]

2.2 The Teaching *of* Phonetics – Pure-obligatory

The largest number of those following a training in phonetics have not chosen it directly, but have been *required* to gain a qualification in it for accreditation in the profession they hope to enter. This is the case, certainly in Britain, for those training as Speech and Language therapists (SLT), and it is ironic that at a time when practical training in pure-elective contexts is in decline, it remains a required component for professional accreditation: the relevant paragraph of the Standards of Proficiency for Speech and Language Therapists published by the UK Health Professions Council says that practitioners must be able to 'describe and analyse clients' abilities and needs using, where appropriate, phonetic transcription . . .' (p. 9)[6].

The relatively large numbers on phonetics courses[7] attached to SLT programmes thus encompass students with a range of motivations and attitudes towards the subject, including at least some who are indifferent, reluctant or even hostile, and this has given rise to pedagogical research which is in some measure *remedial* in its goals. This research touches on attitude, learning styles and possible links between musical and phonetic ability, and is undertaken with a view to improving pedagogical methods and teaching materials, or perhaps furnishing screening procedures for student selection (MacKenzie Beck, 2003; Dankovicová et al., 2007; Knight in press). Recent results from cognitive neuroscience (Golestani et al., 2011) point rather clearly to innate structural differences in the auditory cortex of expert phoneticians compared with matched controls, furnishing a possible physical basis for a predisposition to the subject. This of course relates to the role of aptitude in the teaching of pure phonetics; issues of aptitude and motivation arise in a different form in relation to the teaching of pronunciation (for a review see Rogerson-Revell, 2011).

A perceived need to encourage and support students who did not primarily choose to study phonetics but find it urged upon them as a vocational desideratum also arises in regard to those training to be English as a Foreign Language (EFL) teachers (or trainers of such teachers). This has given rise to a considerable body of pedagogical material aimed at teachers and trainers in which the proportion of motivational and assistive material is high compared with the phonetic content. The aim is often not only to give language teachers some grounding in phonetics, and ideas on how to apply it, but also to argue the case for pronunciation training generally, in a context where it is often sidelined. While much of this material is of considerable merit (Fraser, 2001; Underhill, 2005), the pedagogical benefits of sugaring the (supposed) pill of phonetics may be doubted, seeing that learners form their expectations and prejudices about the relative difficulty of different components of their syllabus on the basis of cues – both overt and implicit – picked up from their teachers (Biggs, 2007). To introduce the topic of pronunciation by means of numerous analogies and mnemonics may be to imply, effectively, 'this topic is difficult, and you're going to find it challenging'.

2.3 Phonetics *in* Teaching – Applied Implicit

Presumably few would doubt that phonetics is the science on which the teaching of pronunciation must be based. But as outlined earlier, phonetic knowledge and research may be applied implicitly or explicitly in such teaching. The types of work just considered, which interpret phonetics for teachers of pronunciation, or for the trainers of such teachers, would tend to lead to implicit use in the actual delivery of pronunciation teaching itself. For one thing, teachers who required encouragement to engage with phonetics and to consider the possibility of systematic pronunciation teaching are hardly likely to feel able to purvey explicit phonetic training and knowledge to their own students. Nevertheless, the implicit application of phonetics by those teaching pronunciation is potentially very valuable, and is likely to include ability to analyse the pronunciation and perception difficulties of students (and to an extent to anticipate them through contrastive analysis), the understanding of issues connected with pronunciation models and identities, the setting of priorities in pronunciation work and the cultivation of an interactive and supportive classroom environment where pronunciation work can flourish. A comprehensive analysis of the ways in which a phonetically trained teacher can apply phonetics in pronunciation teaching, without necessarily resorting to explicit teaching of phonetics, is given by MacCarthy (1978), though his analysis assumes a degree of training and confidence on the part of the teacher which is now rare.

A number of writers have commented on the decoupling of 'L2' research from practical pedagogical concerns (Rogerson-Revell, 2011, p. 16). Liberman (2008) notes a gulf between practice and the research behind it. Much experimental L2 research, if it can lead to applications at all, would have to be applied implicitly. A good example of research successfully applied this way is High Variabilty Phonetic Training (HVPT), an idea which arose from theories of category formation in speech perception. It was explored in detail by Pisoni and colleagues from around 1991 (Logan et al., 1991; see also discussion in Liberman, 2008). They advocate methods which aim to:

> form robust phonetic categories by increasing stimulus variability during learning. Different talkers produce widely varying acoustic output due to differences in vocal tract size and shape, glottal source function, dialect, and speaking rates. This additional stimulus variability may be important for developing stable and robust phonetic categories that show perceptual constancy across different environment. (Logan et al., 1991, p. 876)[8]

An example of HVPT realized as computer software (or smartphone application) is the UCL Vowel Trainer[9] developed by Iverson and Evans (see Iverson &

Evans, 2009 and references therein). The technique is evidently highly success-ful, but it is worth pointing out that it does indeed provide *training* rather than *teaching*. It does not give learners any insight into vowel categorization, or the means to help themselves on future occasions.

2.4 Phonetics *in* Teaching – Applied Explicit

The explicit application of phonetic knowledge in the teaching of pronuncia-tion characterizes the approach associated with Daniel Jones and his various colleagues and students. In this tradition, it is taken for granted that an under-standing of phonetic categorization and terminology, and an ability to read and to write phonetic transcription, are needed even by those whose goal is devel-opment of skill in the pronunciation of a foreign language (It should be pointed out that an emphasis on conscious knowledge of phonetics does not preclude the simultaneous development of unconscious skills or habits by production drilling and ear-training; in practice, the two were always used together).

Phonetic knowledge can of course be explicit without being complete: a pro-nunciation teacher may on occasion use phonetic concepts and terminology where necessary to reinforce a pronunciation point without basing the whole approach on explicit phonetic analysis. The advantage of doing this – rather than using ad hoc or fanciful descriptions which serve only present needs – is that what is imparted to the learner can serve as an interface to further study, whether this is undertaken as independent learning or in a new academic con-text. Good examples of explicit though limited applications of phonetics are MacCarthy (1978), already mentioned above, Morley (1994), and outstanding pronunciation practice books such as Grant (2001) and Gilbert (2005).

3 Relation to General Pedagogical Theory

Finally, it is relevant to consider phonetic pedagogy in the broader context of pedagogical theory. As noted in Ashby (2008), it is interesting to reflect that the mixture of theory and interactive practical training long advocated in the British-style approach to phonetics teaching anticipates many features now for-mally acknowledged as elements of good practice. The following have been suggested as factors in the teaching environment which tend to promote a deep approach to learning:

> Teaching in such a way as to explicitly bring out the structure of the topic or subject;

Teaching to elicit an active response from students, for example, question-
ing, presenting problems, rather than teaching to expound information;
Teaching by building on what students already know;
Confronting and eradicating students' misconceptions;
Assessing for structure rather than for independent facts. (Biggs, 2007,
pp. 16–17)

All of these can be readily exemplified from the interactive, participatory style
of learning which arises when students are guided and encouraged to explore
their own speech patterns, their own unconscious linguistic knowledge and the
capabilities of their own vocal tracts and voices.

Problem-based learning, learning through discovery, the engagement of
multiple sensory modalities and the development of learner autonomy, can
all be traced in familiar exercises such as phonetic transcription, ear-training
dictation and the phonetics practical production class. In fact one of the great
benefits of a pure phonetics training with a large practical component may be
not the practical skills themselves (which many learners may have little further
occasion to deploy), but rather the enhanced understanding of theory which
the approach can bring (very much in the way described by Catford, 2001).

The greatest threats currently facing phonetic pedagogy are those which in
search of economies will cut engagement and interactivity and thus tend to
encourage surface learning in place of the deep learning which many current
and former practitioners were privileged to enjoy.

Notes

1. PTLC proceedings can be consulted online via www.phon.ucl.ac.uk/ptlc/
2. The most recent congress (Lee & Zee, 2011) included two full oral sessions on pedagogy, one being a special session on 'Phonetic teaching and learning' and four sessions with titles which include 'L2'. At the Saarbrücken congress (Trouvain & Barry,
2007) there was a Special Session 'Second Language Acquisition and Exemplar
Theory', three oral sessions on aspects of 'Foreign language acquisition', including
one session on 'new methodology'. At Barcelona in 2003 (Solé et al., 2003) there was a
Symposium 'Tools for teaching phonetics', and both poster and oral sessions devoted
to pedagogy.
3. The International Phonetic Association still offers a Certificate examination in the
Phonetics of English, this being the only current legacy from the association's former
leadership in setting standards.
4. A useful annotated selective list arranged by topic is maintained at: www.unc.
edu/~jlsmith/pht-url.html.
5. There is a minor error over dates in Ladefoged's account. He describes the events as
having taking place at ICPhS XIV – this is impossible, as that congress (Los Angeles)
was in 1999, later than the publication of Ladefoged's letter. He means ICPhS XIII
(Stockholm) in 1995 – and indeed the *Proceedings* of that congress contain Ladefoged's
paper from the session in question.

6. Available at: www.hpc-uk.org/assets/documents/10000529Standards_of_Proficiency_ SLTs.pdf. The requirement is for transcription (i.e. auditory recognition and symbolic representation), not performance, and the once universal expectation that students should be able to perform sounds as well as recognize them has been dropped in some UK training institutions. Ladefoged's informal experiment at ICPhS involved production, though it seems likely that similarly poor results would have been obtained in a listening task.
7. As an illustration, at UCL the annual SLT intake is in the region of 60; by contrast, the number beginning the MA Phonetics is about one-tenth of that.
8. Though the work reported aims at training the phonemic categories of a second or foreign language, there is a clear parallel with the general phonetic 'ear training' that has long formed part of a training in pure phonetics, where the concern is to establish a wide range of sound categories, independently of any one phonemic system. Along with the sources of variability listed by Pisoni and colleagues, one may add those which result from live delivery in a classroom: reverberation, ambient noise, other speech, variation in the location of the source (as the speaker moves around the room), etc.
9. www.phon.ucl.ac.uk/shop/voweltrainer.php

14 An Introduction to Phonetic Technology

Mark Huckvale

1 Applications

Phonetics is not just an academic discipline; phonetic knowledge also underpins a multi-billion dollar speech technology industry. Businesses are selling products *now* that exploit knowledge of phonological structures, allophonic variants and articulatory constraints. Text-to-speech (TTS) conversion systems convert written text into an audio facsimile of speech, as if it were being read by a person. Voice dictation systems produce a written transcript of dictated utterances, captured from a microphone recording. Interactive voice response systems lead customers through business transactions over the telephone, by prompting for and recognizing pieces of spoken information. Speaker verification systems check the identity of a person by comparing characteristics of his or her voice with those on file.

Phonetic knowledge is also found in many emerging applications which are yet to be fully commercialized. Speech-to-speech translation systems will help two speakers of different languages to communicate. Voice conversion systems will give your voice a new identity, or give a computer's voice your identity. Audio and video indexing systems will help track down parts of radio or television broadcasts or video recordings by what was said in them. Concept-to-speech systems will communicate information using spoken descriptions of objects and events found in computer databases.

In this chapter, my aim is to provide an outline of the essential phonetic technologies behind these applications. Rather than provide detailed descriptions of the architecture and operation of each type of system, I will focus on the nature of the phonetic representations they use and how these are processed. In this way, the chapter aims to expose the current state-of-the-art in exploiting phonetic knowledge for technological applications.

2 Transformations

Spoken utterances can be represented in many forms at a number of different linguistic levels: signals, features, phones, segments, words and utterances. For each level we will look at the transformations used to convert between representations, both in terms of analysis and of synthesis. This approach acknowledges an ongoing trend in phonetic technology, that transformations are expressions of the phonetic relationship between levels and are often appropriate to both recognition and generation of speech.

2.1 Transformations between Signals and Features

The majority of speech technology applications do not operate on the acoustic signal directly, but on the basis of a sequence of *feature frames*, where each frame represents the acoustic properties of a short-section of the signal. The reasons are:

(1) to reduce the data rate and remove signal redundancy, by changing from a one-dimensional sequence of samples at a high rate to a two-dimensional table of feature frames at a lower rate,

(2) to obtain representations which are easier to compare – facilitating the use of *distance functions* which deliver estimates of the phonetic similarity of signal sections,

(3) to make possible the modification of properties of the acoustic signal such as fundamental frequency or spectral envelope,

(4) to create representations which match the requirements of subsequent pattern processing stages, such as orthogonality (feature independence), robustness against noise or robustness against speaker variation.

The transformation into frames is performed on overlapping sections of the signal called *windows*, see Figure 14.1. These windows are often fixed in duration, but may also be derived 'pitch-synchronously', that is, at locations which span a fixed number of repetition periods of the signal. The durations of windows are chosen to be sufficiently long for good estimation of the important phonetic properties of the signal, but short enough to cope with rapid changes in properties with time. It is common to generate feature frames every 10 ms, each being based on a 30 ms window of the signal.

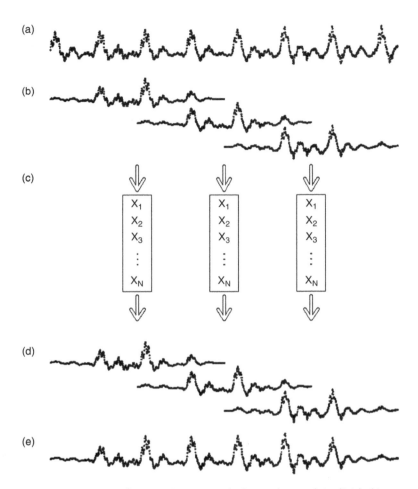

Figure 14.1 For analysis, (a) input sampled speech signal, is divided into (b) overlapping windows, and then analysed into (c) sequence of feature frames. For synthesis, the feature frames are used to recreate (d) signal segments, which are overlapped and added to create (e) output signal

Most feature transformations can also be used for synthesis, that is, there exist methods by which a speech signal can be regenerated from the feature frame sequence. Typically each frame is used to generate a short section of signal which is then overlapped and added to other sections to create a continuous output as in the lower part of Figure 14.1.

Below is a sample from a wide-range of feature representations that have been developed for representing sections of speech signals. See Figure 14.2 for a graphical demonstration of some of these.

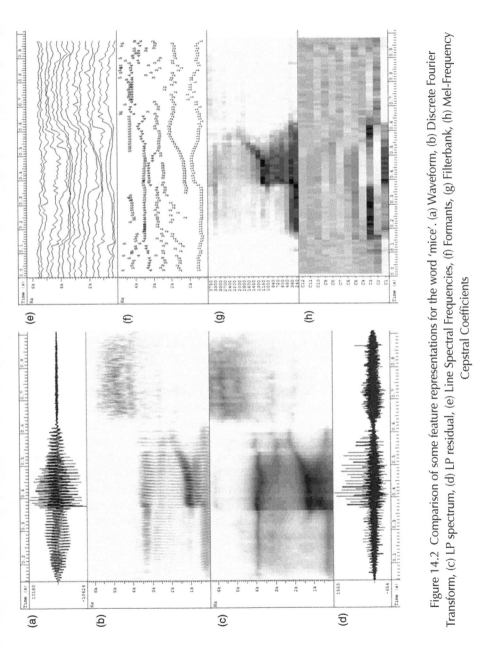

Figure 14.2 Comparison of some feature representations for the word 'mice'. (a) Waveform, (b) Discrete Fourier Transform, (c) LP spectrum, (d) LP residual, (e) Line Spectral Frequencies, (f) Formants, (g) Filterbank, (h) Mel-Frequency Cepstral Coefficients

2.1.1 Discrete Fourier Transform (DFT)

The Discrete Fourier Transform (DFT) converts N signal samples into the amplitudes and phases of N/2 harmonics. These harmonics are the constituent sinewaves which when summed make up the windowed signal section. No information is lost in the transformation, and the signal can be perfectly reconstructed from the feature vector. The DFT is widely used as a means for manipulating the signal in the frequency domain, for equalization, dynamic compression or noise reduction for example.

2.1.2 Sinusoidal Model

Here a limited number of sinusoids are chosen from the DFT, to represent the signal using fewer than N/2 frequencies. These are typically chosen on the basis of a least-squares fit to the waveform (Quatieri & McAulay, 1992). Since the chosen sinusoids are likely to correspond to the harmonics of a periodic sound, they also form the basis for a mechanism to modify the pitch or duration of the reconstructed signal. The sinusoids can be scaled in frequency while maintaining the spectral envelope to change the pitch. Alternatively, frames can be repeated and overlapped to change the speaking rate while keeping pitch constant.

2.1.3 Linear Prediction (LP)

Linear prediction (LP) is a modelling technique which assumes that the observed signal derives from a white (flat spectrum) signal source filtered by an all-pole (all-resonance) filter (Markel & Gray, 1976). The model has a clear relationship to the source-filter model of speech production, where the glottal source is filtered by the vocal tract pipe. LP analysis derives parameters of the filter (expressed either as recursive filter coefficients or as derivatives thereof), and the excitation signal (the signal needed to be input into the filter to generate the observed signal). This excitation is also called the residual, since it expresses the parts of the signal not amenable to linear prediction. In synthesis the residual can be passed back through the filter to recreate the original signal without loss. LP parameters have wide application in speech coding systems, since the filter and residual can be simplified and/or compressed to fewer bits with relatively little loss in quality. Through manipulation of the filter coefficients or the residual, LP analysis has also been widely used for prosody manipulation.

2.1.4 Line Spectral Frequencies (LSF)

One form of the LP filter coefficients that has found favour in voice conversion are Line Spectral Frequencies (LSF) (Kabal & Ramachandran, 1986). This is a way of expressing the LP filter as a set of frequencies in the absence of amplitude information. The amplitude information is captured instead in the spacing between the LSFs (see Figure 14.2). LSFs make it easy to interpolate between two LP filters, which makes them useful in morphing between voices.

2.1.5 Residual Modelling

The residual signal after LP analysis still contains much information about the speech signal. Being the excitation signal that needs to be put through the LP filter to create the speech, it stores information about the energy, the periodicity, and the fundamental frequency of the signal. It also contains some information about the voice quality and hence captures some aspects of speaker identity. There are ongoing attempts to model the information present in the residual so that it can be modified, synthesized or used as a source of speaker identity information. Typically a pitch-synchronous approach is used, whereby one or two periods of the residual are parameterized into a few coefficients. These might be explicitly connected to a model of glottal function through inverse filtering (Wong et al., 1979) or modelled through a process of statistical decomposition (Drugman et al., 2009).

2.1.6 Perceptual Linear Prediction (PLP) and Relative Spectral Transform (RASTA)-PLP

In normal linear prediction, each part of the signal spectrum is weighted equally, and the chosen LP filter best fits the linear spectral magnitudes. In perceptual linear prediction (PLP), the idea is to warp the frequency axis and apply an amplitude compression function before LP modelling, so as to recreate some of the psychoacoustic characteristics of human hearing (Hermansky, 1990). The claim then is that a distance function calculated between PLP vectors should more closely match human judgements of perceptual similarity. In RASTA processing (Hermansky & Morgan, 1994), parameter estimation is made more robust in conditions of noise by assuming that speech features should change slowly in time compared to changes in the noise. A process of averaging features over time provides a simple mechanism for removing short-term parameter fluctuations caused by the noise. The combination of RASTA smoothing and PLP features is widely used for speech recognition in noisy environments.

2.1.7 Filterbanks and MFCC

In many recognition applications it is sufficient to characterize the spectral envelope without regard to the fine temporal structure of the signal. An easy way to do this is to use a bank of band-pass filters with centre frequencies spread across the frequency range of interest. The output of the filters are rectified, smoothed and down-sampled to produce a spectral envelope representation that is quantized in frequency (to say 20 energies) and in time (to say 100 frames/sec). Where such filterbanks have been applied, the bandwidths and centre frequencies of the filters have commonly been adjusted to mimic auditory filters, for example, the 19-channel vocoder (Holmes, 1980). While such filterbank representations form an efficient coding of the envelope, there are still strong correlations between adjacent channels. One way to remove that redundancy is to apply a cosine transform to the filter energy vector across frequency (somewhat like taking the DFT of the spectral envelope). This creates a small number of relatively independent parameters called cepstral coefficients which describe the envelope shape quite well. The combination of an auditory-inspired filterbank and cepstral coefficients is the basis for the mel-scaled cepstral coefficient (MFCC) representation widely used in speech recognition (Davis & Mermelstein, 1980).

2.1.8 STRAIGHT
The STRAIGHT vocoder is a recent development of the idea to decompose the speech signal into a parameterized spectral envelope and a parameterized excitation signal (Kawahara et al., 1999). By performing spectral analysis in a pitch-synchronous manner, STRAIGHT achieves a superior separation of source and filter information, with less source information left in the filter and vice versa. This makes the representation especially suited to applications that require separate manipulation of source and filter characteristics of the voice, such as emotional speech synthesis and voice conversion.

2.2 Transformations between Features and Phones

Whereas feature frames represent short-time sections of the audio signal in a few coefficients, *phones* represent phonetically interesting events that are extended over longer, variable-length regions. Here we will use the term phone to refer to the phonetic realizations of phonological segments, augmented to include non-speech events such as pauses, background noises, lip-smacks, breaths and so on. In this way a whole recording can be considered to be realized as a contiguous sequence of phones. Phones then, are not phonemes (see Jones, this volume). The distinction has the advantage that a single phonological segment can be said to be realized as one of many alternative phones chosen from a large inventory of phone types. It is even possible that one segment could be realized as a sequence of phones.

Since the phone sequence is intermediate between acoustic features and segments, it is at this level that we need to deal with signal variability that is unrelated to the identity of the underlying phonological segments. Such aspects might include pitch changes, additional sound sources present in the audio or speaker-specific characteristics irrelevant to the linguistic interpretation. Thus it is common at this level to see techniques for removing fine temporal structure, adapting to the microphone channel and environment (such as cepstral mean normalization), or adapting to speaker identity (such as vocal tract length normalization, or MLLR transforms of feature vectors (Leggetter & Woodland, 1995)). Conversely, in synthesis, it is at this level that speaker-specific characteristics are added.

The naive approach to the transformation between feature vector sequence and phone sequence assumes a segmentation and labelling of the signal. Segmentation requires finding the temporal boundaries between the phones, and labelling implies choosing a phone from a given inventory of possible phone types.

Attempts have been made to establish a correspondence between feature vector and phone sequence from the 'bottom up', without recourse to phonological information. These employ unsupervised machine learning techniques that group feature vectors by similarity into clusters, then describe the speech signal as a sequence of transitions between clusters. The Kohonen self-organizing map has been found to be useful for this (Kohonen, 1988). Alternatively the probability distribution of the feature vectors themselves can be modelled as being emitted from a collection of multi-variate Gaussian probability distributions: a Gaussian Mixture Model, or GMM (McLachan & Peel, 2000). Each feature vector can then be associated with the probability that it arose from each Gaussian mixture, or the whole sequence of feature vectors can be associated with a probability that it could have arisen from all the mixtures. Such methods are widely applied in speaker recognition, where the interest is in the relative probability that an utterance was produced by a GMM model of one speaker compared to another.

Once a feature frame sequence has been segmented into labelled regions, then each region can be considered an exemplar or a template for a phone label. This has become a popular approach in synthesis, where new utterances are generated from old ones by concatenating labelled regions chosen from a corpus of speech, see Section 3.1. The use of templates for recognition was largely abandoned in the 1970s because they failed to capture phonologically conditioned variability in the phonetic form of speech. However interest in exemplar-based recognition has recently revived with the advent of computer systems of sufficient size and power to perform recognition directly from the training data eschewing the process of statistical modelling (De Wachter et al., 2007).

Undoubtedly the most widespread technique for inter-converting features and phones is the hidden Markov model (HMM) (Rabiner, 1989). Conceptually the idea is simple. The observed feature vector sequence is assumed to have been generated from a finite-state machine – that is from a system comprising a simple network of states and transitions between them. Each state is associated with a distribution over the possible feature frames occurring in some time interval. Each transition is associated with a probability that at each time step the generating system switches from one state to another (see Figure 14.3).

Given an HMM it is straightforward to calculate the probability that it could have generated an observed feature frame sequence. The 'hidden' part of the HMM refers to the fact that this probability can be calculated without deciding on any single association of times and states, that is, without requiring a

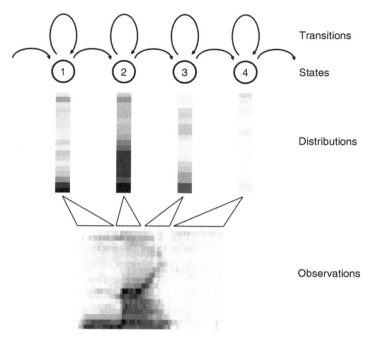

Figure 14.3 A hidden Markov model is a generative model consisting of states to which are associated a distribution of observed spectral frames. Transitions between states capture the ordering and durations of frames. Here four states are used to describe the spectral development of the word 'mice'

segmentation. The probability of an utterance is just the sum of all the ways in which the HMM could have generated the feature vector sequence, over all possible segmentations and alignments. In a phone recognition system, an inventory of phone models is created, where each phone is represented by a small HMM (typically three states), and the set of HMMs are built into one large network of states that also allows transitions between phones (with certain probabilities). The task then is not to find the probability of the utterance, but to find the single best path through the network of states that has the individually highest probability. Since this path travels through a sequence of phone models, the phone sequence is revealed. Note, however, that the search for the best phone sequence is conducted over all possible segmentations; it is not the case that segmentation comes before labelling or vice versa.

It is also possible to translate a given state sequence in an HMM back to a feature vector sequence. This approach is becoming more widely used in speech synthesis. The generation of an acceptable feature vector sequence from an HMM is not straightforward, however. The problem is that each state has knowledge of the range of feature vectors seen at that part of the phone, but it does not know how they should be arranged temporally to ensure a smoothly changing spectral envelope with no discontinuities at the state boundaries. The solution to this problem was discovered by Tokuda (Tokuda et al., 2000), and is in two parts. First, the feature vector is extended to incorporate not just the feature values at each time step, but also the rate-of-change of those values (their velocity or 'deltas'), and also the rate-of-change of the rate-of-change of the values (their acceleration or 'delta-deltas'). Secondly an iterative process can be established to find a vector sequence which respects the distribution of values, velocities and accelerations stored on each state. The result is a vector sequence for an utterance which matches the dynamic characteristics of the speech signals used for training, and is adequate for synthesis.

The statistical parameters stored inside HMMs need to be trained from labelled training data. For example, a set of phone models can be trained from a set of audio examples, each transcribed at the phone level. The quantity of training material depends on the number and complexity of the HMMs, but modern large-vocabulary speech recognition applications are built from hundreds of hours of audio material.

The power of the HMM as a means of modelling the transform between features and phones comes from a unique combination of factors: that a reliable and convergent training procedure is possible, that efficient search techniques are applicable for recognition, that it combines constraints on phone quality with constraints on phone sequence, that recognition of word or phone sequences do not require early segmentation and that it operates probabilistically so as to combine well with other sources of probabilistic information about the nature of utterances, such as probabilistic models of word sequences. Many attempts have been made to improve upon HMMs, but most fail if they give up these important properties. Some success has been made with the use of recurrent neural networks for phone recognition, but usually these just replace the HMM component that estimates the posterior probabilities of an observation vector given the phone. The recognition process after that still exploits the HMM techniques (Robinson, 1994)

2.3 Transformations between Phones and Segments

In the previous section we treated 'phones' as the physical realization of phonological segments. This distinction requires us now to consider the mapping between phones and phonological segments.

In large-vocabulary speech recognition, the pronunciation of a lexical item is defined in terms of a sequence of phonological segments (phonemes), taken from an inventory of about 40 types (for English). A phone sequence is generated from the segment sequence using a 'phone-in-context' model, otherwise known as a 'triphone' model. Each segment is assumed to have a large number of possible phone realizations dependent only upon the identity of the phonological segment to the left and right. Take, for example, the word 'mark' transcribed as /mɑːk/, which would be realized as a sequence of three phones: [#mɑː], [mɑːk] and [ɑːk#]. The first of these represents /m/ in the context of silence and /ɑː/, the second /ɑː/ in the context of /m/ and /k/, and so on.

The restriction on phone identity by segment context has the benefit that in recognition, the constraints on phone sequences are just the same as the constraints on segment sequences. The phone [#mɪ] cannot precede [mɑːk] because the segmental contexts do not match.

The separation of phones and segments also provides a mechanism for dealing with some accent variation, since the choice of phone realizations for a segment can be made dependent on accent (Tjalve, 2007). However, this requires a phone set that covers the realizations of multiple accents, and also training material that has been labelled at the phone level across a range of accents. This has often been considered impractical for large systems.

In phonology, the mapping between phonological and phonetic representations has often been formalized as a set of context-sensitive rewrite rules (Chomsky & Halle, 1968). Thus the realization of 'would you' as [wʊdʒu] might be seen as the application of a rule that realizes /d/ as [dʒ] before /j/, for example: [coronal] ⇨ [palato-alveolar] / _ j.

Such rules would appear to be very important in synthesis and recognition, where knowledge about phonological representations is primarily limited to the lexicon, and the pronunciation of utterances is considered simply as a concatenation of lexical forms. However, their use is not widespread, perhaps because of the difficulty of applying them within the computational structure of the systems, or because no comprehensive set of reliable rules has been found. A possible solution to the first problem is the use of *finite-state transducers* to compile rule sets into an efficient computational formalism (Kaplan & Kay, 1994), and a solution to the second may be to learn these rules from training data. In such a data-driven approach, the mapping between phones and segments is observed for a number of known training utterances, and symbol rewrite rules are derived automatically. Such a system of rules might then accommodate some of the weaknesses in the phone recognizer, for example, it can take into account common phone substitution, insertion or deletion errors. Also it could take into account larger contexts, such as syllables or words so as to exploit structural constraints. One approach to this can be seen in the Kohonen Phonetic Typewriter (Kohonen, 1986).

2.4 Transformations between Segments and Words

By far the dominant method of relating words to phonological segment sequences is through a pronunciation dictionary of word forms. The use of morphological analysis of word forms into lexemes plus inflections has become less prevalent with the advent of large dictionaries with a coverage of over 100,000 word forms for major languages. Earlier uses of morphological diction-aries (Allen et al., 1987) were partly driven by the need to conserve computer memory, something that no longer applies.

Although lexical units of some kind are required in synthesis and recogni-tion to map between semantic and phonological representations, it is not always necessary to use word forms. Sometimes smaller units are appropriate: for example, recognition into morphs (Huckvale & Fang, 2002), sometimes larger units: for example, synthesis from commonly occurring word compounds or phrase templates.

However large the dictionary, it is inevitable that systems will meet out-of-vocabulary (OOV) word forms at some stage. To derive pronunciations for OOV word forms, it is necessary to fall back on some algorithmic process for deriving pronunciation from orthography. There are two basic approaches: letter-to-sound rules which are derived by hand to produce fair attempts at pronunciation, and pronunciation-by-analogy systems, which use the existing dictionary as a resource of knowledge about spelling and sound.

A set of letter-to-sound rules for English were published by Elovitz et al. (1976) and exemplify a common strategy. Each rule is a context-sensitive sym-bol rewrite rule, with a left and a right context (see Figure 14.4). Each letter in the input is matched in turn, left-to-right. The first rule for that letter that matches the context is applied, and the input moves on to the next letter. A final stage of processing may be necessary to clean up illegal phonotactic sequences, for example, to delete any /r/ segments before consonants in a non-rhotic accent of English.

A set of letter-to-sound rules is commonly optimized by testing against a dictionary of known words. However a limited number of rules will only cap-ture a subset of the knowledge in the dictionary. Thus it may be better to use the dictionary itself as a means of finding a pronunciation for an unknown word, by drawing analogies between the unknown and known words. In a pronunciation-by-analogy system (Marchand & Damper, 2000) a network of letter substrings and phoneme substrings is constructed for the unknown word, using matches to the dictionary. Paths through this network are evaluated using a number of possible cost functions, and the best path is chosen as the predicted pronunciation (see Figure 14.5).

Letter Pattern	Phonetics	Example
[CH]^	/k/	CHRISTMAS
^E[CH]	/k/	MECHANIC
[CH]	/tʃ/	CHURCH
S[CI]#	/saɪ/	SCIENCE
[CI]A	/ʃ/	SPECIAL
[CI]O	/ʃ/	PRECIOUS
[CI]EN	/ʃ/	ANCIENT
[C]+	/s/	CEILING
[CK]	/k/	LUCK
[COM]%	/kʌm/	COME
[C]	/k/	CUP

Figure 14.4 Letter-to-sound rules involving the letter 'C' from (Elovitz et al., 1976). The letters inside the square brackets are replaced by the phonetic symbols. Elements to the left and the right of the square brackets indicate contextual constraints. The symbol '^' matches one consonant; '#' matches one or more vowels, '+' matches E, I or Y; '%' matches one of E, ER, ES, ED, ING, ELY

Finally, it is often useful to represent a dictionary not just as a list of word forms and pronunciation strings, but as a computationally efficient data structure that supports rapid search and retrieval. In recognition, for example, the mapping between segment sequences and putative word sequences is helped by constructing a tree structure of nodes representing word prefixes, arcs representing segments and leaf nodes representing word forms. Such a tree allows rapid determination of which phones may extend a partial sentence hypothesis.

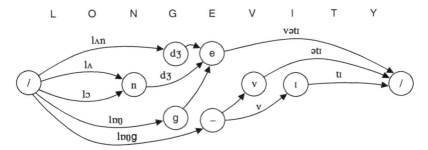

Figure 14.5 Prediction of the pronunciation of 'longevity' by analogy. Matches to the dictionary determine pronunciation possibilities for substrings of the word. Paths through the network of pronunciation fragments determine a number of pronunciation possibilities which are separately evaluated for likelihood. Figure adapted from Marchand and Damper, 2000

2.5 Transformations between Words and Utterances

The analysis and representation of the grammatical and semantic structure of utterances is outside the scope of this chapter, so here we shall concentrate on some phonetic properties of utterances above the level of the word.

In speech synthesis, it is necessary to be able to make a prediction for the durations of words, syllables and segments in an utterance given information about the composition of the utterance and some pragmatic information about the communicative context. Early attempts at this were built on rule-systems connecting linguistic properties to the durations of phonetic units. The Klatt rules for predicting segmental durations in English sentences, for example, modified segment-intrinsic durations on the basis of rules sensitive to segment position in a syllable, syllable position in a word and word position in an utterance (Klatt, 1979). These rule systems have fallen out of favour with the advent of large annotated speech corpora, from which durations can be predicted by a process of statistical modelling. A common strategy is to use a classification-and-regression tree (CART) (Breiman et al., 1984). CART trees have the advantage that they can exploit linguistically derived features of the utterance (such as the ones used by Klatt) to predict duration within a machine-learning framework. Such a tree identifies homogeneous sub-classes of the data on the basis of a set of questions about features of the data; here groups of sounds having similar duration on the basis of their phonetic properties and context. Thus a CART makes good predictions of duration from whatever subset of the provided linguistic knowledge has demonstrated utility in the training data.

Just as machine-learning techniques have been used to predict durations from linguistic features of utterances, so similar ideas have been used in the prediction of pitch contours. However, pitch contour prediction requires some kind of parametric representation of the contour, to interconvert fundamental frequency information specified on individual spectral frames into a few parameters specified at segment, syllable, word, accent-group or intonational phrase (IP) level. Many forms of parameterization have been proposed. An influential model was the Fujisaki model (Fujisaki, 1992) in which a contour for a whole IP is represented in terms of the control signals needed by a generative model. Other models parameterize the shape of the pitch contour directly: for example, the TILT model describes the contour for each pitch accent in terms of six coefficients (Taylor, 1998); while the qTA model describes the contour for each syllable in terms of a pitch target and a damped approximation (Prom-on et al., 2009).

To generate a parametric representation of the contour in synthesis, methods are required to predict the parameters for a given utterance. Input to this process ought to be intonational mark-up for the utterance derived from some understanding of its content and communicative function. However, since such information is rarely available to machines, which commonly operate with unanalysed orthography, intonational prediction is inevitably rather poor, and often limited to a 'neutral' reading. However, given intonational choices for a set of utterances, and the actual parameterized fundamental frequency tracks, it is possible to derive a predictive model using machine-learning techniques, such as CART (Black, 1997).

3 System Examples

Here we give a brief outline of the architecture of modern applications of phonetic technology.

3.1 Text-to-Speech Synthesis

Starting from orthographic text, a modern TTS system performs a stage of text normalization which aims to convert the written text into a form suitable for being spoken. This includes dealing with text formatting, numbers, abbreviations and disambiguation of homographs. Linguistic features relevant to prosody prediction are extracted from a word-class tagging and shallow syntactic analysis. A dictionary plus letter-to-sound rules are used to generate a phonological representation from concatenated lexical forms. A CART system is used to predict the segment durations and the parameters for the pitch contour.

There are two modern types of signal generation used to synthesize an utterance from its phonological specification. Unit-selection involves finding putative signal sections suited to realize elements of the phrase by searching a large labelled corpus. These sections are stored in a transition network and possible paths through the network then represent different ways in which the utterance can be generated from a concatenation of the signal sections. Each path can also be evaluated in terms of two objective measures: a target cost representing how well the phonological specification of the section matches the phonological specification of the part of the utterance it realizes, and a join cost representing how well adjacent sections match in properties like spectral envelope, pitch and speaking rate (Hunt & Black, 1996). The path of lowest cost is used to create the signal (see Figure 14.6).

A second signal generation approach is based on hidden Markov models (Black et al., 2007). A set of phone HMMs can be trained from the labelled corpus, and the phonological specification for the utterance can be translated into a phone sequence and then a state sequence. Predictions of duration and pitch are also brought down to state level. A sequence of acoustic parameters can then be found which best fits the statistical distributions stored on the state sequence as mentioned in Section 2.2.

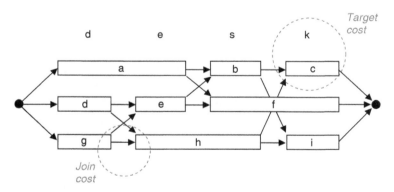

Figure 14.6 The unit selection algorithm. A synthetic version of the word /desk/ is generated by concatenating signal fragments found from a labelled corpus. Each fragment a-i is allocated a 'target cost' on the basis of how well its phonetic labelling matches the target transcription. Each junction between two fragments is allocated a 'join cost' on the basis of how well the two fragments connect together without distortion. The overall best-generated signal lies along the path that connects the sequence of fragments with the lowest combined cost

3.2 Speech Recognition

Modern large-vocabulary speech recognition systems conform to a common architecture in which an 'acoustic model' of pronunciation units is connected through a dictionary to a 'language model' of word sequences (Young, 1996). For the acoustic model, phone-in-context HMMs are a common choice, trained from very large corpora of sentences read by multiple speakers, and labelled solely at the orthographic level. The pronunciation of each training sentence is approximated by concatenated lexical pronunciations from a dictionary, then a phone-in-context model is chosen for each segment according to the identity of neighbouring segments. The statistical distributions of the observations held on each state of the HMM and the transition probabilities between states are then updated using the feature sequence calculated from the sentence recording. Because of the variation across speakers and environments, the distribution of feature vectors for a particular state may be quite complex, so commonly a set of Gaussian mixtures are chosen to represent the probability distribution of the observed features on a single state. Also, since even with a large training corpus some phone models will not occur very often and will not be well trained, a process of smoothing or 'tying' of states is performed to share acoustic data across models.

The language model provides a means to calculate the probability of a word sequence, specifically if it estimates the probability that a sentence prefix can be extended by a particular word. Language models are trained from large text corpora. Particular concern is given to the problem of data sparsity when training a language model, since many possible word sequences will not be present in a training corpus of any practical size. The probabilities of word sequences derived from the language model can be combined with probabilities of the signal given a phone sequence to evaluate the probability of one recognition hypothesis. In recognition, a search procedure is established to search over a large subset of possible sentence hypotheses {W} to find which hypothesis has the highest probability W* for the audio input A. This can be written as follows: where p(W) is the probability of a word sequence from the language model, and p(A|W) is the probability of the acoustic evidence given the word sequence, which is found from the HMM phone models and the dictionary. The power of this approach to recognition is that it allows disparate evidence from text and audio to be combined by expressing both as probabilities. In recognition, multiple hypotheses are built left-to-right: frame-by-frame, state-by-state, phone-by-phone and word-by-word. At each time step, hypotheses with low probabilities are discarded, so that at the end of the utterance, the best scoring hypothesis is the recognized answer.

3.3 Speaker Verification

A speaker verification system makes a decision about whether cooperative speakers are who they say they are on the basis of their voice. The task is slightly easier than speaker recognition, where the identity of the speaker may have to be chosen from a large number of possible speakers, and where the speaker may not want to be recognized.

In a typical speaker verification system each user is enrolled using some known text, such as digit sequences. A model of the sounds typically used by that speaker is then built, which will allow the system to estimate the probability that a new utterance could have been produced by this speaker. A GMM is commonly used for this (Reynolds, 1995). This probability needs to be compared to the probability that the utterance could have been produced by someone else. This normalization is normally achieved by also building a background or 'population' model from utterances of many training speakers. The probability of the utterance given the purported speaker identity can then be compared to the probability of the utterance given the population model. If this ratio is bigger than some threshold then the speaker is verified. The threshold can be adjusted to set the rate of false acceptances (or false rejections) desired by the application.

3.4 Voice Conversion

A voice conversion system aims to convert the speaker identity in a recording, while leaving the linguistic content unchanged. Such systems have application in customizing TTS systems, and in speech-to-speech translation systems, where it is generally acknowledged that it would be better to have the foreign language output spoken in the source speaker's voice.

Voice conversion systems are typically trained using parallel utterances spoken by the source speaker and the target speaker. These utterances can be aligned and a large number of matching spectral frames can be extracted. In the voice conversion method proposed by Stylianou (Stylianou & Moulines, 1998), the source speaker's frames are modelled by a GMM having 32 or more mixtures. The mixtures divide the frames into a number of phonetic classes by their spectral similarity. For each mixture a single linear transform is estimated from training data, such that the difference between the transformed frames and the target frames is minimized for those source frames that are best described by that mixture. In conversion of a new utterance, each incoming frame is matched to each mixture, and a weighted combination of the linear transforms is applied according to the probability that the frame fits each mixture.

Line spectral frequencies (LSF) are commonly used in voice conversion applications. This is because the LSF features can be readily estimated from the signal and reused for synthesis, and because they are amenable to interpolation and extrapolation. A weakness of the approach is the remaining differences in the linear-prediction residual between speakers. The residual is less easy to transform, even though it is likely to contain much speaker-specific information about pitch and voice quality.

4 Conclusions

We have seen in this chapter a wide range of technologies that are being used in commercial applications of phonetic technology. Perhaps the most important are linear prediction analysis, Gaussian mixture models, hidden Markov models, unit selection and classification-and-regression trees. Each of these technologies has a well-developed mathematical treatment which can be found by following the references given. Modern students of Phonetics need to be aware of the capabilities of these technologies, even if they do not care to understand the mathematics behind them. Fortunately, there are many computer toolkits available for exploring the capabilities of these technologies, and experience in these should be considered essential for anyone seeking to exploit their Phonetics skills in the modern technological marketplace.

15 New Directions in Speech Perception

Rachel Smith

1 Introduction

The speech signals that we hear in daily life are part of the flux of sensory information that we take in and use to guide our own actions in the world. For skilled perceivers, phonetic perception of the sounds of speech blends seamlessly into understanding the linguistic messages and social signals that speech conveys, shaped by the speaker's intentions, the interactional context and a host of other factors. This chapter discusses what contemporary phonetic research is uncovering about the types of information available to listeners from speech signals, and points up the congruence of these currents in phonetics with discoveries from psycholinguistics and cognitive neuroscience about the capacities of the listening brain to exploit this information.

Speech perception can be defined narrowly, as the set of processes involved in identifying and discriminating individual sounds and syllables in abstraction from meaning; or broadly, to encompass any/all processes whereby speech gives rise to perceived meaning of some kind, from the strictly linguistic to the social and situational. This chapter adopts a broad definition, taking the view that perceiving speech in meaningless versus meaningful contexts are very different tasks, which can give rise to divergent results and which probably recruit partially different brain processes; and that meaningful contexts are the more ecologically valid. While most research has been done on the recognition of units the size of the word or smaller, future progress in the field depends on understanding that recognition of words takes place in a broader context in which people are behaving not only as listeners, categorizers and comprehenders of speech sounds, but simultaneously as speakers, conversationalists and social agents. Here the focus is on perception by skilled adult listeners in their first language.

2 Information and Variability in the Speech Signal

To understand how speech is perceived, we first have to appreciate what types of information are present in the speech signal and potentially accessible to listeners. While it is tempting to focus solely on basic information about simple phonological units such as phonemes, all research into speech perception has to cope with the problem of the 'lack of invariance' in the speech signal. Coarticulation, prosodic environment, speech style, speaker and situational factors, among others, introduce variability into the realization of phonological units. Increasingly, this variability has come to be seen not so much as a problem for the listener, but rather – because much of it is systematic – as a source of valuable information (see Jones, this volume). Below, some of the types of information in speech are reviewed along with evidence of how listeners exploit them perceptually.

2.1 Basic Phonological Units

Historically, much research has focused on uncovering perceptual cues to the phonological categories and contrasts that serve to distinguish words, and understanding how the various cues combine and are weighted by listeners. Psycholinguistic research has tended to focus on cues to phoneme-sized units, while phonetic research usually breaks these down further into their component phonological distinctive features (e.g. Stevens, 2002) or articulatory gestures (e.g. Fowler & Rosenblum, 1991). Despite much progress it has not been possible to identify cues to distinctive features (or gestures or phonemes) that are present on all occasions regardless of the context, speech style and speaker. Indeed, Stevens and Keyser (2010) acknowledge that the defining acoustic attributes of features are usually enhanced by other articulatory strategies whose acoustic consequences strengthen perceptual distinctiveness, and that in running speech, a defining feature may be absent and its contrast cued only by the presence of enhancing features.

2.2 Coarticulatory Variability

The phonetic context in which a segment is produced inevitably affects its realization, sometimes radically, due to coarticulation (see Harrington et al. and

Tabain, this volume). Listeners clearly know about the acoustic consequences of coarticulation, compensate perceptually for it and use coarticulatory information to predict upcoming sounds (e.g. Warren & Marslen-Wilson, 1987, 1988; Marslen-Wilson & Warren, 1994). Importantly, coarticulatory information can be available some considerable time before and after the segment it relates to. For example, long-term 'r-resonances' can facilitate perception of /r/ in noisy listening conditions (Heinrich et al., 2010) and some listeners can detect coarticulatory [i]-colouring in vowels up to three vowels distant from a critical [i] (Grosvald, 2009). Long-domain cues to features may be widespread (Coleman, 2003; Hawkins & Nguyen, 2004), which highlights the impossibility of exhaustively parsing speech signals into chunks each cuing one, and no more than one, phoneme-sized segment.

2.3 Prosodically Conditioned Variability

The position of segments in prosodic structure – that is, the degree of prominence associated with the syllable they are in, and their location with respect to boundaries between constituents such as words and prosodic phrases – affects their realization in complex yet systematic ways (Fletcher, 2010). For example, the duration and F0 of a syllable like /ham/ are affected by whether it constitutes a monosyllabic word (*ham*), or part of a polysyllable (*hamster*). Davis et al. (2002) and Salverda et al. (2003) showed that listeners are more likely to perceive a polysyllabic word from short-duration syllables, and a monosyllabic word from long-duration ones. Similar results have been found for phrases (e.g. Christophe et al., 2004). With regard to prominence, phonetic detail cueing lexical stress placement helps to disambiguate pairs of Dutch words like *OCtopus* versus *OkTOber* before the words diverge segmentally (Reinisch et al., 2010; though see Cutler, 1986 for contrasting results for English). Prosodically conditioned variability can, like coarticulation, affect perceptual decisions over very long domains: Dilley and McAuley (2008) demonstrate that the parsing of an ambiguous sequence (e.g. *notebook worm* vs. *note bookworm*) is affected by the prosodic structure of material several syllables previous.

2.4 Morphologically and Grammatically Conditioned Variability

A word's morphological structure may be reflected in phonetic detail which can in turn assist listeners in recovering the intended word and morphology. For example, the duration of Dutch noun stems is longer in singular compared to plural forms (e.g. *boek/boeken*, book/books), and listeners take duration into account when deciding whether word fragments belong to singular or plural nouns (Kemps et al., 2005). Phoneme strings can also differ in realization when they function as affixes versus part of stems: for example, /dɪsp/ is realized as a less reduced syllable, and with longer VOT in /p/, when *dis* is a true prefix (e.g. *displease*) than a pseudo-prefix (*displays*; Smith et al., 2012; see Sugahara & Turk, 2009). Listeners look earlier and longer at pictures of events (e.g. a swan *displaying* its feathers) when phonetic detail is correct for a word's prefix status (Hawkins, 2011).

2.5 Rate-conditioned Variability

Many cues to segmental identity and suprasegmental structure are durational, and changes in rate of speech alter both the absolute and relative values of these cues. Rate-induced changes affect listeners' judgements about segmental identity (e.g. Liberman et al., 1956; Miller & Liberman, 1979), and also about suprasegmental properties like stress (Reinisch et al., 2011). Dilley and Pitt (2010) have shown that entire words can disappear or appear perceptually as a function of the speaking rate of their context, illustrating the fundamental nature of the perceptual shifts that can result from tracking speech rate over time.

2.6 Variability in Speech Style

In casual speech, a high proportion of the phonemes expected in a canonical pronunciation of a word – up to 40 per cent by some estimates – may be unrealized, realized by weak cues or massively reorganized (Johnson, 2004; Schuppler et al., 2011). While speech reduction can be extreme, especially in high-frequency and/or function words, its effects are phonetically gradient and not best captured in simplistic terms like 'deletion' of segments. Instead:

> reduced sections of speech often seem to contain clear cues to some phonological features (e.g., one perceives nasalization clearly, or perceives rhotacization somewhere in the word, or perceives non-back vocalic material), but one cannot definitively localize these features or identify them as segments. (Ernestus & Warner, 2011, p. 255)

These reorganizations present many interesting issues for perception. Some studies suggest that canonical tokens of words are more easily processed than casual tokens, even though most of the listeners' experience consists of *non*-canonical tokens (Pitt et al., 2011; Tucker, 2011). However, difficulty comprehending reduced tokens is most pronounced when tokens lack context. A viable phonological context promotes recovery of an 'underlying' assimilated or deleted segment (Gaskell & Marslen-Wilson, 1996; Mitterer & McQueen, 2009; Mitterer, 2011). Even extremely reduced tokens become relatively easy to understand if sufficient context is heard (Pollack & Pickett, 1963; Ernestus et al., 2002). Niebuhr and Kohler (2011) investigated the German modal particle *eigentlich* ('actually'), canonically [aɪɡn̩tlɪç] but reducible to [aĩ]. They manipulated the duration of the non-palatal and palatal portions of [aĩ] in meaningful sentence stimuli, and showed that longer palatal sections increased the likelihood of perceiving *eigentlich* relative to the competitor *eine* ('one'). In this case, residual cues to underlying structure seem to preserve a 'phonetic essence' sufficient to support accurate perception.

2.7 Socio-indexical Variability

Vast phonetic variation results from organic and learned individual differences, and from social factors: not only the broad descriptive categories of age, gender, regional accent and socio-economic status but also the stances people wish to project in particular situations, and the 'communities of practice' (Wenger, 1998) within which they conduct their working and social lives. For overviews, see, for example, Foulkes et al. (2010) and Di Paolo and Yaeger-Dror (2010). While most perceptual work in sociophonetics concerns how listeners use phonetic detail to make *social* judgements, experiments also show that decisions about segmental and lexical identity are affected by indexical variation. Segmental categorization is sensitive, for example, to information about gender and regional accent, whether this is in the signal, induced by instructions to imagine speaker characteristics (Johnson et al., 1999; Niedzelski, 1999) or even primed by the experimenter's dialect or a socially meaningful object such as a stuffed toy kiwi or kangaroo (Hay & Drager, 2010).

2.8 Interactionally Conditioned Variability

In spontaneous conversation, the realization of words varies systematically according to aspects of the structure of the interaction, such as the system of turn-taking between interlocutors, and the particular kind of social action that is being performed. For example, released word-final plosives seem to encourage a change of speaking turn, compared to unreleased ones (Local, 2003b); increased rate at the transition between one conversational action (e.g. a request) and another indicates that a speaker is unwilling to relinquish the turn (Local & Walker, 2004); and agreement or disagreement can be indicated by phonetic 'upgrading' or 'downgrading' of pitch, intensity and articulatory clarity

(Ogden, 2006). Although studies of naturally occurring conversation suggest that people pay attention to these phenomena, only one study has experimentally investigated perception of interactional variability. De Ruiter et al. (2006) found that phonetic cues were less important than syntactic cues in determining when listeners expect the end of a speaking turn to occur. However, their study only tested one phonetic cue, the pitch contour, and does not rule out the possibility that other information like duration and segmental realization could play a role (Local & Walker, forthcoming).

2.9 Summary

Several themes emerge from the above review. Listeners use all relevant information as soon as it becomes available, and in proportion to its reliability. The many sources of variability in speech inform simultaneously not just about phonological contrasts and word identity, but also about prosodic meaning, the speaker's social characteristics and the progress of the interaction. Information is integrated over a range of different time-domains, including some that are very long. Perception of temporally smeared cues and holistic patterns is probably the norm, and exhaustive parsing of the signal into segment-sized chunks the exception. With these points in mind, the following sections discuss some of the cognitive processes and representations at work in speech perception.

3 Processes, Representations and Pathways

This section shows that there is – in principle at least – no conflict between the systematic variability of speech, and the psychological and neural mechanisms that process it. While many details remain to be worked out, it is becoming clear that listening brains cope easily and naturally with uncertainty and variability, process signals with respect to multiple functions simultaneously and are exquisitely sensitive to the social context within which stimulation occurs.

3.1 Probabilistic Processing under Conditions of Uncertainty

Speech perception, and perception in general, is *probabilistic* in nature. When we encounter a speech signal we simultaneously consider a range of hypotheses as to its interpretation, and choose the one that is the most probable, in terms of two aspects: its match with the sensory signal and its congruence with our expectations. Speech signal information is continuously evaluated across all sensory modalities (audition, vision, touch, etc.), while expectations are determined by our understanding of the linguistic context and the situation: what we expect people to say and do in meetings at work, when speaking on the telephone about social plans, while doing the dishes at home, etc. While the precise nature of the relative contributions made by the signal (sometimes referred to as 'bottom-up' information) and the listener's expectation ('top-down' information) has aroused enormous controversy over the years, there is broad agreement that both affect decisions (for reviews, see, for example, Dahan & Magnuson, 2006; McQueen, 2007; McQueen & Cutler, 2010; for position statements, see McClelland & Elman, 1986; Norris, et al., 2000; McClelland et al., 2006).

A key emerging direction in speech perception research is to think about probabilistic processing in terms of a set of statistical concepts known as Bayesian inference (Scharenborg et al., 2005; Clayards et al., 2008; Norris & McQueen, 2008; Feldman et al., 2009). Bayes' theorem expresses how decisions can be made based on knowledge or expectation in combination with evidence. Fundamental to the approach is the idea that hypotheses are associated with *prior probability distributions* ('priors' for short), which give probabilities of any hypothesis being true. Priors are based on existing knowledge, and are independent of the current evidence for a hypothesis. For instance, if I select a word from a corpus of spoken English at random, then without any evidence about which word I have selected, you know that it is more likely to be *the* than *unification* – simply because *the* is a more frequent word. *Posterior probability distributions*, on the other hand, reflect the probability of a hypothesis being true given the current evidence. They are calculated by combining the prior probability associated with a hypothesis, with the probability distribution of observing the evidence given that the hypothesis is true, which is also known as the *likelihood*.

An important aspect of Bayes' theorem is that probability of any single hypothesis is affected by those of all other candidate hypotheses. Thus a word that has many and/or highly probable *neighbours* (words similar to it) may be harder to recognize than one with few neighbours, based on their relative prior probabilities, independent of the evidence in any particular case. Another key point is that where the evidence favours a particular hypothesis the role of the evidence in determining the outcome is relatively great; on the other hand, if the evidence fails to discriminate between multiple hypotheses, then there is an increase in reliance on priors. This amounts to saying that signal evidence is always used to the extent available, but as the ambiguity of the signal increases (e.g. in noise), so does the reliance on previously existing knowledge.

3.1.1 A Model of Phonetic Category Structure and Recovery of Phonetic Detail

Feldman et al.'s (2009) model of phonetic categorization illustrates these ideas. According to this model, when a listener is presented with a stimulus, her task is twofold: to ascertain which phonetic category the stimulus belongs to, and to recover the target pattern of phonetic detail that the speaker intended, in order to reconstruct coarticulatory and non-linguistic information. Phonetic categories are defined as normal (Gaussian) distributions over particular parameter(s), such as formant frequencies and VOT. When someone speaks, they choose a target production of a sound sampled from such a distribution, with the target's exact location being influenced by factors such as coarticulation, speech rate and affect. However, the actual sound experienced by a listener is not exactly the speaker's target production: it is slightly distorted in transmission by articulatory, acoustic and perceptual noise. These distortions are modelled by treating the actual, noisy, sound as sampled from a normal distribution around the speaker's target production.

When a sound is heard, the listener uses knowledge of category structures and category locations in her language to infer not only the intended category, but the target production. Feldman et al. neatly show that Bayesian inference can explain an interesting aspect of phonetic categorization known as the *perceptual magnet effect* (PME; Kuhl et al., 1992; Iverson & Kuhl, 1995). The PME is an empirical phenomenon whereby perceptual space is 'warped' such that stimuli close to a category mean are less discriminable than stimuli close to the category boundaries. For example, listeners are poor at telling apart pairs of /i/ sounds that are close to a 'prototypical' /i/ in their language, but good at telling apart pairs of /i/s that, while no more distinct from each other acoustically, happen to be less similar to the prototype. This is explained in the model as a consequence of prior knowledge about the structure of categories. That is, experienced listeners know that they are more likely to hear sounds near the centre of categories than sounds far from the centre. They use this knowledge to compensate for noise in the speech signal, by biasing perception towards the centre of a category, where the target production is most likely to be located. The extent of the bias depends upon beliefs about category membership. The more certain a listener is that a stimulus comes from a particular category, the stronger the 'pull' of the mean of that category. If the stimulus' category affiliation is ambiguous, the influence of each possible category is weighted according to the probability that the sound came from that category. Thus, for sounds further from the prototype, and closer to category boundaries, the amount of perceptual warping decreases, giving rise to the characteristic patterns of the PME.

This discussion illustrates how a relatively simple rule for combining information from the signal with expectations based on stored knowledge can account for complex observations about perceptual decisions. The Bayesian framework can account well for classic demonstrations of the importance of expectation in speech perception – for example, that we can recognize predictable words at less favourable signal-to-noise ratios than less predictable words (Kalikow et al., 1977). A Bayesian approach also correctly predicts that listeners will take the whole stimulus distribution, including the variability among stimuli, into account in making decisions (Clayards et al., 2008).

3.2 Variable Signals, Variable Representations

The last 20 years have seen the understanding of systematic variability in the speech signal begin to radically affect fundamental ideas about the way speech is represented perceptually. Prior to the 1990s, the dominant theoretical position was that the representations of words stored in memory were highly abstract, consisting, for example, of phoneme strings (e.g. Halle, 1985). Speaker characteristics were not represented, and allophonic detail was predictable by rule. In contrast, the broad consensus today is that much of the variability in the signal is learned about and encoded in memory, but that this specificity is not incompatible with a degree of abstraction.

The best evidence that variability is encoded in stored category structure comes from experiments demonstrating *perceptual learning*. This is the way that people seem to automatically learn about some quite detailed properties of stimuli that they are exposed to, even when the task does not require attention to these properties. Now classic experiments showed that theoretically irrelevant information about the speaker's voice is remembered and used when decoding linguistic messages: listeners identify degraded speech better when the speaker characteristics are familiar (Nygaard et al., 1994; Nygaard & Pisoni, 1998) and are more likely to remember that they have heard a word before if it is presented in the same voice on first and second hearings (Palmeri et al., 1993). Memory for voices appears to include mean F0 and aspects of intonation (Church & Schacter, 1994), amplitude, vocal effort and rate of speech (Bradlow et al., 1999) as well as individual variation in segmental realization (Norris et al., 2003).

Exemplar approaches to speech perception (also known as non-analytic or episodic approaches) explain perceptual learning by assuming that individual instances, or exemplars, of speech are stored in memory. When a new speech signal is heard, it is matched simultaneously against all stored exemplar traces in memory, which are activated in proportion to the goodness of match, and the aggregate of these activations produces a response. There is no need for storage of abstract forms, and linguistic categories are simply the distributions of items that a listener encounters, encoded in terms of values of parameters in a multidimensional phonetic space.

3.2.1 Linguistic Units in Exemplar Models

There has been much debate about whether exemplar representations are holistic 'episodes', of flexible size and structure, or bear closer correspondence to particular types of linguistic unit. A widespread assumption is that stored exemplars correspond to *words* because, as Johnson (2006, p. 492) puts it, 'words lie at the intersection of form and meaning and thus generate coordinated patterns of activity in both sensory and higher level areas of cognition'. Norris et al. (2003), Pierrehumbert (2002, 2006) and Goldinger (2007) discuss problems with this idea. For one thing, it necessitates accounting for how word tokens are pre-segmented from running speech before being matched against traces in memory. For another, it leaves words' internal phonological structure unrepresented, making it difficult to explain how people generalize from particular words to the 'same' (or similar) sounds in other words.

3.3 Hybrid Models

Because of the above considerations, it is becoming widely accepted that representation of linguistic categories is hybrid, that is, involves both exemplar storage and sufficient abstraction to explain generalization of learning across words; and consequently that multiple levels of representation are necessary. That is, we may store words or larger chunks, but we also know about the internal structure of these chunks. The evidence to date suggests a role for features (Kraljic & Samuel, 2006; Nielsen, 2011) and allophonic variation specific to position-in-syllable and -word (Dahan & Mead, 2010; Smith & Hawkins, 2012) as well as for phonemes (McQueen et al., 2006). In principle, people could also learn about how a speaker habitually realizes phrase boundaries, makes constituents prosodically prominent or uses phonetic detail to signal other aspects of functional and interactional meaning. Conversely, properties lacking linguistic or functional relevance may be difficult to learn (Nygaard et al., 2000; Sommers & Barcroft, 2006).

To date no perceptual model implements multi-level exemplar representation in a computationally explicit, testable way. However, Polysp (Hawkins & Smith, 2001; Hawkins, 2003, 2010) shares principles of hierarchical organization with explicit multi-level models in the speech production literature (e.g. Pierrehumbert, 2002, 2006; Walsh et al., 2010). Sounds are always considered in the context of their position in a broader, hierarchical linguistic structure (akin to a prosodic tree, with links to grammar and meaning) and heard sounds are argued to be able to map directly to any level of this structure (or to multiple levels simultaneously), with 'higher' levels and larger patterns being more accessible for skilled perceivers.

3.4 Parallel Processing in Neural Pathways for Speech Understanding

Research into the neurobiology of speech perception has burgeoned over the last 15 to 20 years with the development of electrophysiological, magnetoencephalographic and neuroimaging techniques (see Knight & Hawkins, this volume). This field now presents a vastly more complex and fascinating picture than the idea that Broca's and Wernicke's areas in the left hemisphere are the key sites of linguistic processing. Nevertheless, there remains a long way to go to marry neurobiological with phonetic and psycholinguistic research. As Poeppel and Monahan (2008, p. 83) observe, 'it remains entirely unclear how the putative primitives of speech (e.g. feature, syllable, etc.) map onto the putative primitives of the biological substrate (e.g., neuron, synapse, oscillation, etc)'.

One of the clearest themes to emerge from neurobiological speech perception research is the idea that there is massive parallelism and redundancy in the way the brain processes speech (e.g. Grossberg, 2000; Scott & Johnsrude, 2003; Hickok & Poeppel, 2007), such that the same signal information is processed by different streams across many brain areas, while the same function (e.g. lexical access) can be performed by different parts of the brain, acting usually in concert, but independently under some circumstances. This redundancy explains how some brain lesions, even to 'core' language areas, can spare speech perception functions to a surprising degree, and seems likely to be central to an account of how the same signal subserves extraction of meanings of many different kinds.

3.4.1 'What' and 'How' Streams

There are (at least) two main processing streams, one dealing primarily with sound-to-meaning mappings (a 'what' stream), and the other primarily with sound-to-motor mappings (a 'how' and/or 'where' stream; Scott & Johnsrude, 2003; Hickok & Poeppel, 2007; Scott et al., 2009). Accounts of the cortical organization and functions of these streams vary, but some points are generally agreed upon. Both streams begin in the primary auditory cortex and both share neural tissue in the superior temporal gyrus (especially in the left hemisphere). However, they diverge anatomically and specialize for different aspects of speech processing. The anterior 'what' stream, running ventrally along the superior and middle temporal lobes, and encompassing parts of the auditory association cortex in the superior temporal gyrus and the inferior frontal gyrus, is thought to be especially important for speech recognition tasks – that is, for converting sound to meaning.

The 'how' and/or 'where' stream involves parts of the posterior superior temporal gyrus, the inferior parietal cortex (supramarginal gyrus), motor and somatosensory areas and the inferior frontal gyrus. This posterior pathway has been suggested to be engaged in sensorimotor integration and spatial processing. While some of the tasks classically used to study speech perception – for example, phoneme and syllable discrimination – appear to implicate it, it may be rather little involved in ordinary listening to speech for meaning. This view is developed by Scott et al. (2009) with specific regard to the role of the motor cortex in speech understanding. Scott et al. argue that imaging, lesion and developmental data fail to support the idea that motor cortex is essential for perceiving spoken language (Liberman & Mattingly, 1985). Instead the motor activation seen during speech perception may relate to other factors: semantic and syntactic processing, meta-linguistic task requirements or responding to the motor information expressed in speech and other sounds. Scott et al. hypothesize that the motor system is involved in a sound-to-action pathway that is not speech-specific, but that is highly refined in human language to allow for the smooth coordination of turn-taking in conversation, for synchronous behaviour, and for interpersonal convergence.

3.4.2 Hemispheric Lateralization

A left-hemisphere bias for speech processing has been observed across many studies, yet its nature and basis is controversial (McGettigan & Scott, 2012). Zatorre and colleagues (e.g. Zatorre et al., 2002) argue that the left hemisphere is specialized for processing of rapid temporal information, and the right hemisphere for spectral information such as pitch, rather like the difference between wide-band and narrow-band spectrography. A similar view is that neuronal ensembles in the two cerebral hemispheres differ in terms of the preferred timescales over which they integrate information: longer windows (150–300 ms) in the right hemisphere, and shorter ones (20–50 ms) in the left hemisphere (Hickok & Poeppel, 2007; Poeppel et al., 2008). However, there is at best partial empirical support for these views (McGettigan & Scott, 2012): fast information is processed bilaterally, and both hemispheres process pitch, although the right hemisphere shows an advantage for processing pitch *variation* and possibly voices and emotional vocalizations (e.g. Belin et al., 1998, 2000). A different view is that hemispheric lateralization does not primarily reflect different *acoustic* sensitivities. Rosen et al. (2011), using cleverly manipulated stimuli that varied in spectral modulation, amplitude modulation and intelligibility, failed to find a hemispheric preference for either type of signal manipulation. Instead, they found that the left hemisphere showed much greater involvement to intelligible speech. These results suggest that the hemispheric difference may only be partly to do with preferences for different types of signal; the left hemisphere may preferentially process speech that is intelligible, or perhaps more generally, be involved in categorizing and extracting meaning from stimuli.

Many questions persist concerning how the brain responds to different combinations of signal properties and meanings. Some light may be shed in the future by careful investigation of the processing of phonetic information with different types of function. Pitch, for example, is often thought of as gradient, but it can also be highly categorical when linguistic prosody (intonation) is at issue. Likewise, voice information is frequently considered gradient and non-abstract, yet voices can also be very clearly (covertly or overtly) categorized, for example, as sharing or not sharing the accent of the speaker, or belonging or not belonging to some prestigious or stigmatized group; and these judgements are informed by short-domain segmental features as well as by voice pitch and quality. Similar considerations apply to vocal emotion (Schirmer & Kotz, 2006). Findings of a right-hemisphere bias for the processing of pitch, voice and vocal emotion may relate to the fact that abstraction and categorization are not as widespread, clear-cut or essential for these as for word identification. Alternatively, it may simply be that researchers have not yet found the relevant type of tasks for accessing categorical responses to social and emotional information.

3.4.3 Multi-time Resolution Processing in the Brain

Poeppel et al. (2008) propose that speech perception is a multi-time resolution process, with perceptual analyses occurring concurrently on two timescales commensurate with (sub)segmental and syllabic analyses, respectively (see Section 3.3.2). Poeppel et al. do not claim that these two rates are aligned uniquely with linguistic units of a particular size, although they point out an affinity between short-window analysis and distinctive features, and long-window analysis and syllabic and suprasegmental attributes. Nevertheless, many properties in speech do not belong clearly to one level or the other (see Section 2). Almost certainly more than two rates are needed because speech contains information at a far wider range of timescales, from a few milliseconds for some segmental attributes, up to the order of seconds for phrases and speaking turns.

3.4.4 Dynamic and Rhythmic Attention

Attention may be intrinsically rhythmically organized (Large & Jones, 1999). Cortical networks can display oscillatory behaviour (Buzsáki & Draguhn, 2004) which is endogenous (self-generated) and occurs at various timescales, even at rest. These oscillations can entrain, or lock, to external events, such that brain activity falls into phase with the signal activity; and they can be hierarchically organized such that different rates of oscillation influence each other. When entrainment happens, certain advantages for processing ensue, including the ability to predict upcoming important events and target a window of enhanced attentional activity upon them; and the ability to sustain perception of a regular beat, despite fluctuation in the surface realization of the rhythm. The neural correlates of rhythmic attending are beginning to be well worked out for simple and more complex musical rhythms (Large, 2008). For speech, these issues have been much less explored. In the future, considering the dynamic nature of attention may shed some light on the paradoxical nature of speech rhythm: There is little regularity in the surface duration of any linguistic unit (see Fletcher, 2010), and much information is conveyed by deviations from isochrony (e.g. Aylett & Turk, 2004). Yet listeners seem inclined to hear speech as rhythmic, and when metrical or temporal regularity can be induced, it does improve identification and discrimination performance (Pitt & Samuel, 1990) and arguably serves persuasive, interactional and mnemonic functions (Auer et al., 1999).

3.5 Active Perception by the Social Brain

The discussion in Sections 3.1 and 3.2 showed that listeners closely track statistical distributions of information in the environment, yet people listening to speech are not mere passive receivers of information. Instead, much current research suggests a more active role for the listener. The Bayesian framework discussed in Section 3.1 is becoming the cornerstone of a range of emerging theories which have in common the radical view that the brain does much more by predicting, and less by merely reacting to sensory information. For example, Poeppel and Monahan (2011) propose a framework in terms of 'analysis by synthesis' (Stevens, 1960; Halle & Stevens, 1962; Stevens & Halle, 1967). An initial, basic sensory analysis is used to generate hypotheses about the structure of the signal, and the listener then uses her internal models of how speech is produced to 'synthesize' expected patterns, which are tested against the incoming signal. The distance between expected and observed patterns is used to refine hypotheses and to guide learning. Similar ideas are advanced in the 'predictive coding' and 'free energy' accounts of neural processing (Schultz & Dickinson, 2000; Bar, 2009; Friston, 2010) while Gagnepain et al. (2012) report positive preliminary tests of these theories as applied to spoken word recognition.

Though these views of cognition have yet to stand the test of time, they are exciting because they afford a central role for prediction. It is becoming apparent that listeners do use early signal information to predict upcoming information, even when doing so is not essential to the task (Hawkins, 2011). Moreover, the notion of analysis by synthesis opens up interesting avenues for considering the relation of a listener's perceptual analysis to his/her own production. If perceptual analysis involves synthesis, according to the listener's internal models, of an expected signal, and comparison of this expectation to the actual signal produced by an interlocutor, then we have an obvious mechanism whereby the producer's and perceiver's speech might influence one another. This is the pattern documented in studies of phonetic convergence, where in natural or experimental situations, participants' speech can become more similar to that of a recorded model or a live interlocutor. Convergence is difficult to quantify, and not observed in all situations – indeed *di*vergent behaviour, with specific social causes and consequences, also occurs. Yet it is clear that interlocutors do affect each other's behaviour in various domains, from breath control (Rochet-Capellan et al., 2012) to segmental articulation (Pardo et al., 2011; Babel, 2012) to non-speech interactional signals (Delaherche et al., 2012), and across a range of situations from passive listening (e.g. Delvaux & Soquet, 2007; Nielsen, 2011) to artificial 'synchronous speaking' and shadowing tasks (Cummins, 2003; Shockley et al., 2004) to spontaneous conversation (Local, 2003b; Pardo et al., 2011). By placing prediction at the centre of perceptual analysis, it seems possible to achieve a deeper understanding of how individuals' speech patterns can become yoked together.

4 Conclusion

This chapter has reviewed the systematic variability of speech, its perceptual relevance and some ways in which variable speech signals might be represented, categorized and processed by the brain. As these phenomena become better understood, a paradox emerges for speech perception research. The dominant research paradigms use, as stimuli, relatively carefully produced tokens of isolated syllables and words, minimizing many sources of variability (see Knight & Hawkins, this volume). Yet people's sensitivity to different types of variation in speech suggests that we should be shifting to a different norm, using speech that is casual, highly coarticulated and shaped segmentally and prosodically so as to communicate with an interlocutor in a socially natural context. Standard tasks in which listeners respond to stimuli by making computerized judgements may not be sufficient for this type of speech; methodological ingenuity will be required to design tasks that more closely approximate what listener-speakers do in ordinary communicative situations (see the preliminary steps taken by, for example, Niebuhr & Kohler, 2011; de Ruiter et al., 2006). If appropriate methodological advances can be achieved, we can hope for considerable progress to be made in understanding how speech is perceived in the context of shared action in everyday life.

16 New Directions in Speech Production

Jonathan Harrington, Phil Hoole and Marianne Pouplier

Chapter Overview

---

1 Introduction

Studying speech production from a phonetic perspective can be considered on the one hand to form part of the task in cognitive science and psycholinguistics of explaining how a speaker's intention to produce an utterance is related to its physical instantiation, that is, to the movements of the vocal organs that give rise to an acoustic signal. But it also shares with phonology and linguistics the goal of explaining why the sounds of languages are shaped the way that they are. These two obviously related aims can nevertheless be differentiated by the kinds of questions that are asked in studying speech production. For example, a question that is more directly relevant to the first task of explaining how the sounds of speech are transmitted between a speaker and a hearer in conversation might be: what kinds of control structures are invoked by the speaker so that a listener perceives sounds to have both a certain serial order and a grouping into structures such as syllables and words? Questions that are more applicable to the second goal of finding the physiological bases to the way that sounds are distributed and pattern in the world's languages might be: how do aerodynamic and voicing constraints contribute to the relative paucity in languages of voiced velar stops? And how do articulatory and perceptual characteristics influence the relatively greater likelihood of a vowel and consonant being blended in a sound change when the consonant is syllable-final than syllable-initial (e.g. Ohala, 1990)?

Both of these approaches to speech production are evident in studies of *coarticulation* in which the task is to develop a model of the way in which sounds overlap, or are blended, with each other in time. Research on *assimilation* deals with broadly similar issues to those of coarticulation, but they have given somewhat greater emphasis methodologically to the types of variability that occur to the production of speech across the major types of juncture (in particular word boundaries) and theoretically to whether segments that are perceived to be deleted really are deleted in speech production. These issues are also central to analyses of *consonant clusters*: but here there has been somewhat greater emphasis on the way that prosodic (and especially syllabic) structure influences the relative overlap between consonants and vowels.

One of the reasons why coarticulation, assimilation and consonant clusters remain important for understanding speech production is because all such analyses require both an explicit modelling of the dynamics of speech as well as an understanding of some of the different ways that speech dynamics can be phonologized. Currently, we lack sufficient information about how dynamics are incorporated into a language's phonology, partly because there are too few empirical studies of the dynamics of speech in the different languages of the world, but also because speech production has been shaped by the idea inherent in much of generative phonology (Clements, 1985) and psycholinguistics (Levelt, 1989) that phonological information precedes and is mapped onto an independent component that deals with the biophysical aspects of speech production (see also Pierrehumbert, 1990, for a critique of this position). Considerable progress against this view has been made through the development of articulatory phonology (AP) in the last 20 years in which gestures function both as phonological primitives and as dynamic action units of the vocal tract: in this model, time is inherent in phonological representations and there is no division between the specification of a phonological plan and its execution in speech production (see also Fowler, 1981, 1984). One of the major challenges in the future will be to extend the AP model so that it can incorporate the subtle ways in which the temporal control and coordination of speech vary between languages and its varieties. Another challenge which is important in the context of modelling the relationships between synchronic variation and diachronic change will be to evaluate more closely than before how dynamic information is transmitted between a speaker and a hearer. As will be discussed below, these are some of the reasons why recent studies of speech dynamics are beginning to give greater emphasis to crosslinguistic physiological comparisons of typologically rare combinations of consonants and vowels (e.g. Pouplier & Beňuš, 2011), and why all three sections presented below are at various points concerned with the perceptual consequences of the production of coarticulation, assimilation and of consonant clusters.

2 Coarticulation

Modelling coarticulation can be considered to be part of the wider problem of how phonology and phonetics are connected. The phonetics-phonology dichotomy comes about because on the one hand it seems undeniable that words can be combined from a smaller set of abstract units – the features, phonemes and syllables of a language – which can be permuted in a rule-governed way to create new words. A central aspect of this combinatorial possibility and indeed of the flexibility to add new words to the lexicon is that the units are *context-independent*: thus, the same units – the phonemes – are presumed to form part of the constitution of the words *tip* and *pit*. However, almost any analysis of the speech signal shows that speech communication is highly *context-dependent*: that is, the ways in which the raising of the tongue dorsum for the vowel and the closure and release of /t/ are timed relatively to each other are very different even when these monosyllables are produced in isolation by the same speaker (Krakow, 1999). Modelling coarticulation is central to understanding how the context-independent units suggested by phonology and the dynamic, context-dependent characteristics of speech communication are related to each other.

For various reasons, it is not possible to explain the production of coarticulation without also considering its perception. Moreover, the relationship between them also forms a key part of relating synchronic variation in speech to diachronic sound change. Some of these issues are discussed in further detail below.

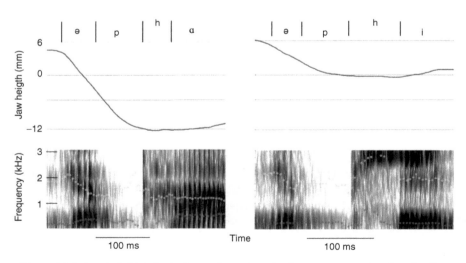

Figure 16.1 Jaw height trajectories and synchronized spectrogram showing the first two formant frequencies with superimposed acoustic phonetic segment boundaries of /əpɑ/ (left) and /əpi/ (right) produced by a female speaker of Standard German

2.1 The Production of Coarticulation

Figure 16.1 shows an instance of so-called transconsonantal vowel coarticulation, first studied systematically by Öhman (1966) and Perkell (1969), in which the vowels influence each other in a VCV sequence across an intervening consonant. The evidence for VCV coarticulation in Figure 16.1 is that the differences in jaw height in the final vowels of /əpɑ/ and /əpi/ are already anticipated across the medial /p/ and during the initial schwa: thus the jaw height is lower throughout the extent (and certainly by the offset) of the schwa of /əpɑ/ than that of /əpi/. Öhman's (1966) study showed that VCV coarticulation is possible (also across non-labial consonants) because vowel and consonant movements are generally controlled by different sets of muscles.

In so-called translation accounts of coarticulation of the 1960s and 1970s (e.g. Henke, 1966; Daniloff & Hammarberg, 1973), the nasalization of /a/ in a nasal context such as *man* was effected by a context-sensitive rule that changed /a/ into a nasal variant [ã]. By contrast, Fowler (1981) developed a context-invariant explanation of coarticulation as coproduction in which consonants and vowels are controlled by autonomous articulatory coordinative structures that overlap with each other in time. Vowel nasalization in this example comes about according to Fowler (1981) not because the vowel is modified by context, but instead because the nasal consonant is overlaid at some phase during the production of the vowel and without these articulatory strategies actually influencing or changing each other.

Many of these ideas have been incorporated into Browman and Goldstein's (1991, 1992) model of Articulatory Phonology in which coarticulation is explained as the temporal layering of gestures. Articulatory strength, which defines how resistant a segment is to coarticulatory influences (Fowler & Saltzman, 1993), is a key part of this model: in general, the more resistant a segment, the greater its influence on neighbouring segments (i.e. coarticulatory resistance and dominance are roughly inversely proportional). Articulatory resistance is quantified by Recasens (1999) in terms of a consonant's degree of articulatory constraint (DAC). Fowler and Brancazio (2000) provide support for one of the findings in Recasens (1984) that although consonants with a high DAC may affect the magnitude of coarticulation, they have little effect on its temporal extent. They also show that a consonant restricts vowel-to-vowel coarticulation only in the vicinity of the medial consonant (see also Fowler, 2005).

Data such as these form the basis for Fowler's argument that the coarticulatory influence of the consonant V_1CV_2 sequences is unlikely to be directly planned, since otherwise a speaker would have to plan first for a large degree of V_2 on V_1 coarticulatory influence (at the onset of V_1) but then plan to reduce it close to the consonant. It seems instead more likely that the extent of observable coarticulation is a function of the waxing and waning of the consonant (Fowler,

1984): that is, in the middle of the VCV, the vowels' gestures are largely covered up or hidden by the consonant during the phase at which it is maximally prominent; but they are then more in evidence at the consonant's margins during which its articulation is less prominent. It is this type of articulatory waxing and waning that is also used to explain many types of acoustic shortening. For example, polysyllabic shortening, in which /beɪ/ is shorter in *baby* than in *bay* comes about, not because the speaker plans a shorter first syllable, but instead because of the coproduction of the two syllables as a result of which the first syllable is progressively covered up by the second as it wanes towards its margin (Fowler & Thompson, 2010).

Coarticulation resistance also forms a central part of Keating's (1990) window model of coarticulation. A window in this model defines the range of allowable articulatory variation of different features that make up a segment: in the production of /u/, there is, then, a window specifying the extent to which the tongue body can vary along a front-back dimension, and a separate window that defines how much allowable variation there can be in lip-rounding and so on for all of the features that make up /u/. Essentially, the narrower the window for any feature, the greater the coarticulatory resistance. The width of windows is presumed to be influenced by phonology: thus the window width for the feature nasal is much narrower in French than for English (as a result of which the coarticulatory influence of flanking nasal consonants on oral vowels is small) because French, but not English, makes a phonological contrast between oral and nasal vowels.

2.2 The Perception of Coarticulation

A study by Alfonso and Baer (1982) showed that listeners could identify V_2 when presented with the initial /əC/ from /əCV_2/ sequences. Compatibly, listeners' reactions to identifying V_2 in V_1CV_2 were found to be slowed (Martin & Bunnell, 1982) when V_1 provided conflicting as opposed to valid coarticulatory information about V_2 (see also Fowler & Smith, 1986). These experiments provide evidence both that the source of coarticulation is perceptible, and that it contributes to phonetic identification (since identification is impaired when it is removed, as in these cross-spliced stimuli). As discussed in Fowler (2005), there are two different ways in which listeners could make use of this coarticulatory information about an upcoming segment. One of them is context-sensitive in which the different variants of schwa due to coarticulation are perceived to be different. The other is context-invariant in which listeners perceive directly the layered gestures that are produced by the speaker. Based on a series of discrimination tests, Fowler (2005) provides evidence for the second context-independent mode of perception: thus, listeners hear the different phonetic variants as the same because they subtract, or factor out, the variation in attributing it to its source, the final vowel.

Experiments on the compensation for coarticulation provide further evidence for this context-independent mode of perception. For example, Mann and Repp (1980) showed that when a continuum between /s/ and /ʃ/ is synthesized by lowering the spectral centre of gravity of the fricative and prepending it to a vowel, then listeners' responses are biased towards /s/ when the vowel is rounded (in /su-ʃu/) compared with when it is not (/sa-ʃa/). This is because the spectral centre of gravity is not only a positive cue for /ʃ/ but is also a consequence of the anticipatory coarticulatory influence of a following rounded vowel. Thus listeners attribute some of the spectral centre of gravity lowering in the fricative to /u/ and factor it out: as a result, they hear more /s/ tokens from the same /s-ʃ/ continuum when it is prepended to rounded /u/ than to unrounded /a/. Similar effects of perceptual compensation for nasal coarticulation are demonstrated in Beddor et al. (1986).

2.3 Language-specific Coarticulatory Effects

The earlier discussion of Keating's window model suggests that coarticulation is influenced by a language's phonology. Öhman (1966) also showed that the extent of transconsonantal vowel coarticulation is less in Russian than in English or Swedish: his explanation is that a large displacement of the tongue dorsum in the production of the consonant due to vowel coarticulation might compromise the phonological opposition which exists in Russian (but not English or Swedish) between palatalized and non-palatalized consonants. There is also some evidence that V-on-V coarticulatory influences are related to the size of the vowel inventory: since phonetic variation in the production of a vowel needs to be contained if a language has a phonologically crowded vowel system (in order for vowels not to encroach upon each others' space), then languages with a large number of phonemic vowel oppositions are predicted to be affected less by coarticulation than those with fewer contrasts (Manuel, 1999 for a review); however other studies (Beddor et al., 2002; Mok, 2010) have found no evidence in support of this relationship between inventory size and the magnitude of coarticulation (see also Jones, this volume).

One of the difficulties in comparing the size of coarticulation crosslinguistically is that observed differences in coarticulation between two languages may come about because of phonetic differences in the segments that gives rise to coarticulation, rather than to differences in the magnitude and timing of coarticulation per se. Suppose it were found that the measured differences between schwas in /əCi/ and /əCu/ are greater in German than English. This may come about, not necessarily because of learned, language-specific coarticulatory differences, but instead because the vowels in English are less peripheral than in German, as a result of which the anticipatory front-back influence on schwa is less. One way to begin to resolve this difficulty is with perception experiments in order to test whether listeners of different languages respond differently to coarticulation when presented with the same stimuli. This issue was addressed in a study by Beddor and Krakow (1999) who showed that native listeners of Thai both compensated less for the anticipatory nasalization in vowels than did English listeners to the same continua and showed less anticipatory nasal coarticulation in their production. More recent crosslinguistic studies of VCV coarticulation in Shona and English and other studies of nasal coarticulation in English and Thai have provided some further evidence that coarticulation is language-specific in production and that listeners are sensitive to these language-specific effects in perception (Beddor et al., 2002). This different sensitivity to perceived coarticulation depending on production differences has also been shown for two age groups of the same variety of Standard British English in Harrington et al. (2008): in this study, older subjects both compensated more for the coarticulatory influences on /u/ and (compatibly) exhibited a greater influence of context in their production of /u/ than younger subjects of the same variety.

2.4 Coarticulatory Variation and Change

Coarticulation has been shown to be speaker-specific (van den Heuvel et al., 1996; Magen, 1997; Grosvald, 2009). Part of the reason for this type of variability may well be because coarticulation is affected by speaking style (Krull, 1989). Another is that if phonological generalizations over phonetic detail depend statistically on learning experience (Pierrehumbert, 2003, 2006), then, given that no two speakers are ever exposed exactly to the same speaking situations, phonetic detail and therefore coarticulation also are likely to vary slightly from speaker to speaker.

Variation in speaking style and coarticulation are linked in Lindblom's (1990) H&H theory because words that are unpredictable for the listener tend to be hyperarticulated with the result that they are produced with greater clarity (Wright, 2003). Hyperarticulation is a form of segment strengthening which, as discussed earlier, can be linked to coarticulation resistance. Thus since in Germanic languages prosodically accented words often signal new and unpredictable information in an utterance, they tend to be hyperarticulated (de Jong, 1995) and their segments are less prone to coarticulatory influences than those in unaccented words (Harrington et al., 1995; Cho, 2004; Lindblom et al., 2007). Another prosodic variable that influences coarticulation is speaking rate (Bakran & Mildner, 1995) and sometimes in a way that can also be related to H&H theory (Agwuele et al., 2008).

Listeners have been shown to vary in their perception of coarticulation even when they respond to the same stimuli: for example, some experiments have shown that listeners are not consistent in the extent to which they compensate for nasal coarticulation in VN (Fowler & Brown, 2000) nor for vowel-to-vowel coarticulation in VCV stimuli (Beddor et al., 2001, 2002). Thus different listeners perceive the same coarticulated segment differently, if they vary in the extent to which they factor out coarticulation perceptually (Beddor, 2007; Kleber et al., 2012).

According to Ohala (1981, 1993), it is just this type of perceptual ambiguity that is the origin of sound-change: for example, the diachronic development of contrastive oral-nasal vowel phonemes in French and vowel harmony are two types of sound change that originate from under-parsing in which insufficient coarticulatory information is attributed to the source. A sound change such as the loss of the first /w/ from Latin /kwɪnkwe/ in its evolution into Italian /tʃɪnkwe/ (*five*) is presumed to come about because listeners overcompensate for coarticulation: thus, the presence of the initial /w/ is erroneously attributed by the listener to the anticipatory, coarticulatory lip-rounding and backing influence of the second /w/ and then (erroneously) factored out (ultimately resulting in its deletion if these perceptual effects are carried over to production).

3 Assimilation

Assimilation is a phenomenon related to coarticulation, in that it captures how the underlying specification of a sound may change under the influence of neighbouring sounds, either through lexical derivation (e.g. *in* – *probable* → *improbable*) or conditioned by fluent speech processes (e.g. *Paris show* → *Pari*[ʃʃ]*ow*). Here we will mainly be concerned with the latter type of assimilation. There have been (at least) three broad approaches to understanding assimilation. For one, assimilation has been modelled as a symbolic phonological restructuring process independent of phonetics. Another approach, primarily represented by Articulatory Phonology sees the origins of assimilation in the overlap of articulatory gestures, while a third view emphasizes the perceptual roots of assimilation. Although these three views have their origins in different phonological and phonetic models, they are by no means mutually exclusive, and no single approach has as of yet been able to account for the whole range of assimilation phenomena that is observed empirically.

In non-linear approaches to phonology such as Autosegmental Phonology or Feature Geometry, assimilation occurs when a distinctive feature (or subset of features) within a segment changes to agree with the feature(s) of an adjacent segment. This is achieved through linking and delinking of features (Goldsmith, 1976; Clements, 1985; McCarthy, 1988). By way of an example, in fluent speech, the word boundary cluster /d#b/ as in the phrase *road boy* may be (audibly) pronounced with the final coronal being assimilated to the following labial. Schematically this can be represented as in Figure 16.2: The place feature [labial] spreads to the preceding Place node and the feature [coronal] is delinked, with the result of the assimilated sequence being specified as [labial] only.

In this type of model, assimilation is by definition categorical (all-or-none) and happens prior to the computation of the physical properties of the utterance. Therefore in articulation, the coronal is predicted to be categorically absent, that is, it has been replaced completely by the labial feature specification and is not produced. Articulatory recordings of assimilated sequences have shown that this prediction is not necessarily borne out: for example, articulatory records in the phrase *perfect memory* revealed that although *perceptually* the final /t/ was completely assimilated to the following labial, the coronal constriction was in fact still produced, but came to be hidden by the temporally overlapping labial articulation (Browman & Goldstein, 1990a; Tiede et al., 2001). This is schematically illustrated in Figure 16.3, where each box represents the time during which

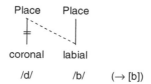

Figure 16.2 A representation of assimilation as spreading and delinking in Feature Geometry

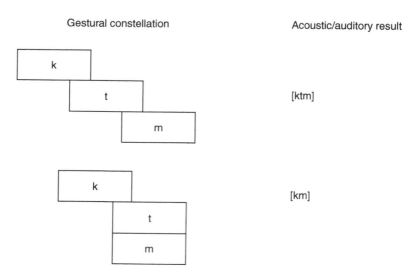

Figure 16.3 Overlap of gestures in Articulatory Phonology

a given constriction gesture (lips, tongue tip, etc.) is active. The tongue tip and the lips can perform their constrictions independently of each other and compatibly they occupy different 'tiers' in the gestural score. This means that even though the gestures may overlap in time in fluent speech, they can both be fully articulated, but it is the acoustic and perceptual consequences of the gestures that will change, resulting in *perfe[km]emory*.

In other cases of assimilation it could be shown that the spatial magnitude of the overlapped tongue tip gesture is reduced along a continuum of values (Surprenant & Goldstein, 1998). These findings seem to refute purely symbolic approaches to assimilation in which one feature specification is in a wholesale fashion replaced by another one. Note that a specification of a Place node as both coronal and labial, that is, linking without delinking, would specify a contour segment rather than gradient assimilation (Hayes, 1992; Nolan, 1992).

The *perfect memory* example illustrates how an articulatorily unassimilated sequence may be *perceived* as assimilated. Specifically *articulatory* assimilation is seen when the temporally coproduced gestures control the same articulator, that is when the gestures overlap spatially. For example, in the phrase *ten themes* both the final and initial consonant are produced with a tongue tip gesture. If the gestural activation intervals overlap in time, conflicting demands will govern the tongue tip with the result of a blended output, in this case a dental /n/ (more examples and a detailed discussion can be found in Browman & Goldstein, 1990a). Another case in point are English [ʃ#j] sequences, such as *miss you*, which can be pronounced as [mɪʃju] in connected speech. This [ʃ]-like percept is caused by the temporal overlap of the tongue tip gesture for /s/ and a tongue body raising gesture for /j/. Articulatorily and acoustically, the assimilated [ʃ] differs from the production of an underlying /ʃ/, since the assimilated fricative is a blend of the two simultaneously realized targets /s, j/ (Zsiga, 1995). For lexically derived forms, however, such as *impression*, Zsiga finds no evidence of [ʃ] arising from a coproduction of /s#j/ gestures. She therefore proposes that assimilation in lexically derived forms arises through symbolic (de)linking of features, while postlexical assimilation arises from gestural overlap.

According to the gestural overlap account of assimilation, (apparent) deletions, assimilation and weakening are all traced back to a single underlying principle: different degrees of gestural overlap, which may or may not be accompanied by a gradient reduction of the overlapped gesture. Depending on whether the overlapping gestures involve the same or different articulators, different consequences are observed. The hypothesis that fluent speech phenomena never involve a symbolic restructuring of phonological units (most explicitly stated in Browman & Goldstein, 1992), but can be exclusively understood as variation in timing and spatial magnitude of overlapping gestures has been quite controversial.

For one, several studies have shown that assimilation may indeed be categorical in that the assimilated gestures may be consistently and categorically absent (not produced), as predicted by the symbolic (de)linking account. For example, the tongue tip gesture for word-final alveolar /n/ in Castilian Spanish (e.g. *diga*[*n*] → *diga*[*m*] *paja*) is categorically reduced and the lip aperture gesture is temporally extended (Honorof, 1999). However, the categorical assimilation only occurs when there is a following non-coronal, whereas for following coronals, a blended output is observed in line with the gestural overlap approach. For Korean, Son et al. (2007) showed that in word-medial /pk/ clusters, the /p/ is either fully present or categorically not produced (but see Jun, 1996). While these cases of consistent and categorical assimilation might be viewed from a diachronic perspective in that a formerly gradient, fluent-speech assimilation process has become lexicalized and is independent of postlexical factors such as speech rate which usually condition gradient assimilation, there are several studies demonstrating that categorical and gradient assimilations truly coexist for connected speech processes.

Ellis and Hardcastle (2002) investigated /n#k/ sequences in English and found that some speakers produced an assimilatory continuum between [nk] and [ŋk], yet others showed a binary opposition between unassimilated [nk] or fully assimilated [ŋk], with no evidence for a non-velar target contributing to the output articulation. Experiments on English [s#ʃ] sibilant assimilation by Nolan et al. (Holst & Nolan, 1995; Nolan et al., 1996) confirmed that for some tokens a blended articulation between /s/ and /ʃ/ could be observed, as predicted by the gestural overlap account. Yet for other tokens, /s/ assimilated to /ʃ/ such that there was neither acoustically nor articulatorily any trace of a partially articulated [s] (as judged by tongue-palate contact data, EPG). The key argument against the gestural view comes from the durational properties of the assimilated sequence: importantly, the duration of the assimilated sibilant was longer compared to an underlying singleton [ʃ]: therefore, so the argument goes, the assimilated fricative cannot be the result of complete gestural overlap but must instead arise through a symbolic restructuring of features. Figure 16.4 illustrates schematically why increasing gestural overlap predicts, all else being equal, a reduced duration in assimilated sequences (the question of what constitutes a reference duration is not straightforward however – see Kühnert & Hoole, 2004).

Interestingly Nolan and colleagues also observe intermediate assimilation patterns for many tokens as predicted by gestural overlap, but they do not offer

Figure 16.4 Schematic illustration of the durational effects of gestural overlap

an account of these assimilation patterns or how the occurrence of one or the other type of assimilation might be conditioned (for a recent discussion and extended study on s-ʃ assimilation, see Pouplier et al., 2011). Other studies describe a similar range of speaker behaviour, and assimilation data that are consistent with a symbolic linking-delinking view have emerged side-by-side with gradient assimilation and gestural hiding and blending phenomena (e.g. Barry, 1991; Nolan, 1999; Kühnert & Hoole, 2004; Kochetov & Pouplier, 2008).

While the gestural approach has sought to explain how different assimilation patterns may follow from the spatio-temporal overlap of gestures, neither Articulatory Phonology nor non-linear phonologies inherently make predictions about why certain types of assimilations are more frequently observed than other types.[1] For example, coronal stops are most likely to assimilate, while fricatives are less likely to assimilate. Several researchers (among others, Kohler, 1990; Ohala, 1990; Jun, 1995; Steriade, 2001, 2009) have pointed out that there is a dimension of assimilatory behaviour which cannot be captured on the basis of articulatory considerations only. Rather, it seems that the perceptibility of the consonant undergoing assimilation is inversely correlated with the propensity for assimilation to occur. A common view therefore holds that assimilation will be most frequently observed if the assimilated consonant is perceptually 'weak': fricatives do not assimilate where stops do because the former are perceptually more salient. Moreover, the regressive nature of assimilation is seen as falling out from perceptual factors, since word-final sounds are less perceptually salient compared to word-initial sounds. That perceptibility may be a predictor of place assimilation patterns is shown by Hura et al. (1992) (see also Ohala, 1990). In a perception experiment they show that the consonants that are generally most likely to be assimilated are the ones that were most frequently misperceived in their study, even though the misperceptions revealed in their study are mostly non-assimilatory in nature.

Opinions differ in the interpretation of these types of results. Some ascribe these perceptually determined assimilation patterns to functional considerations of the speaker. The speakers 'knows' about the contextually conditioned differences in the perceptibility of sounds and will choose to overlap and reduce articulations only in circumstances in which the change is likely to go unperceived or does not endanger lexical contrast. Therefore, word-final sounds are more likely to assimilate than word-initial sounds – word-initial sounds are crucial for lexical access. Conservation of articulatory effort is seen as the driving force of the speaker's behaviour (Kohler, 1990; Lindblom, 1990; Jun, 2004). To predict the circumstances under which assimilation may not be perceptually salient is of course not entirely straightforward, but concepts like Steriade's P-Map (Steriade, 2009) represent ways of turning this general concept into testable hypotheses. Others take a non-teleological view on the perceptual origins of assimilation, but relate assimilation to inadvertent perceptual errors.

Assimilation then becomes an inevitable by-product of (psycho)acoustic ambiguities resulting from nonlinearities in the articulatory-acoustic relationship. If a consonant is perceptually ambiguous in a certain context, it may be perceived as assimilated (even though potentially still produced by the speaker). Since speakers imitate each other, listeners will perpetuate the perceived assimilation in their own productions (Ohala, 1981; Chen, 2003).

In sum, assimilation as a pervasive phenomenon in spoken language remains a touchstone issue for different approaches to speech production in phonology as much as in phonetics. Overall, it has become clear that numerous factors influence the occurrence of assimilation for any given utterance, such as the phonetic context (Farnetani & Busà, 1994; Recasens & Pallarès, 2001; Kochetov & Pouplier, 2008), assumed casualness of speech (Lindblom, 1990; Jun, 1995) and also factors not discussed here such as lexical and co-occurrence frequency (Bybee, 2001; Pierrehumbert, 2001; Stephenson, 2003; Jaeger & Hoole, 2011).

4 Consonant Clusters

Consonant clusters represent some of the motorically most complex behaviour in speech, and their analysis has contributed to our understanding of the relationship between linguistic structure and speech as coordinated behaviour. Much evidence has shown that the coordination of onset clusters with the following vowel is different from that of coda clusters with the preceding vowel (Byrd, 1995; Honorof & Browman, 1995). An influential model of these effects was proposed by Browman and Goldstein (2000) and further developed in a computational framework in Goldstein et al. (2010). In their model, phasing relations between gestures make heaviest use of patterns that are motorically intrinsically stable, namely in-phase and anti-phase. For coda consonants, it is assumed that only the left-most consonant is directly coordinated with the preceding vowel (in an anti-phase relation) and that additional coda consonants are coordinated (also anti-phase) with the preceding one. By contrast, all onset consonants are coordinated in-phase with the vowel. To prevent the onset consonants being synchronous (and thus unrecoverable by the listener) they are assumed to be coupled anti-phase with each other. This results in a competitive coupling topology that expresses itself in a compromise timing pattern at the articulatory surface often referred to as the C-centre pattern (Browman & Goldstein, 2000). The arithmetic mean of the temporal location of the midpoints of all consonants stays in a stable timing relation to the vowel gesture: put another way, the right edge of the right-most consonant in the onset overlaps the vowel more and more as consonants are added to the onset (see Figure 16.5).

One of the most extensive recent investigations that explicitly compares onset and coda clusters is that of Marin and Pouplier (2010). Although they

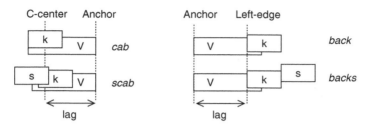

Figure 16.5 Illustration of hypothetical alignment of onset and coda consonants with the vowel and with each other (from Marin & Pouplier, 2010)

provided very clear evidence for the hypothesized C-centre timing pattern, they also found more variability in the coda timing patterns, that is, it was less clear that all possible codas prefer a purely sequential principle of organization. This greater stability of the onset is consistent with Nam's (2007) coupled oscillator model: a topology in which consonants are linked directly both to the vowel as well as to each other constitutes a more constrained topology than one in which the vowel and the consonants are simply linked serially to their neighbour. This may in turn be related to findings showing that codas are more sensitive to the influence of prosodic variation than are onsets (Bombien et al., 2010; Byrd & Choi, 2010; Hoole et al., 2010).

The idea of a C-centre has been used to advance arguments for or against syllable constituency. For example, Goldstein et al. (2007) found differences in timing between Berber and Georgian for superficially similar sequences of pre-vocalic consonants: since Georgian showed the C-centre pattern but Berber did not, they reasoned that the consonant sequences formed complex syllable onsets in Georgian, whereas Berber marked the presence of syllable divisions within the consonant sequences. Similarly, Shaw et al. (2009) found support for the assumption that in Arabic only simple syllable onsets are allowed, since forms such as /b/, /sb/, /ksb/ did not show the C-centre pattern (again a syllable boundary would be assumed before the /b/ in the clusters). Hermes et al. (2012) also argued that the so-called impure /s/ in Italian is not integrated into the C-centre pattern otherwise found for Italian syllable onsets, confirming its special status within Italian syllable structure.

The previous examples already show how relevant aspects of linguistic structure may be reflected in coordination patterns. Other recent work has indicated the need for further refinement in models of coordination relations. For example, based again on Georgian, Chitoran et al. (2002) documented an influencing factor on overlap patterns in consonants that has become known as the place-order effect (see also, for example, Gafos et al., 2010, for Arabic): in clusters of two plosive consonants, there is less overlap when C_1's place of articulation is posterior to that of C_2 (e.g. /tp/), than in the reverse case (e.g. /pt/). This has been attributed to the necessity of ensuring the recoverability of information on C_1 by the listener: that is, there is a greater likelihood of the release of C_1 being acoustically obscured when the C_2 constriction is anterior to that of C_1.

In recent versions of the coupled oscillator model (Nam, 2007), the differences in overlap have been captured by expanding the possible range of coupling topologies, specifically by dividing consonantal gestures into a closure and a release gesture. For the high overlap (front-back) clusters, a default pattern can be used in which the closure gestures of C_1 and C_2 are coupled with the vowel. For the back-front clusters, the lower overlap can be achieved by coupling the *release* gesture of C_1 with the vowel (Goldstein et al., 2010). The differences in the coordination relations between the two cluster types can be associated with differences in phonological behaviour: specifically, the low-overlap clusters permit greater complexity in the laryngeal adjustments associated with the cluster. This may not be entirely surprising: a wider spacing of the consonants simply gives the speaker more time to change the laryngeal configuration and adjust to possibly conflicting aerodynamic requirements. The crucial point here is that an understanding of what are preferred patterns in one part of the speech production system (here the laryngeal specification) can depend on coordination relations in an apparently quite different part of the system (see Gafos et al., 2010 and Pouplier & Beňuš, 2011, for the related issue of cross-language differences in preferred coordination relations). In general, studies such as these provide a better understanding of why certain sound sequences are preferred in languages. Thus the sonority sequencing generalization in which consonants of increasing sonority are preferred nearer the vowel nucleus can be reinterpreted in terms of two phonetic principles: as discussed in Chitoran et al. (2002), preferred sound structures are those that allow a good compromise between parallel transmission of segmental information (efficient for the speaker) and clear modulation of the resulting acoustic signal (efficient for the listener).

The articulatory analysis of German consonant clusters in Hoole et al. (2010) provides further evidence that physiological and acoustic principles can explain both synchronic phonological patterns and diachronic change. Their results show that there is less overlap in /C_1n/ (e.g. German *Kneipe*) than in /C_1l/ (e.g. German *Claudia*) clusters: these differences may come about because premature lowering of the soft palate might destroy important acoustic properties of the plosive burst. The differences between these clusters could be modelled in a similar way to those for Georgian: for /C_1l/, there is a default coupling in which the closure of the initial stop is synchronized with the vowel whereas for /C_1n/ it is the initial consonant release that is synchronized with the nasal consonant. Thus, /C_1n/ clusters may be physiologically costly because they require a departure from the default coordination patterns (they may be additionally costly because of the need to increase the stiffness of the velar opening gesture to ensure a sufficiently abrupt transition from closed position for the plosive to open position for the nasal). Compatibly, /C_1n/ initial clusters are not only rarer in the world's languages than /C_1l/, but they are also more prone to diachronic changes (Vennemann, 2000) such as the loss of the initial velar in /C_1n/ clusters (*knock, gnome*) around the seventeenth Century in English.

At the same time, cross-linguistic comparisons suggest that it may be premature to conclude that speech production is constructed around a small set of basic coordination patterns. For example, although Hoole et al. (2010) found a similar trend for less overlap in /C_1n/ clusters in French, the effect was much less clear-cut than in German and showed greater between-speaker variation (Hoole et al., 2010). Perhaps these differences can be related to the different organization of voicing in French and German, which might produce differences in the acoustic transition between consonants of an initial cluster. Thus this could be another case in which details of coordination patterns emerge from the interaction of different parts of the speech production system. Articulatory synthesis should be able to play an important role in future in elucidating the perceptual consequences of different patterns of overlap.

We would like to conclude this section with a brief summary of four topics that do not directly involve clusters in the narrow sense, but which are likely to contribute to the overall theme of the relationship between linguistic structure and coordinated behaviour in the immediate future.

4.1 Tonal Aspects of Syllable Structure

Gao (2009) has recently proposed that tones in Mandarin Chinese can be considered as tone gestures (T) that enter into a C-centre topology with the consonant and vowel of CV syllables: C and T are both coupled in-phase to the vowel but anti-phase to each other; thus C and T together act like an onset cluster. This is intriguing given the relevance of consonants for the emergence of tones in tonogenesis (see Sun, 2003, for links between consonant cluster simplification and tonal development), but it will be an enormous task to determine how well this concept generalizes to other tone languages, given their number and variety.

4.2 Syllabic Consonants

An unresolved issue is whether the gestural patterning of syllabic consonants is similar to that of vowels. Research by Pouplier and Beňuš (2011) on Slovakian suggests that consonant sequences containing a syllabic consonant are kinematically quite like consonant clusters. But much remains to be learnt here (see also Fougeron & Ridouane, 2008 and Ridouane, 2008 on Berber).

4.3 The Production of Schwa

Studies of pre-tonic schwa deletion within a gestural framework (i.e. in English words such as *police/please*, *support/sport* – see especially Davidson, 2006) suggest that schwa deletion is a gradient process that may be better modelled as the outcome of changes in gestural overlap rather than segmental deletion. Under an even more radical proposal, schwa may emerge as a result of differences in gestural coupling instead of being specified as part of the underlying representation: thus *police* and *please* would share the same cluster under this approach whose hyperarticulation produces the greater asynchrony (and perceived schwa) in the former (see Geng et al., 2010, for a recent discussion and Browman & Goldstein, 1990b, on targetless schwa).

4.4 Coordination and Morphology

Gafos et al. (2010) found that the extent of overlap of homoganic clusters of Arabic was low (i.e. they were produced with two distinct closures) when produced within the same morphological template, but high (i.e. produced as a single long closure) across an affixal boundary. The influence of morphology on articulatory timing was also found for Korean by Cho (2001). We suspect that there are many more phenomena of this kind still to be investigated.

5 Conclusions

One of the main conclusions to emerge from the above brief review is that linguistic structure needs to incorporate time not just in what Gafos (2002) has called its trivial sense, that is, serial order, but in the much richer sense of coordinated behaviour. Indeed, studying coordinated behaviour has the potential not only to provide a common basis for both the production and perception of speech as research on coarticulation shows, but it can also – as the studies reviewed under assimilation suggest – challenge commonly held views about continuous speech processes that are based on hearing (and transcribing) speech as a sequence of serially ordered consonants and vowels. Finally, empirically based research on coordination and speech production can advance our understanding of phonological patterning and diachronic change as many of the studies summarized in the final section on clusters have shown.

A central theme in all of the preceding three sections is that modelling transmission of dynamical information between speakers and listeners forms an essential part of understanding the relationship between the infinite variation in speech signals and phonological categories. In the future, the listener's parsing of coarticulatory patterns in speech production will need to be tested on speaker groups such as children (Zharkova et al., 2011) and in contexts such as weak syllables in which coarticulation is likely to be more extensive or more variable. Moreover, modelling production-perception relationships will continue to be important for understanding how consonants are subjected to assimilation across word and other prosodic boundaries as well as the ways in which consonant clusters are influenced by different prosodic constituents such as onsets and coda (Marin & Pouplier, 2010, Pouplier, in press). All of these issues can shed further light on why syllable types and phonotactic combinations vary in their frequency of occurrence in the world's languages.

Another main theme of the preceding three sections is that sound change may be more likely if the production and perception of speech provide different and divergent solutions about how dynamical information is associated with phonological categories. Thus the first two sections emphasized how sound change is perhaps more likely to come about when coarticulatory or assimilatory information is ambiguously transmitted between a speaker and a hearer. A further currently unresolved issue will be to explain how dynamic activity that is unstable in either or both production and perception can nevertheless be phonologized and acquired by children, albeit in a minority of languages. To do so will require a closer analysis of physiological-perceptual relationships and of a wider range of syllable types drawn from many more languages than have been studied in the past.

Note

1. Resistance to coarticulation (Recasens & Pallarès, 2001; Recasens, 2006) has offered some insights into asymmetries in assimilatory patterns based on articulatory considerations.

Bibliography

Abercrombie, D. (1965). 'Conversation and spoken prose'. In D. Abercrombie (ed.). *Studies in Phonetics and Linguistics*. London: Oxford University Press, pp. 1–9.

—. (1965). *Studies in Phonetics and Linguistics*. London: Oxford University Press.

—. (1967). *Elements of General Phonetics*. Edinburgh: Edinburgh University Press.

Adank, P., Evans, B. G., Stuart-Smith, J. and Scott, S. K. (2009). 'Comprehension of familiar and unfamiliar native accents under adverse listening conditions'. *Journal of Experimental Psychology: Human Perception and Performance* 35: 520–9.

Adank, P., Smits, R. and van Hout, R. (2004). 'A comparison of vowel normalization procedures for language variation research'. *Journal of the Acoustical Society of America* 116: 3099–107.

Agwuele, A., Sussman, H. and Lindblom B. (2008). 'The effect of speaking rate on consonant vowel coarticulation'. *Phonetica* 65: 194–209.

Allbright, R. W. (1958). *The International Phonetic Alphabet: Its Backgrounds and Development*. Bloomington, Indiana: Indiana University Research Center in Anthropology, Folklore and Linguistics.

Alfonso, P. and Baer, T. (1982). 'Dynamics of vowel articulation'. *Language and Speech* 25: 151–73.

Alhawary, M. T. (2003). 'Elicitation techniques and considerations in data collection in early arabic grammatical tradition'. *Journal of Arabic Linguistics Tradition* 1: 1–24.

Allen, J., Hunnicutt, S., Klatt, D., Armstrong, R. and Pisoni, D. (1987). *From Text to Speech: The MITalk System*. New York: Cambridge University Press.

Allen, W. S. (1953). *Phonetics in Ancient India*. London: Oxford University Press.

—. (1981). 'The Greek contribution to the history of phonetics'. In R. E. Asher and E. J. A. Henderson (eds). *Towards a History of Phonetics*. Edinburgh: Edinburgh University Press, pp. 115–22.

Allopenna, P. D., Magnuson, J. S. and Tanenhaus, M. K. (1998). 'Tracking the time course of spoken word recognition using eye movements: Evidence for continuous mapping models'. *Journal of Memory and Language* 38: 419–39.

Al-Nassir, A. A. (1993). *Sibawayh the Phonologist*. London: Kegan Paul International.

Amorosa, H., von Benda, U., Wagner, E. and Keck, A. (1985). 'Transcribing phonetic detail in the speech of unintelligible children: A comparison of procedures'. *British Journal of Disorders of Communication* 20: 281–7.

Anderson, A., Bader, M., Bard, E., Boyle, E., Doherty, G., Garrod, S., Isard, S., Kowtko, J., McAllister, J., Miller, J., Sotillo, C., Thompson, H. and Weinert, R. (1991). 'The HCRC map task corpus'. *Language and Speech* 34: 351–66.

Anderson, S. W. and Cooper, W. E. (1986). 'Fundamental frequency patterns during spontaneous picture description'. *Journal of the Acoustical Society of America* 794: 1172–4.

Anderson, V. B. (2000). *Giving Weight to Phonetic Principles: The Case of Place of Articulation in Western Arrernte*. PhD dissertation, University of California, Los Angeles [available at: www2.hawaii.edu/~vanderso/AndersonDiss.pdf]

—. (2008). 'Static palatography for language fieldwork'. *Language Documentation and Conservation* 2 [Retrieved on 30 June 2010 from: http://hdl.handle.net/10125/1808]

Anwar, M. S. (1983). 'The legitimate fathers of speech errors'. In H. M.Cornelis, E. F. Versteegh, K. Koerner and H.-J. Niederehe (eds). *The History of Linguistics in the Near East*. Amsterdam and Philadelphia: John Benjamins, pp. 13–29.

Aristotle. (1963). *De Interpretatione*. Ackrill, J. L. (ed. and trans.). Oxford: Clarendon Press.
—. (1993). *De Anima*. Hamlyn, D. W. (ed. and trans.). Oxford: Clarendon Press.
Armstrong, S. and Ainley, M. (1988). *The South Tyneside Assessment of Phonology*. Northumberland: Stass.
Arvaniti, A. (2009). 'Rhythm, timing and the timing of rhythm'. *Phonetica* 66: 46–63.
Arvaniti, A. and Ladd, D. R. (1995). 'Tonal alignment and the representation of accentual targets'. *Proceedings of the 13th International Congress of Phonetic Sciences*. Stockholm: 220–3.
Arvaniti, A., Ladd, D. R. and Mennen, I. (1998). 'Stability of tonal alignment: the case of Greek prenuclear accents'. *Journal of Phonetics* 26: 3–25.
Ashby, M. (2008). 'New directions in learning, teaching and assessment for phonetics'. *Estudios de Fon ética Experimental* XVII: 19–44.
Ashby, M. and Maidment, J. A. (2005). *Introducing Phonetic Science*. Cambridge introductions to language and linguistics. Cambridge: Cambridge University Press.
Ashby, M., Figueroa-Clark, M., Seo, E. and Yanagisawa, K. (2005). 'Innovations in practical phonetics teaching and learning'. *Proceedings of the Phonetics Teaching and Learning Conference*. London: 1–4.
Ashby, M., House J., Huckvale, M., Maidment, J. A. and Yanagisawa, K. (2007). 'A distance e-learning course in phonetics'. In J. Trouvain and W. J. Barry (eds). *Proceedings of the 16th International Congress of Phonetic Sciences*. Saarbrücken: pp. 1713–16.
Ashby, P. (2005). *Speech Sounds* (2nd edn). Language workbooks. London: Routledge.
—. (2011). *Understanding Phonetics*. London: Hodder Education.
Aslin, R. N., Saffran, J. R. and Newport, E. L. (1998). 'Computation of conditional probability statistics by 8-month-old infants'. *Psychological Science* 9: 321–4.
Assmann, P. F. and Summerfield, A. Q. (2004). 'The perception of speech under adverse conditions'. In S. Greenberg, W. A. Ainsworth, A. N. Popper and R. R. Fay (eds). *Speech Processing in the Auditory System*. Volume 14. New York: Springer Handbook of Auditory Research, pp. 231–308.
Auer, P., Couper-Kuhlen, E. and Müller, F. (1999). *Language in Time: The Rhythm and Tempo of Spoken Interaction*. Oxford: Oxford University Press.
AusTalk. (2011). AusTalk: An audio-visual corpus of Australian English [Retrieved on 20 January 2011 from: https://austalk.edu.au/]
Australian Government – National Health and Medical Research Council. (2010). National ethics application form [Retrieved on 26 June 2010 from: www.nhmrc.gov.au/health-ethics/australian-health-ethics-committee-ahec/neaf-national-ethics-application-form]
Awan, N. S. (2006). 'The aging female voice: acoustic and respiratory data'. *Clinical Linguistics and Phonetics* 20: 171–80.
Aylett, M. and Turk, A. (2004). 'The smooth signal redundancy hypothesis: A functional explanation for relationships between redundancy, prosodic prominence, and duration in spontaneous speech'. *Language and Speech* 47: 31–56.
Baayen, R. H. and Milin, P. (2010). 'Analyzing reaction times'. *International Journal of Psychological Research* 3: 12–28.
Babel, M. (2012). 'Evidence for phonetic and social selectivity in spontaneous phonetic imitation'. *Journal of Phonetics* 40: 177–89.
Bacsfalvi, P. and Bernhardt, B. (2011). 'Long-term outcomes of speech therapy for seven adolescents with visual feedback technologies: Ultrasound and electropalatography'. *Clinical Linguistics and Phonetics* 25: 1034–43.
Baddeley, A. D., Thomson, N. and Buchanan, M. (1975). 'Word length and the structure of short term memory'. *Journal of Verbal Learning and Verbal Behaviour* 14: 575–89.
Badecker, W. (2005). 'Speech perception after focal brain injury'. In D. Pisoni and R. Remez (eds). *The Handbook of Speech Perception*. Oxford: Blackwell, pp. 524–45.

Bailey, B. (1996). 'Laryngoscopy and laryngoscopes – Who's first: The forefathers/four fathers of laryngology'. *The Laryngoscope* 106: 939–43.

Baines, J. (2004). 'The earliest Egyptian writing: Development, context, purpose'. In S. Houston (ed.). *First Writing*. Cambridge: Cambridge University Press, pp. 150–89.

Bakalla, M. H. (1982). *Ibn Jinnī: An early Arab Muslim phonetician*. Taipei: European Language Publications.

Baker, E. (2010). 'The experience of discharging children from phonological intervention'. *International Journal of Speech-Language Pathology* 12: 325–8.

Bakran, J. and Mildner, V. (1995). 'Effect of speech and coarticulation strategies on the locus equation determination'. *Proceedings of the 13th International Congress of Phonetic Sciences*. Stockholm, 26–9.

Ball, M. J. (1993). *Phonetics for speech pathology* (2nd edn). London: Whurr.

—. (2008). 'Transcribing disordered speech: By target or by production?' *Clinical Linguistics and Phonetics* 22: 864–70.

—. (2009). 'Response to Barry and Trouvain 2008'. *Journal of the International Phonetic Association* 39: 233–4.

Ball, M. J. and Lowry, O. (2001). *Methods in Clinical Phonetics*. London: Whurr.

Ball, M. J. and Müller, N. (2005). *Phonetics for Communication Disorders*. Mahwah, NJ and London: Lawrence Erlbaum Associates.

Ball, M. J. and Rahilly, J. (1999). *Phonetics. The Science of Speech*. London: Edward Arnold.

Bar, M. (2009). 'The proactive brain: Memory for predictions'. *Philosophical Transactions of the Royal Society B* 364.1521: 1235–43.

Barr, D. (2008). 'Analyzing "visual world" eyetracking data using multilevel logistic regression'. *Journal of Memory and Language* 59: 457–74.

Barreda, S. and Nearey, T. (2012). 'The direct and indirect roles of fundamental frequency in vowel perception'. *Journal of the Acoustical Society of America* 131: 466–77.

Barry, M. C. (1991). 'Temporal modeling of gestures in articulatory assimilation'. *Proceedings of the 12th International Congress of Phonetic Sciences* 4: 14–17.

Barry, W. and Andreeva, B. (2001). 'Cross-language similarities and differences in spontaneous speech patterns'. *Journal of the International Phonetic Association* 31: 51–66.

Barry, W. J. (1997). 'Another R-tickle'. *Journal of the International Phonetic Association* 27: 35–45.

Barry, W. J. and Trouvain, J. (2008). 'Do we need a symbol for a central open vowel?' *Journal of the International Phonetic Association* 38: 349–57.

Bates, E. and Liu, H. (1996). 'Cued-shadowing'. In F. Grosjean and U. Frauenfelder (eds). *A Guide to Spoken Word Recognition Paradigms*. Hove: Psychology press, pp. 577–82.

Beach, D. M. (1938). *The Phonetics of the Hottentot Language*. Cambridge: W. Heffer and Sons.

Beal, J. (1999). *English Pronunciation in the Eighteenth Century*. Oxford: Oxford University Press.

—. (2009). 'Pronouncing Dictionaries – I Eighteenth and early Nineteenth Centuries'. In A. P. Cowie (ed.). *The Oxford History of English Lexicography, Volume II: Specialized Dictionaries*. Oxford: Clarendon Press, pp. 149–75.

Beal, J., Burbano-Elizondo, L. and Llamas, C. (2012). *Urban North-Eastern English: Tyneside to Teesside. Edinburgh Dialects of English Series*. Edinburgh: Edinburgh University Press.

Beck, J. M. (2003). 'Is it possible to predict students' ability to develop skills in practical phonetics?' In M.-J. Solé, D. Recasens and J. Romero (eds). *Proceedings of the 15th International Congress of the Phonetic Sciences*. Barcelona, pp. 2833–6.

—. (2010). 'Organic variation of the vocal apparatus'. In W. J. Hardcastle, J. Laver and F. Gibbon (eds). *The Handbook of Phonetic Sciences*. Oxford: Wiley-Blackwell, pp. 155–201.

Beddor, P. (2007). 'Nasals and nasalization: the relation between segmental and coarticulatory timing'. In J. Trouvain and W. J. Barry (eds). *Proceedings of the 16th International Congress of Phonetic Sciences*. Saarbrücken, pp. 249–54.

Beddor, P., Harnsberger, J. and Lindemann, S. (2002). 'Language-specific patterns of vowel-to-vowel coarticulation: acoustic structures and their perceptual correlates'. *Journal of Phonetics* 30: 591–627.

Beddor, P. and Krakow, R. (1999). 'Perception of coarticulatory nasalization by speakers of English and Thai: Evidence for partial compensation'. *Journal of the Acoustical Society of America* 106: 2868–87.

Beddor, P., Krakow, R. and Goldstein, L. (1986). 'Perceptual constraints and phonological change: a study of nasal vowel height'. *Phonology Yearbook* 3: 197–217.

Beddor, P., Krakow, R. and Lindemann, S. (2001). 'Patterns of perceptual compensation and their phonological consequences'. In E. Hume and K. Johnson (eds). *The Role of Speech Perception in Phonology*. Academic Press: San Diego, pp. 55–78.

Belin, P., Zatorre, R. J., Lafaille, P., Ahad, P. and Pike, B. (2000). 'Voice-selective areas in human auditory cortex'. *Nature* 403: 309–12.

Belin, P., Zilbovicius, M., Crozier, S., Thivard, L., Fontaine, A., Masure, M.-C. and Samson, Y. (1998). 'Lateralization of speech and auditory temporal processing'. *Journal of Cognitive Neuroscience* 10: 536–40.

Bell, A. M. (1867). *Visible Speech*. London: Simpkin Marshall.

Benner, A., Grenon, I. and Esling, J. H. (2007). 'Infants' phonetic acquisition of voice quality parameters in the first year of life'. In J. Trouvain and W. J. Barry (eds). *Proceedings of the 16th International Congress of Phonetic Sciences*. Saarbrücken: 2073–6.

Beranek, L. L. (1949). *Acoustic Measurements*. New York: McGraw-Hill.

Berinstein, A. E. (1979). 'A cross-linguistic study on the perception and production of stress'. *UCLA Working Papers in Phonetics* 47: 1–59.

Bernthal, J. E. and Bankson, N. W. (1998). *Articulation and Phonological Disorders* (2nd edn). Englewood Cliffs, NJ: Prentice Hall.

Best, C. T. and Tyler, M. D. (2007). 'Nonnative and second-language speech perception: Commonalities and complementarities'. In M. J. Munro and O.-S. Bohn (eds). *Second Language Speech Learning: The Role of Language Experience in Speech Perception and Production*. Amsterdam: John Benjamins, pp. 13–34.

Best, C. T., McRoberts, G. and Sithole, N. M. (1988). 'Examination of perceptual reorganization for nonnative speech contrasts: Zulu click discrimination by English-speaking adults and infants'. *Journal of Experimental Psychology: Human Perception and Performance* 14: 45–60.

Biggs, John B. (2007). *Teaching for Quality Learning at University: What the Student Does* (3rd edn). Maidenhead: McGraw-Hill/Society for Research into Higher Education and Open University Press.

Bijeljac-Babic, R., Bertoncini, J. and Mehler, J. (1993). 'How do 4-day-old infants categorize multisyllabic utterances?' *Developmental Psychology* 29: 711–21.

Black, A. (1997). 'Predicting the intonation of discourse segments from examples in dialogue speech'. In Y. Sagisaka, N. Campbell and N. Higuchi (eds). *Computing Prosody*. Berlin: Springer-Verlag, pp. 117–27.

Black, A., Zen, H. and Tokuda, K. (2007). 'Statistical parametric speech synthesis'. *ICASSP*. Honolulu, HI: IEEE, pp. 1229–32.

Blevins, J. (2007). 'Interpreting misperception: Beauty is in the ear of the beholder'. In M.-J. Solé, P., Beddor, S. and M. Ohala (eds). *Experimental Approaches to Phonology*. Oxford: Oxford University Press, pp. 144–54.

—. (2008). 'Natural and unnatural sound patterns: a pocket field guide'. In K. Willems and L. de Cuypere (eds). *Naturalness and Iconicity in Language*. Amsterdam: John Benjamins, pp. 121–48.

Bloothooft, G. (1997). *The Landscape of Future Education in Speech Communication Sciences. 2 Proposals for European Education in Phonetics, Spoken Language Engineering, Speech and Language Therapy.* Utrecht, the Netherlands: Utrecht Institute of Linguistics OTS Publications.

Boersma, P. and Hamann, S. (2008). 'The evolution of auditory dispersion in bidirectional constraint grammars'. *Phonology* 25: 217–70.

Boersma, P. and Weenink, D. (2011). 'Praat: doing phonetics by computer [Computer program]'. Version 5. 2. 26 [Retrieved on 24 May 2011 from www.praat.org/]

Bolinger, D. (1965). *Forms of English: Accent, Morpheme, Order.* Cambridge, MA: Harward University Press.

Bombien, L., Mooshammer, C., Hoole, P. and Kühnert, B. (2010). 'Prosodic and segmental effects on EPG contact patterns of word-initial German clusters'. *Journal of Phonetics* 38: 388–403.

Bornstein, M. H. (1973). 'Color vision and color naming: a psychophysiological hypothesis of cultural difference'. *Psychological Bulletin* 80: 257–85.

Bowen, C. (2009). *Children's Speech Sound Disorders.* Chichester: Wiley-Blackwell.

—. (2011). *Speech Sound Disorders: The Basics and Beyond II.* Course held in York, England.

Bowern, C. (2008). *Linguistic Field Work: A Practical Guide.* Houndmills and New York: Palgrave MacMillan.

Boyce, S. E. and Menn, L. (1979). 'Peaks vary, endpoints don't: Implications for intonation theory'. *Proceedings of the 5th Annual Meeting of the Berkeley Linguistic Society* 5: 373–84.

Boyd, Z. (2005). 'Slips of the ear'. In D. Pisoni and R. Remez (eds). *The Handbook of Speech Perception.* Oxford: Blackwell, pp. 290–310.

Brace, C. L. (1986). 'Egg on the face, *f* in the mouth, and the overbite'. *American Anthropologist* 88: 695–7.

Bradley, D. and Forster, K. (1987). 'A reader's view of listening'. In U. Frauenfelder and L. Tyler (eds). *Spoken Word Recognition.* Cambridge: MIT press, pp. 103–34.

Bradlow, A. (1995). 'A comparative acoustic study of English and Spanish vowels'. *Journal of the Acoustical Society of America* 97: 1916–24.

Bradlow, A. R. and Alexander, J. A. (2007). 'Semantic-contextual and acoustic-phonetic enhancements for English sentence-in-noise recognition by native and non-native listeners'. *Journal of the Acoustical Society of America* 121: 2339–49.

Bradlow, A. R., Nygaard, L. C. and Pisoni, D. B. (1999). 'Effects of talker, rate and amplitude variation on recognition memory for spoken words'. *Perception and Psychophysics* 61: 206–19.

Braun, A. (1996). 'Age estimation by different listener groups'. *Forensic Linguistics: The International Journal of Speech, Language and the Law* 3: 65–73.

Breiman, L., Friedman, J. H., Olshen, R. A. and Stone, C. J. (1984). *Classification and Regression Trees.* Monterey, CA: Wadsworth and Brooks.

Brent, M. and Siskind, J. (2001). 'The role of exposure to isolated words in early vocabulary development'. *Cognition* 81: 33–44.

Bressman, T. (2006). 'Speech adaptation to a self-inflicted cosmetic tongue-split: perceptual and ultrasonographic analysis'. *Clinical Linguistics and Phonetics* 20: 205–10.

Britain, D. (ed.) (2007). *Language in the British Isles.* Cambridge: Cambridge University Press.

Broomfield, J. and Dodd, B. (2004). 'The nature of referred subtypes of primary speech disability'. *Child Language Teaching and Therapy* 20: 135–51.

Brosnahan, L. F. (1961). *The Sounds of Langauge.* Cambridge: Heffer.

Browman, C. P. and Goldstein, L. M. (1989). 'Articulatory gestures as phonological units'. *Phonology* 6: 201–51.

—. (1990a). 'Tiers in Aticulatory Phonology, with some implications for casual speech'. In J. Kingston and M. E. Beckman (eds). *Papers in Laboratory Phonology I*. Cambridge: Cambridge University Press, pp. 340–76.

—. (1990b). 'Gestural specification using dynamically defined articulatory structures'. *Journal of Phonetics* 18: 299–320.

—. (1991). 'Gestural structures: distinctiveness, phonological processes, and historical change'. In I. Mattingly and M. Studdert-Kennedy (eds). *Modularity and the Motor Theory of Speech Perception*. Mahwah NJ: Lawrence Erlbaum, pp. 313–38.

—. (1992). 'Articulatory phonology: An overview'. *Phonetica* 49: 155–80.

—. (2000). 'Competing constraints on intergestural coordination and self-organization of phonological structure'. *Les Cahiers de l'ICP* 5: 25–34.

Brown, G. (1981). *Listening to Spoken English*. London: Longman.

Brown, R. (1973). *A First Language: The Early Stages*. London: George Allen and Unwin Ltd.

Bruce, G. (1977). *Swedish Word Accents in Sentence Perspective*. Lund: Gleerup.

Brunelle, M. (2011). 'Perception in the field'. In R. Pieraccini and A. Colombo (eds). *Proceedings of the 12th Annual Conference of the International Speech Communication Association*. Bonn: International Speech Communication Association, pp. 80–3.

Brunelle, M., Nguyên, D. D. and Nguyên, K. H. (2010). 'A laryngographic and laryngoscopic study of Northern Vietnamese tones'. *Phonetica* 67: 147–69.

Brunner, J., Fuchs, S. and Perrier, P. (2009). 'On the relationship between palate shape and articulatory behavior'. *Journal of the Acoustical Society of America* 125: 3936–49.

Burton-Roberts, N., Carr, P. and Docherty, G. (eds) (2000). *Phonological Knowledge*. Oxford: Oxford University Press.

Butcher A. R. (1995). 'The phonetics of neutralisation: the case of Australian coronals'. In J. Windsor Lewis (ed.). *Studies in General and English Phonetics. Essays in honour of Professor J.D. O'Connor*. London: Routledge, pp. 10–38.

—. (1999). 'What speakers of Australian aboriginal languages do with their velums and why: the phonetics of the nasal/oral contrast'. In J. J. Ohala, Y. Hasegawa, M. Ohala, D. Granville and A. C. Bailey (eds). *Proceedings of the XIV International Congress of Phonetic Sciences*. Berkeley: ICPhS, pp. 479–82.

—. (2004). '"Fortis/Lenis" revisited one more time: the aerodynamics of some oral stop contrasts in three continents'. *Clinical Linguistics and Phonetics* 18: 547–57.

Butcher, A. R. and Loakes, D. E. (2008). 'Enhancing the left edge: the phonetics of prestopped sonorants in Australian languages. (A)'. 156th Meeting of the Acoustical Society of America, Miami, Florida. *Journal of the Acoustical Society of America* 124: 2527.

Butcher, A. R. and Tabain, M. (2004). 'On the back of the tongue: contrasting dorsal sounds in Australian languages'. *Phonetica* 61: 22–52.

Buzsáki, G. and Draguhn, A. (2004). 'Neuronal oscillations in cortical networks'. *Science* 304: 1926–9.

Bybee, J. H. (2001). *Phonology and Language Use*. Cambridge: Cambridge University Press.

Byrd, D. (1995). 'C-centers revisited'. *Phonetica* 52: 285–306.

Byrd, D. and Choi, S. (2010). 'At the juncture of prosody, phonology, and phonetics – The interaction of phrasal and syllable structure in shaping the timing of consonant gestures'. In C. Fougeron, B. Kühnert, M. D'Imperio and N. Vallée (eds). *Laboratory Phonology 10: Variability, Phonetic Detail and Phonological Representation*. Berlin: Mouton de Gruyter, pp. 31–59.

Byrd, D., Flemming, E., Muller, C. and Tan, C. (1995). 'Using regions and indices in EPG data reduction'. *Journal of Speech and Hearing Research* 38: 821–7.

Byrd, D., Tobin, S., Bresch, E. and Narayanan, S. (2009). 'Timing effects of syllable structure and stress on nasals: a real-time MRI examination'. *Journal of Phonetics* 37: 97–110.

Byrne, C. and Foulkes, P. (2004). 'The "Mobile Phone Effect" on vowel formants'. *International Journal of Speech, Language and the Law* 11: 83–102.

Cabeza, R. and Kingstone, K. (eds) (2006). *Handbook of Functional Neuroimaging of Cognition*. Cambridge, MA: MIT Press

Campbell, F., Gick, B., Wilson, E. and Vatikiotis-Bateson, E. (2010). 'Spatial and temporal properties of gestures in North American English /r/'. *Language and Speech* 53: 49–69.

Canavan, A., Graff, D. and Zipperlen, G. (1997). *CALLHOME American English speech*. Philadelphia: Linguistic Data Consortium.

Carr, P. 1999. *English Phonetics and Phonology: An Introduction*. Oxford: Blackwell.

Carter, P. and Local, J. (2007). 'F2 variation in Newcastle and Leeds English liquid systems'. *Journal of the International Phonetic Association* 37: 183–99.

Caruso, A. and Strand, E. (1999). *Clinical Management of Motor Speech Disorders in Children*. New York: Thieme.

Catford, J. C. (1964). 'Phonation types: The classification of some laryngeal components of speech production'. In D. Abercrombie, D. B. Fry, P. A. D. McCarthy, N. C. Scott and J. L. M. Trim (eds). *In Honour of Daniel Jones*. London: Longman, pp. 26–37.

—. (1968). 'The articulatory possibilities of man'. In B. Malmberg (ed.). *Manual of Phonetics*. Amsterdam: North-Holland Publishing Company, pp. 309–33.

—. (1977). *Fundamental Problems in Phonetics*. Edinburgh: Edinburgh University Press.

—. (1997). 'The myth of the primordial click'. In I. Hegedüs, P. A. Michalors and A. Manaster Ramer (eds). *Indo-European, Nostratic and Beyond: Festschrift for Vitalij V. Shevorshkin. Journal of Indo-European Studies Monograph* 22: 51–71.

—. (2001). *A Practical Introduction to Phonetics* (2nd edn). Oxford: Oxford University Press.

Catford, J. C. and Esling, J. H. (2006). 'Articulatory phonetics'. In K. Brown (ed.). *Encyclopedia of Language and Linguistics* (2nd edn), vol. 9. Oxford: Elsevier, pp. 425–42.

Cecioni, C. G. (1980). 'Sir Thomas Smith's "De recta et emendata linguae anglicae scriptione diologus". (1568)'. In K. Koerner (ed.). *Progress in Linguistic Historiography*. Amsterdam: John Benjamins, pp. 87–93.

Chelliah, S. L. and de Reuse, W. J. (2011). *Handbook of Descriptive Linguistic Fieldwork*. Dordrecht: Springer.

Chen, L. (2003). 'The origins in overlap of place assimilation'. In G. Garding and M. Tsujimura (eds). *West Coast Conference of Formal Linguistics* 22. San Diego, CA: pp. 137–50.

Chen, M. (1970). 'Vowel length variation as a function of the voicing of the consonant environment'. *Phonetica* 22: 129–59.

Cheshire, J., Fox, S, Kerswill, P. and Torgersen, E. (2008). 'Ethnicity, friendship network and social practices as the motor of dialect change: Linguistic innovation in London'. In U. Ammon and K. J. Mattheier (eds). *Sociolinguistica: International Yearbook of European Sociolinguistics*. Tübingen: Max Niemeyer Verlag, pp. 1–23.

Chiat, S. and Roy, P. (2007). 'The preschool repetition test: An evaluation of performance in typically developing and clinically referred children'. *Journal of Speech, Language, and Hearing Research* 50: 429–43.

Chiba, T. and Kajiyama, M. (1958). *The Vowel, its Nature and Structure*. Tokyo: Phonetics Society of Japan.

Chitoran, I., Goldstein, L. and Byrd, D. (2002). 'Gestural overlap and recoverability: Articulatory evidence from Georgian'. In C. Gussenhoven and N. Warner (eds). *Papers in Laboratory Phonology 7*. Berlin: Mouton de Gruyter, pp. 419–48.

Cho, T. (2001). 'Effects of morpheme boundaries on intergestural timing: Evidence from Korean'. *Phonetica* 58: 129–62.

—. (2004) 'Prosodically conditioned strengthening and vowel-to-vowel coarticulation in English'. *Journal of Phonetics* 32: 141–76.

Cho, T. and Ladefoged, P. (1999). 'Variation and universals in VOT: evidence from 18 languages'. *Journal of Phonetics* 27: 207–29.

Cho, T., Lee, Y. and Kim, S. (2011). 'Communicatively driven versus prosodically driven hyper-articulation in Korean'. *Journal of Phonetics* 39: 344–61.

Chomsky, N. and Halle, M. (1968). *The Sound Pattern of English*. New York: Harper and Row.

Christophe, A., Peperkamp, S., Pallier, C., Block, E. and Mehler, J. (2004). 'Phonological phrase boundaries constrain lexical access: I. Adult data'. *Journal of Memory and Language* 51: 523–47.

Church, B. A. and Schacter, D. L. (1994). 'Perceptual specificity of auditory priming: Implicit memory for voice intonation and fundamental frequency'. *Journal of Experimental Psychology: Learning, Memory, and Cognition* 20: 521–33.

Cieri, C. (2010). 'Making a field recording'. In M. Di Paolo and M. Yaeger-Dror (eds). *Sociophonetics: A Student's Guide*. London: Routledge, pp. 24–35.

Clark, J., Yallop, C. and Fletcher, J. (2007). *An Introduction to Phonetics and Phonology* (3rd edn). Blackwell textbooks in linguistics 9. Malden, MA: Blackwell.

Clayards, M., Tanenhaus, M. K., Aslin, R. N. and Jacobs, R. A. (2008). 'Perception of speech reflects optimal use of probabilistic speech cues'. *Cognition* 108: 804–9.

Clements, G. N. (1985). 'The geometry of phonological features'. *Phonology Yearbook* 2: 225–52.

Clopper, C. G. and Pierrehumbert, J. B. (2008). 'Effects of semantic predictability and regional dialect on vowel space reduction'. *Journal of the Acoustical Society of America* 124: 1682–8.

Cohn, A. C. (1993). 'Nasalisation in English: phonology or phonetics'. *Phonology* 10: 43–81.

Cohn, A. C., Ham, W. H. and Podesva, R. J. (1999). 'The phonetic realization of singleton-geminate contrasts in three languages of Indonesia'. In J. J. Ohala, Y. Hasegawa, M. Ohala, D. Granville and A. C. Bailey (eds). *Proceedings of the XIV International Congress of Phonetic Sciences*. Berkeley: ICPhS, pp. 587–90.

Coleman, J. (2003). 'Discovering the acoustic correlates of phonological contrasts'. *Journal of Phonetics* 31: 351–72.

Collins, B. and Mees, I. M. (1999). *The Real Professor Higgins: The Life and Career of Daniel Jones*. Berlin: Mouton de Gruyter.

—. (2008). *Practical Phonetics and Phonology: A Resource Book for Students* (2nd edn). London: Routledge.

Connell, B. (2002). 'Tone languages and the universality of intrinsic F0: evidence from Africa'. *Journal of Phonetics* 30: 101–29.

Cooper, F. S., Delattre, P. C., Liberman, A. M., Borst, J. M. and Gerstman, L. J. (1952). 'Some experiments on the perception of synthetic speech sounds'. *Journal of the Acoustical Society of America* 24: 597–606.

Cooper, R. P. and Aslin, R. N. (1994). 'Developmental differences in infant attention to the spectral properties of infant-directed speech'. *Child Development* 65: 1663–77.

Coulmas, F. (2003). *Writing Systems*. Cambridge: Cambridge University Press.

Couper-Kuhlen, E. and Ford, C. E. (eds) (2004). *Sound Patterns in Interaction. Cross-linguistic Studies from Conversation. Typological Studies in Language*. Amsterdam: John Benjamins.

Couper-Kuhlen, E. and Selting, M. (eds) (1996). *Prosody in Conversation*. Cambridge: Cambridge University Press.

Cristià, A. (2010). 'Phonetic enhancement of sibilants in infant-directed speech'. *Journal of the Acoustical Society of America* 128: 424–34.

Crowley, T. (2007). *Field Linguistics: A Beginner's Guide*. Oxford: Oxford University Press.

Cruttenden, A. (1997). *Intonation* (2nd edn). Cambridge: Cambridge University Press.

Crystal, D. (1985). *A Dictionary of Linguistics and Phonetics* (2nd edn). Oxford: Blackwell.

Cummins, F. (2003a). 'Practice and performance in speech produced synchronously'. *Journal of Phonetics* 31: 139–48.

—. (2003b). 'Rhythmic grouping in word lists: competing roles of syllables, words and stress feet'. In M.-J. Solé, D. Recasens and J. Romero (eds). *Proceedings of the 15th International Congress of the Phonetic Sciences*. Barcelona, pp. 325–8.

—. (2009). 'Rhythm as entrainment: The case of synchronous speech'. *Journal of Phonetics* 37: 16–28.

Cutler, A. (1986). 'Forbear is a homophone: lexical prosody does not constrain lexical access'. *Language and Speech* 29: 201–20.

—. (2005). 'Lexical stress'. In D. B. Pisoni and R. E. Remez (eds). *The Handbook of Speech Perception*. Oxford: Blackwell, pp. 264–89.

Cutler, A. and Butterfield, S. (1992). 'Rhythmic cues to speech segmentation: Evidence from juncture misperception'. *Journal of Memory and Language* 31: 218–36.

Dahan, D. and Magnuson, J. S. (2006). 'Spoken-word recognition'. In M. J. Traxler and M. A. Gernsbacher (eds). *Handbook of Psycholinguistics*. Amsterdam: Academic Press, pp. 249–83.

Dahan, D. and Mead, R. L. (2010). 'Context-conditioned generalization in adaptation to distorted speech'. *Journal of Experimental Psychology: Human Perception and Performance* 36: 704–28.

Dain, S. J., Cassimaty, V. T. and Psarakis, D. T. (2004). 'Differences in FM100-Hue test performance related to iris colour may be due to pupil size as well as presumed amounts of macular pigmentation'. *Clinical and Experimental Optometry* 87: 322–5.

Danielsson, B. (1955). *John Hart's Works on English Orthography and Pronunciation, Part II: Phonology*. Stockholm: Almqvist and Wiksell.

Daniloff, R. and Hammarberg, R. (1973). 'On defining coarticulation'. *Journal of Phonetics* 1: 239–48.

Dankovičová, J., House, J., Crooks, A. and Jones, K. (2007). 'The relationship between musical skills, music training, and intonation analysis skills'. *Language and Speech* 50: 177–225.

Darch, J., Milner, B., Shao, X., Vaseghi, S. and Yan, Q. (2005). 'Predicting formant frequencies from MFCC vectors'. *Proceedings of the IEEE International Conference on Acoustics, Speech, and Signal Processing (ICASSP)*. Philadelphia, March 2005, pp. 941–4.

Dart, S. (1991). *Articulatory and Acoustic Properties of Apical and Laminal Articulations*. PhD dissertation, University of California, Los Angeles [available as *UCLA Working Papers in Phonetics* 79].

Daubert, V. (1993). Merrell Dow Pharmaceuticals, Inc., 509 U.S. 579, 585.

Dauer, R. M. (1983). 'Stress-timing and syllable-timing re-analysed'. *Journal of Phonetics* 11: 51–62.

—. (1987). 'Phonetic and phonological components of language rhythm'. *Proceedings of the 11th International Congress of Phonetic Sciences*. Talinn, pp. 447–50.

Davenport, M. and Hannahs, S. J. (2010). *Introducing Phonetics and Phonology* (3rd edn). London: Hodder Education.

Davidson, L. (2006). 'Schwa elision in fast speech: segmental deletion or gestural overlap?' *Phonetica* 63: 79–112.

Davis, M. H., Marslen-Wilson, W. D. and Gaskell, M. G. (2002). 'Leading up the lexical garden-path: segmentation and ambiguity in spoken word recognition'. *Journal of Experimental Psychology: Human Perception and Performance* 28: 218–44.

Davis, S. and Mermelstein, P. (1980). 'Comparison of parametric representations for monosyllabic word recognition in continuously spoken sentences'. *IEEE Trans. Acoustics, Speech and Signal Processing* 28: 357–66.

de Jong, K. (1995). 'The supraglottal articulation of prominence in English: Linguistic stress as localized hyperarticulation'. *Journal of the Acoustical Society of America* 97: 491–504.

de Pinto, O. and Hollien, H. (1982). 'Speaking fundamental frequency characteristics of Australian women: then and now'. *Journal of Phonetics* 10: 367–75.

De Ruiter, J. P., Mitterer, H. and Enfield, N. J. (2006). 'Projecting the end of a speaker's turn: a cognitive cornerstone of conversation'. *Language* 82: 515–35.

De Wachter, M., Matton, M., Demuynck, K., Wambacq, P., Cools, R. and Van Compernolle, D. (2007). 'Template-Based Continuous Speech Recognition'. *IEEE Transactions on Audio, Speech, and Language Processing* 15: 1377–90.

DeCasper, A. J. and Fifer, W. P. (1980). 'Of human bonding: Newborns prefer their mothers' voices'. *Science* 208: 1174–6.

DeCasper, A., Lecanuet, J. P., Busnel, M.-C., Granier-Deferre, C. and Maugeais, R. (1994). 'Fetal reactions to recurrent maternal speech'. *Infant Behavior and Development* 17: 159–64.

DeCasper, A. J. and Spence, M. (1986). 'Prenatal maternal speech influences newborns' perception of speech sounds'. *Infant Behavior and Development* 9: 133–50.

Delaherche, E., Chetouani, M., Mahdhaoui, A., Saint-Georges, C., Viaux, S. and Cohen, D. (forthcoming). 'Interpersonal synchrony: A survey of evaluation methods across disciplines'. *IEEE Transactions on Affective Computing*.

Delattre, P., Liberman, A. M. and Cooper, F. S. (1955). 'Acoustic loci and transitional cues for consonants'. *Journal of the Acoustical Society of America* 27: 769–74.

Dellwo, V. (2006). 'Rhythm and speech rate: A variation coefficient for deltaC'. In P. Karnowski and I. Szigeti (eds). *Sprache und Sprachverarbeitung / Language and Language-Processing*. Frankfurt am Main: Peter Lang, pp. 231–41.

Delvaux, V. and Soquet, A. (2007). 'The influence of ambient speech on adult speech productions through unintentional imitation'. *Phonetica* 64: 145–73.

Demolin, D. (2011). 'Aerodynamic techniques for phonetic fieldwork'. *Proceedings of the 17th International Congress of Phonetic Sciences*. Hong Kong, pp. 84–7.

Denes, P. B. and Pinson, E. N. (1993). *The Speech Chain: Physics and Biology of Spoken Language*. Basingstoke: W.H. Freeman and Co.

Di Paolo, M. and Yaeger-Dror, M. (eds) (2011). *Sociophonetics: A Student's Guide*. London: Routledge.

Dilley, L. C. and McAuley, J. D. (2008). 'Distal prosodic context affects word segmentation and lexical processing'. *Journal of Memory and Language* 59: 294–311.

Dilley, L. C. and Pitt, M. (2010). 'Altering context speech rate can cause words to appear or disappear'. *Psychological Science* 21: 1664–70.

Disner, S. F. (1980). 'Evaluation of vowel normalization procedures'. *Journal of the Acoustical Society of America* 67: 253–61.

Dobson, E. J. (1957). *The Phonetic Writings of Robert Robinson*. London: Oxford University Press.

Docherty, G. J. (1992). *The Timing of Voicing in British English Obstruents*. Berlin: Foris.

Docherty, G. J., Watt, D., Llamas, C., Hall, D. and Nycz, J. (2011). 'Variation in voice onset time along the Scottish-English border'. *Proceedings of the 17th International Congress of Phonetic Sciences*. Hong Kong, pp. 591–4.

Dodd, B. (1995). *The Differential Diagnosis and Treatment of Children with Speech Disorder*. London: Whurr.

—. (2005). *The Differential Diagnosis and Treatment of Children with Speech Disorder* (2nd edn). London: Whurr.

Dodd, D., Hua, Z., Crosbie, S., Holm, A. and Ozanne, A. (2002). *Diagnostic Evaluation of Articulation and Phonology (DEAP) Manual*. San Antonio, Texas: Harcourt Assessment.

Doke, C. M. (1931). *Comparative Study in Shona Phonetics*. Johannesburg: University of Witwatersrand Press.

Drugman, T., Wilfart, G. and Dutoit, T. (2009). *A Deterministic plus Stochastic Model of the Residual Signal for Improved Parametric Speech Synthesis*. Interspeech. Brighton, UK

Duckworth, M., Allen, G., Hardcastle, W. and Ball, M. (1990). 'Extensions to the International Phonetic Alphabet for the transcription of atypical speech'. *Clinical Linguistics and Phonetics* 4: 273–80.

Dudley, H. and Gruenz, O. O. (1946). 'Visible speech translators with external phosphors'. *Journal of the Acoustical Society of America* 18: 62–73.

Duffy, J. (2005). *Motor Speech Disorders: Substrates, Differential Diagnosis, and Management* (2nd edn). St Louis: Mosby.

Dunn, C., Noble, W., Tyler, R., Kordus, M., Gantz, B. and Ji, H. (2010). 'Bilateral and unilateral cochlear implant users compared on speech perception in noise'. *Ear and Hearing* 31: 296–8.

Edmondson, J. A. and Esling, J. H. (2006). 'The valves of the throat and their functioning in tone, vocal register, and stress: Laryngoscopic case studies'. *Phonology* 23: 157–91.

Eilers, R. E. and Minifie, F. D. (1975). 'Fricative discrimination in early infancy'. *Journal of Speech and Hearing Research* 18: 158–67.

Eimas, P. D., Siqueland, E. R., Jusczyk, P. and Vigorito, J. (1971). 'Speech perception in infants'. *Science* 171: 303–6.

Elliott, R. W. V. (1954). 'Isaac Newton as phonetician'. *The Modern Language Review* 49: 5–12.

Ellis, A. J. (1869). *On Early English Pronunciation*. London: Asher and Co.

Ellis, L. and Hardcastle, W. (2002). 'Categorical and gradient properties of assimilation in alveolar to velar sequences: evidence from EPG and EMA data'. *Journal of Phonetics* 30: 373–96.

Ellis, S. (1994). 'The Yorkshire ripper enquiry: Part I'. *Forensic Linguistics: The International Journal of Speech, Language and the Law* 1: 197–206.

Elovitz, H., Johnson, R., McHugh, A. and Shore, J. (1976). 'Letter-to-sound rules for automatic translation of English text to phonetics'. *IEEE Trans. Acoustics, Speech and Signal Processing* 24: 446–59.

Enderby, P. and Phillipp, R. (1986). 'Speech and language handicap: Towards knowing the size of the problem'. *British Journal of Disorders of Communication* 21: 151–65.

Engstrand, O., Frid, J. and Lindblom, B. (2007). 'A perceptual bridge between coronal and dorsal /r/'. In M.-J. Solé, P. S. Beddor and M. Ohala (eds). *Experimental Approaches to Phonology*. Oxford: Oxford University Press, pp. 175–91.

Eriksson, A. and Lacerda, F. (2007). 'Charlatanry in forensic speech science: A problem to be taken seriously'. *International Journal of Speech, Language and the Law* 14: 169–93.

Ernestus, M. (2012). 'Segmental within-speaker variation'. In A. C. Cohn, C. Fougeron and M. K. Huffman (eds). *The Oxford Handbook of Laboratory Phonology*. Oxford: Oxford University Press, pp. 93–102.

Ernestus, M. and Warner, N. (2011). 'An introduction to reduced pronunciation variants'. *Journal of Phonetics* 39: 253–60.

Ernestus, M., Baayen, H. and Schreuder, R. (2002). 'The recognition of reduced word forms'. *Brain and Language* 81: 162–73.

Esling, J. H. (1978). 'The identification of features of voice quality in social groups'. *Journal of the International Phonetic Association* 8: 18–23.

—. (1996). 'Pharyngeal consonants and the aryepiglottic sphincter'. *Journal of the International Phonetic Association* 26: 65–88.

—. (1999). 'The IPA categories "pharyngeal" and "epiglottal": Laryngoscopic observations of pharyngeal articulations and larynx height'. *Language and Speech* 42: 349–72.

—. (2005). 'There are no back vowels: The laryngeal articulator model'. *Canadian Journal of Linguistics* 50: 13–44.

—. (2009). 'The control of laryngeal constriction and the emergence of speech in infants in the first year of life'. In G. Fant, H. Fujisaki and J. Shen (eds). *Frontiers in Phonetics and Speech Science, Festschrift for Wu Zongji*. Beijing: Commercial Press, pp. 191–203.

—. (2010). 'Phonetic notation'. In W. J. Hardcastle, J. Laver and F. Gibbon (eds). *The Handbook of Phonetic Sciences*. Oxford: Wiley-Blackwell, pp. 678–702.

Esling, J. H. and Edmondson, J. A. (2002). 'The laryngeal sphincter as an articulator: Tenseness, tongue root and phonation in Yi and Bai'. In A. Braun and H. R. Masthoff (eds). *Phonetics and its Applications: Festschrift for Jens-Peter Köster on the Occasion of his 60th Birthday*. Stuttgart: Franz Steiner Verlag, pp. 38–51.

—. (2011). 'Acoustical analysis of voice quality for sociophonetic purposes'. In M. Di Paolo and M. Yaeger-Dror (eds). *Sociophonetics: A Student's Guide*. London and New York: Routledge, pp. 131–48.

Esling, J. H. and Moisik, S. R. (2011). 'Multimodal observation and measurement of larynx height and state during pharyngeal sounds'. *Proceedings of the 17th International Congress of Phonetic Sciences*. Hong Kong, pp. 643–6.

Esling, J. H., Fraser, K. E. and Harris, J. G. (2005). 'Glottal stop, glottalized resonants, and pharyngeals: a reinterpretation with evidence from a laryngoscopic study of Nuuchahnulth (Nootka)'. *Journal of Phonetics* 33: 383–410.

Evett, I. W. (1998). 'Towards a uniform framework for reporting opinions in forensic science casework'. *Science and Justice* 38: 198–202.

Fabricius, A. H., Watt, D. and Johnson, D. E. (2009). 'A comparison of three speaker-intrinsic vowel formant frequency normalization algorithms for sociophonetics'. *Language Variation and Change* 21: 413–35.

Fant, G. (1960). *Acoustic Theory of Speech Production*. The Hague: Mouton.

Farkas, L. G., Katic, M. J. and Forrest, C. R. (2005). 'International anthropometric study of facial morphology in various ethnic groups/races'. *The Journal of Craniofacial Surgery* 16: 615–46.

Farnetani, E. and Busà, M. G. (1994). 'Italian clusters in continuous speech'. *Proceedings of the International Congress on Spoken Language Processing*. Yokohama, pp. 359–61.

Feldman, N. H., Griffiths, T. L. and Morgan, J. L. (2009). 'The influence of categories on perception: Explaining the perceptual magnet effect as optimal statistical inference'. *Psychological Review* 116: 752–82.

Fernald, A. (1989). 'Intonation and communicative intent in mother's speech to infants: Is the melody the message?' *Child Development* 60: 1497–1510.

Fernald, A. and Mazzie, C. (1991). 'Prosody and focus in speech to infants and adults'. *Developmental Psychology* 27: 209–21.

Ferragne, E. and Pellegrino, F. (2004). 'A comparative account of the suprasegmental and rhythmic features of British English dialects'. *Proceedings of Modelisations pour l'Identification des Langues*. Paris, pp. 121–6.

Firth, J. R. (1935). 'The technique of semantics'. *Transactions of the Philological Society* XX: 36–72.

—. (1957). 'The English school of phonetics'. In J. R. Firth. *Papers in Linguistics 1934–1951*. London: Oxford University Press, pp. 92–120.

Fitch, W. T. and Giedd, J. (1999). 'Morphology and development of the human vocal tract: a study using magnetic resonance imaging'. *Journal of the Acoustical Society of America* 106: 1511–22.

Flege, J. E. (1999). 'Age of learning and second language speech'. In D. Birdsong (ed.). *Second Language Acquisition and the Critical Period Hypothesis*. Mahwah, NJ: Lawrence Erlbaum Associates, pp. 101–31.

Fletcher, J. (2010). 'The prosody of speech: Timing and rhythm'. In W. J. Hardcastle, J. Laver and F. Gibbon (eds). *The Handbook of Phonetic Sciences* (2nd edn). Oxford: Blackwell, pp. 523–602.

Fletcher, S. G. (1992). *Articulation: A Physiological Approach*. San Diego: Singular.

Floccia, C., Christophe, A. and Bertoncini, J. (1997). 'High-amplitude sucking and new-borns: The quest for underlying mechanisms'. *Journal of Experimental Child Psychology* 64: 175–98.

Floccia, C., Goslin, J., Girard, F. and Konopczynski, G. (2006). 'Does a regional accent perturb speech processing?' *Journal of Experimental Psychology. Human Perception and Performance* 32: 1276–93.

Flynn, N. and Foulkes, P. (2011). 'Comparing vowel formant normalisation procedures'. *Proceedings of the 17th International Congress of Phonetic Sciences*. Hong Kong, pp. 683–6.

Forrest, K., Weismer, G., Milenkovic, P. and Dougall, R. N. (1988). 'Statistical analysis of word-initial voiceless obstruents: Preliminary data'. *Journal of the Acoustical Society of America* 84: 115–23.

Fougeron, C. and Ridouane, R. (2008). 'On the phonetic implementation of syllabic consonants and vowel-less syllables in Tashlhiyt'. *Estudios de Fonética Experimental* 18: 139–75.

Foulkes, P. and Docherty, G. (eds) (1999). *Urban Voices: Accent Studies in the British Isles*. London: Arnold.

Foulkes, P. and Docherty, G. J. (2001). 'Another chapter in the story of /r/: "labiodental" variants in British English'. *Journal of Sociolinguistics* 4: 30–59.

Foulkes, P. and French, J. P. (2001). 'Forensic phonetics and sociolinguistics'. In R. Mesthrie (ed.). *Concise Encyclopaedia of Sociolinguistics*. Amsterdam: Elsevier Press, pp. 329–32.

—. (2012). 'Forensic speaker comparison: A linguistic-acoustic perspective'. In L. Solan and P. Tiersma (eds). *Oxford Handbook of Language and Law*. Oxford: Oxford University Press, pp. 557–72.

Foulkes, P., Scobbie, J. M. and Watt, D. (2010). 'Sociophonetics'. In W. J. Hardcastle, J. Laver and F. Gibbon (eds). *The Handbook of Phonetic Sciences* (2nd edn). Oxford: Blackwell, pp. 703–54.

Fourcin, A. and Abberton, E. (1971). 'First applications of a new laryngograph'. *Medical and Biological Illustration* 21: 172–82.

Fowler, C. (1981). 'Production and perception of coarticulation among stressed and unstressed vowels'. *Journal of Speech and Hearing Research* 24: 127–39.

—. (1984). 'Segmentation of coarticulated speech in perception'. *Perception and Psychophysics* 36: 359–68.

—. (2005). 'Parsing coarticulated speech in perception: Effects of coarticulation resistance'. *Journal of Phonetics* 33: 199–213.

Fowler, C. A. and Brancazio, L. (2000). 'Coarticulation resistance of American English consonants and its effects on transconsonantal vowel-to-vowel coarticulation'. *Language and Speech* 43: 1–41.

Fowler, C. A. and Brown, J. M. (2000). 'Perceptual parsing of acoustic consequences of velum lowering from information for vowels'. *Perception & Psychophysics* 62: 21–32.

Fowler, C. A. and Housum, J. (1987). 'Talkers' signaling of "new" and "old" words in speech and listeners' perception and use of the distinction'. *Journal of Memory and Language* 26: 489–504.

Fowler, C. A. and Rosenblum, L. D. (1991). 'Perception of the phonetic gesture'. In I. G. Mattingly and M. Studdert-Kennedy (eds). *Modularity and the Motor Theory*. Hillsdale, NJ: Lawrence Erlbaum, pp. 33–59.

Fowler, C. A. and Saltzman, E. (1993). 'Coordination and coarticulation in speech production'. *Language and Speech* 36: 171–95.

Fowler, C. A. and Smith, M. (1986). 'Speech perception as "vector analysis": An approach to the problems of segmentation and invariance'. In J. Perkell and D. Klatt (eds). *Invariance and Variability of Speech Processes*. Hillsdale, NJ: Lawrence Erlbaum Associates, pp. 123–36.

Fowler, C. A. and Thompson, J. (2010). 'Listeners' perception of compensatory shortening'. *Perception and Psychophysics* 72: 481–91.

Fraser, H. (2001). *Teaching Pronunciation: A Handbook for Teachers and Trainers. Three Frameworks for an Integrated Approach*. New South Wales Department of Education and Training. Available from www.dest.gov.au/archive/ty/litnet/docs/teaching_pronunciation.pdf

—. (2003). 'Issues in transcription: factors affecting the reliability of transcripts as evidence in legal cases'. *International Journal of Speech, Language and the Law* 10: 203–26.

Fraser, H., Stevenson, B. and Marks, T. (2011). 'Interpretation of a crisis call: Persistence of a primed perception of a disputed utterance'. *International Journal of Speech Language and the Law* 18: 261–92.

Frauenfelder, U. H. and Tyler, L. K. (1987). 'The process of spoken word recognition: an introduction'. *Cognition* 25: 1–20.

French, P. (1990). 'Analytic procedures for the determination of disputed utterances'. In H. Kniffka (ed.). *Texte zu Theorie und Praxis forensischer Linguistik*. Tübingen: Niemeyer Verlag, pp. 201–13.

—. (1998). 'Mr. Akbar's nearest ear versus the Lombard reflex: a case study in forensic phonetics'. *International Journal of Speech, Language and the Law* 5: 58–68.

French, P. and Harrison, P. (2006). 'Investigative and evidential applications of forensic speech science'. In A. Heaton-Armstrong, E. Shepherd, G. Gudjonsson and D. Wolchover (eds). *Witness Testimony: Psychological, Investigative and Evidential Perspectives*. Oxford: Oxford University Press, pp. 247–62.

—. (2007). 'Position statement concerning use of impressionistic likelihood terms in forensic speaker comparison cases'. *International Journal of Speech, Language and the Law* 14: 137–44.

French, P., Harrison, P. and Windsor Lewis, J. (2006). 'Case report. R -v- John Samuel Humble: The Yorkshire ripper hoaxer trial'. *International Journal of Speech, Language and the Law* 13: 255–73.

French, P., Harrison, P., Cawley, L. and Bhagdin, A. (2009). 'Evaluation of the BATVOX automatic speaker recognition system for use in UK based forensic speaker comparison casework'. Paper presented at the *International Association for Forensic Phonetics and Acoustics Annual Conference*, Cambridge, UK, August 2009.

French, P., Nolan, F., Foulkes, P., Harrison, P. and McDougall, K. (2010). 'The UK position statement on forensic speaker comparison; a rejoinder to Rose and Morrison'. *International Journal of Speech Language and the Law* 17: 143–52.

Friston, K. (2010). 'The free-energy principle: a unified brain theory?' *Nature Reviews Neuroscience* 11: 127–38.

Fry, D. B. (1955). 'Duration and intensity as physical correlates of linguistic stress'. *Journal of the Acoustical Society of America* 274: 765–8.

—. (1958). 'Experiments in the perception of stress'. *Language and Speech* 1: 126–52.

Fry, D. B. (ed.) (1976). *Acoustic Phonetics: A Course of Basic Readings*. Cambridge: Cambridge University Press.

Fujisaki, H. (1992). 'Modelling the process of fundamental frequency contour generation'. In Y. Tohkura, E. Vatikiotis-Bateson and Y. Sagisasaka (eds). *Speech Perception, Production and Linguistic Structure*. Amsterdam: IOS Press, pp. 313–28.

Gafos, A. (2002). 'A grammar of gestural coordination'. *Natural Language and Linguistic Theory* 20: 169–337.

Gafos, A., Hoole, P., Roon, K. and Zeroual, C. (2010). 'Variation in timing and phonological grammar in Moroccan Arabic clusters'. In C. Fougeron, B. Kühnert, M. D'Imperio and N. Vallée (eds). *Laboratory Phonology 10: Variability, Phonetic Detail and Phonological Representation*. Berlin: Mouton de Gruyter, pp. 657–98.

Gagnepain, P., Henson, R. N. and Davis, M. H. (2012). 'Temporal predictive codes for spoken words in auditory cortex'. *Current Biology* 22: 615–21.

Gandolfo, M. D. (1998). 'Renaissance linguistics: Roman slavdom'. In G. Lepschy (ed.). *History of Linguistics volume III: Renaissance and Early Modern Linguistics*. London: Longman, pp. 108–23.

Ganong, W. F. (1980). 'Phonetic categorization in auditory word perception'. *Journal of Experimental Psychology: Human Perception and Performance* 6: 110–25.

Gao, M. (2009). 'Gestural coordination among vowel, consonant and tone gestures in Mandarin Chinese'. *Chinese Journal of Phonetics* 2: 43–50.

Gardiner, A. H. (1916). 'The Egyptian origin of the Semitic alphabet'. *Journal of Egyptian Archaeology* 3: 1–16.

Garlock, V., Walley, A. and Metsala, J. (2001). 'Age-of-acquisition, word frequency, and neighborhood density effects on spoken word recognition by children and adults'. *Journal of Memory and Language* 45: 468–92.

Gaskell, M. G. and Marslen-Wilson, W. D. (1996). 'Phonological variation and inference in lexical access'. *Journal of Experimental Psychology: Human Perception and Performance* 22: 144–58.

Gauffin, J. (1977). 'Mechanisms of larynx tube constriction'. *Phonetica* 34: 307–9.

Gelb, I. J. (1963). *A Study of Writing* (rev. edn). Chicago: University of Chicago Press.

Geng, C., Mooshammer, C., Nam, H. and Hoole, P. (2010). 'Schwa deletion under varying prosodic conditions: Results of a pilot study'. In S. Fuchs, M. Zygis, C. Mooshammer and P. Hoole (eds). *Between the Regular and the Particular in Speech and Language*. Frankfurt am Main: Peter Lang, pp. 145–69.

Gerken, L. A. and Aslin, R. N. (2005). 'Thirty years of research on infant speech perception: The legacy of Peter W. Jusczyk'. *Language Learning and Development* 1: 5–21

Gibbon, F. and Nicolaidis, K. (1999). 'Palatography'. In W. Hardcastle and N. Hewlett (eds). *Coarticulation: Data, Theory and Techniques*. Cambridge: Cambridge University Press, pp. 229–45.

Gick, B. (2002a). 'An x-ray investigation of pharyngeal constriction in American English schwa'. *Phonetica* 59: 38–48.

—. (2002b). 'The use of ultrasound for linguistic phonetic fieldwork'. *Journal of the International Phonetic Association* 32: 113–22.

Gick, B., Wilson, I., Koch, K. and Cook, C. (2004). 'Language-specific articulatory settings: evidence from inter-utterance rest position'. *Phonetica* 61: 220–33.

Gierut, J. A., Morrisette, M. L., Hughes, M. T. and Rowland, S. (1996). 'Phonological treatment efficacy and developmental norms'. *Language, Speech and Hearing Services in Schools* 27: 215–30.

Gilbert, J. B. (2005). *Clear Speech: Basic Pronunciation and Listening Comprehension in North American English. Student's Book* (3rd edn). Cambridge: Cambridge University Press.

Gili-Fivela, B. and Savino, M. (2003). 'Segments, syllables and tonal alignment: a study on two varieties of Italian'. In M.-J. Solé, D. Recasens and J. Romero (eds). *Proceedings of the 15th International Congress of the Phonetic Sciences*. Barcelona, pp. 2933–6.

Gilkerson, J. and Richards, J. A. (2007). *The Infoture Natural Language Study, Technical Report itr-02–1*. Technical Report. Boulder, CO: Infoture, Inc.

Gimson, A. C. (1975). *An Introduction to the Pronunciation of English* (3rd edn). London: Arnold.

Glenn, J. R. (1991). 'The sound recordings of john p. harrington: a report on their disposition and state of preservation'. *Anthropological Linguistics* 33: 357–66.

Gobl, C. and Ní Chasaide, A. (2010). 'Voice source variation and its communicative functions'. In W. J. Hardcastle, J. Laver and F. E. Gibbon (eds). *The Handbook of Phonetic Sciences* (2nd edn). Oxford: Blackwell, pp. 378–423.

Gold, E. (2012). 'Considerations for the analysis of interlocutors' speech in forensic speech science casework'. Paper presented at the *International Association for Forensic Phonetics and Acoustics Annual Conference*, Santander, Spain, August 2012.

Gold, E. and French, P. (2011a). 'An international investigation of forensic speaker comparison practices'. *Proceedings of the 17th International Congress of Phonetic Sciences*. Hong Kong, pp. 751–4.

—. (2011b). 'International practices in forensic speaker comparison'. *The International Journal of Speech, Language and the Law* 18: 293–307.

Goldinger, S. (1996). 'Auditory lexical decision'. In F. Grosjean and U. Frauenfelder (eds). *A Guide to Spoken Word Recognition Paradigms*. Hove: Psychology Press, pp. 559–68.

—. (2007). 'A complementary-systems approach to abstract and episodic speech perception'. In J. Trouvain and W. J. Barry (eds). *Proceedings of the 16th International Congress of Phonetic Sciences*. Saarbrücken, pp. 49–54.

Goldinger, S., Luce, P., Pisoni, D. and Marcario, J. (1992). 'Form-based priming in spoken word recognition: the roles of competition and bias'. *Journal of Experimental Psychology Learning Memory and Cognition* 18: 1211–38.

Goldsmith, J. (1976). *Autosegmental Phonology*. PhD dissertation, MIT.

Goldstein, L., Chitoran, I. and Selkirk, E. (2007). 'Syllable structure as coupled oscillator modes: Evidence from Georgian vs. Tashlhiyt Berber'. In J. Trouvain and W. J. Barry (eds). *Proceedings of the 16th International Congress of Phonetic Sciences*. Saarbrücken, 241–4.

Goldstein, L., Nam, H., Saltzman, E. and Chitoran, I. (2010). 'Coupled oscillator planning model of speech timing and syllable structure'. In G. Fant, H. Fujisaki and J. Shen (eds). *Frontiers in Phonetics and Speech Science, Festschrift for Wu Zongji*. Beijing: Commercial Press, pp. 239–50.

Golestani, N., Price, C. J. and Scott, S. K. (2011). 'Born with an ear for dialects? Structural plasticity in the "expert" phonetician brain'. *The Journal of Neuroscience* 31: 4213–20.

Gonzalez, J. (2004). 'Formant frequencies and body size of speaker: A weak relationship in adult humans'. *Journal of Phonetics* 32: 277–87.

Gordon, M., Barthmaier, P. and Sands, K. (2002). 'A cross-linguistic acoustic study of voiceless fricatives'. *Journal of the International Phonetic Association* 32: 141–74.

Gordon-Salant, S. and Fitzgibbons, P. (1995). 'Recognition of multiply degraded speech by young and elderly listeners'. *Journal of Speech and Hearing Research* 38: 1150–6.

Goswami, U., Gerson, D. and Astruc, L. (2010). 'Amplitude envelope perception, phonology, prosodic sensitivity in children with developmental dyslexia'. *Reading and Writing* 238: 995–1019.

Gósy, M. and Horváth, V. (2010). 'Changes in articulation accompanying functional changes in word usage'. *Journal of the International Phonetic Association* 40: 135–61.

Gow, D. W. and McMurray, B. (2007). 'Word recognition and phonology: The case of English coronal place assimilation'. In J. Cole and J. Hualde (eds). *Papers in Laboratory Phonology 9*. Berlin: Mouton de Gruyter, pp. 173–200.

Grabe, E. and Low, E.-L. (2002). 'Durational variability in speech and the rhythm class hypothesis'. In C. Gussenhoven and N. Warner (eds). *Papers in Laboratory Phonology 7*. Berlin: Mouton de Gruyter, pp. 515–46.

Grabe, E., Post, B. and Nolan, F. (2001). *The IViE Corpus*. Department of Linguistics, University of Cambridge. The corpus is now held at the Phonetics Laboratory, University of Oxford: www.phon.ox.ac.uk/~esther/ivyweb

Grabe, E., Post, B., Nolan, F. and Farrar, K. (2000). 'Pitch accent realisation in four varieties of British English'. *Journal of Phonetics* 28: 161–85.

Graf Estes, K. (2009) 'From tracking statistics to learning words: statistical learning and lexical acquisition'. *Language and Linguistics Compass* 3: 1379–89.

Grant, L. (2001). *Well Said: Pronunciation for Clear Communication* (2nd edn). Boston: Heinle and Heinle Publishers.

Greisbach, R. (1999). 'Estimation of speaker height from formant frequencies'. *International Journal of Speech, Language and the Law* 6: 265–77.

Grosjean, F. (1980). 'Spoken word recognition processes and the gating paradigm'. *Perception and Psychophysics* 28: 267–83.

—. (1997). 'Gating'. In F. Grosjean and U. Frauenfelder (eds). *A Guide to Spoken Word Recognition Paradigms*. Hove: Psychology Press, pp. 597–604.

Grossberg, S. (2000). 'The complementary brain: unifying brain dynamics and modularity'. *Trends in Cognitive Sciences* 4: 233–46.

Grosvald, M. (2009). 'Interspeaker variation in the extent and perception of long-distance vowel-to-vowel coarticulation'. *Journal of Phonetics* 37: 173–88.

Grunwell, P. (1985). *Phonological Assessment of Child Speech (PACS)*. Windsor: NFER-Nelson.

—. (1987). *Clinical Phonology* (2nd edn). London: Croom Helm.

Guay, A. H., Maxwell, D. L. and Beecher, R. (1978). 'A radiographic study of tongue posture at rest and during the phonation of /s/ in Class III malocclusion'. *Angle Orthodontist* 48: 10–22.

Gussenhoven, C. (2004). *The Phonology of Tone and Intonation*. Cambridge: Cambridge University Press.

Hall, T. A., Hamann, S. and Zygis, M. (2006). 'The phonetic motivation for phonological stop assibilation'. *Journal of the International Phonetic Association* 36: 59–81.

Halle, M. (1985). 'Speculation about the representation of words in memory'. In V. A. Fromkin (ed.). *Phonetic Linguistics: Essays in Honor of Peter Ladefoged*. Orlando, FL: Academic Press, pp. 101–14.

Halle, M. and Stevens, K. N. (1962). 'Speech recognition: A model and a program for research'. *IRE Transactions of the PGIT* IT-8: 155–9.

Halliday, M. A. K. (1967). *Intonation and Grammar in British English*. Mouton, The Hague.

Hardcastle, W. (1972). 'The use of electropalatography in phonetic research'. *Phonetica* 25: 197–215.

—. (1981). 'Experimental studies in lingual coarticulation'. In R. E. Asher and E. Henderson (eds). *Towards a History of Phonetics*. Edinburgh: Edinburgh University Press, pp. 50–66.

—. (1999). 'Electromyography'. In W. Hardcastle and N. Hewlett (eds). *Coarticulation: Data, Theory and Techniques*. Cambridge: Cambridge University Press, 270–83.

Hardcastle, W., Gibbon, F. and Nicolaidis, K. (1991). 'EPG data reduction methods and their implications for studies of lingual coarticulation'. *Journal of Phonetics* 19: 251–66.

Harrington, J. (2010a). *Phonetic Analysis of Speech Corpora*. Oxford: Blackwell.

—. (2010b). 'Acoustic phonetics'. In W. J. Hardcastle, J. Laver and F. E. Gibbon (eds). *The Handbook of Phonetic Sciences* (2nd edn). Oxford: Blackwell, pp. 81–129.

Harrington, J., Fletcher, J. and Roberts, C. (1995). 'An analysis of truncation and linear rescaling in the production of accented and unaccented vowels'. *Journal of Phonetics* 23: 305–22.

Harrington, J., Kleber, F. and Reubold, U. (2008). 'Compensation for coarticulation, /u/-fronting, and sound change in Standard Southern British: An acoustic and perceptual study.' *Journal of the Acoustical Society of America* 123: 2825–35.

Harrington, J., Palethorpe, S. and Watson, C. I. (2007). 'Age-related changes in fundamental frequency and formants: a longitudinal study of four speakers'. *Interspeech-2007* Antwerp, August 2007, pp. 2753–6.

Harrison, P. (2011). *Formant Measurements from Real Speech*. Paper presented at the 20th Conference of the International Association for Forensic Phonetics and Acoustics, Vienna. [Online resource: http: //harrison2011. notlong. com]

Harrison, P. and French, P. (2010). 'Assessing the suitability of Batvox for use in UK based forensic speaker comparison casework Part II'. Paper presented at the *International Association for Forensic Phonetics and Acoustics Annual Conference*, Trier, Germany, July 2010.

Hart, J. (1569). 'An Orthographie'. In B. Danielsson (ed.). *John Hart's Works on English Orthography Part I: Biographical and Bibliographical Introductions, Texts and Index Verborum*. Stockholm: Almqvist and Wiksell (1955), pp. 165–228.

Haugen, E. (1972). *First Grammatical Treatise: An Edition, Translation and Commentary* (2nd edn). London: Longman.

Hawkins, S. (1999a). 'Looking for invariant correlates of linguistic units: two classical theories of speech perception'. In J. Pickett (ed.). *The Acoustics of Speech Communication*. Boston: Allyn and Bacon, pp. 198–231.

—. (1999b). 'Re-evaluating assumptions about speech perception'. In J. Pickett (ed.). *The Acoustics of Speech Communication*. Boston: Allyn and Bacon, pp. 232–88.

—. (1999c). 'Auditory capacities and phonological development: Animal, baby, and foreign listeners'. In J. Pickett (ed.). *The Acoustics of Speech Communication*. Boston: Allyn and Bacon, pp. 188–94.

—. (2003). 'Roles and representations of systematic fine phonetic detail in speech understanding'. *Journal of Phonetics* 31: 373–405.

—. (2010). 'Phonetic variation as communicative system: Perception of the particular and the abstract'. In C. Fougeron, B. Kühnert, M. D'Imperio and N. Vallée (eds). *Laboratory Phonology 10: Variability, Phonetic Detail and Phonological Representation*. Berlin: Mouton de Gruyter, pp. 479–510.

—. (2011). 'Does phonetic detail guide situation-specific speech recognition?' *Proceedings of the 17th International Congress of Phonetic Sciences*. Hong Kong, pp. 9–18.

Hawkins, S. and Nguyen, N. (2004). 'Influence of syllable-coda voicing on the acoustic properties of syllable-onset /l/ in English'. *Journal of Phonetics* 32: 199–231.

Hawkins, S. and Smith, R. (2001). 'Polysp: A polysystemic, phonetically-rich approach to speech understanding'. *Rivista di Linguistica* 13: 99–188.

Hay, J. and Drager, K. (2010). 'Stuffed toys and speech perception'. *Linguistics* 48: 865–92.

Hay, J., Nolan, A. and Drager, K. (2006). 'From fush to feesh: Exemplar priming in speech perception'. *The Linguistic Review* 23: 351–79.

Hayes, B. (1992). 'Comments on the paper by Nolan'. In G. J. Docherty and D. R. Ladd (eds). *Papers in Laboratory Phonology II: Gesture, Segment, Prosody*. Cambridge: Cambridge University Press, Cambridge, pp. 280–6.

Hayward, K. and Hayward, R. J. (1999). 'Amharic'. In IPA. *Handbook of the International Phonetic Association: A Guide to the Use of the International*. Cambridge: Cambridge University Press, pp. 45–50.

Heid, S. and Hawkins, S. (2000). 'An acoustical study of long-domain /r/ and /l/ coarticulation'. *Proceedings of the 5th ISCA Seminar on Speech Production: Models and Data*. Kloster Seeon, Germany, pp. 77–80.

Heinrich, A., Flory, Y. and Hawkins, S. (2010). 'Influence of English r-resonances on intelligibility of speech in noise for native English and German listeners'. *Speech Communication* 52: 1038–1055.

Henke, W. L. (1966). *Dynamic Articulatory Model of Speech Production using Computer Simulation*. Unpublished doctoral diss. Cambridge, MA: MIT.

Hepper, P. G. and Shahidullah, S. (1994). 'The development of fetal hearing'. *Fetal and Maternal Medicine Review* 6: 167–79.

Hermansky, H. (1990). 'Perceptual linear predictive (PLP) analysis of speech'. *Journal of the Acoustical Society of America* 87: 1738–52.

Hermansky, H. and Morgan, N. (1994). 'RASTA processing of speech'. *IEEE Transactions on Speech and Audio Processing* 2: 578–89.

Hermes, A., Grice, M., Mücke, D. and Niemann, H. (2012: in press). 'Articulatory coordination and the syllabification of word initial consonant clusters in Italian'. In P. Hoole, L. Bombien, M. Pouplier, C. Mooshammer and B. Kühnert (eds). *Consonant Clusters and Structural Complexity*. Berlin and New York: de Gruyter.

Heselwood, B. and Hassan, Z. M. (in press). 'Introduction'. In Z. M. Hassan and B. Heselwood (eds). *Instrumental Studies in Arabic Phonetics*. Amsterdam: John Benjamins.

Hewlett, N. (1988). 'Acoustic properties of /k/ and /t/ in normal and phonologically disordered speech'. *Clinical Linguistics and Phonetics* 2: 29–45.

Hewlett, Nigel and Mackenzie Beck, J. (2006). *An Introduction to the Science of Phonetics*. Mahwah, NJ: Lawrence Erlbaum Associates.

Hickok, G. and Poeppel, D. (2007). 'The cortical organization of speech processing'. *Nature Reviews Neuroscience* 8: 393–402.

Hiki, S. and Itoh, H. (1986). 'Influence of palate shape on lingual articulation'. *Speech Communication* 5: 141–58.

Hilkhuysen, G. and Huckvale, M. (2010a). 'Adjusting a commercial speech enhancement system to optimize intelligibility'. Paper presented at the *AES Conference on Audio Forensics*, Copenhagen, Denmark, June 2010.

—. (2010b). 'Signal properties reducing intelligibility of speech after noise reduction'. Paper presented at the *European Conference on Signal Processing (EUSIPCO)*, Aalborg, Denmark, August 2010.

Hirson, A,. French, P and Howard, D. M. (1994). 'Speech fundamental frequency over the telephone and face-to face: some implications for forensic phonetics'. In J. Windsor Lewis (ed.). *Studies in General and English Phonetics*. London: Routledge, pp. 230–40.

Hirson, A., Holmes, F. and Coulthrust, B. (2003). 'Street Talk'. Paper presented at the *International Association for Forensic Phonetics and Acoustics Annual Conference*, Vienna, Austria.

Hoit, J. D., Pearl Solomon, N. and Hixon, T. J. (1993). 'Effect of lung volume on voice onset time (VOT)'. *Journal of Speech and Hearing Research* 36: 516–21.

Holder, W. (1669). *Elements of Speech*. Facsimile reprint. (1967). R. C. Alston (ed.). Menston: The Scolar Press.

Hollien, H. (1971). 'Three major vocal registers: a proposal'. *Proceedings of the 7th International Congress of Phonetic Sciences*. Montreal, pp. 320–31.

Hollien, H. and Michel, J. F. (1968). 'Vocal fry as a phonational register'. *Journal of Speech and Hearing Research* 11: 600–4.

Hollien, H., Moore, P., Wendahl, R. W. and Michel, J. F. (1966). 'On the nature of vocal fry'. *Journal of Speech and Hearing Research* 9: 245–7.

Hollien, H. and Shipp, T. (1972). 'Speaking fundamental frequency and chronological age in males'. *Journal of Speech and Hearing Research* 15: 155–9.

Holmes, J. (1980). 'The JSRU channel vocoder'. *Communications, Radar and Signal Processing, IEE Proceedings F* 127: 53–60.

Holmes, J. and Holmes, W. (2001). *Speech Synthesis and Recognition*. New York: Taylor and Francis.

Holst, T. and Nolan, F. (1995). 'The influence of syntactic structure on [s] to [ʃ] assimilation'. In B. Connell and A. Arvaniti (eds). *Phonology and Phonetic Evidence. Papers in Laboratory Phonology IV*. Cambridge: Cambridge University Press, pp. 315–33.

Honikman, B. (1964). 'Articulatory settings'. In D. Abercrombie, D. B. Fry, P. A. D. McCarthy, N. C. Scott and J. L. M. Trim (eds). *In Honour of Daniel Jones*. London: Longman, pp. 73–84.

Honorof, D. (1999). *Articulatory Gestures and Spanish Nasal Assimilation*. PhD dissertation, Yale University.

Honorof, D. and Browman, C. P. (1995). 'The center or the edge: How are consonant clusters organized with respect to the vowel?' *Proceedings of the 13th International Congress of Phonetic Sciences*. Stockholm, 552–5.

Hoole, P. and Nguyen, N. (1999). 'Electromagnetic articulography'. In W. Hardcastle and N. Hewlett (eds). *Coarticulation: Data, Theory and Techniques*. Cambridge: Cambridge University Press, pp. 260–9.

Hoole, P., Bombien, L., Kühnert, B. and Mooshammer, C. (2010). 'Intrinsic and prosodic effects on articulatory coordination in initial consonant clusters'. In G. Fant, H. Fujisaki and J. Shen (eds). *Frontiers in Phonetics and Speech Science, Festschrift for Wu Zongji*. Beijing: Commercial Press, pp. 281–91.

Hoole, P., Kühnert, B. and Pouplier, M. (2012). 'System-related variation'. In A. C. Cohn, C. Fougeron and M. K. Huffman (eds). *The Oxford Handbook of Laboratory Phonology*. Oxford: Oxford University Press, pp. 115–30.

Hooper, J. B. (1976). 'Word frequency in lexical diffusion and the source of morphophonological change'. In W. Christie (ed.). *Current Progress in Historical Linguistics*. North Holland, Amsterdam, pp. 96–105.

House, A. S. and Fairbanks, G. (1953). 'The influence of consonant environment upon the secondary acoustical characteristics of vowels'. *Journal of the Acoustical Society of America* 25: 105–13.

Houston, D. M. and Jusczyk, P. W. (2000). 'The role of talker-specific information in word segmentation by infants'. *Journal of Experimental Psychology: Human Perception and Performance* 26: 1570–82.

Howard, S. J. and Heselwood, B. C. (2002). 'Learning and teaching phonetic transcription for clinical purposes'. *Clinical Linguistics and Phonetics* 16: 371–401.

Howard, S. and Heselwood, B. (2011). 'Instrumental and perceptual phonetic analyses: The case for two-tier transcriptions'. *Clinical Linguistics and Phonetics* 25: 940–8.

Howes, D. (1957). 'On the Relation between the Intelligibility and Frequency of Occurrence of English Words'. *Journal of the Acoustical Society of America* 29: 296–305.

Hsu, P. P., Tan, A. K. L., Chan, Y. H., Lu, P. K. S. and Blair, R. L. (2005). 'Clinical predictors in obstructive sleep apnoea patients with calibrated cephalometric analysis – a new approach'. *Clinical Otolaryngology* 30: 234–41.

Huckvale, M. and Fang, A. (2002). 'Using Phonologically-Constrained Morphological Analysis in Speech Recognition'. *Computer Speech and Language* 16: 165–81.

Hudson, T., de Jong, G., McDougall, K., Harrison, H. and Nolan, F. (2007). 'F0 statistics for 100 young male speakers of Standard Southern British English'. In J. Trouvain and W. J. Barry (eds). *Proceedings of the 16th International Congress of Phonetic Sciences*. Saarbrücken, 1809–12.

Huettig, F., Rommers, J. and Meyer, A. (2011). 'Using the visual world paradigm to study language processing: A review and critical evaluation'. *Acta Psychologica* 137: 151–71.

Hughes, A., Trudgill, P. and Watt, D. (2012). *English Accents and Dialects: An Introduction to Social and Regional Varieties of English in the British Isles* (5th edn). London: Hodder Education.

Hunt, A. and Black, A. (1996). 'Unit Selection in a Concatenative Speech Synthesis System Using a Large Speech Database'. *ICASSP*. Atlanta, Georgia: IEEE, pp. 373–6.

Huotilainena, M., Shestakova, A. and Hukkid, J. (2008) 'Using magnetoencephalography in assessing auditory skills in infants and children'. *International Journal of Psychophysiology* 68: 123–9.

Hura, S. L., Lindblom, B. and Diehl, R. L. (1992). 'On the role of perception in shaping phonological assimilation rules'. *Language and Speech* 35: 59–72.

Hurford, J. R. (1968a). 'The range of contoidal articulations in a dialect'. *Orbis* 17: 389–95.

—. (1968b). ŋglıʃ: kɒkni. *Le Maître Phonétique*: 32–4.

—. (1969). ŋglıʃ: kɒkni. *Le Maître Phonétique*: 41–3.

—. (1970). ŋglıʃ: kɒkni. *Le Maître Phonétique*: 38–9.

Huss, V. (1978). 'English word stress in the postnuclear position'. *Phonetica* 35: 86–105.

Hyman, L. M. (2008). 'Universals in phonology'. *The Linguistic Review* 25: 83–137.

Infante, P. F. (1975). 'An epidemiologic study of decidious molar relations in preschool children'. *Journal of Dental Research* 54: 723–7.

Innes, B. (2011). 'Case Report. R -v- David Bain – a unique case in New Zeal and legal and linguistic history'. *International Journal of Speech, Language and the Law* 18: 145–55.

IPA. (1999). *Handbook of the International Phonetic Association: A Guide to the Use of the International Phonetic Alphabet*. Cambridge: Cambridge University Press.

IPDS. (1995–7). *The Kiel Corpus of Spontaneous Speech, vols. 1–3*. Kiel: Institut für Phonetik und digitale Sprachverarbeitung.

Iverson, P. and Kuhl, P. K. (1995). 'Mapping the perceptual magnet effect for speech using signal detection theory and multidimensional scaling'. *Journal of the Acoustical Society of America* 97: 553–62.

Iverson, Paul and Evans, B. G. (2009). 'Learning English vowels with different first-language vowel systems II: Auditory training for native Spanish and German speakers'. *Journal of the Acoustical Society of America* 126 (2): 866.

Jacewicz, E., Fox, R. A., O'Neill, C. and Salmons, J. (2009). 'Articulation rate across dialect, age, and gender'. *Language Variation and Change* 21: 233–56.

Jaeger, M. and Hoole, P. (2011). 'Articulatory factors influencing regressive place assimilation across word-boundaries in German'. *Journal of Phonetics* 39: 413–28.

James, D. K. (2010). 'Fetal learning: A critical review'. *Infant and Child Development* 19: 45–54.

Jefferson, G. (1983). 'On a failed hypothesis: "Conjunctionals" as overlap- vulnerable'. *Tilburg Papers in Language and Literature* 28: 29–33.

Jessen, M. (2008). 'Forensic phonetics'. *Language and Linguistics Compass* 2: 671–711.

Joffe, V. and Pring, T. (2008). 'Children with phonological problems: A survey of clinical practice'. *International Journal of Language and Communication Disorders* 43: 154–64.

Johnson, K. (2004). 'Massive reduction in conversational American English'. In K. Yoneyama and K. Maekawa (eds). *Spontaneous Speech: Data and Analysis*. Tokyo: The National International Institute for Japanese Language, pp. 29–54.

—. (2006). 'Resonance in an exemplar-based lexicon: The emergence of social identity and phonology'. *Journal of Phonetics* 34: 485–99.

—. (2011). *Acoustic and Auditory Phonetics* (3rd edn). Oxford: Blackwell.

Johnson, K., Strand, E. A. and D'Imperio, M. (1999). 'Auditory-visual integration of talker gender in vowel perception'. *Journal of Phonetics* 27: 359–84.

Jones, D. (1972). *An Outline of English Phonetics*. Cambridge: W. Heffer and Sons. (Originally published 1918).

Jones, M. J. and Llamas, C. (2008). 'Fricated realisations of /t/ in Dublin and Middlesbrough English: An acoustic analysis of plosive frication and surface fricative contrasts'. *English Language and Linguistics* 12: 419–43.

Jones, M. J. and McDougall, K. (2009). 'The acoustic character of fricated /t/ in Australian English: A comparison with /s/ and /ʃ/'. *Journal of the International Phonetic Association* 39: 265–89.

Jongman, A., Blumstein, S. E. and Lahiri, A. (1985). 'Acoustic properties for dental and alveolar stop consonants: A cross-language study'. *Journal of Phonetics* 13: 235–51.

Jongman, A., Wayland, R. and Wong, S. (2000). 'Acoustic characteristics of English frica-tives'. *Journal of the Acoustical Society of America* 108: 1252–63.

Jun, J. (1995). *Perceptual and Articulatory Factors in Place Assimilation: An Optimality Theoretic Approach*. Unpublished PhD dissertation, University of California, Los Angeles.

—. (1996). 'Place assimilation is not the result of gestural overlap: Evidence from Korean and English'. *Phonology* 13: 377–407.

—. (2004). 'Place assimilation'. In B. Hayes, R. Kirchner and D. Steriade (eds). *The Phonetic Basis of Markedness*. Cambridge: Cambridge University Press, pp. 58–86.

Jun, S. A. (2005). *Prosodic Typology: The Phonetics of Intonation and Phrasing*. Oxford: Oxford University Press.

Junqua, J. (1996). 'The influence of acoustics on speech production: a noise-induced stress phenomenon known as the Lombard reflex'. *Speech Communication* 20: 13–22.

Jusczyk, P. W. (1999). 'How infants begin to extract words from speech'. *Trends in Cognitive Science* 3: 323–8.

Jusczyk, P. W. and Aslin, R. N. (1995). 'Infants' detection of the sound patterns of words in fluent speech'. *Cognitive Psychology* 29: 1–23.

Jusczyk, P. W., Luce, P. A. and Charles-Luce, J. (1994). 'Infants' sensitivity to phonotactic patterns in the native language'. *Journal of Memory and Language* 33: 630–45.

Jusczyk, P. W., Friederici, A. D., Wessels, J. M., Svenkerud, V. Y. and Jusczyk, A. M. (1993). 'Infants' sensitivity to the sound patterns of native language words'. *Journal of Memory and Language* 32: 402–20.

Kabal, K. and Ramachandran, R. P. (1986). 'The computation of line spectral frequencies using chebyshev polynomials'. *IEEE Trans. Acoustics, Speech, Signal Processing* 34: 1419–26.

Kalikow, D. N., Stevens, K. N. and Elliott, L. L. (1977). 'Development of a test of speech intelligibility in noise using sentence materials with controlled word predictability'. *Journal of the Acoustical Society of America* 61: 1337–51.

Kamide, Y., Altmann, G. and Haywood, S. (2003). 'The time-course of prediction in incre-mental sentence processing: evidence from anticipatory eye movements'. *Journal of Memory and Language* 49: 133–59

Kaplan, P. S., Bachorowski, J.-A., Smoski, M. J. and Hudenko, W. J. (2002). 'Infants of depressed mothers, although competent learners, fail to learn in response to their own mothers' infant-directed speech'. *Psychological Science* 13: 268–71.

Kaplan, P. S., Sliter, J. K. and Burgess, A. P. (2007). 'Infant-directed speech pro-duced by fathers with symptoms of depression: Effects on associative learning in a conditioned-attention paradigm'. *Infant Behavior and Development* 30: 535–45.

Kaplan, R. and Kay, M. (1994). 'Regular models of phonological rule systems'. *Computational Linguistics* 20: 331–78.

Kawahara, H., Masuda-Katsuse, I. and de Cheveigne, A. (1999). 'Restructuring speech representations using a pitch-adaptive time-frequency smoothing and an instantaneous-frequency-based F0 extraction: Possible role of a repetitive structure in sounds'. *Speech Communication* 27: 187–207.

Keating, P. A. (1984). 'Phonetic and phonological representation of stop consonant voicing'. *Language* 60: 286–319.

—. (1990). 'The window model of coarticulation: Articulatory evidence'. In J. Kingston and M. E. Beckman (eds). *Papers in Laboratory Phonology I*. Cambridge: Cambridge University Press, pp. 451–70.

—. (2005). D-prime (signal detection). analysis. www.linguistics.ucla.edu/faciliti/facili-ties/statistics/dprime.htm

Keefe, D. H., Bulen, J. C., Arehart, K. H. and Burns, E. M. (1993). 'Ear-canal impedance and reflection coefficient in human infants and adults'. *Journal of the Acoustical Society of America* 94: 2617–38.

Keller, E. and Ostry, D. J. (1983). 'Computerized measurement of tongue dorsum movements with pulsed-echo ultrasound'. *Journal of the Acoustical Society of America* 73: 1309–15.

Kemp, A. (2006). 'Phonetics: Precursors to Modern Approaches'. In K. Brown (ed.). *Encyclopedia of Language and Linguistics vol. 9*. Amsterdam: Elsevier, pp. 470–89.

Kemp, J. A. (1972). *John Wallis's Grammar of the English Language*. London: Longman.

—. (2001). 'The development of phonetics from the late 18th to the late 19th centuries'. In S. Auroux, E. F. K. Koerner, H.-J. Niederehe and K. Versteegh (eds). *History of the Language Sciences*. Berlin: Walter de Gruyter, pp. 1468–80.

Kemps, R. J. J. K., Ernestus, M., Schreuder, R. and Baayen, R. H. (2005). 'Prosodic cues for morphological complexity: The case of Dutch plural nouns'. *Memory and Cognition* 33: 430–46.

Kent, R. D. (1996). 'Hearing and believing: Some limits to the auditory-perceptual assessment of speech and voice disorders'. *American Journal of Speech-Language Pathology* 5: 7–23.

Kewley Port, D. (1999). 'Speech recognition by machine'. In J. Pickett (ed.). *The Acoustics of Speech Communication*. Boston: Allyn and Bacon, pp. 335–44.

Khouw, E. and Ciocca, V. (2007). 'Perceptual correlates of Cantonese tones'. *Journal of Phonetics* 35: 104–17.

Kirchhübel, C., Howard, D. M. and Stedmon, A. W. (2011). 'Acoustic correlates of speech when under stress: Research, methods and future directions'. *International Journal of Speech, Language and the Law* 18: 75–98.

Kirchner, R. (1998). *An Effort-based Approach to Consonant Lenition*. PhD thesis, University of California, Los Angeles.

Kirchner, R., Moore, R. K. and Chen, T.-Y. (2010). 'Computing phonological generalizations over real speech exemplars'. *Journal of Phonetics* 38: 540–7.

Kirk, P. L., Ladefoged, J. and Ladefoged, P. (1993). 'Quantifying acoustic properties of modal, breathy, and creaky vowels in Jalapa Mazatec'. In A. Mattina and T. Montler (eds). *American Indian Linguistics and Ethnography in Honor of Laurence C. Thompson*. Missoula, MT: University of Montana Press, pp. 435–50.

Klatt, D. H. (1973). 'Interaction between two factors that influence vowel duration'. *Journal of the Acoustical Society of America* 54: 1102–4.

—. (1979). 'Synthesis by rule of segmental durations in English sentences'. In B. Lindblom and S. Öhman (eds). *Frontiers of Speech Communication Research*. London: Academic Press, pp. 287–300.

Kleber, F., Harrington, J. and Reubold, U. (2012: in press) 'The relationship between the perception and production of coarticulation during a sound change in progress'. *Language and Speech*.

Kluender, K. R. and Walsh, M. A. (1992). 'Amplitude rise time and the perception of the voiceless affricate/fricative distinction'. *Perception and Psychophysics* 51: 328–33.

Kluender, K. R., Diehl, R. L. and Wright, B. A. (1988). 'Vowel-length differences before voiced and voiceless consonants: an auditory explanation'. *Journal of Phonetics* 16: 153–69.

Knight, R.-A. (2010a). 'Sounds for study: Speech and language therapy students' use and perception of exercise podcasts for phonetics'. *International Journal of Teaching and Learning in Higher Education* 22: 269–76.

—. (2010b). 'Transcribing nonsense words: The effect of numbers of voices and repetitions'. *Clinical Linguistics and Phonetics* 24: 473–84.

—. (2011c). 'Assessing the temporal reliability of rhythm metrics'. *Journal of the International Phonetic Association* 41: 271–81.

Knight, R.-A., Villafaña Dalcher, C. and Jones, M. J. (2007). 'A real-time case study of rhotic acquisition in Southern British English'. In J. Trouvain and W. J. Barry (eds). *Proceedings of the 16th International Congress of Phonetic Sciences*. Saarbrücken, 1581–4.

Knowles, G. (1978). *Scouse, the Urban Dialect of Liverpool*. Unpublished PhD thesis, University of Leeds.

Kochetov, A. and Pouplier, M. (2008). 'Phonetic variability and grammatical knowledge. An articulatory study of Korean place assimilation'. *Phonology* 25: 399–431.

Koenig, L. L. (2000). 'Laryngeal factors in voiceless consonant production in men, women, and 5-year olds'. *Journal of Speech, Language, and Hearing Research* 43: 1211–28.

Koenig, W., Dunn, H. K. and Lacy, L. Y. (1946). 'The sound spectrograph'. *Journal of the Acoustical Society of America* 18: 19–49.

Kohler, K. (1990). 'Segmental reduction in connected speech in German: Phonological facts and phonetic explanations'. In W. J. Hardcastle and A. Marchal (eds). *Speech Production and Speech Modelling*. Dordrecht: Kluwer, pp. 69–92.

Kohler, K. J. and Simpson, A. P. (eds) (2001). 'Patterns of speech sounds in unscripted communication: Production – Perception – Phonology'. *Journal of the International Phonetic Association*. Vol. 31.1.

Kohn, M. E. and Farrington, C. (2012). 'Evaluating acoustic speaker normalization algorithms: Evidence from longitudinal child data'. *Journal of the Acoustical Society of America* 131: 2237–48.

Kohonen, T. (1986). 'Dynamically expanding context with application to the correction of symbol strings in the recognition of continuous speech'. *Eighth International Conference Pattern Recognition*. Washington DC, USA: IEEE Computer Society, pp. 1148–51.

—. (1988). 'The "Neural" Phonetic Typewriter'. *Computer* 21: 11–22.

Kovacs, T. and Finan, D. S. (2006). 'Effects of midline tongue piercing on spectral centroid frequencies of sibilants'. *Proceedings of Interspeech* 2006: 977–80.

Krakow, R. (1999). 'Physiological organization of syllables: A review'. *Journal of Phonetics* 27: 23–54.

Kraljic, T. and Samuel, A. G. (2006). 'Generalization in perceptual learning for speech'. *Psychonomic Bulletin and Review* 13: 262–8.

Kreiman, J. and Gerratt, B. R. (2011). 'Comparing two methods for reducing variability in voice quality measurements'. *Journal of Speech, Language and Hearing Research* 54: 803–12.

Krull, D. (1989). 'Second formant locus patterns and consonant-vowel coarticulation in spontaneous speech'. *Phonetic Experimental Research at the Institute of Linguistics University of Stockholm (PERILUS)* 10: 87–108.

Kuhl, P. K. and Miller, J. D. (1978). 'Speech perception by the chinchilla: Identification functions for synthetic VOT stimuli'. *Journal of the Acoustical Society of America* 63: 905–17.

Kuhl, P. K., Tsao. F.-M. and Liu, H.-M. (2003). 'Foreign-language experience in infancy: Effects of short-term exposure and social interaction on phonetic learning'. *Proceedings of the National Academy of Sciences* 100: 9096–9101.

Kuhl, P. K., Andruski, J. E., Chistovich, I. A., Chistovich, L. A., Kozhevnikova, E. V., Ryskina, V. L., Stolyarova, E. I., Sundberg, U. and Lacerda, F. (1997). 'Cross-language analysis of phonetic units in language addressed to infants'. *Science* 277: 684–6

Kuhl, P. K., Stevens, E., Hayashi, A., Deguchi, T., Kiritani, S. and Iverson, P. (2006). 'Infants show facilitation for native language phonetic perception between 6 and 12 months'. *Developmental Science* 9: 13–21.

Kuhl, P. K., Williams, K. A., Lacerda, F., Stevens, K. N. and Lindblom, B. (1992). 'Linguistic experience alters phonetic perception in infants by 6 months of age'. *Science* 255: 606–8.

Kühnert, B. and Hoole, P. (2004). 'Speaker-specific kinematic properties of alveolar reductions in English and German'. *Clinical Linguistics and Phonetics* 18: 559–75.

Künzel, H. J. (1997). 'Some general phonetic and forensic aspects of speaking tempo'. *Forensic Linguistics: International Journal of Speech, Language and the Law* 4: 48–83.

—. (2001). 'Beware the "telephone effect": The influence of telephone transmission on the measurement of formant frequencies'. *International Journal of Speech, Language and the Law* 8: 80–99.

Kurowski, K. and Blumstein, S. E. (1987). 'Acoustic properties for place of articulation in nasal consonants'. *Journal of the Acoustical Society of America* 81: 1917–27.

Kutas, M. and Federmeier, K. (2011). 'Thirty years and counting: Finding meaning in the N400 component of the event-related brain potential (ERP)'. *Annual Review Psychology* 62: 621–47.

Ladd, D. R. (1996). *Intonational Phonology*. Cambridge: Cambridge University Press.

—. (2008). *Intonational Phonology*. Cambridge: Cambridge University Press.

Ladd, D. R., Dediu, D. and Kinsella, A. R. (2008). 'Languages and genes: reflections on biolinguistics and the nature-nurture question'. *Biolinguistics* 2: 114–26.

Ladd, D. R., Mennen, I. and Schepman, A. (2000). 'Phonological conditioning of peak alignment in rising pitch accents in Dutch'. *Journal of the Acoustical Society of America* 107: 2685–96.

Ladd, D. R., Schepman, A., White, L., Quarmby, L. M. and Stackhouse, R. (2009). 'Structural and dialectal effects on pitch peak alignment in two varieties of British English'. *Journal of Phonetics* 37: 146–61.

Ladefoged, P. (1968) *A Phonetic Study of West African Languages*. Cambridge: Cambridge University Press.

—. (1984). 'Out of chaos comes order: Physical, biological, and structural patterns in phonetics'. *Proceedings of the 10th International Congress of Phonetic Sciences*. Utrecht, pp. 83–95.

—. (1997). 'David Abercrombie and the changing field of phonetics'. *Journal of Phonetics* 25: 85–91.

—. (1997). 'Instrumental techniques for phonetic fieldwork'. In W. J. Hardcastle and J. Laver (eds). *The Handbook of Phonetic Sciences*. Oxford: Blackwell, pp. 137–66.

—. (2003). *Phonetic Data Analysis: An Introduction to Fieldwork and Instrumental Techniques*. Oxford: Blackwell.

Ladefoged, P. and Maddieson, I. (1996). *The Sounds of the World's Languages*. Oxford: Blackwell.

Ladefoged, P. and Johnson, K. (2011). *A Course in Phonetics* (6th edn). Boston: Cengage.

Ladefoged, P., Maddieson, I. and Jackson, M. (1988). 'Investigating phonation types in different languages'. In O. Fujimura (ed.). *Vocal Fold Physiology: Voice Production, Mechanisms and Functions*. New York: Raven Press, pp. 297–317.

Laeng, B., Brennan, T., Elden, Å., Paulsen, H. G., Banerjee, A. and Lipton, R. (2007). 'Latitude-of-birth and season-of-birth effects on human color vision in the Arctic'. *Vision Research* 47: 1595–1607.

Large, E. W. (2008). 'Resonating to musical rhythm: Theory and experiment'. In S. Grondin (ed.). *The Psychology of Time*. West Yorkshire: Emerald, 189–232.

Large, E. W. and Riess Jones, M. (1999). 'The dynamics of attending: how people track time-varying events'. *Psychological Review* 106: 119–59.

Larkey, L. (1983). 'Reiterant speech: an acoustic and perceptual validation'. *Journal of the Acoustical Society of America* 73: 1337–45.

Lass, R. (1984). *Phonology. An Introduction to Basic Concepts*. Cambridge: Cambridge University Press.

Laumann, A. E. and Derick, A. J. (2006). 'Tattoos and body piercings in the Unites States: A national data set'. *Journal of the American Academy of Dermatology* 55: 413–21.

Laver, J. (1980). *The Phonetic Description of Voice Quality*. Cambridge: Cambridge University Press.

—. (1994). *Principles of Phonetics*. Cambridge: Cambridge University Press.

Laver, J., Wirz, S., Mackenzie, J. and Hillier, S. M. (1981). 'A perceptual protocol for the analysis of vocal profiles'. *Edinburgh University Department of Linguistics Work in Progress* 14: 139–55.

Lavoie, L. M. (2002). 'Subphonemic and suballophonic consonant variation: The role of the phoneme inventory'. *ZAS Papers in Linguistics* 28: 39–54.

Lawson, E., Stuart-Smith, J., Scobbie, J. M., Yaeger-Dror, M. and Maclagan, M. (2010). 'Analyzing liquids'. In M. Di Paolo and M. Yaeger-Dror (eds). *Sociophonetics: A Student's Guide*. London: Routledge, pp. 72–86.

Lecanuet, J.-P., Granier-Deferre. C, Jacquet, A. Y., Capponi, I. and Ledru, L. (1993). 'Prenatal discrimination of male and female voice uttering the same sentence'. *Early Development and Parenting* 2: 217–28.

Lee, S., Potamianos, A. and Narayanan, S. (1999). 'Acoustics of children's speech: developmental changes of spectral and temporal parameters'. *Journal of the Acoustical Society of America* 105: 1455–68.

Lee, W.-S., and Zee, E. (2011). *Proceedings of the 17th International Congress of the Phonetic Sciences. Hong Kong* (available online at http://icphs2011.hk/ICPHS_CongressProceedings.htm).

Leggetter, C. and Woodland, P. (1995). 'Maximum likelihood linear regression for speaker adaptation of continuous density hidden Markov models'. *Computer Speech and Language* 9: 171–85.

Lehiste, I. (1964). *Acoustical Characteristics of Selected English Consonants*. The Hague: Mouton.

—. (1977). *Suprasegmentals* (3rd edn). Cambridge, MA: MIT Press.

Lehto, L. (1969). *English Stress and its Modification by Intonation: An Analytic and Synthetic Study of Acoustic Parameters*. Suomalaisen tiedeakatemian Toimituksia. Helsinki: Annales Academiae Scientiarum Fennicae, B. 1644.

Lepsius, R. (1863). *Standard Alphabet for Reducing Unwritten Languages and Foreign Graphic Systems to a Uniform Orthography in European Letters* (2nd edn). J. A. Kemp (ed.). Amsterdam: John Benjamins. (1981).

Levelt, W. J. M. (1983). Monitoring and self-repair in speech. *Cognition* 14: 41–104.

—. (1989). *Speaking: From Intention to Articulation*. Cambridge, MA: MIT Press.

Levi, S. (2005). 'Acoustic correlates of lexical accent in Turkish'. *Journal of the International Phonetic Association* 35: 73–97.

Li, F., Menon, A. and Allen, J. B. (2010). 'A psychoacoustic method to find the perceptual cues of stop consonants in natural speech'. *Journal of the Acoustical Society of America* 127: 2599–610.

Liberman, A. M. and Mattingly, I. G. (1985). 'The motor theory of speech perception revised'. *Cognition* 21: 1–36.

Liberman, A. M., Delattre, P. C., Gerstman, L. J. and Cooper, F. S. (1956). 'Tempo of frequency change as a cue for distinguishing classes of speech sounds'. *Journal of Experimental Psychology* 52: 127–37.

Liberman, M. (2008). HVPT. http: //languagelog.ldc.upenn.edu/nll/?p=328

Liberman, M. and Pierrehumbert, J. (1984). 'Intonational invariance under changes in pitch range and length'. In M. Aronoff and R. T. Oehrle (eds). *Language Sound Structure: Studies in Phonology Presented to Morris Halle by his Teacher and Students*. Cambridge, MA: MIT Press, pp. 157–233.

Lickley, R. J., Schepman, A. and Ladd, D. R. (2005). 'Alignment of "phrase accent" lows in Dutch falling rising questions: theoretical and methodological considerations'. *Language and Speech* 48: 157–83.

Lieberman, P. (1960). 'Some acoustic correlates of word stress in American English'. *Journal of the Acoustical Society of America* 32: 451–4.

—. (1963). 'Some effects of semantic and grammatical context on the production and perception of speech'. *Language and Speech* 6: 172–87.

Liederman, J., Gilbert, K., McGraw Fisher, J., Mathews, G., Frye, R. E. and Joshi, P. (2011). 'Are women more influenced than men by top-down semantic information when listening to disrupted speech?' *Language and Speech* 54: 33–48.

Liljencrants, J. and Lindblom, B. (1972). 'Numerical simulation of vowel quality systems: the role of perceptual contrast'. *Language* 48: 839–62.

Lindau, M. (1985). 'The story of /r/'. In V. A. Fromkin (ed.). *Phonetic Linguistics: Essays in Honor of Peter Ladefoged*. Orlando, FL: Academic Press, pp. 157–68.

Lindblom, B. (1963). 'Spectrographic study of vowel reduction'. *Journal of the Acoustical Society of America* 35: 1773–81.

—. (1967). 'Vowel duration and a model of lip mandible coordination'. *STL-QPSR* 8: 1–29. www.speech.kth.se/prod/publications/files/qpsr/1967/1967_8_4_001–029.pdf

—. (1983). 'Economy of speech gestures'. In P. F. MacNeilage (ed.). *The Production of Speech*. New York: Springer, pp. 217–46.

—. (1990). 'Explaining phonetic variation: a sketch of the H&H theory'. In W. J. Hardcastle and A. Marchal (eds). *Speech Production and Speech Modelling*. Dordrecht: Kluwer, pp. 403–39.

Lindblom, B., Agwuele, A., Sussman, H. and Cortes E. (2007). 'The effect of emphatic stress on consonant vowel coarticulation'. *Journal of the Acoustical Society of America* 121: 3802–13.

Liu, H.-M., Kuhl, P. K. and Tsao, F.-M. (2003). 'An association between mother's speech clarity and infants' speech discrimination skills'. *Developmental Science* 6: F1–F10.

Liu, H.-M., Tsao, F.-M. and Kuhl, P. K. (2009). 'Age-related changes in acoustic modifications of Mandarin maternal speech to preverbal infants and five-year-old children: A longitudinal study'. *Journal of Child Language* 36: 909–22.

Llamas, C. and Watt, D. (eds) (2010). *Language and Identities*. Edinburgh: Edinburgh University Press.

Local, J. K. (2003a). 'Phonetics and talk-in-interaction'. In J. Trouvain and W. J. Barry (eds). *Proceedings of the 16th International Congress of Phonetic Sciences*. Saarbrücken: 115–18.

—. (2003b). 'Variable domains and variable relevance: interpreting phonetic exponents'. *Journal of Phonetics* 31: 321–39.

Local, J. K. and Kelly, J. (1986). 'Projection and "silences": Notes on phonetic detail and conversational structure'. *Human Studies* 9: 185–204.

Local, J. K., Kelly, J. and Wells, W. H. G. (1986). 'Some phonetic aspects of turn-delimitation in the speech of Urban Tynesiders'. *Journal of Linguistics* 22: 411–37.

Local, J. and Walker, G. (2004). 'Abrupt-joins as a resource for the production of multi-unit, multi-action turns'. *Journal of Pragmatics* 36: 1375–403.

—. (2005). 'Methodological imperatives for investigating the phonetic organization and phonological structures of spontaneous speech'. *Phonetica* 62: 120–30.

—. (forthcoming). 'How phonetic features project more talk'. *Journal of the International Phonetic Association*.

Lodge, K. F. (1984). *Studies in Colloquial English*. Beckenham: Croom Helm.

Lodwick, F. (1686). 'An essay towards an universal alphabet'. In V. Salmon (ed.). *The Works of Francis Lodwick*. London: Longman, pp. 235–42.

Logan, J. S., Lively, S. E. and Pisoni, D. B. (1991). 'Training Japanese listeners to identify English /r/ and /l/: a first report'. *Journal of the Acoustical Society of America* 89: 874–86.

Loizou, P. and Kim, G. (2011). 'Reasons why current speech-enhancement algorithms do not improve speech intelligibility and suggested solutions'. *IEEE Transactions on Audio, Speech and Language Processing* 19: 47–56.

Lotto, A. J., Kluender, K. R. and Holt, L. L. (1997). 'Animal models of speech perception phenomena'. In K. Singer, R. Eggert and G. Anderson (eds), *Chicago Linguistic Society* 33: 357–67.

Low, E. L., Grabe, E. and Nolan, F. (2000). 'Quantitative characterisations of speech rhythm: "Syllable-timing" in Singapore English'. *Language and Speech* 43: 377–401.

Luce, P. A. and Pisoni, D. B. (1998). 'Recognizing spoken words: The neighborhood activation model'. *Ear and Hearing* 19: 1–36.

Luce, R. (1991). *Response Times: Their Role in Inferring Elementary Mental Organization.* New York: Oxford University Press.

MacCarthy, Peter. 1978. *The Teaching of Pronunciation*. Cambridge: Cambridge University Press,.

Mackenzie Beck, J. (1988). *Organic Variation and Voice Quality*. Unpublished PhD thesis, University of Edinburgh.

Macmillan, N. A. and Creelman, C. D. (2005). *Detection Theory: A User's Guide* (2nd edn). Mahwah, NJ: Lawrence Erlbaum Associates.

MacWhinney, B. (2000). *The CHILDES Project: Tools for Analyzing Talk.* Mahwah, NJ: Lawrence Erlbaum Associates.

Maddieson, I. (1984). *Patterns of Sounds*. Cambridge: Cambridge University Press.

—. (1997). 'Phonetic universals'. In W. J. Hardcastle and J. Laver (eds). *The Handbook of Phonetic Sciences.* Oxford: Blackwell, pp. 619–39.

Magen, H. (1997) 'The extent of vowel-to-vowel coarticulation in English'. *Journal of Phonetics* 25: 187–205.

Magnuson, T. J. (2007). 'The story of /r/ in two vocal tracts'. In J. Trouvain and W. J. Barry (eds). *Proceedings of the 16th International Congress of Phonetic Sciences.* Saarbrücken: 1193–6.

Majerus, S., Ponceleta, M., Béraulta, A., Audreya, S., Zesigere, P., Serniclaes, W. and Barisnikove, K. (2011). 'Evidence for atypical categorical speech perception in Williams syndrome'. *Journal of Neurolinguistics* 24: 249–67.

Mann, V. A. and Repp, B. H. (1980). 'Influence of vocalic context on perception of the [ʃ]-[s] distinction'. *Perception and Psychophysics* 28: 213–28.

Manuel, S. (1990). 'The role of contrast in limiting vowel-to-vowel coarticulation in different languages'. *Journal of the Acoustical Society of America* 88: 1286–98.

—. (1999). 'Cross-language studies: relating language-particular coarticulation patterns to other language-particular facts'. In W. Hardcastle and N. Hewlett (eds). *Coarticulation: Data, Theory and Techniques.* Cambridge: Cambridge University Press, pp. 179–98.

Marchand, Y. and Damper, R. (2000). 'A multistrategy approach to improving pronunciation by analogy'. *Computational Linguistics* 26: 195–219.

Marcus, G. F., Vijayan, S., Rao, S. B and Vishton, P. M. (1999). 'Rule learning by 7-month-old infants'. *Science* 283: 77–80.

Marin, S. and Pouplier, M. (2010). 'Temporal organization of complex onsets and codas in American English: Testing the predictions of a gestural coupling model'. *Motor Control* 14: 380–407.

Markel, J. and Gray, A. (1976). *Linear Prediction of Speech*. New York: Springer Verlag.

Marslen-Wilson, W. D. and Warren, P. (1994). 'Levels of perceptual representation and process in lexical access – words, phonemes, and features'. *Psychological Review* 101: 653–75.

Martin, J. and Bunnell, H. (1982). 'Perception of anticipatory coarticulation effects in vowel-stop consonant-vowel sequences'. *Journal of Experimental Psychology: Human Perception and Performance* 8: 473–88.

Marton, K. (2006). 'Do nonword repetition errors in children with specific language impairment reflect a weakness in an unidentified skill specific to nonword repetition or a deficit in simultaneous processing?' *Applied Psycholinguistics* 27: 569–73.

Matthews, P. (1994). 'Greek and Roman linguistics'. In G. Lepschy (ed.). *History of Linguistics Volume II: Classical and Medieval Linguistics*. London: Longman, pp. 1–133.

Maye, J., Werker, J. F. and Gerken, L. (2002). 'Infant sensitivity to distributional information can affect phonetic discrimination'. *Cognition* 82: B101–B111.

McCarthy, J. J. (1988). 'Feature geometry and dependency: A review'. *Phonetica* 45: 84–108.

McClelland, J. L. and Elman, J. L. (1986). 'The TRACE model of speech perception'. *Cognitive Psychology* 18: 1–86.

McClelland, J. L., Mirman, D. and Holt, L. L. (2006). 'Are there interactive processes in speech perception?' *Trends in Cognitive Sciences* 10: 363–9.

McDonough, J. and Ladefoged, P. (1993). 'Navajo stops'. *UCLA Working Papers in Phonetics* 84: 151–64.

McDougall, K. (2004). 'Speaker-specific formant dynamics: An experiment on Australian English /aɪ/'. *International Journal of Speech, Language and the Law* 11: 103–30.

McGettigan, C. and Scott, S. K. (2012). 'Cortical asymmetries in speech perception: what's wrong, what's right and what's left?' *Trends in Cognitive Sciences* 16: 269–76.

McLachan, G. and Peel, D. (2000). *Finite Mixture Models*. Hoboken, NJ: Wiley.

Mcleod, S. and Bleile, K. (2003) 'Neurological and developmental foundations of speech acquisition'. *American Speech-Language-Hearing Association Convention*. Chicago, USA. [available online at www.speech-language-therapy.com/pdf/docs/ ASHA03McLeodBleile.pdf]

McQueen, J. M. (1997). 'Phonetic categorisation'. In F. Grosjean and U. Frauenfelder (eds). *A Guide to Spoken Word Recognition Paradigms*. Hove: Psychology Press, pp. 655–64.

—. (2007). 'Eight questions about spoken-word recognition'. In M. G. Gaskell (ed.). *The Oxford Handbook of Psycholinguistics*. Oxford: Oxford University Press, pp. 37–53.

McQueen, J. M. and Cutler, A. (2010). 'Cognitive processes in speech perception'. In W. J. Hardcastle, J. Laver and F. E. Gibbon (eds) *The Handbook of Phonetic Sciences* (2nd edn). Oxford: Blackwell, pp. 489–520.

McQueen, J. M., Cutler, A. and Norris, D. (2006). 'Phonological abstraction in the mental lexicon'. *Cognitive Science* 30: 1113–26.

Mehiri, A. (1973). *Les Théories Grammaticales d'Ibn Jinnī*. Tunis: Publications de l'Université de Tunis.

Mehler, J. and Christophe, A. (1995). 'Maturation and learning of language in the first year of life'. In M. S. Gazzaniga (ed.), *The Cognitive Neurosciences*. Cambridge, MA: MIT Press, pp. 943–54.

Mehler, J., Jusczyk, P. W., Lambertz, G., Halsted, N., Bertoncini, J., Amiel-Tison, C. (1988). 'A precursor of language acquisition in young infants'. *Cognition* 29: 143–78.

Menzerath, P. and Lacerda, A. (1933). *Koartikulation, Steuerung und Lautabgrenzung*. Berlin: F. Dümmler.

Miller, A. and Finch, K. (2011). 'Corrected high frame rate anchored ultrasound with software alignment'. *Journal of Speech, Language and Hearing Research* 54: 471–86.

Miller, G. and Nicely, P. (1955). 'An analysis of perceptual confusions among some English consonants'. *Journal of the Acoustical Society of America* 27: 338–52.

Miller, J. L. and Liberman, A. M. (1979). 'Some effects of later-occurring information on the perception of stop consonant and semivowel'. *Perception and Psychophysics* 46: 505–12.

Mitani, S., Kitama, T. and Sato, Y. (2006). 'Voiceless affricate/fricative distinction by frication duration and amplitude rise slope'. *Journal of the Acoustical Society of America* 120: 1600–7.

Mitterer, H. (2011). 'Recognizing reduced forms: Different processing mechanisms for similar reductions'. *Journal of Phonetics* 39: 298–303.

Mitterer, H. and McQueen, J. M. (2009). 'Processing reduced word-forms in speech perception using probabilistic knowledge about speech production'. *Journal of Experimental Psychology: Human Perception and Performance* 35: 244–63.

Möbius, B. (2003). 'Gestalt psychology meets phonetics – an early experimental study of intrinsic F0 and intensity'. In M.-J. Solé, D. Recasens and J. Romero (eds). *Proceedings of the 15th International Congress of the Phonetic Sciences*. Barcelona, pp. 2677–80.

Moisik, S. R., Esling, J. H. and Crevier-Buchman, L. (2010). 'A high-speed laryngoscopic investigation of aryepiglottic trilling'. *Journal of the Acoustical Society of America*, 127: 1548–59.

Mok, P. (2010). 'Language-specific realizations of syllable structure and vowel-to-vowel coarticulation'. *Journal of the Acoustical Society of America* 128: 1346–56.

Mompeán, J. A., Ashby, M. and Fraser, H. (2011). 'Phonetics teaching and learning: an overview of recent trends and directions'. *Proceedings of the 17th International Congress of Phonetic Sciences*. Hong Kong, pp. 96–9.

Montgomery, C. R. and Clarkson, M. G. (1997). 'Infants' pitch perception: Masking by low- and high-frequency noises'. *Journal of the Acoustical Society of America* 102: 3665–72.

Moore, B. C. J. and Glasberg, B. R. (1983). 'Suggested formulae for calculating auditory-filter bandwidths and excitation patterns'. *Journal of the Acoustical Society of America* 74: 750–3.

Mooshammer, T. (2010). 'Acoustic and laryngographic measures of the laryngeal reflexes of linguistic prominence and vocal effort in German'. *Journal of the Acoustical Society of America* 127: 1047–58.

Morales, M., Mundy, P., Delgado, C., Yale, M., Neal, R. and Schwartz, H. K. (2000). 'Gaze following, temperament, and language development in 6-month-olds: A replication and extension'. *Infant Behavior and Development* 23: 231–6.

Morley, J. (1994). *Pronunciation Pedagogy and Theory: New Views, New Directions*. Alexandria, VA: Teachers of English to Speakers of Other Languages.

Morris, R. J., McCrea, C. R. and Herring, K. D. (2008). 'Voice onset time differences between adult males and females: Isolated syllables'. *Journal of Phonetics* 36: 308–17.

Morrison, G. S. (2009a). 'Forensic voice comparison and the paradigm shift'. *Science and Justice* 49: 298–308.

—. (2009b). 'Likelihood-ratio forensic voice comparison using parametric representations of the formant trajectories of diphthongs'. *Journal of the Acoustical Society of America* 125: 2387–97.

Morrongiello, B. A. and Trehub, S. E. (1987). 'Age-related changes in auditory temporal perception'. *Journal of Experimental Child Psychology* 44: 413–26.

Morton, J., Marcus, S. and Frankish, C. (1976). 'Perceptual centers'. *Psychological Review* 83: 405–8.

Müller, N. and Damico, J. S. (2002). 'A transcription toolkit: Theoretical and clinical considerations'. *Clinical Linguistics and Phonetics* 16: 299–316.

Munson, B. and Brinkman, K. N. (2004). 'The influence of multiple presentations on judgments of children's phonetic accuracy'. *American Journal of Speech-Language Pathology* 13: 341–54.

Munson, B., Edwards, J. and Beckman, M. E. (2005). 'Relationships between nonword repetition accuracy and other measures of linguistic development in children with phonological disorders'. *Journal of Speech, Language, and Hearing Research* 48: 61–78.

Myers, S. (2005). 'Vowel duration and neutralization of vowel length contrasts in Kinyarwanda'. *Journal of Phonetics* 33: 427–46.

Myers, S. and Hansen, B. B. (2005). 'The origin of vowel-length neutralisation in vocoid sequences: Evidence from Finnish speakers'. *Phonology* 22: 317–44.

Nábelek, A. K. (1988). 'Identification of vowels in quiet, noise, and reverberation: Relationships with age and hearing loss'. *Journal of the Acoustical Society of America* 84: 476–84.

Nam, H. (2007). 'A competitive, coupled oscillator model of moraic structure: Split-gesture dynamics focusing on positional asymmetry'. In J. Cole and J. Hualde (eds). *Papers in Laboratory Phonology 9*. Berlin: Mouton de Gruyter, pp. 483–506.

Negus, V. E. (1949). *The Comparative Anatomy and Physiology of the Larynx*. London: William Heinemann Medical Books Ltd. Reprinted (1962).

Neiman, G. S. and Applegate, J. A. (1990). 'Accuracy of listener judgments of perceived age relative to chronological age in adults'. *Folia Phoniatrica*, 42, 327–30.

Nelson, M. A. and Hodge, M. M. (2000). 'Effects of facial paralysis and audiovisual information on stop place identification'. *Journal of Speech, Language and Hearing Research* 43: 158–71.

Nespor, I. and Vogel, M. (1986). *Prosodic Phonology*. Dordrecht: Foris. (Republished 2007, Berlin: Mouton de Gruyter).

Newman, P. and Ratliff, M. (eds) (2001). *Linguistic Fieldwork*. Cambridge: Cambridge University Press.

Niebuhr, O. and Kohler, K. J. (2011). 'Perception of phonetic detail in the identification of highly reduced words'. *Journal of Phonetics* 39: 319–29.

Niedzelski, N. (1999). 'The effect of social information on the perception of sociolinguistic variables'. *Journal of Language and Social Psychology* 18: 62–85.

Nielsen, K. Y. (2011). 'Specificity and abstractness of VOT imitation'. *Journal of Phonetics* 39: 132–42.

Nolan, F. (1983). *The Phonetic Bases of Speaker Recognition*. Cambridge: Cambridge University Press.

—. (1992). 'The descriptive role of segments: evidence from assimilation'. In G. J. Docherty and D. R. Ladd (eds). *Laboratory Phonology II*. Cambridge: Cambridge University Press, pp. 261–80.

—. (1997). 'Speaker recognition and forensic phonetics'. In W. J. Hardcastle and J. Laver (eds). *The Handbook of Phonetic Sciences*. Oxford: Blackwell, pp. 744–67.

—. (1999). 'The devil is in the detail'. In J. J. Ohala, Y. Hasegawa, M. Ohala, D. Granville and A. C. Bailey (eds). *Proceedings of the XIV International Congress of Phonetic Sciences*. Berkeley: ICPhS, pp. 1–8.

—. (2003). 'Intonational equivalence: an experimental evaluation of pitch scales'. In M.-J. Solé, D. Recasens and J. Romero (eds). *Proceedings of the 15th International Congress of the Phonetic Sciences*. Barcelona, pp. 771–4.

—. (2011). 'Phonetic degrees of freedom: an argument for native speakers in LADO'. Paper presented at *ESRC LADO Network Seminar #2: 'The Role of Native Speakers in LADO'*. Colchester, UK, November 2011.

—. (2012). 'The phonetic case for the involvement of native speakers in LADO'. Paper presented at *British Association of Academic Phoneticians Conference*. Leeds, UK, March 2012.

Nolan, F. and Asu, E.-L. (2009). 'The Pairwise Variability Index and coexisting rhythms in language'. *Phonetica* 66: 64–77.

Nolan, F. and Oh, T. (1996). 'Identical twins, different voices'. *Forensic Linguistics* 3: 39–49.

Nolan, F., Holst, T. and Kühnert, B. (1996). 'Modelling [s] to [ʃ] accommodation in English'. *Journal of Phonetics* 24: 113–37.

Nolan, F., McDougall, K., de Jong, G. and Hudson, T. (2009). 'The DyViS Database: Style-controlled recordings of 100 homogeneous speakers for forensic phonetic research'. *International Journal of Speech Language and the Law* 16: 31–57.

Norman, G. (2010). 'Likert scales, levels of measurement and the "laws" of statistics'. *Advances in Health Science Education* 15: 625–32.

Norris, D. and McQueen, J. M. (2008). 'Shortlist B: A Bayesian model of continuous speech recognition'. *Psychological Review* 115: 357–95.

Norris, D., McQueen, J. M. and Cutler, A. (2000). 'Merging information in speech recognition: feedback is never necessary'. *Behavioral and Brain Sciences* 23: 299–370.

—.(2003). 'Perceptual learning in speech'. *Cognitive Psychology* 47: 204–38.

Nossair, Z. B. and Zahorian, S. A. (1991). 'Dynamic spectral shape features as acoustic correlates for initial stop consonants'. *Journal of the Acoustical Society of America* 89: 2978–91.

Nozza, R. J. and Henson, A. M. (1999). 'Unmasked thresholds and minimum masking in infants and adults: Separating sensory from nonsensory contributions to infant-adult differences in behavioural thresholds'. *Ear and Hearing* 20: 483–96.

Nygaard, L. C. and Pisoni, D. B. (1998). 'Talker-specific learning in speech perception'. *Perception and Psychophysics* 60: 355–76.

Nygaard, L. C., Burt, S. A. and Queen, J. S. (2000). 'Surface form typicality and asymmetric transfer in episodic memory for spoken words'. *Journal of Experimental Psychology: Learning, Memory and Cognition* 26: 1228–44.

Nygaard, L. C., Sommers, M. S. and Pisoni, D. B. (1994). 'Speech perception as a talker-contingent process'. *Psychological Science* 5: 42–6.

O'Connor, J. D. and Arnold, G. F. (1973). *Intonation of Colloquial English*. Bristol: Longman.

Ochs, E. (1979). 'Transcription as theory'. In E. Ochs and B. Schievelin (eds). *Developmental Pragmatics*. New York: Academic Press, pp. 43–72.

Ogden, R. (2001). 'Turn transition, creak and glottal stop in Finnish talk-in- interaction'. *Journal of the International Phonetic Association* 31: 139–52.

—. (2006). 'Phonetics and social action in agreements and disagreements'. *Journal of Pragmatics* 38: 1752–75.

—. (2009). *An Introduction to English Phonetics*. Edinburgh textbooks on the English language. Edinburgh: Edinburgh University Press.

Ogden, R., Hawkins, S., House, J., Huckvale, M., Local, J., Carter, P., Dankovičová, J. and Heid, S. (2000). 'Prosynth: An integrated prosodic approach to device-independent, natural-sounding speech synthesis'. *Computer Speech and Language* 14: 177–210.

Ohala, J. J. (1981). 'The listener as a source of sound change'. In C. S. Masek, R. A. Hendrick and M. F. Miller (eds). *Papers from the Parasession on Language and Behavior*. Chicago: Chicago Linguistic Society, pp. 178–203.

—. (1983). 'The origin of sound patterns in vocal tract constraints'. In P. F. MacNeilage (ed.). *The Production of Speech*. New York: Springer, pp. 189–216.

—. (1990). 'The phonetics and phonology aspects of assimilation'. In J. Kingston and M. E. Beckman (eds). *Papers in Laboratory Phonology I*. Cambridge University Press: Cambridge, pp. 258–75.

—. (1993). 'The phonetics of sound change'. In C. Jones (ed.). *Historical Linguistics: Problems and Perspectives*. Longman: London, pp. 237–78.

—. (2003). 'Phonetics and historical phonology'. In B. D. Joseph and R. D. Janda (eds). *The Handbook of Historical Linguistics*. Oxford: Blackwell, pp. 669–86.

—. (2004). 'Phonetics and phonology then, and then, and now'. In H. Quené and V. van Heuven (eds). *On Speech and Language: Studies for Sieb Nooteboom*. Utrecht: LOT Netherlands Graduate Occasional Series, 133–40.

Öhman, S. (1966). 'Coarticulation in VCV utterances: spectrographic measurements'. *Journal of the Acoustical Society of America* 39: 151–68.

Olsho, L. W. (1984). 'Infant frequency discrimination as a function of frequency'. *Infant Behavior and Development* 7: 27–35.

Olson, K. S. and Hajek, J. (1999). 'The phonetic status of the labial flap'. *Journal of the International Phonetic Association* 29: 101–14.

Ortega-Llebaría, M. (2004). 'Interplay between phonetic and inventory constraints in the degree of spirantization of voiced stops, comparing intervocalic /b/ and intervocalic /g/ in Spanish and English'. In T. L. Face (ed.). *Laboratory Approaches to Spanish Phonology*. Berlin: Mouton de Gruyter, pp. 237–53.

Ozanne, A. (2005). 'Childhood apraxia of speech'. In B. Dodd (ed.). *Differential Diagnosis and Treatment of Children with Speech Disorders*. London: Whurr, pp. 71–82.

Palmeri, T. J., Goldinger, S. D. and Pisoni, D. B. (1993). 'Episodic encoding of voice attributes and recognition memory for spoken words'. *Journal of Experimental Psychology: Learning, Memory, and Cognition* 19: 309–28.

Panconcelli-Calzia, G. (1924). *Die experimentelle Phonetik in ihrer Anwendung auf die Sprachwissenschaft*. Berlin: W. de Gruyter and Co.

Pardo, J., Gibbons, R., Suppes, A. and Krauss, R. M. (2012). 'Phonetic convergence in college roommates'. *Journal of Phonetics* 40: 190–7.

Pascoe, M. Stackhouse, J. and Wells, B. (2006). *Persisting Speech Difficulties in Children*. Book 3 in series Children's Speech and Literacy Difficulties. Chichester: Wiley.

Pätzold, M. and Simpson, A. P. (1995). 'An acoustic analysis of hesitation particles in German'. *Proceedings of the 13th International Congress of Phonetic Sciences*. Stockholm, 512–15.

Pegg, J. E. and Werker, J. F. (1997). 'Adult and infant perception of two English phones'. *Journal of the Acoustical Society of America* 102: 3742–53.

Pelucchi, B., Hay, J. F. and Saffran, J. R. (2009). 'Statistical learning in a natural language by 8 month-old infants'. *Child Development* 80: 674–85.

Peppe, S. and McCann, J. (2003). 'Assessing intonation and prosody in children with atypical language development: The PEPS-C test and the revised version. Selected papers from ICPLA 2002'. *Clinical Linguistics and Phonetics* 17: 345–54.

Perkell, J. (1969). *Physiology of Speech Production: Results and Implications of a Quantitative Cineradiographic Study*. Cambridge, MA: MIT Press.

Perkell, J., Cohen, M., Svirsky, M., Matthies, M., Garabieta, I. and Jackson, M. (1992). 'Electro-magnetic midsagittal articulometer (EMMA) systems for transducing speech articulatory movements'. *Journal of the Acoustical Society of America* 92: 3078–96.

Perrier, P., Payan, Y., Zandipour, M. and Perkell, J. (2003). 'Influences of tongue biomechanics on speech movements during the production of velar stop consonants: a modelling study'. *Journal of the Acoustical Society of America* 114: 1582–99.

Peter, W. A. (1996). 'The history of laryngology'. *Otolaryngology – Head and Neck Surgery* 114: 343–54.

Peterson, G. E. and Lehiste, I. (1960). 'Duration of syllable nuclei in English'. *Journal of the Acoustical Society of America* 32: 693–703.

Petrova, O., Plapp, R., Ringen, C. and Szentgyörgyi, S. (2006). 'Voice and aspiration: Evidence from Russian, Hungarian, German, Swedish, and Turkish'. *The Linguistic Review* 23: 1–35.

Pierrehumbert, J. (1980). *The Phonology and Phonetics of English Intonation*. PhD thesis, MIT. http: //faculty.wcas.northwestern.edu/~jbp/publications/Pierrehumbert_PhD.pdf

—. (1990). 'Phonological and phonetic representation'. *Journal of Phonetics* 18: 375–94.

—. (2001). 'Exemplar dynamics: Word frequency, lenition and contrast'. In J. Bybee and P. Hopper (eds). *Frequency Effects and the Emergence of Linguistic Structure*. Amsterdam: John Benjamins, pp. 137–57.

—. (2002). 'Word-specific phonetics'. In C. Gussenhoven and N. Warner (eds). *Papers in Laboratory Phonology 7*. Berlin: Mouton de Gruyter, pp. 101–40.

—. (2003). 'Phonetic diversity, statistical learning, and acquisition of phonology'. *Language and Speech* 46: 115–54.

—. (2006). 'The next toolkit'. *Journal of Phonetics* 34: 516–30.

Pierrehumbert, J., Beckman, M. E. and Ladd, D. R. (2000). 'Conceptual foundations of phonology as a laboratory science'. In N. Burton-Roberts, P. Carr and G. Docherty (eds). *Phonological Knowledge*. Oxford: Oxford University Press, pp. 273–303.

Pierrehumbert, J., Bent, T., Munson, B., Bradlow, A. R. and Bailey, J. M. (2004). 'The influence of sexual orientation on vowel production'. *Journal of the Acoustical Society of America* 116: 1905–8.

Pike, K. L. (1945). *The Intonation of American English*. Ann Arbor: University of Michigan Press.

Pisoni, D. B. (1977). 'Identification and discrimination of the relative onset time of two component tones: implications for voicing perception in stops'. *Journal of the Acoustical Society of America* 61: 1352–61.

Pitt, M. A. and Samuel, A. G. (1990). 'The use of rhythm in attending to speech'. *Journal of Experimental Psychology: Human Perception and Performance* 16: 564–73.

Pitt, M. A., Dilley, L. and Tat, M. (2011). 'Exploring the role of exposure frequency in recognizing pronunciation variants'. *Journal of Phonetics* 39: 304–11.

Pitt, M. A., Johnson, K., Hume, E., Kiesling, S. and Raymond, W. (2005). 'The Buckeye corpus of conversational speech: Labeling conventions and a test of transcriber reliability'. *Speech Communication* 45: 89–95.

Plato. (1973). *Theaetetus*. J. McDowell (ed. and trans.). Oxford: Clarendon Press.

Plichta, B. (2010). *Improving Signal Acquisition*. [Online resource: http: //bartus.org/akustyk/signal. php]

Plug, L. and Ogden, R. (2003). 'A parametric approach to the phonetics of postvocalic /r/ in Dutch'. *Phonetica* 60: 159–86.

Poeppel, D. and Monahan, P. J. (2008). 'Speech perception: Cognitive foundations and cortical implementation'. *Current Directions in Psychological Science* 17: 80–5.

—. (2011). 'Feedforward and feedback in speech perception: Revisiting analysis-by-synthesis'. *Language and Cognitive Processes* 26: 935–51.

Poeppel, D., Idsardi, W. J. and van Wassenhove, V. (2008). 'Speech perception at the interface of neurobiology and linguistics'. In B. Moore, L. Tyler and M. Marslen-Wilson (eds). *The Perception of Speech: From Sound to Meaning*. Special Edition of the Philosophical Transactions of the Royal Society, vol. 363: 1071–86.

Pollack, I. and Pickett, J. M. (1963). 'The intelligibility of excerpts from conversational speech'. *Language and Speech* 6: 165–71.

Pols, L. C. W. (2004). 'Expanding phonetics'. In H. Quené and V. van Heuven (eds). *On Speech and Language: Studies for Sieb Nooteboom*. Utrecht: LOT Netherlands Graduate Occasional Series, pp. 141–8.

Port, R. (2007). 'How are words stored in memory? Beyond phones and phonemes'. *New Ideas in Psychology* 25: 143–70.

Potisuk, S., Gandour, J. and Harper, M. P. (1996). 'Acoustic correlates of stress in Thai'. *Phonetica* 53: 200–20.

Pouplier, M. (in press). 'The gestural approach to syllable structure: Universal, language- and cluster-specific aspects'. In S. Fuchs, M. Weirich, D. Pape and P. Perrier (eds). *Speech Planning and Dynamics*. Frankfurt: Peter Lang.

Pouplier, M. and Beňuš, Š. (2011). 'On the phonetic status of syllabic consonants: Evidence from Slovak'. *Laboratory Phonology* 2: 243–73.

Pouplier, M., Hoole, P. and Scobbie, J. (2011). 'Investigating the asymmetry of English sibilant assimilation: acoustic and EPG data'. *Journal of Laboratory Phonology* 2: 1–33.

Preston, J. L., Ramsdell, H. L., Oller, D. K., Edwards, M. L. and Tobin, S. J. (2011). 'Developing a weighted measure of speech sound accuracy'. *Journal of Speech, Language, and Hearing Research* 54: 1–18.

Prieto, P. and Torreira, F. (2007). 'The segmental anchoring hypothesis revisited. Syllable structure and speech rate effects on peak timing in Spanish'. *Journal of Phonetics* 35: 473–500.

Prieto, P., Vanrell, M. M., Astruc, L., Payne, E. and Post, B. (2012). 'Phonotactic and phrasal properties of speech rhythm. Evidence from Catalan, English, and Spanish'. *Speech Communication* 54: 681–702.

Proffit, W. R. (1975). 'Muscle pressures and tooth position: North American Whites and Australian Aborigines'. *Angle Orthodontist* 45: 1–11.

Prom-on, S., Xu, Y. and Thipakorn, B. (2009). 'Modeling tone and intonation in Mandarin and English as a process of target approximation'. *Journal of the Acoustical Society of America* 125: 405–24.

Pye, C., Wilcox, K. A. and Siren, K. A. (1988). 'Refining transcriptions: The significance of transcriber "errors"'. *Journal of Child Language* 15: 17–37.

Quatieri, T. and McAulay, R. (1992). 'Shape invariant time-scale and pitch modifiation of speech'. *IEEE Transactions on Signal Processing* 40: 497–510.

Rabiner, L. (1989). 'A tutorial on Hidden Markov Models and selected applications in speech recognition'. *Proceedings of the IEEE* 77: 257–86.

Ramus, F. and Mehler, J. (1999). 'Language identification with suprasegmental cues: a study based on speech resynthesis'. *Journal of the Acoustical Society of America* 105: 512–21.

Ramus, F., Nespor, M. and Mehler, J. (1999). 'Correlates of linguistic rhythm in the speech signal'. *Cognition* 73: 265–92.

Ramus, F., Hauser, M., Miller, C., Morris, D. and Mehler, J. (2000). 'Language discrimination by human newborns and by cott on-top tamarind monkeys'. *Science* 288: 349–51.

RCSLT (2011). *RCSLT Policy Statement Developmental Verbal Dyspraxia. Royal College of Speech and Language Therapists*. (available online at http://speech-language-therapy.com/pdf/papers/rcslt2011dvdPolicyStatement.pdf).

Recasens, D. (1984). V-to-C coarticulation in Catalan VCV sequences: an articulatory and acoustical study. *Journal of Phonetics* 12: 61–73.

—. (1999). 'Lingual coarticulation'. In W. Hardcastle and N. Hewlett (eds). *Coarticulation: Data, Theory and Techniques*. Cambridge: Cambridge University Press, pp. 80–104.

—. (2006). 'Integrating coarticulation, blending and assimilation into a model of articulatory constraints'. In L. Goldstein, D. Whalen and C. Best (eds). *Laboratory Phonology 8*. Berlin-New York: Mouton de Gruyter, pp. 611–34.

—. (2009). 'Response to Barry and Trouvain 2008'. *Journal of the International Phonetic Association* 39: 231–3.

Recasens, D. and Espinosa, A. (2005). 'Articulatory, positional and coarticulatory characteristics for clear /l/ and dark /l/: evidence from two Catalan dialects'. *Journal of the International Phonetic Association* 35: 1–25.

Recasens, D. and Pallarès, M. (2001). 'Coarticulation, assimilation and blending in Catalan consonant clusters'. *Journal of Phonetics* 29: 273–301.

Reetz, H. and Jongman, A. 2009. *Phonetics: Transcription, Production, Acoustics and Perception*. Blackwell textbooks in linguistics 22. Malden, MA: Blackwell.

Reimchen, T. E. (1987). 'Human color vision deficiencies and atmospheric twilight'. *Social Biology* 34: 1–11.

Reinisch, E., Jesse, A. and McQueen, J. M. (2010). 'Early use of phonetic information in spoken word recognition: Lexical stress drives eye movements immediately'. *Quarterly Journal of Experimental Psychology* 63: 772–83.

—. (2011). 'Speaking rate affects the perception of duration as a suprasegmental lexical-stress cue'. *Language and Speech* 54: 147–65.

Remijsen, B. (2002). *Word-prosodic systems of Raja Ampat languages*. PhD Dissertation, Graduate School of Linguistics, University of Leiden. LOT Dissertation Series vol 49. [www.papuaweb.org/dlib/s123/remijsen/_phd.html]

Rendall, D., Kollias, S., Ney, C. and Lloyd, P. (2005). 'Pitch (F0) and formant profiles of human vowels and vowel-like baboon grunts: The role of vocalizer body size and voice-acoustic allometry'. *Journal of the Acoustical Society of America* 117: 944–55.

Reynolds, D. (1995). 'Speaker identification and verification using gaussian mixture models'. *Speech Communication* 17: 91–108.

Ridouane, R. (2008). 'Syllables without vowels: phonetic and phonological evidence from Tashlhiyt Berber'. *Phonology* 25: 1–39.

Rietveld, A. C. M.; and Gussenhoven, C. (1995). 'On the relation between pitch excursion size and prominence'. *Journal of Phonetics* 13: 299–308.

Rinkenauer, G., Osman, A., Ulrich, R., Muller-Gethmann, H. and Mattes, S. (2004). 'On the locus of speed-accuracy trade-off in reaction time: Inferences from the lateralized readiness potential'. *Journal of Experimental Psychology: General* 133: 261–82.

Ripley, K., Daines, B. and Barrett, J. (1997). *Dyspraxia: A Guide for Teachers and Parents.* London: David Fulton.

Roach, P. (1982). 'On the distinction between "stress-timed" and "syllable-timed" languages'. In D. Crystal (ed.). *Linguistic Controversies.* London: Arnold, pp. 73–9.

—. (2009). *English Phonetics and Phonology: A Practical Course* (4th edn). Cambridge: Cambridge University Press.

Robb, M., Gilbert, H. and Lerman, J. (2005). 'Influence of gender and environmental setting on voice onset time'. *Folia Phoniatrica et logopaedica* 57: 125–33.

Robertson, B. and Vignaux, G. A. (1995). *Interpreting Evidence.* Chichester: Wiley.

Robins, R. H. (1990). *A Short History of Linguistics* (3rd edn). London: Longman.

Robinson, A. J. (1994). 'An application of recurrent nets to phone probability estimation'. *IEEE Transactions on Neural Networks* 5: 298–305.

Robinson, R. (1617). *The Art of Pronunciation.* Facsimile reprint. (1969). R. C. Alston (ed.). Menston: The Scolar Press.

Rochet-Capellan, A., Fuchs, S. and Perrier, P. (2012). 'How listeners' respiration changes while listening to speech'. Paper presented at *Perspectives on Rhythm and Timing,* Glasgow, 19–21 July 2012.

Rogerson-Revell, P. 2011. *English Phonology and Pronunciation Teaching.* London: Continuum.

Rose, P. (2002). *Forensic Speaker Identification.* London: Taylor and Francis.

Rosen, S., Wise, R. J. S., Chadha, S., Conway, E.-J. and Scott, S. K. (2011). 'Hemispheric asymmetries in speech perception: Sense, nonsense and modulations'. *PLoS ONE* 6: e24672.

Rousselot, P. J. (1897–1908). *Principes de Phonétique Expérimentale.* Paris: H. Welter.

Roy, B. C., Frank, M. C. and Roy, D. (2009). 'Exploring word learning in a high-density longitudinal corpus'. *Proceedings of the 31st Annual Meeting of the Cognitive Science Society.* Amsterdam, Netherlands. 29 July–1 August 2009, pp. 2106–11.

Roy, D. (2009). 'New horizons in the study of child language acquisition'. *Proceedings of Interspeech 2009.* Brighton, England, 6–10 September 2009, pp. 13–20.

Rozelle, L. (1997). 'The effects of stress on vowel length in Aleut'. *UCLA Working papers in Phonetics* 95: 91–101.

Rubin, P., Turvey, M. T. and Van Gelder, P. (1976). 'Initial phonemes are detected faster in spoken words than in spoken nonwords'. *Perception and Psychophysics* 19: 394–8.

Russell, A., Penny, L. and Pemberton, C. (1995). 'Speaking fundamental frequency changes over time in women: a longitudinal study'. *Journal of Speech and Hearing Research* 38: 101–9.

Ryalls, J., Zipprer, A. and P. Baldauff, P. (1997). 'A preliminary investigation of the effects of gender and race on voice onset time'. *Journal of Speech, Language, and Hearing Research* 40: 642–5.

Sacks, H. (1992). *Lectures on Conversation.* Vol. 1 and 2. Blackwell, Maldon, MA.

Sacks, H., Schegloff, E. and Jefferson, G. (1974). 'A simplest systematics for the organization of turn-taking for conversation'. *Language* 50: 696–735.

Saffran, J. R. (2003). 'Statistical language learning: Mechanisms and constraints'. *Current Directions in Psychological Science* 12: 110–14

Saffran, J. R. and Thiessen, E. D. (2003). 'Pattern induction by infant language learners'. *Developmental Psychology* 39: 484–94.

Saffran, J. R., Werker, J. F. and Werner, L. A. (2006). 'The infant's auditory world: Hearing, speech, and the beginnings of language'. In R. Siegler and D. Kuhn (eds), *Handbook of Child Psychology: Vol.2, Cognition, perception and language* (6th edn). New York: Wiley, pp. 58–108.

Salverda, A. P., Dahan, D. and McQueen, J. M. (2003). 'The role of prosodic boundaries in the resolution of lexical embedding in speech comprehension'. *Cognition* 90: 51–89.

Sawsuch, J. (1996). 'Instrumentation and methodology for the study of speech perception'. In N. Lass (ed.). *Principles of Experimental Phonetics*. St Louis: Mosby, pp. 525–50.

Scarborough, R. (2010). 'Lexical and contextual predictability: Confluent effects on the production of vowels'. In C. Fougeron, B. Kühnert, M. D'Imperio and N. Vallée (eds). *Laboratory Phonology 10: Variability, Phonetic Detail and Phonological Representation*. Berlin: Mouton de Gruyter, pp. 557–86.

Scharenborg, O., Norris, D., ten Bosch, L. and McQueen, J. M. (2005). 'How should a speech recognizer work?' *Cognitive Science* 29: 867–918.

Schirmer, A. and Kotz, S. A. (2006). 'Beyond the right hemisphere: brain mechanisms mediating vocal emotional processing'. *Trends in Cognitive Sciences* 10: 24–30.

Schneider, B. A., Morrongiello, B. A. and Trehub, S. E. (1990). 'The size of the critical band in infants, children, and adults'. *Journal of Experimental Psychology: Human Perception and Performance* 16: 642–52.

Schultz, W. and Dickinson, A. (2000). 'Neuronal coding of prediction errors'. *Annual Review of Neuroscience* 23: 473–500.

Schuppler, B., Ernestus, M., Scharenborg, O. and Boves, L. (2011). 'Acoustic reduction in conversational Dutch: A quantitative analysis based on automatically generated segmental transcriptions'. *Journal of Phonetics* 39: 96–109.

Schwartz, J.-L., Abry, C., Boë, L.-J., Ménard, L. and Vallée, N. (2005). 'Asymmetries in vowel perception, in the context of the dispersion-focalisation theory'. *Speech Communication* 45: 425–34.

Schweitzer, N. J. and Saks, M. J. (2007). 'The CSI effect: Popular fiction about forensic science affects the public's expectations about real forensic science'. *Jurimetrics* 47: 357–64.

Scobbie, J., Turk, A. E. and Hewlett, N. (1999). 'Morphemes, phonetics and lexical items: The case of the Scottish vowel length rule'. In J. J. Ohala, Y. Hasegawa, M. Ohala, D. Granville and A. C. Bailey (eds). *Proceedings of the XIV International Congress of Phonetic Sciences*. Berkeley: ICPhS, pp. 1617–20.

Scott, S. K. (1998). 'The point of P-centres'. *Psychological Research* 61: 4–11.

Scott, S. K. and Johnsrude, I. S. (2003). 'The neuroanatomical and functional organization of speech perception'. *Trends in Neuroscience* 26: 100–7.

Scott, S. K., McGettigan, C. and Eisner, F. (2009). 'A little more conversation, a little less action – candidate roles for the motor cortex in speech perception'. *Nature Reviews Neuroscience* 10: 295–302.

Scott, S. and Wise, R. (2004). 'The functional neuroanatomy of prelexical processing in speech perception'. *Cognition* 92: 13–45.

Scripture, E. W. (1902). *The Elements of Experimental Phonetics*. London: Edward Arnold.

Selkirk, E. 1978. 'On prosodic structure in relation to syntactic structure'. In T. Fretheim (ed). *Nordic Prosody* 2. TAPIR, Trondheim, Norway, pp. 111–40.

Shadle, C. (2010). 'The aerodynamics of speech'. In W. J. Hardcastle, J. Laver and F. E. Gibbon (eds). *The Handbook of Phonetic Sciences* (2nd edn). Oxford: Blackwell, pp. 39–80.

Shadle, C. H., Badin, P. and Moulinier, A. (1991). 'Towards the spectral characteristics of fricative consonants'. *Proceedings of the 12th International Congress of Phonetic Sciences*. Aix-en-Provence, pp. 42–5.

Shahidullah, S. and Hepper, P. G. (1994). 'Frequency discrimination by the fetus'. *Early Human Development* 36: 13–26.

Shaw, J., Gafos, A., Hoole, P. and Zeroual, C. (2009). 'Temporal evidence for syllabic structure in Moroccan Arabic: Theory, experiment, model'. *Phonology* 26: 187–215.

Shi, R. and Werker, J. F. (2001). 'Six-month-old infants' preference for lexical over grammatical words'. *Psychological Science* 12: 70–5.

Shi, R., Werker, J. and Cutler, A. (2006). 'Recognition and representation of function words in English-learning infants'. *Infancy* 10: 187–98

Shipp, T., Qi, Y., Huntley, R. and Hollien, H. (1992). 'Acoustic and temporal correlates of perceived age'. *Journal of Voice* 6: 211–16.

Shockey, L. (2003). *Sound Patterns of Spoken English*. Oxford: Blackwell.

Shockley, K., Sabadini, L. and Fowler, C. A. (2004). 'Imitation in shadowing words'. *Perception and Psychophysics* 66: 422–9.

Shriberg, E. E. (2001). 'To "errrr" is human: ecology and acoustics of speech disfluencies'. *Journal of the International Phonetic Association* 31: 153–69.

Shriberg, L. D. (2006). 'Research in idiopathic and symptomatic childhood apraxia of speech'. *5th International Conference on Speech Motor Control*. Nijmegen, the Netherlands [www.waisman.wisc.edu/phonology/presentations/PRES39.pdf]

Shriberg, L. D., Austin, D., Lewis, B. A., McSweeny, J. L. and Wilson, D. L. (1997). 'The Percentage of Consonants Correct (PCC) metric: Extensions and reliability data'. *Journal of Speech, Language, and Hearing Research* 40: 708–22.

Shriberg, L. D., Kwiatkowski, J. and Hoffmann, K. (1984). 'A procedure for phonetic transcription by consensus'. *Journal of Speech and Hearing Research* 27: 456–65.

Shriberg, L. and Lof, G. (1991). 'Reliability studies in broad and narrow phonetic transcription'. *Clinical Linguistics and Phonetics* 5: 225–79.

Sievers, E. (1901). *Grundzüge der Phonetik* (5th edn). Leipzig: Breitkopf & Härtel.

Simonet, M. (2010). 'Dark and clear laterals in Catalan and Spanish: Interaction of phonetic categories in early bilinguals'. *Journal of Phonetics* 38: 664–79.

Simpson, A. P. (1992). 'Casual speech rules and what the phonology of connected speech might really be like'. *Linguistics* 30: 535–48.

—. (2001a). 'Does articulatory reduction miss more patterns than it accounts for?' *Journal of the International Phonetic Association* 31: 29–40.

—. (2001b). 'Dynamic consequences of differences in male and female vocal tract dimensions'. *Journal of the Acoustical Society of America* 109: 2153–64.

—. (2002). 'Gender-specific articulatory-acoustic relations in vowel sequences'. *Journal of Phonetics* 30: 417–35.

—. (2006). 'Phonetic processes in discourse'. In K. Brown (ed.). *Encyclopedia of Language and Linguistics* (2nd edn). Vol. 9. Elsevier, Amsterdam, pp. 379–85.

—. (2007). 'Phonetische Motivation für Lenition: Gebrauch oder Missbrauch von phonetischen Erklärungen?' In Gallmann, P., Lehmann, C. and Lühr, R. (eds). *Sprachliche Motivation. Zur Interdependenz von Inhalt und Ausdruck*. Tübinger Beiträge zur Linguistik, Band 502. Narr, Tübingen, pp. 211–23.

—. (2009). 'Phonetic differences between male and female speech'. *Language and Linguistics* Compass 3: 621–40.

Simpson, S. A. and Cooke, M. (2005). 'Consonant identification in N-talker babble is a nonmonotonic function of N'. *Journal of the Acoustical Society of America* 118: 2775–8.

Singh, S. and Singh, K. S. (2006). *Phonetics Principles and Practices* (3rd edn). San Diego: Plural Publishing.

Sluijter, A. M. C. and van Heuven, V. J. J. P. (1996). 'Spectral balance as an acoustic correlate of linguistic stress'. *Journal of the Acoustical Society of America* 100: 2471–85.

Sluijter, A. M. C., van Heuven, V. J. J. P. and Pacilly, J. J. A. (1997). 'Spectral balance as a cue in the perception of linguistic stress'. *Journal of the Acoustical Society of America* 101: 503–13.

Smith, R. and Hawkins, S. (2012). 'Production and perception of speaker-specific phonetic detail at word boundaries'. *Journal of Phonetics* 40: 213–33.

Smith, R., Baker, R. and Hawkins, S. (2012). 'Phonetic detail that distinguishes prefixed from pseudo-prefixed words'. *Journal of Phonetics* 40: 689–705.

Smith, S. L., Gerhardt, K. J., Griffiths, S. K. and Huang, X. (2003). 'Intelligibility of sentences recorded from the uterus of a pregnant ewe and from the fetal inner ear'. *Audiology and Neuro Otology* 8: 347–53.

Smith, T. (1568). *De recta et emendata linguae anglicae scriptione*. B. Danielsson (ed. and trans.). Stockholm: Almqvist and Wiksell (1983).

Snodgrass, J., Levy-Berger, G. and Haydon, M. (1985). *Human Experimental Psychology*. Oxford: Oxford University Press.

Soh, J., Sandham, A. and Chan, Y. H. (2005). 'Occlusal status in Asian male adults: prevalence and ethnic variation'. *Angle Orthodontist* 75: 814–20.

Solé, M.-J. (1992) 'Phonetic and phonological processes: The case of nasalization'. *Language and Speech* 35: 29–43.

—. (2007). 'Controlled and mechanical properties in speech'. In M.-J. Solé, P. S. Beddor and M. Ohala (eds). *Experimental Approaches to Phonology*. Oxford: Oxford University Press, pp. 302–21.

Solé, M.-J and Ohala, J. J. (2012). 'What is and what is not under the control of the speaker: Intrinsic vowel duration'. In C. Fougeron, B. Kühnert, M. D'Imperio and N. Vallée (eds). *Laboratory phonology 10: Variability, Phonetic Detail and Phonological Representation*. Berlin: Mouton de Gruyter, pp. 607–55.

Solé, M.-J., Recasens, D. and Romero, J. (eds) (2003). *Proceedings of the 15th International Congress of the Phonetic Sciences*. Barcelona. Causal Productions.

Sommers, M. S. and Barcroft, J. (2006). 'Stimulus variability and the phonetic relevance hypothesis: effects of variability in speaking style, fundamental frequency, and speaking rate on spoken word identification'. *Journal of the Acoustical Society of America* 119: 2406–16.

Son, M., Kochetov, A. and Pouplier, M. (2007). 'The role of gestural overlap in perceptual place assimilation in Korean'. In J. Cole and J. Hualde (eds). *Papers in Laboratory Phonology 9*. Berlin: Mouton de Gruyter, pp. 507–34.

Spence, T. (1775). *The Grand Repository of the English Language*. Facsimile reprint. (1968). R. C. Alston (ed.). Menston: The Scolar Press.

Stackhouse, J. and Wells, B. (1997). *Children's Speech and Literacy Difficulties 1: A Psycholinguistic Framework*. London: Whurr.

Stager, C. L. and Werker, J. F. (1997). 'Infants listen for more phonetic detail in speech perception than in word-learning tasks'. *Nature* 388: 381–2.

Stampe, D. (1979). *A Dissertation on Natural Phonology*. New York: Garland.

Starr-Marshall, T. (2010). *Recordings of Disordered Speech: The Effect of 3 Different Modes of Audiovisual Presentation on Transcription Agreement*. Unpublished MSc dissertation, City University London.

Steele, J. (1775). *An Essay towards Establishing the Melody and Measure of Speech to be Expressed and Perpetuated by Peculiar Symbols*. Facsimile reprint. (1969). R. C. Alston (ed.). Menston: The Scolar Press.

Stephens, M. I. and Daniloff, R. (1977). 'A methodological study of factors affecting the judgment of misarticulated /s/'. *Journal of Communication Disorders* 10: 207–20.

Stephenson, L. (2003). 'An EPG study of repetition and lexical frequency effects in alveolar to velar assimilation'. In M.-J. Solé, D. Recasens and J. Romero (eds). *Proceedings of the 15th International Congress of the Phonetic Sciences*. Barcelona, pp. 1891–4.

Steriade, D. (2001). 'Directional asymmetries in place assimilation: A perceptual account'. In E. Hume and K. Johnson (eds). *The Role of Speech Perception in Phonology*. San Diego: Academic Press, pp. 219–50.

—. (2009). 'The phonology of perceptibility effects: the P-map and its consequences for constraint organization'. In S. Inkelas and K. Hanson (eds) *On the Nature of the Word. Studies in Honor of Paul Kiparsky*. Cambridge, MA: MIT Press, pp. 151–80.

Stetson, R. H. (1951). *Motor Phonetics: A Study of Speech Movements in Action*. Amsterdam: North Holland. (first published in *Archives néerlandaises de phonétique expérimentale* 1928).

Stevens, K. N. (1960). 'Toward a model for speech recognition'. *Journal of the Acoustical Society of America* 32: 47–55.

—. (1998). *Acoustic Phonetics*. Cambridge, MA: MIT Press.

—. (2002). 'Toward a model for lexical access based on acoustic landmarks and distinctive features'. *Journal of the Acoustical Society of America* 111: 1872–91.

Stevens, K. N. and Blumstein, S. E. (1978). 'Invariant cues for place of articulation in stop consonants'. *Journal of the Acoustical Society of America* 64: 1358–68.

Stevens, K. N. and Halle, M. (1967). 'Remarks on analysis by synthesis and distinctive features'. In W. Wathen-Dunn (ed.). *Models for the Perception of Speech and Visual Form*. Cambridge, MA: MIT Press, pp. 88–102.

Stevens, K. N. and Keyser, S. J. (2010). 'Quantal theory, enhancement and overlap'. *Journal of Phonetics* 38: 10–19.

Stevens, L. and French, P. (2012). 'Voice quality in studio quality and telephone transmitted recordings'. Paper presented at the *British Association of Academic Phonetics Conference*, Leeds, UK, March 2012.

Stoakes H., Fletcher J. M. and Butcher A. R. (2006). 'Articulatory variability of intervocalic stop articulation in Bininj Gun-wok'. In P. Warren and C. I. Watson (eds). *Proceedings of the 11th Australasian International Conference on Speech Science and Technology*. Canberra: Australasian Speech Science and Technology Association Inc., pp. 182–6. [available at: www.assta.org/sst/2006/sst2006–98.pdf]

—. (2007). 'An acoustic and articulatory study of Bininj Gun-wok stop consonants'. In J. Trouvain and W. J. Barry (eds). *Proceedings of the 16th International Congress of Phonetic Sciences*. Saarbrücken, pp. 869–72.

Stoel-Gammon, C. (1988). *Evaluation of Phonological Skills in Pre-school Children*. New York: Thieme Medical Publishers.

Stoel-Gammon, C. and Dunn, C. (1985). *Normal and Disordered Phonology in Children*. Baltimore: University Park Press.

Stoel-Gammon, C., Williams, K. and Buder, E. (1994). 'Cross-language differences in phonological acquisition: Swedish and American /t/'. *Phonetica* 51: 146–58.

Stone, M. (1991). 'Toward a three dimensional model of tongue movement'. *Journal of Phonetics* 19: 309–20.

—. (1999). 'Imaging techniques'. In W. Hardcastle and N. Hewlett (eds). *Coarticulation: Data, Theory and Techniques*. Cambridge: Cambridge University Press, pp. 246–59.

—. (2005). 'A guide to analysing tongue motion from ultrasound images'. *Clinical Linguistics and Phonetics* 19: 455–502.

Stone, M., Faber, A., Raphael, L. J. and Shawker, T. H. (1992). 'Cross-sectional tongue shape and linguopalatal contact patterns in [s],[ʃ], and [l]'. *Journal of Phonetics:* 20 253–70.

Strange, W. and Halwes, T. (1971). 'Confidence ratings in speech perception research: Evaluation of an efficient technique for discrimination testing'. *Attention, Perception, and Psychophysics* 9: 182–6.

Stuart-Smith, J. (1999). 'Glasgow: Accent and voice quality'. In P. Foulkes and G. Docherty (eds). *Urban Voices*. London: Arnold, pp. 203–22.

—. (2007). 'Empirical evidence for gendered speech production: /s/ in Glaswegian'. In J. Cole and J. Hualde (eds). *Papers in Laboratory Phonology 9*. Berlin: Mouton de Gruyter, pp. 65–86.

Studdert-Kennedy, M. and Whalen, D. H. (1999). 'A brief history of speech perception research in the United States'. In J. J. Ohala, A. J. Bronstein, M. Grazia Busà, J. A. Lewis and W. F. Weigel (eds). *A Guide to the History of the Phonetic Sciences in the United States*. Berkeley, CA: University of California Press, pp. 21–5.

Stylianou, Y. and Moulines, E. (1998). 'Continuous probabilistic transform for voice conversion'. *IEEE Transactions on Speech and Audio Processing* 6: 131–42.

Sugahara, M. and Turk, A. (2009). 'Durational correlates of English sublexical constituent structure'. *Phonology* 26: 477–524.

Sumera, M. (1981). 'The keen prosodic ear: A comparison of the notations of rhythm of Joshua Steele, William Thomson and Morris Croll'. In R. E. Asher and E. Henderson (eds). *Towards a History of Phonetics*. Edinburgh: Edinburgh University Press, pp. 100–12.

Summer, W. V., Pisoni, D. B., Bernacki, R. H., Pedlow, R. I. and Stokes, M. A. (1988). 'Effects of noise on speech production: acoustic and perceptual analyses'. *Journal of the Acoustical Society of America* 84: 917–28.

Summerfield, Q. and Haggard, M. (1977). 'On the dissociation of spectral and temporal cues to the voicing distinction in initial stop consonants'. *Journal of the Acoustical Society of America* 62: 435–48.

Sun, J. T.-S. (2003). 'Variegated tonal developments in Tibetan'. In D. Bradley, R. LaPolla, B. Michailovsky and G. Thurgood (eds). *Language Variation: Papers on Variation and Change in the Sinosphere and in the Indosphere in Honour of James A. Matisoff*. Canberra, Australia, A.N.U. (Pacific Linguistics. Series C – 87), pp. 35–51.

Surprenant, A. M. and Goldstein, L. (1998). 'The perception of speech gestures'. *Journal of the Acoustical Society of America* 104: 518–29.

Sweet, H. (1877). *Handbook of Phonetics*. Oxford: Clarendon Press.

Swingley, D. (2009). 'Contributions of infant word learning to language development'. *Philosophical Transactions of the Royal Society B* 364: 3617–22.

Swingley, D. and Aslin, R. N. (2000) 'Spoken word recognition and lexical representation in very young children'. *Cognition* 76: 147–66.

—.(2002). 'Lexical neighborhoods and the word-form representations of 14-month-olds'. *Psychological Science* 13: 480–4.

t' Hart, J., Collier, R. and Cohen, A. (1990). *A Perceptual Study of Intonation: An Experimental-phonetic Approach to Speech Melody*. Cambridge: Cambridge University Press.

Tabain, M. (2009). 'An EPG study of the alveolar vs. retroflex apical contrast in Central Arrernte'. *Journal of Phonetics* 37: 486–501.

—. (2011). 'EPG data from Central Arrernte: a comparison of the new Articulate palate with the standard Reading palate'. *Journal of the International Phonetic Association* 41: 343–67.

Tabain, M., Fletcher, J. M. and Butcher, A. R. (2011). 'An EPG study of palatal consonants in two Australian languages'. *Language and Speech* 54: 265–82.

Tabri, D., Abou Chacra, K. M. and Pring, T. (2011). 'Speech perception in noise by monolingual, bilingual and trilingual listeners'. *International Journal of Language and Communication Disorders* 46: 411–22.

Takano, S., Honda, K. and Masaki, S. (2006). 'Observation of tongue-larynx interaction using improved MRI techniques'. In J. Harrington and M. Tabain (eds). *Speech Production: Models, Phonetic Processes, Techniques*. Hove: Psychology Press, pp. 331–40.

Tanenhaus, M. and Brown-Schmidt, S. (2008). 'Language processing in the natural world'. In B. Moore, L. Tyler and M. Marslen-Wilson (eds). *The Perception of Speech:*

From Sound to Meaning. Special Edition of the Philosophical Transactions of the Royal Society, vol. 363: 1105–22.

Tavoni, M. (1998). 'Renaissance linguistics: Western Europe'. In G. Lepschy (ed.). *History of Linguistics volume III: Renaissance and Early Modern Linguistics.* London: Longman, pp. 4–108.

Taylor, P. (1998). 'The Tilt intonation model'. *International Conference on Spoken Language Processing.* Sydney, Australia, pp. 1383–138.

Thieberger N. (ed.) (2012). *The Oxford Handbook of Linguistic Fieldwork.* Oxford: Oxford University Press.

Thiessen, E. D. and Saffran, J. R. (2003). 'When cues collide: Use of statistical and stress cues to word boundaries by 7- and 9-month-old infants'. *Developmental Psychology* 39: 706–16.

Thomas, E. R. (2011). *Sociophonetics.* Basingstoke: Palgrave Macmillan.

Thomas, E. R. and Kendall, T. (2007). *NORM: The Vowel Normalization and Plotting Suite.* [Online resource: http://ncslaap.lib.ncsu.edu/tools/norm/]

Tiede, M., Perkell, J., Zandipour, M. and Matthies, M. (2001). 'Gestural timing effects in the "perfect memory" sequence observed under three rates by electromagnetometry'. *Journal of the Acoustical Society of America* 110: 2657 [Abstract].

Tillmann, H. G. (1995). 'Early modern instrumental phonetics'. In E. F. Koerner and R. E. Asher (eds). *Concise History of the Language Sciences: From the Sumerians to the Cognitivists.* New York: Pergamon, pp. 401–16.

Titze, I. R. (1989). 'Physiologic and acoustic differences between male and female voices'. *Journal of the Acoustical Society of America* 85: 1699–1707.

—. (1990). 'Interpretation of the electroglottographic signal'. *Journal of Voice* 4: 1–9.

Tjalve, M. (2007). *Accent Features and Idiodictionaries: On Improving Accuracy for Accented Speakers in ASR.* PhD Thesis, London: University College London.

Tokuda, K., Yoshimura, T., Masuko, T., Kobayashi, T. and Kitamura, T. (2000). 'Speech parameter generation algorithms for HMM-based speech synthesis'. *ICASSP.* Istanbul, Turkey: IEEE, pp. 1315–18.

Tomiak, G. R. (1990). *An Acoustic and Perceptual Analysis of the Spectral Moments Invariant with Voiceless Fricative Obstruents.* Unpublished PhD dissertation, State University of New York at Buffalo.

Torre III, P. and Barlow, J. A. (2009). 'Age-related changes in acoustic characteristics of adult speech'. *Journal of Communication Disorders* 42: 324–33.

Traunmüller, H. (1981). 'Perceptual dimension of openness in vowels'. *Journal of the Acoustical Society of America* 69: 1465–75.

—. (1990). 'Analytical expressions for the tonotopic sensory scale'. *Journal of the Acoustical Society of America* 88: 97–100.

Trouvain, J. and Barry, W. (2007). *Proceedings of the 16th International Congress of the Phonetic Sciences.* Saarbrücken (available online at http://www.icphs2007.de/).

Trudgill, P. (1974). *The Social Differentiation of English in Norwich.* Cambridge: Cambridge University Press.

Tucker, B. V. (2011). 'The effect of reduction on the processing of flaps and /g/ in isolated words'. *Journal of Phonetics* 39: 312–18.

Turk, A. E., Nakai, S. and Sugahara, M. (2006). 'Acoustic segment durations in prosodic research: A practical guide'. In S. Sudhoff, D. Lenertová, R. Meyer, S. Pappert, P. Augurzky, I. Mleinek, N. Richter and J. Schließer (eds). *Methods in Empirical Prosody Research.* Berlin: Mouton de Gruyter, pp. 1–28.

Tyler, L., Voice, J. and Moss, H. (2000). 'The interaction of meaning and sound in spoken word recognition'. *Psychonomic Bulletin and Review* 7: 320–6.

Underhill, A. (2005). *Sound Foundations: Learning and Teaching Pronunciation.* [Revised and expanded.]. Oxford: Macmillan.

Utman, J. A. and Blumstein, S. E. (1994). 'The influence of language on the acoustic properties of phonetic features, a study of the feature [strident] in Ewe and English'. *Phonetica* 51: 221–38.

Vaissière, J. (2003). 'New Tools for Teaching Phonetics'. In M.-J. Solé, D. Recasens and J. Romero (eds). *Proceedings of the 15th International Congress of the Phonetic Sciences.* Barcelona, pp. 309–12.

van den Berg, J. (1968). 'Mechanism of the larynx and the laryngeal vibrations'. In B. Malmberg (ed.). *Manual of Phonetics.* Amsterdam: North-Holland Publishing Company, pp. 278–308.

van den Heuvel, H., Cranen, B. and Rietveld, T. (1996). 'Speaker variability in the coarticulation of /a, i, u/'. *Speech Communication* 18: 113–30.

van Dommelen, W. A. and Moxness, B. H. (1995). 'Acoustic parameters in speaker height and weight identification: sex-specific behaviour'. *Language and Speech* 38: 267–87.

van Dommelen, W. A. and Nilsen, R. A. (2002). 'Toneme realization in two North Norwegian dialects'. *Proceedings of FonetikTMH-QPSR* 44: 21–4.

Van Donselaar, W. (1996). 'Mispronunciation detection'. In F. Grosjean and U. Frauenfelder (eds). *A Guide to Spoken Word Recognition Paradigms.* Hove: Psychology Press, pp. 611–20.

Van Donselaar, W., Koster, M. and Cutler, A. (2005). 'Exploring the role of lexical stress in lexical recognition'. *Quarterly Journal of Experimental Psychology* 58A: 251–73.

van Heuven, V. J. J. P. and Sluijter, A. C. M. (1996). 'Notes on the phonetics of word prosody'. In R. Goedemans, H. van der Hulst and E. Visch (eds). *Stress Patterns of the World, Part 1: Background, HIL Publications volume 2.* The Hague: Holland Institute of Generative Linguistics, Leiden/Holland Academic Graphics, pp. 233–69.

Van Hoof, S. and Verhoeven, J. (2011). 'Intrinsic vowel F0, the size of vowel inventories and second language acquisition'. *Journal of Phonetics* 39: 168–77.

Van Petten, C., Coulson, S., Rubin, S,. Plante, E. and Parks, M. (1999). 'Time course of word identification and semantic integration in spoken language'. *Journal of Experimental Psychology Learning Memory and Cognition* 25: 394–417.

van Santen, J. P. H. and Hirschberg, J. (1994). 'Segmental effects on timing and height of pitch contours'. *Proceedings of ICSLP-94, International Conference on Speech and Language Processing,* pp. 719–22.

Varma, S. (1961). *Critical Studies in the Phonetic Observations of Indian Grammarians.* Delhi: Munshi Ram Manohar Lal.

Vennemann, T. (2000). 'Triple-cluster reduction in Germanic: Etymology without sound laws?' *Historische Sprachforschung (Historical Linguistics)* 113: 239–58.

Verhoeven, J., Hirson, A. and Basavraj, K. (2011). 'Fricative devoicing in standard Southern British English'. *Proceedings of the 17th International Congress of Phonetic Sciences.* Hong Kong, pp. 2070–3.

Vicenik, C. (2010). 'An acoustic study of Georgian stop consonants'. *Journal of the International Phonetic Association* 40: 59–92.

Villing, R. (2010). *Hearing the Moment: Measures and Models of the Perceptual Centre.* PhD thesis, National University of Ireland Maynooth. http://eprints.nuim.ie/2284/

Vineis, E. and Maierú, A. (1994). 'Medieval linguistics'. In G. Lepschy (ed.). *History of Linguistics volume II: Classical and Medieval Linguistics.* London: Longman, pp. 134–346.

Vouloumanos, A. and Werker, J. F. (2004). 'Tuned to the signal: The privileged status of speech for young infants'. *Developmental Science* 7: 270–6.

—. (2007). 'Listening to language at birth: Evidence for a bias for speech in neonates'. *Developmental Science* 10: 159–64.

Wadnerkar, M. B., Cowell, P. E. and Whiteside, S. P. (2006). 'Speech across the menstrual cycle: A replication and extension study'. *Neuroscience Letters* 408: 21–4.

Walker, G. (2003). '"Doing a rush-through" – A phonetic resource for holding the turn in everyday conversation'. In M.-J. Solé, D. Recasens and J. Romero (eds). *Proceedings of the 15th International Congress of the Phonetic Sciences*. Barcelona, pp. 1847–50.

Walker, J. (1791). *A Critical Pronouncing Dictionary*. Facsimile reprint. (1968). R. C. Alston (ed.). Menston: The Scolar Press.

Wallis, J. (1653). 'Tractatus de Loquela'. In J. A. Kemp (ed. and trans.). *John Wallis's Grammar of the English Language* (1972). London: Longman, pp. 128–211.

Walsh, M., Möbius, B., Wade, T. and Schütze, H. (2010). 'Multilevel exemplar theory'. *Cognitive Science* 34: 537–82.

Ward, I. C. (1933). *The Phonetic and Tonal Structure of Efik*. Cambridge: W. Heffer and Sons.

Waring, R. and Knight, R. A. (2013). 'How should children with speech sound disorders of unknown origin be classified? A review and critical evaluation of current classification systems'. *International Journal of Language and Communication Disorders* 48(1): 25-40.

Warren, P. and Marslen-Wilson, W. D. (1987). 'Continuous uptake of acoustic cues in spoken word recognition'. *Perception and Psychophysics* 41: 262–75.

—. (1988). 'Cues to lexical choice: discriminating place and voice'. *Perception and Psychophysics* 43: 21–30.

Warren, R. (1968). 'Verbal transformation effect and auditory perceptual mechanisms'. *Psychological Bulletin* 70: 261–70.

Warren, R. and Warren, R. (1970). 'Auditory illusions and confusions'. *Scientific American* 223: 30–6.

Watson, C. and Harrington, J. (1999). 'Acoustic evidence for dynamic formant trajectories in Australian English vowels'. *Journal of the Acoustical Society of America* 106: 458–68.

Watt, D. and Fabricius, A. H. (2002). 'Evaluation of a technique for improving the mapping of multiple speakers' vowel spaces in the F1~F2 plane'. *Leeds Working Papers in Linguistics and Phonetics* 9: 159–73. [Online resource: http://wattfab2002. notlong.com]

—. (2011). 'A measure of variable planar locations anchored on the centroid of the vowel space: A sociophonetic research tool'. *Proceedings of the 17th International Congress of Phonetic Sciences*. Hong Kong, pp. 2102–5.

Watt, D., Fabricius, A. H. and Kendall, T. (2010). 'More on vowels: Plotting and normalization'. In M. Di Paolo and M. Yaeger-Dror (eds). *Sociophonetics: A Student's Guide*. London: Routledge, pp. 107–18.

Watt, D., Llamas, C., Nycz, J. and Hall, D. (2010). *Voice Onset Time and the Scottish Vowel Length Rule along the Scottish-English Border*. Paper presented at the 2010 Conference of the British Association of Academic Phoneticians, London.

Watt, D. and Yurkova, J. (2007). 'Voice onset time and the Scottish Vowel Length Rule in Aberdeen English'. In J. Trouvain and W. J. Barry (eds). *Proceedings of the 16th International Congress of Phonetic Sciences*. Saarbrücken: 1521–4.

Welby, P. and Loevenbruck, H. (2005). 'Segmental "anchorage" and the French late rise'. *Proceedings of INTERSPEECH 2005*, pp. 2369–72.

Wells, J. C. (1982). *Accents of English*. Cambridge: Cambridge University Press.

Wenger, E. (1998). *Communities of Practice: Learning, Meaning, and Identity*. Cambridge: Cambridge University Press.

Werker, J. F. and Tees, R. C. (1983). 'Developmental changes across childhood in the perception of nonnative speech sounds'. *Canadian Journal of Psychology* 57: 278–86.

—. (1984). 'Cross-language speech perception: Evidence for perceptual reorganization during the first year of life'. *Infant Behavior and Development* 7: 49–63.

Werker, J. F., Polka, L. and Pegg, J. (1997). 'The conditioned head turn procedure as a method for testing infant speech perception'. *Early Development and Parenting* 6: 171–8.

Werker, J. F., Fennell, C. T., Corcoran, K. M. and Stager, C. L. (2002). 'Infants' ability to learn phonetically similar words: Effects of age and vocabulary size'. *Infancy* 3: 1–30.

West, P. (2000). 'Perception of distributed coarticulatory properties of English /l/ and /r/'. *Journal of Phonetics* 27: 405–25.

Westbury, J. (1994). *X-ray Microbeam Speech Production Database User's Handbook.* University of Wisconsin, Madison, WI: Waisman Center on Mental Retardation and Human Development.

Whalen, D. H. and Levitt, A. G. (1995). 'The universality of intrinsic F0 of vowels'. *Journal of Phonetics* 23: 349–66.

White, L. and Mattys, S. L. (2007). 'Calibrating rhythm: First language and second language studies'. *Journal of Phonetics* 35: 501–22.

White, L. and Turk, A. E. (2010). 'English words on the Procrustean bed: Polysyllabic shortening reconsidered'. *Journal of Phonetics* 38: 459–71.

White, L., Payne, E. and Mattys, S. L. (2009). 'Rhythmic and prosodic contrast in Venetan and Sicilian Italian'. *Amsterdam Studies in the Theory and History of Linguistic Science. Series IV, Current Issues in Linguistic Theory* 306: 137–58.

Wichmann, A., House, J. and Rietveld, T. (2000). 'Discourse constraints on F0 peak timing in English'. In A. Botinis (ed.). *Intonation: Analysis, Modelling and Technology.* Dordrecht, The Netherlands: Kluwer Academic Publishers, pp. 163–82.

Wiget, L., White, L., Schuppler, B., Grenon, I., Rauch, O. and Mattys, S. L. (2010). 'How stable are acoustic metrics of contrastive speech rhythm?' *Journal of the Acoustical Society of America* 127: 1559–69.

Wilcox, K. A. and Horii, Y. (1980). 'Age and changes in vocal jitter'. *Journal of Gerontology* 35: 194–8.

Wilkins, J. (1668). *An Essay towards a Real Character and a Philosophical Language.* London: Sa. Gellibrand.

Williams, A., Mcleod, S. and McCauley, R. (eds) (2010). *Interventions for Speech Sound Disorders in Children.* Baltimore: Paul H. Brookes.

Windsor, F. (2011). 'The broad or narrow way?' *Speech and Language Therapy in Practice* Winter: 14–16.

Wong, D., Markel, J. and Gray, A. (1979). 'Least squares glottal inverse filtering from an acoustic speech wave'. *IEEE Trans. Acoustics, Speech and Signal Processing* 27: 350–5.

Woo, G. C. and Lee, M.-H. (2002). 'Are ethnic differences in the F.-M 100 scores related to macular pigmentation?' *Clinical and Experimental Optometry* 85: 372–7.

Wrench, A. (2007). 'Advances in EPG palate design'. *Advances in Speech-Language Pathology* 9: 3–12.

Wright, R. (2003). 'Lexical competition and reduction in speech'. In J. Local, R. Ogden and R. Temple (eds). *Phonetic Interpretation: Papers in Laboratory Phonology VI.* Cambridge: Cambridge University Press, pp. 75–87.

Xu, Y. (2009). 'Timing and coordination in tone and intonation – an articulatory-functional perspective'. *Lingua* 119: 906–27.

—. (2010). 'In defence of lab speech'. *Journal of Phonetics* 38: 329–36.

Xu, Y. and Sun, X. (2002). 'Maximum speed of pitch change and how it may relate to speech'. *Journal of the Acoustical Society of America* 111: 1399–413.

Xue, S. A. and Hao, G. J. (2003). 'Changes in the human vocal tract due to aging and the acoustic correlates of speech production: A pilot study'. *Journal of Speech, Language, and Hearing Research* 46: 689–701.

Xue, S. A. and Hao, J. G. (2006). 'Normative standards for vocal tract dimensions by race as measured by acoustic pharyngometry'. *Journal of Voice* 20: 391–400.

Xue, S. A., Cheng, R. W. C. and Ng, L. M. (2010). 'Vocal tract dimensional develop-ment of adolescents: An acoustic reflection study'. *International Journal of Pediatric Otorhinolaryngology* 74: 907–12.

Yigezu, M. (2002). 'Articulatory and acoustic effects of lip-plate speech in Chai and its implications for phonological theory'. *Journal of the International Phonetic Association* 31: 203–21.

Young, S. (1996). 'A review of large vocabulary continuous speech recognition'. *IEEE Signal Processing Magazine* 13: 45–57.

Zajac, D. J. and Yates, C. C. (1997). 'Speech aerodynamics'. In M. J. Ball and C. Code (eds). *Instrumental Clinical Phonetics*. London: Whurr Publishers, pp. 87–118.

Zatorre, R. J., Belin, P. and Penhune, V. B. (2002). 'Structure and function of the human auditory cortex: music and speech'. *Trends in Cognitive Sciences* 6: 37–46.

Zerbian, S., Downing, L. J. and Kügler, F. (2009). 'Introduction: tone and intonation from a typological perspective'. *Lingua* 119: 817–26.

Zharkova, N., Hewlett, N. and Hardcastle, W. (2011). 'Coarticulation as an indicator of speech motor control development in children: an ultrasound study'. *Motor Control* 15: 118–40.

Ziegler, J., Pech-Georgel, C., George, F. and Lorenzi, C. (2009). 'Speech-perception-in-noise deficits in dyslexia'. *Developmental Science* 12: 732–45.

Zsiga, E. (1995). 'An acoustic and electropalatographic study of lexical and postlexical palatalization in American English'. In B. Connell and A. Arvaniti (eds). *Phonology and Phonetic Evidence. Papers in Laboratory Phonology IV*. Cambridge: Cambridge University Press, pp. 282–302.

Zwaan, K., Muysken, P. and Verrips, M. (eds) (2010). *Language and Origin: The Role of Language in European Asylum Procedures: A Linguistic and Legal Survey*. Nijmegen: Wolf Legal Publishers.

Index